SCIENCE OF HORSES

By

Dr. Amita Sarkar

Deptt. of Zoology
Agra College, Agra
(Uttar Pradesh)
(India)

DISCOVERY PUBLISHING HOUSE PVT. LTD.
NEW DELHI-110 002

Published by:
Tilak Wasan

DISCOVERY PUBLISHING HOUSE PVT. LTD.
4383/4B, Ansari Road, Darya Ganj
New Delhi-110 002 (India)
Phone : +91-11-23279245, 43596064-65
Fax : +91-11-23253475
E-mail : discoverypublishinghouse@gmail.com
sales@discoverypublishinggroup.com
parul.wasan@gmail.com
web : www.discoverypublishinggroup.com

First Edition: **2013**

ISBN: 978-93-5056-300-7

Science of Horses

Printed at:
Aditi Fine Art Press
Delhi

Preface

The horse (*Equus ferus caballus*) is one of two extant subspecies of *Equus ferus*, or the wild horse. It is a single-hooved (ungulate) mammal belonging to the taxonomic family Equidae. The horse has evolved over the past 45 to 55 million years from a small multi-toed creature into the large, single-toed animal of today. Humans began to domesticate horses around 4000 BC, and their domestication is believed to have been widespread by 3000 BC. Horses in the subspecies *caballus* are domesticated, although some domesticated populations live in the wild as feral horses. These feral populations are not true wild horses, as this term is used to describe horses that have never been domesticated, such as the endangered Przewalski's Horse, a separate subspecies, and the only remaining true wild horse. There is an extensive, specialized vocabulary used to describe equine-related concepts, covering everything from anatomy to life stages, size, colours, markings, breeds, locomotion, and behaviour.

Horses' anatomy enables them to make use of speed to escape predators and they have a well-developed sense of balance and a strong fight-or-flight instinct. Related to this need to flee from predators in the wild is an unusual trait: horses are able to sleep both standing up and lying down. Female horses, called mares, carry their young for approximately 11 months, and a young horse, called a foal, can stand and run shortly following birth. Most domesticated horses begin training under saddle or in harness between the ages of two and four. They reach full adult development by age five, and have an average lifespan of between 25 and 30 years.

Horse breeds are loosely divided into three categories based on general temperament: spirited 'hot bloods' with speed and endurance; 'cold bloods', such as draft horses and some ponies, suitable for slow, heavy work; and 'warmbloods', developed from crosses between hot bloods and cold bloods often focusing on creating breeds for specific riding purposes, particularly in Europe. There are over 300 breeds of horses in the world today, developed for many different uses.

Horses and humans interact in a wide variety of sport competitions and non-competitive recreational pursuits, as well as in working activities such as police work, agriculture, entertainment, and therapy. Horses were historically used in warfare, from which a wide variety of riding and driving techniques developed, using many different styles of equipment and methods of control. Many products are derived from horses, including meat, milk, hide, hair, bone, and pharmaceuticals extracted from the urine of pregnant mares. Humans provide domesticated horses with food, water and shelter, as well as attention from specialists such as veterinarians and farriers.

Horses are grazing animals, and their major source of nutrients is good-quality forage from hay or pasture. They can consume approximately 2 per cent to 2.5 per cent of their body weight in dry feed each day. Therefore, a 450-kilogram (990 lb) adult horse could eat up to 11 kilograms (24 lb) of food. Sometimes, concentrated feed such as grain is fed in addition to pasture or hay, especially when the animal is very active. When grain is fed, equine nutritionists recommend that 50 per cent or more of the animal's diet by weight should still be forage.

Horses require a plentiful supply of clean water, a minimum of 38 L to 45 L per day. Although horses are adapted to live outside, they require shelter from the wind and precipitation, which can range from a simple shed or shelter to an elaborate stable.

Horses require routine hoof care from a farrier, as well as vaccinations to protect against various diseases, and dental examinations from a veterinarian or a specialized equine dentist. If horses are kept inside in a barn, they require regular daily exercise for their physical health and mental well-being. When turned outside, they require well-maintained, sturdy fences to be safely contained. Regular grooming is also helpful to help the horse maintain good health of the hair coat and underlying skin.

—Author

Contents

CHAPTER 1

Introduction

The horse (*Equus ferus caballus*) is one of two extant subspecies of *Equus ferus*, or the wild horse. It is a single-hooved (ungulate) mammal belonging to the taxonomic family Equidae. The horse has evolved over the past 45 to 55 million years from a small multi-toed creature into the large, single-toed animal of today. Humans began to domesticate horses around 4000 BC, and their domestication is believed to have been widespread by 3000 BC. Horses in the subspecies *caballus* are domesticated, although some domesticated populations live in the wild as feral horses. These feral populations are not true wild horses, as this term is used to describe horses that have never been domesticated, such as the endangered Przewalski's Horse, a separate subspecies, and the only remaining true wild horse. There is an extensive, specialized vocabulary used to describe equine-related concepts, covering everything from anatomy to life stages, size, colours, markings, breeds, locomotion, and behaviour.

Horses' anatomy enables them to make use of speed to escape predators and they have a well-developed sense of balance and a strong fight-or-flight instinct. Related to this need to flee from predators in the wild is an unusual trait: horses are able to sleep both standing up and lying down. Female horses, called mares, carry their young for approximately 11 months, and a young horse, called a foal, can stand and run shortly following birth. Most domesticated horses begin training under saddle or in harness between the ages of two and four. They reach full adult development by age five, and have an average lifespan of between 25 and 30 years.

Horse breeds are loosely divided into three categories based on general temperament: spirited 'hot bloods' with speed and endurance; 'cold bloods', such as draft horses and some ponies, suitable for slow, heavy work; and 'warmbloods', developed from crosses between hot bloods and cold bloods, often focusing on creating breeds for specific riding purposes, particularly in

Europe. There are over 300 breeds of horses in the world today, developed for many different uses.

Horses and humans interact in a wide variety of sport competitions and non-competitive recreational pursuits, as well as in working activities such as police work, agriculture, entertainment, and therapy. Horses were historically used in warfare, from which a wide variety of riding and driving techniques developed, using many different styles of equipment and methods of control. Many products are derived from horses, including meat, milk, hide, hair, bone, and pharmaceuticals extracted from the urine of pregnant mares. Humans provide domesticated horses with food, water and shelter, as well as attention from specialists such as veterinarians and farriers.

Specific terms and specialized language is used to describe Horse anatomy, different life stages, colours and breeds.

Lifespan and Life Stages

Depending on breed, management and environment, the modern domestic horse has a life expectancy of 25 to 30 years. It is uncommon, but a few animals live into their 40s and, occasionally, beyond. The oldest verifiable record was 'Old Billy', a 19th-century horse that lived to the age of 62. In modern times, Sugar Puff, who had been listed in the Guinness Book of World Records as the world's oldest living pony, died in 2007 at age 56.

Regardless of a horse's actual birth date, for most competition purposes an animal is considered a year older on January 1 of each year in the northern hemisphere and August 1 in the southern hemisphere. The exception is in endurance riding, where the minimum age to compete is based on the animal's actual calendar age.

The following terminology is used to describe horses of various ages:

- *Foal:* A horse of either sex less than one year old. A nursing foal is sometimes called a *suckling* and a foal that has been weaned is called a *weanling*. Most domesticated foals are weaned at 5 to 7 months of age, although foals can be weaned at 4 months with no adverse physical effects.
- *Yearling:* A horse of either sex that is between one and two years old.
- *Colt:* A male horse under the age of four. A common terminology error is to call any young horse a 'colt', when the term actually only refers to young male horses.
- *Filly:* A female horse under the age of four.
- *Mare:* a female horse four years old and older.
- *Stallion:* A non-castrated male horse four years old and older. Some people, particularly in the UK, refer to a stallion as a 'horse'.
- *Gelding:* A castrated male horse of any age.

In horse racing, these definitions may differ: For example, in the British Isles, Thoroughbred horse racing defines colts and fillies as less than five years old. However, Australian Thoroughbred racing defines colts and fillies as less than four years old.

The height of horses is measured at the highest point of the withers, where the neck meets the back. This point was chosen because it is a stable point of the anatomy, unlike the head or neck, which move up and down.

The English-speaking world measures the height of horses in hands and inches. One hand is equal to 4 inches (101.6 mm). The height is expressed as the number of full hands, followed by a point, then the number of additional inches, then the abbreviation 'h' or 'hh' (for 'hands high'). Thus, a horse described as '15.2 h' is 15 hands (60 inches, 152 cm) plus 2 inches (5.1 cm), for a total of 62 inches (157.5 cm) in height.

The size of horses varies by breed, but also is influenced by nutrition. Light riding horses usually range in height from 14 to 16 hands (56 to 64 inches, 142 to 163 cm) and can weigh from 380 to 550 kilograms (840 to 1,200 lb). Larger riding horses usually start at about 15.2 hands (62 inches, 157 cm) and often are as tall as 17 hands (68 inches, 173 cm), weighing from 500 to 600 kilograms (1,100 to 1,300 lb). Heavy or draft horses are usually at least 16 to 18 hands (64 to 72 inches, 163 to 183 cm) high and can weigh from about 700 to 1,000 kilograms (1,500 to 2,200 lb).

The largest horse in recorded history was probably a Shire horse named Mammoth, who was born in 1848. He stood 21.2½ hands high (86.5 in/220 cm), and his peak weight was estimated at 1,500 kilograms (3,300 lb). The current record holder for the world's smallest horse is Thumbelina, a fully mature miniature horse affected by dwarfism. She is 17 inches (43 cm) tall and weighs 57 pounds (26 kg).

The general rule for height distinguishing between a horse and a pony at maturity is 14.2 hands (58 inches, 147 cm). An animal 14.2 h or over is usually considered to be a horse and one less than 14.2 h a pony. However, there are many exceptions to the general rule. In Australia, ponies measure under 14 hands (56 inches, 142 cm). The International Federation for Equestrian Sports, which uses metric measurements, defines the cutoff between horses and ponies at 148 centimetres (58.27 in) (just over 14.2 h) without shoes and 149 centimetres (58.66 in) (just over 14.2½ h) with shoes. Some breeds which typically produce individuals both under and over 14.2 h consider all animals of that breed to be horses regardless of their height. Conversely, some pony breeds may have features in common with horses, and individual animals may occasionally mature at over 14.2 h, but are still considered to be ponies.

The distinction between a horse and pony is not simply a difference in height, but other aspects of *phenotype* or appearance, such as conformation and temperament. Ponies often exhibit thicker manes, tails, and overall coat. They also have proportionally shorter legs, wider barrels, heavier bone, shorter and thicker necks, and short heads with broad foreheads. They may have calmer temperaments than horses and also a high level of equine intelligence that may or may not be used to cooperate with human handlers. In fact, small size, by itself, is sometimes not a factor at all. While the Shetland pony stands on average 10 hands (40 inches, 102 cm), the Falabella and other miniature horses, which can be no taller than 30 inches (76 cm), the size of a medium-sized dog, are classified by their respective registries as very small horses rather than as ponies.

Horses exhibit a diverse array of coat colours and distinctive markings, described with a specialized vocabulary. Often, a horse is classified first by its coat colour, before breed or sex. Horses of the same colour may be distinguished from one another by white markings, which, along with various spotting patterns, are inherited separately from coat colour.

Many genes that create horse coat colours have been identified, although research continues to further identify factors that result in specific traits. One of the first genetic relationships to be understood was that between recessive 'red' (chestnut) and dominant 'black' allele that is controlled by the Melanocortin 1 receptor, also known as the 'extension gene' or 'red factor'. Additional genes control suppression of base red and black colour to point colouration as seen in bay, spotting patterns such as pinto or leopard, dilutions such as palomino or dun, as well as graying, and all the other factors that create the dozens of possible coat colours found in horses. These colours can be modified by at least ten other genes to create all other colours.

Horses which have a white coat colour are often mislabeled; a horse that looks 'white' is usually a middle-aged or older gray. Grays are born a darker shade, get lighter as they age, and usually have black skin underneath their white hair coat (with the exception of pink skin under white markings). The only horses properly called white are born with a white hair coat and have predominantly pink skin, a fairly rare occurrence. Different and unrelated genetic factors can produce white coat colours in horses, including several different alleles of dominant white and the sabino-1 gene. However, there are no 'albino' horses, defined as having both pink skin and red eyes. Gestation lasts for approximately 335-340 days and usually results in one foal. Twins are rare. Horses are a precocial species, and foals are capable of standing and running within a short time following birth.

Horses, particularly colts, sometimes are physically capable of reproduction at about 18 months, but domesticated horses are rarely allowed to breed before the age of three, especially females. Horses four years old are considered mature, although the skeleton normally continues to develop until the age of six; maturation also depends on the horse's size, breed, sex, and quality of care. Also, if the horse is larger, its bones are larger; therefore, not only do the bones take longer to actually form bone tissue, but the epiphyseal plates are also larger and take longer to convert from cartilage to bone. These plates convert after the other parts of the bones, and are crucial to development.

Depending on maturity, breed, and work expected, horses are usually put under saddle and trained to be ridden between the ages of two and four. Although Thoroughbred race horses are put on the track as young age two in some countries, horses specifically bred for sports such as dressage are generally not put under saddle until they are three or four years old, because their bones and muscles are not solidly developed. For endurance riding competition, horses are not deemed mature enough to compete until they are a full 60 calendar months (5 years) old.

Horses have a skeleton that averages 205 bones. A significant difference between the horse skeleton and that of a human, is the lack of a collarbone—the horse's forelimbs are attached to the spinal column by a powerful set of muscles, tendons, and ligaments that attach the shoulder blade to the torso. The horse's legs and hooves are also unique structures. Their leg bones are proportioned differently from those of a human. For example, the body part that is called a horse's 'knee' is actually made up of the carpal bones that correspond to the human wrist. Similarly, the hock contains bones equivalent to those in the human ankle and heel. The lower leg bones of a horse correspond to the bones of the human hand or foot, and the fetlock (incorrectly called the 'ankle') is actually the proximal sesamoid bones between the cannon bones (a single equivalent to the human metacarpal or metatarsal bones) and the proximal phalanges, located where one finds the 'knuckles' of a human. A horse also has no muscles in its legs below the knees and hocks, only skin, hair, bone, tendons, ligaments, cartilage, and the assorted specialized tissues that make up the hoof.

The critical importance of the feet and legs is summed up by the traditional adage, 'no foot, no horse'. The horse hoof begins with the distal phalanges, the equivalent of the human fingertip or tip of the toe, surrounded by cartilage and other specialized, blood-rich soft tissues such as the laminae. The exterior hoof wall and horn of the sole is made of essentially the same material as a human fingernail. The end result is that a horse, weighing on average 500 kilograms (1,100 lb), travels on the same bones as would a human on tiptoe. For the protection of the hoof under certain conditions, some horses have horseshoes placed on their feet by a professional farrier. The hoof continually grows, and in most domesticated horses needs to be trimmed (and horseshoes reset, if used) every five to eight weeks, though the hooves of horses in the wild wear down and regrow at a rate suitable for their terrain.

Teeth

Horses are adapted to grazing. In an adult horse, there are 12 incisors at the front of the mouth, adapted to biting off the grass or other vegetation. There are 24 teeth adapted for chewing, the premolars and molars, at the back of the mouth. Stallions and geldings have four additional teeth just behind the incisors, a type of canine teeth called 'tushes'. Some horses, both male and female, will also develop one to four very small vestigial teeth in front of the molars, known as 'wolf' teeth, which are generally removed because they can interfere with the bit. There is an empty interdental space between the incisors and the molars where the bit rests directly on the gums, or 'bars' of the horse's mouth when the horse is bridled.

An estimate of a horse's age can be made from looking at its teeth. The teeth continue to erupt throughout life and are worn down by grazing. Therefore, the incisors show changes as the horse ages, but a distinct wear and growth pattern, and changes in the angle at which the chewing surfaces meet. This allows a very rough estimate of a horse's age, although diet and veterinary care can also affect the rate of tooth wear.

Horses are herbivores with a digestive system adapted to a forage diet of grasses and other plant material, consumed steadily throughout the day. Therefore, compared to humans, they have a relatively small stomach but very long intestines to facilitate a steady flow of nutrients. A 450-kilogram (990 lb) horse will eat 7 to 11 kilograms (15 to 24 lb) of food per day and, under normal use, drink 38 litres (8.4 imp gal; 10 US gal) to 45 litres (9.9 imp gal; 12 US gal) of water. Horses are not ruminants, so they have only one stomach, like humans, but unlike humans, they can digest cellulose, a major component of grass. Cellulose digestion occurs in the cecum, or 'water gut', which food goes through before reaching the large intestine. Unlike humans, horses cannot vomit, so digestion problems can quickly cause colic, a leading cause of death.

The horse's senses are generally superior to those of a human. As prey animals, they must be aware of their surroundings at all times. They have the largest eyes of any land mammal, and are lateral-eyed, meaning that their eyes are positioned on the sides of their heads. This means that horses have a range of vision of more than 350°, with approximately 65° of this being binocular vision and the remaining 285° monocular vision. Horses have excellent day and night vision, but they have two-colour, or dichromatic vision; their colour vision is somewhat like red-green colour blindness in humans, where certain colours, especially red and related colours, appear as a shade of green.

A horse's hearing is good, and the pinna of each ear can rotate up to 180°, giving the potential for 360° hearing without having to move the head. Their sense of smell, while much better than that of humans, is not their strongest asset; they rely to a greater extent on vision.

Horses have a great sense of balance, due partly to their ability to feel their footing and partly to highly developed proprioception—the unconscious sense of where the body and limbs are at all times. A horse's sense of touch is well developed. The most sensitive areas are around the eyes, ears, and nose. Horses sense contact as subtle as an insect landing anywhere on the body.

Horses have an advanced sense of taste that allows them to sort through fodder to choose what they would most like to eat, and their prehensile lips can easily sort even the smallest grains. Horses generally will not eat poisonous plants. However, there are exceptions and horses will occasionally eat toxic amounts of poisonous plants even when there is adequate healthy food.

All horses move naturally with four basic gaits: the four-beat walk, which averages 6.4 kilometres per hour (4.0 mph); the two-beat trot or jog at 13 to 19 kilometres per hour (8.1 to 12 mph) (faster for harness racing horses); the canter or lope, a three-beat gait that is 19 to 24 kilometres per hour (12 to 15 mph); and the gallop. The gallop averages 40 to 48 kilometres per hour (25 to 30 mph), but the world record for a horse galloping over a short, sprint distance is 88 kilometres per hour (55 mph). Besides these basic gaits, some horses perform a two-beat pace, instead of the trot. There also are several four-beat "ambling" gaits that are approximately the speed of a trot or pace, though smoother to ride. These include the lateral rack, running walk, and tölt as well as the diagonal fox trot. Ambling gaits are often genetic in some breeds, known collectively as gaited horses. Often, gaited horses replace the trot with one of the ambling gaits.

Horses are prey animals with a strong fight-or-flight response. Their first reaction to threat is to startle and usually flee, although they will stand their ground and defend themselves when flight is not possible or if their young are threatened. They also tend to be curious; when startled, they will often hesitate an instant to ascertain the cause of their fright, and may not always flee from something that they perceive as non-threatening. Most light horse riding breeds were developed for speed, agility, alertness and endurance; natural qualities that extend from their wild ancestors. However, through selective breeding, some breeds of horses are quite docile, particularly certain draft horses. Horses are herd animals, with a clear hierarchy of rank, led by a dominant individual, usually a mare. They are also social creatures who are able to form companionship attachments to their own species and to other animals, including humans. They communicate in various ways, including vocalizations such as nickering or whinnying, mutual grooming, and body language. Many horses will become difficult to manage if they are isolated, but with training, horses can learn to accept a human as a companion, and thus be comfortable away from other horses. However, when confined with insufficient companionship, exercise, or stimulation, individuals may develop stable vices, an assortment of bad habits, mostly stereotypies of psychological origin, that include wood chewing, wall kicking, 'weaving' (rocking back and forth), and other problems.

Intelligence and Learning

In the past, horses were considered unintelligent, with no abstract thinking ability, unable to generalize, and driven primarily by a herd mentality. However, modern studies show that they perform a number of cognitive tasks on a daily basis, meeting mental challenges that include food procurement and social system identification. They also have good spatial discrimination abilities. Studies have assessed equine intelligence in the realms of problem solving, learning speed, and knowledge retention. Results show that horses excel at simple learning, but also are able to solve advanced cognitive challenges that involve categorization and concept learning. They learn from habituation, desensitization, Pavlovian conditioning, and operant conditioning. They respond to and learn from both positive and negative reinforcement. Recent studies even suggest horses are able to count if the quantity involved is less than four.

Domesticated horses tend to face greater mental challenges than wild horses, because they live in artificial environments that stifle instinctive behaviour while learning tasks that are not natural. Horses are creatures of habit that respond and adapt well to regimentation, and respond best when the same routines and techniques are used consistently. Some trainers believe that 'intelligent' horses are reflections of intelligent trainers who effectively use response conditioning techniques and positive reinforcement to train in the style that fits best with an individual animal's natural inclinations. Others who handle horses regularly note that personality also may play a role separate from intelligence in determining how a given animal responds to various experiences.

Horses are mammals, and as such are 'warm-blooded' creatures, as opposed to cold-blooded reptiles. However, these words have developed a separate meaning in the context of equine terminology, used to describe temperament, not body temperature. For example, the 'hot-bloods', such as many race horses, exhibit more sensitivity and energy, while the 'cold-bloods', such as most draft breeds, are quieter and calmer. Sometimes 'hot-bloods' are classified as 'light horses' or 'riding horses', with the 'cold-bloods' classified as 'draft horses' or 'work horses'.

'Hot blooded' breeds include 'oriental horses' such as the Akhal-Teke, Arabian horse, Barb and now-extinct Turkoman horse, as well as the Thoroughbred, a breed developed in England from the older oriental breeds. Hot bloods tend to be spirited, bold, and learn quickly. They are bred for agility and speed. They tend to be physically refined—thin-skinned, slim, and long-legged. The original oriental breeds were brought to Europe from the Middle East and North Africa when European breeders wished to infuse these traits into racing and light cavalry horses.

Muscular, heavy draft horses are known as 'cold bloods', as they are bred not only for strength, but also to have the calm, patient temperament needed to pull a plow or a heavy carriage full of people. They are sometimes nicknamed 'gentle giants'. Well-known draft breeds include the Belgian and the Clydesdale. Some, like the Percheron are lighter and livelier, developed to pull carriages or to plow large fields in drier climates. Others, such as the

Shire, are slower and more powerful, bred to plow fields with heavy, clay-based soils. The cold-blooded group also includes some pony breeds.

'Warmblood' breeds, such as the Trakehner or Hanoverian, developed when European carriage and war horses were crossed with Arabians or Thoroughbreds, producing a riding horse with more refinement than a draft horse, but greater size and milder temperament than a lighter breed. Certain pony breeds with warmblood characteristics have been developed for smaller riders. Warmbloods are considered a 'light horse' or 'riding horse'.

Today, the term 'Warmblood' refers to a specific subset of sport horse breeds that are used for competition in dressage and show jumping. Strictly speaking, the term "warm blood' refers to any cross between cold-blooded and hot-blooded breeds. Examples include breeds such as the Irish Draught or the Cleveland Bay. The term was once used to refer to breeds of light riding horse other than Thoroughbreds or Arabians, such as the Morgan horse.

Horses are able to sleep both standing up and lying down. In an adaptation from life in the wild, horses are able to enter light sleep by usıng a 'stay apparatus' in their legs, allowing them to doze without collapsing. Horses sleep better when in groups because some animals will sleep while others stand guard to watch for predators. A horse kept alone will not sleep well because its instincts are to keep a constant eye out for danger.

Unlike humans, horses do not sleep in a solid, unbroken period of time, but take many short periods of rest. Horses spend four to fifteen hours a day in standing rest, and from a few minutes to several hours lying down. Total sleep time in a 24-hour period may range from several minutes to a couple of hours, mostly in short intervals of about 15 minutes each. The average sleep time in a 24-hour period of a domestic horse is said to be 2.9 hours.

Horses must lie down to reach REM sleep. They only have to lie down for an hour or two every few days to meet their minimum REM sleep requirements. However, if a horse is never allowed to lie down, after several days it will become sleep-deprived, and in rare cases may suddenly collapse as it involuntarily slips into REM sleep while still standing. This condition differs from narcolepsy, although horses may also suffer from that disorder.

The horse adapted to survive in areas of wide-open terrain with sparse vegetation, surviving in an ecosystem where other large grazing animals, especially ruminants, could not. Horses and other equids are odd-toed ungulates of the order Perissodactyla, a group of mammals that was dominant during the Tertiary period. In the past, this order contained 14 families, but only three—Equidae (the horse and related species), the tapir, and the rhinoceros—have survived to the present day. The earliest known member of the Equidae family was the *Hyracotherium,* which lived between 45 and 55 million years ago, during the Eocene period. It had 4 toes on each front foot, and 3 toes on each back foot. The extra toe on the front feet soon disappeared with the *Mesohippus*, which lived 32 to 37 million years ago. Over time, the extra side toes shrank in size until they vanished. All that remains of them in modern horses is a set of small vestigial bones on the leg below the knee, known informally as splint bones. Their legs also lengthened as their toes disappeared until they were a hooved animal capable of running at great speed. By about 5 million years ago, the modern *Equus* had evolved. Equid teeth also evolved from browsing on soft, tropical plants to adapt to browsing of drier plant material, then to grazing of tougher plains grasses. Thus proto-horses changed from leaf-eating forest-dwellers to grass-eating inhabitants of semi-arid regions worldwide, including the steppes of Eurasia and the Great Plains of North America.

By about 15,000 years ago, *Equus ferus* was a widespread holarctic species. Horse bones from this time period, the late Pleistocene, are found in Europe, Eurasia, Beringia, and North America. Yet between 10,000 and 7,600 years ago, the horse became extinct in North America and rare elsewhere. The reasons for this extinction are not fully known, but one theory notes that extinction in North America paralleled human arrival. Another theory points to climate change, noting that approximately 12,500 years ago, the grasses characteristic of a steppe ecosystem gave way to shrub tundra, which was covered with unpalatable plants.

A truly wild horse is a species or subspecies with no ancestors that were ever domesticated. Therefore, most 'wild' horses today are actually feral horses, animals that escaped or were turned loose from domestic herds and the descendants of those animals. Only two never-domesticated subspecies, the Tarpan and the Przewalski's Horse, survived into recorded history.

The only true wild horse alive today is the Przewalski's Horse (*Equus ferus przewalskii*), named after the Russian explorer Nikolai Przhevalsky. It is a rare Asian animal, also known as the Mongolian Wild Horse; Mongolian people know it as the *taki*, and the Kyrgyz people call it a *kirtag*. The species was presumed extinct in the wild between 1969 and 1992, while a small breeding population survived in zoos around the world. In 1992, it was reestablished in the wild due to the conservation efforts of numerous zoos. Today, a small wild breeding population exists in Mongolia. There are additional animals still maintained at zoos throughout the world.

The Tarpan or European Wild Horse (*Equus ferus ferus*) was found in Europe and much of Asia. It survived into the historical era, but became extinct in 1909, when the last captive died in a Russian zoo. Thus, the genetic line was lost. Attempts have been made to recreate the Tarpan, which resulted in horses with outward physical similarities, but nonetheless descended from domesticated ancestors and not true wild horses.

Periodically, populations of horses in isolated areas are speculated to be relict populations of wild horses, but generally have been proven to be feral or domestic. For example, the Riwoche horse of Tibet was proposed as such, but testing did not reveal genetic differences with domesticated horses, Similarly, the Sorraia of Portugal was proposed as a direct descendant of the Tarpan based on shared characteristics, but genetic studies have shown that the Sorraia is more closely related to other horse breeds and that the outward similarity is an unreliable measure of relatedness.

Besides the horse, there are seven other species of genus *Equus* in the Equidae family. These are the ass or donkey, *Equus asinus*; the mountain zebra, *Equus zebra*; plains zebra, *Equus quagga*; Grévy's zebra, *Equus grevyi*; the kiang, *Equus kiang*; and the onager, *Equus hemionus*.

Horses can crossbreed with other members of their genus. The most common hybrid is the mule, a cross between a 'jack' (male donkey) and a mare. A related hybrid, a hinny, is a cross between a stallion and a jenny (female donkey). Other hybrids include the zorse, a cross between a zebra and a horse. With rare exceptions, most hybrids are sterile and cannot reproduce.

Domestication of the horse most likely took place in central Asia prior to 3500 BC. Two major sources of information are used to determine where and when the horse was first domesticated and how the domesticated horse spread around the world. The first source is based on palaeological and archaeological discoveries, the second source is a comparison of DNA obtained from modern horses to that from bones and teeth of ancient horse remains.

The earliest archaeological evidence for the domestication of the horse comes from sites in Ukraine and Kazakhstan, dating to approximately 3500-4000 BC. By 3000 BC, the horse was completely domesticated and by 2000 BC there was a sharp increase in the number of horse bones found in human settlements in northwestern Europe, indicating the spread of domesticated horses throughout the continent. The most recent, but most irrefutable evidence of domestication comes from sites where horse remains were interred with chariots in graves of the Sintashta and Petrovka cultures c. 2100 BC.

Domestication is also studied by using the genetic material of present day horses and comparing it with the genetic material present in the bones and teeth of horse remains found in archaeological and palaeological excavations. The variation in the genetic material shows that very few wild stallions contributed to the domestic horse, while many mares were part of early domesticated herds. This is reflected in the difference in genetic variation between the DNA that is passed on along the paternal, or sire line (Y-chromosome) versus that passed on along the maternal, or dam line (mitochondrial DNA). There are very low levels of Y-chromosome variability, but a great deal of genetic variation in mitochondrial DNA. There is also regional variation in mitochondrial DNA due to the inclusion of wild mares in domestic herds. Another characteristic of domestication is an increase in coat colour variation. In horses, this increased dramatically between 5000 and 3000 BC.

Before the availability of DNA techniques to resolve the questions related to the domestication of the horse, various hypothesis were proposed. One classification was based on body types and conformation, suggesting the presence of four basic prototypes that had adapted to their environment prior to domestication. Another hypothesis held that the four prototypes originated from a single wild species and that all different body types were entirely a result of selective breeding after domestication. However, the lack of a detectable substructure in the horse has resulted in a rejection of both hypotheses.

Feral Populations

Feral horses are born and live in the wild, but are descended from domesticated animals. Many populations of feral horses exist throughout the world. Studies of feral herds have provided useful insights into the behaviour of prehistoric horses, as well as greater understanding of the instincts and behaviours that drive horses that live in domesticated conditions.

There are also semi-feral horses in many parts of the world, such as Dartmoor and the New Forest in the UK, where the animals are all privately owned but live for significant amounts of time in 'wild' conditions on undeveloped, often public, lands. Owners of such animals often pay a fee for grazing rights.

Breeds

Horse breeds are groups of horses with distinctive characteristics that are transmitted consistently to their offspring, such as conformation, colour, performance ability, or disposition. These inherited traits result from a combination of natural crosses and artificial selection methods. Horses have been selectively bred since their domestication. Breeds developed due to a need for 'form to function', the necessity to develop certain characteristics in order to perform a particular type of work. Thus, powerful but refined breeds such as the Andalusian developed as riding horses that also had a great aptitude for dressage, while heavy draft horses such as the Clydesdale developed out of a need to perform demanding farm work and pull heavy wagons. Other horse breeds developed specifically for light agricultural work, carriage and road work, various sport disciplines, or simply as pets. Some breeds developed through centuries of crossings with other breeds, while others, such as Tennessee Walking Horses and Morgans, descended from a single foundation sire. There are more than 300 horse breeds in the world today.

However, the concept of purebred bloodstock and a controlled, written breed registry only became of significant importance in modern times.

Sometimes purebred horses are called Thoroughbreds, which is incorrect; 'Thoroughbred' is a specific breed of horse, while a 'purebred' is a horse (or any other animal) with a defined pedigree recognized by a breed registry. An early example of people who practiced selective horse breeding were the Bedouin, who had a reputation for careful practices, keeping extensive pedigrees of their Arabian horses and placing great value upon pure bloodlines. These pedigrees were originally transmitted via an oral tradition. In the 14th century, Carthusian monks of southern Spain kept meticulous pedigrees of bloodstock lineages still found today in the Andalusian horse. One of the earliest formal registries was General Stud Book for Thoroughbreds, which began in 1791 and traced back to the foundation bloodstock for the breed.

Interaction with Humans

Worldwide, horses play a role within human cultures and have done so for millennia. Horses are used for leisure activities, sports, and working purposes. The Food and Agriculture Organisation (FAO) estimates that in 2008, there were almost 59,000,000 horses in the world, with around 33,500,000 in the Americas, 13,800,000 in Asia and 6,300,000 in Europe and smaller portions in Africa and Oceania. There are estimated to be 9,500,000 horses in the United States alone. The American Horse Council estimates that horse-related activities have a direct impact on the economy of the United States of over $39 billion, and when indirect spending is considered, the impact is over $102 billion. In a 2004 'poll' conducted by Animal Planet, more than 50,000 viewers from 73 countries voted for the horse as the world's 4th favourite animal.

Communication between human and horse is paramount in any equestrian activity; to aid this process horses are usually ridden with a saddle on their backs to assist the rider with balance and positioning, and a bridle or related headgear to assist the rider in maintaining control. Sometimes horses are ridden without a saddle, and occasionally, horses are trained to perform without a bridle or other headgear. Many horses are also driven, which requires a harness, bridle, and some type of vehicle.

Historically, equestrians honed their skills through games and races. Equestrian sports provided entertainment for crowds and honed the excellent horsemanship that was needed in battle. Many sports, such as dressage, eventing and show jumping, have origins in military training, which were focused on control and balance of both horse and rider. Other sports, such as rodeo, developed from practical skills such as those needed on working ranches and stations. Sport hunting from horseback evolved from earlier practical hunting techniques. Horse racing of all types evolved from impromptu competitions between riders or drivers. All forms of competition, requiring demanding and specialized skills from both horse and rider, resulted in the systematic development of specialized breeds and equipment for each sport. The popularity of equestrian sports through the centuries has resulted in the preservation of skills that would otherwise have disappeared after horses stopped being used in combat.

Horses are trained to be ridden or driven in a variety of sporting competitions. Examples include show jumping, dressage, three-day eventing, competitive driving, endurance riding, gymkhana, rodeos, and fox hunting. Horse shows, which have their origins in medieval European fairs, are held around the world. They host a huge range of classes, covering all of the mounted and harness disciplines, as well as "In-hand" classes where the horses are led, rather than ridden, to be evaluated on their conformation. The method of judging varies with the discipline, but winning usually depends on style and ability of both horse and rider. Sports such as polo do not judge the horse itself, but rather use the horse as a partner for human competitors as a necessary part of the game. Although the horse requires specialized training to participate, the details of its performance are not judged, only the result of the rider's actions—be it getting a ball through a goal or some other task. Examples of these sports of partnership between human and horse include jousting, in which the main goal is for one rider to unseat the other, and buzkashi, a team game played throughout Central Asia, the aim being to capture a goat carcass while on horseback.

Horse racing is an equestrian sport and major international industry, watched in almost every nation of the world. There are three types: 'flat' racing; steeplechasing, i.e. racing over jumps; and harness racing, where horses trot or pace while pulling a driver in a small, light cart known as a sulky. A major part of horse racing's economic importance lies in the gambling associated with it.

There are certain jobs that horses do very well, and no technology has yet developed to fully replace them. For example, mounted police horses are still effective for certain types of patrol duties and crowd control. Cattle ranches still require riders on horseback to round up cattle that are scattered across remote, rugged terrain. Search and rescue organisations in some countries depend upon mounted teams to locate people, particularly hikers and children, and to provide disaster relief assistance. Horses can also be used in areas where it is necessary to avoid vehicular disruption to delicate soil, such as nature reserves. They may also be the only form of transport allowed in wilderness areas. Horses are quieter than motorized vehicles. Law enforcement officers such as park rangers or game wardens may use horses for patrols, and horses or mules may also be used for clearing trails or other work in areas of rough terrain where vehicles are less effective.

Although machinery has replaced horses in many parts of the world, an estimated 100 million horses, donkeys and mules are still used for agriculture and transportation in less developed areas. This number includes around 27 million working in Africa alone. Some land management practices such as cultivating and logging can be efficiently performed with horses. In agriculture, less fossil fuel is used and increased environmental conservation occurs over time with the use of draft animals such as horses. Logging with horses can result in reduced damage to soil structure and less damage to trees due to more selective logging.

Modern horses are often used to reenact many of their historical work purposes. Horses are used, complete with equipment that is authentic or a meticulously recreated replica, in various live action historical reenactments of specific periods of history, especially recreations of famous battles. Horses are also used to preserve cultural traditions and for ceremonial purposes. Countries such as the United Kingdom still use horse-drawn carriages to convey royalty and other VIPs to and from certain culturally significant events. Public exhibitions are another example, such as the Budweiser Clydesdales, seen in parades and other public settings, a team of draft horses that pull a beer wagon similar to that used before the invention of the modern motorized truck.

Horses are frequently seen in television and films. They are sometimes featured as a major character in films about particular animals, but also used as visual elements that assure the accuracy of historical stories. Both live horses and iconic images of horses are used in advertising to promote a variety of products. The horse frequently appears in coats of arms in heraldry. The horse can be represented as standing, walking (passant), trotting, running (courant), rearing (rampant or forcine) or springing (salient). The horse may be saddled and bridled, harnessed, or without any apparel whatsoever. The horse also appears in the 12-year cycle of animals in the Chinese zodiac related to the Chinese calendar. According to Chinese folklore, each animal is associated with certain personality traits, and those born in the year of the horse are intelligent, independent, and free-spirited.

People of all ages with physical and mental disabilities obtain beneficial results from association with horses. Therapeutic riding is used to mentally and physically stimulate disabled persons and help them improve their lives through improved balance and coordination, increased self-confidence, and a greater feeling of freedom and independence. The benefits of equestrian activity for people with disabilities has also been recognized with the addition of equestrian events to the Paralympic Games and recognition of para-equestrian events by the International Federation for Equestrian Sports (FEI). Hippotherapy and therapeutic horseback riding are names for different physical, occupational, and speech therapy treatment strategies that utilize equine movement. In hippotherapy, a therapist uses the horse's movement to improve their patient's cognitive, coordination, balance, and fine motor skills, whereas therapeutic horseback riding uses specific riding skills.

Horses also provide psychological benefits to people whether they actually ride or not. 'Equine-assisted' or 'equine-facilitated' therapy is a form of experiential psychotherapy that uses horses as companion animals to assist people with mental illness, including anxiety disorders, psychotic disorders, mood disorders, behavioural difficulties, and those who are going through major life changes. There are also experimental programmes using horses in prison settings. Exposure to horses appears to improve the behaviour of inmates and help reduce recidivism when they leave.

Horses in warfare have been seen for most of recorded history. The first archaeological evidence of horses used in warfare dates to between 4000 to 3000 BC, and the use of horses in warfare was widespread by the end of the Bronze Age. Although mechanization has largely replaced the horse as a weapon of war, horses are still seen today in limited military uses, mostly for ceremonial purposes, or for reconnaissance and transport activities in areas of rough terrain where motorized vehicles are ineffective. Horses have been used in the 21st century by the Janjaweed militias in the War in Darfur.

Products

Horses are raw material for many products made by humans throughout history, including byproducts from the slaughter of horses as well as materials collected from living horses.

Products collected from living horses include mare's milk, used by people with large horse herds, such as the Mongols, who let it ferment to produce kumis. Horse blood was once used as food by the Mongols and other nomadic tribes, who found it a convenient source of nutrition when traveling. Drinking their own horses' blood allowed the Mongols to ride for extended periods of time without stopping to eat. The drug Premarin is a mixture of estrogens extracted from the urine of pregnant mares (pregnant mares' urine), and was previously a widely used drug for hormone replacement therapy. The tail hair of horses can be used for making bows for string instruments such as the violin, viola, cello, and double bass.

Horse meat has been used as food for humans and carnivorous animals throughout the ages. It is eaten in many parts of the world, though consumption is taboo in some cultures, and a subject of political controversy in others. Horsehide leather has been used for boots, gloves, jackets, baseballs, and baseball gloves. Horse hooves can also be used to produce animal glue. Horse bones can be used to make implements. Specifically, in Italian cuisine, the horse tibia is sharpened into a probe called a *spinto*, which is used to test the readiness of a (pig) ham as it cures. In Asia, the saba is a horsehide vessel used in the production of kumis.

Horses are grazing animals, and their major source of nutrients is good-quality forage from hay or pasture. They can consume approximately 2 per cent to 2.5 per cent of their body weight in dry feed each day. Therefore, a 450-kilogram (990 lb) adult horse could eat up to 11 kilograms (24 lb) of food. Sometimes, concentrated feed such as grain is fed in addition to pasture or hay, especially when the animal is very active. When grain is fed, equine nutritionists recommend that 50 per cent or more of the animal's diet by weight should still be forage.

Horses require a plentiful supply of clean water, a minimum of 10 US gallons (38 L) to 12 US gallons (45 L) per day. Although horses are adapted to live outside, they require shelter from the wind and precipitation, which can range from a simple shed or shelter to an elaborate stable.

Horses require routine hoof care from a farrier, as well as vaccinations to protect against various diseases, and dental examinations from a veterinarian or a specialized equine dentist. If horses are kept inside in a barn, they require regular daily exercise for their physical health and mental well-being. When turned outside, they require well-maintained, sturdy fences to be safely contained. Regular grooming is also helpful to help the horse maintain good health of the hair coat and underlying skin.

CHAPTER 2

Evolution of the Horse

The evolution of the horse pertains to the phylogenetic ancestry of the modern horse from the small dog-sized, forest-dwelling *Hyracotherium* over geologic time scales. Paleozoologists have been able to piece together a more complete picture of the modern horse's evolutionary lineage than that of any other animal.

The horse belongs to an order known as Perissodactyla, or 'odd-toed ungulates', which all share hoofed feet and an odd number of toes on each foot, as well as mobile upper lips and a similar tooth structure. This means that horses share a common ancestry with tapirs and rhinoceroses. The perissodactyls originally arose in the late Paleocene, less than 10 million years after the Cretaceous-Tertiary extinction event. This group of animals appears to have been originally specialized for life in tropical forests, but whereas tapirs and, to some extent, rhinoceroses, retained their jungle specializations, modern horses are adapted to life on drier land in the much-harsher climatic conditions of the steppes. Other species of *Equus* are adapted to a variety of intermediate conditions.

The early ancestors of the modern horse walked on several spread-out toes, an accommodation to life spent walking on the soft, moist grounds of primeval forests. As grass species began to appear and flourish, the equids' diets shifted from foliage to grasses, leading to larger and more durable teeth. At the same time, as the steppes began to appear, the horse's predecessors needed to be capable of greater speeds to outrun predators. This was attained through the lengthening of limbs and the lifting of some toes from the ground in such a way that the weight of the body was gradually placed on one of the longest toes, the third.

Horses were absent from the Americas until the Spanish brought domestic horses from Europe, beginning in 1493, and escaped horses quickly established large wild herds. The early naturalist Buffon suggested in the

1760s that this was an indication of inferiority of fauna in the New World, then later reconsidered this idea. William Clark's 1807 expedition to Big Bone Lick found 'leg and foot bones of the Horses' which were included with other fossils sent to Thomas Jefferson and evaluated by the anatomist Caspar Wistar, but neither commented on the significance of this find.

The first equid fossil was found in the gypsum quarries in Montmartre, Paris in the 1820s. The tooth was sent to the Paris Conservatory, where it was identified by Georges Cuvier who identified it as a browsing equine related to the tapir. His sketch of the entire animal matched later skeletons found at the site.

During the *Beagle* survey expedition the young naturalist Charles Darwin had remarkable success with fossil hunting in Patagonia. On 10 October 1833 at Santa Fe, Argentina, he was 'filled with astonishment' when he found a horse's tooth in the same stratum as fossil giant armadillos, and wondered if it might have been washed down from a later layer, but concluded that this was 'not very probable'. After the expedition returned in 1836, the anatomist Richard Owen confirmed the tooth was from an extinct species which he subsequently named *Equus curvidens*, and remarked that "This evidence of the former existence of a genus, which, as regards South America, had become extinct, and has a second time been introduced into that Continent, is not one of the least interesting fruits of Mr. Darwin's palæontological discoveries".

In 1848 a study *On the fossil horses of America* by Joseph Leidy systematically examined Pleistocene horse fossils from various collections, including that of the Academy of Natural Sciences and concluded at least two ancient horse species had existed in North America: *Equus curvidens* and another which he named *Equus americanus*. A decade later, however, he found the latter name had already been taken and renamed it *Equus complicatus*. In the same year, he visited Europe and was introduced by Owen to Darwin.

The original sequence of species believed to have evolved into the horse was based on fossils discovered in North America in the 1870s by paleontologist Othniel Charles Marsh. The sequence, from *Hyracotherium* (popularly called *Eohippus*) to the modern horse (*Equus*), was popularized by Thomas Huxley and became one of the most widely-known examples of a clear evolutionary progression. The horse's evolutionary lineage became a common feature of biology textbooks, and the sequence of transitional fossils was assembled by the American Museum of Natural History into an exhibit which emphasized the gradual, 'straight-line' evolution of the horse.

Since then, as the number of equid fossils has increased, the actual evolutionary progression from *Hyracotherium* to *Equus* has been discovered to be much more complex and multi-branched than was initially supposed. The straight, direct progression from the former to the latter has been replaced by a more elaborate model with numerous branches in different directions, of which the modern horse is only one of many. It was first recognized by

George Gaylord Simpson in 1951 that the modern horse was not the 'goal' of the entire lineage of equids, it is simply the only genus of the many horse lineages that has survived.

Detailed fossil information on the rate and distribution of new equid species has also revealed the progression between species was not as smooth and consistent as was once believed. Although some transitions, such as that of *Dinohippus* to *Equus*, were indeed gradual progressions, a number of others, such as that of *Epihippus* to *Mesohippus*, were relatively abrupt and sudden in geologic time, taking place over only a few million years. Both anagenesis (gradual change in an entire population's gene frequency) and cladogenesis (a population 'splitting' into two distinct evolutionary branches) occurred, and many species coexisted with 'ancestor' species at various times. The change in equids' traits was also not always a 'straight line' from *Hyracotherium* to *Equus*: some traits reversed themselves at various points in the evolution of new equid species, such as size and the presence of facial *fossae*, and it is only in retrospect that certain evolutionary trends can be recognized.

The earliest animal to bear recognizably horse-like anatomy was the *Hyracotherium* ('hyrax-like beast'). Its scientific name is derived from initial confusion over early partial fossils' relationship with living species: Richard Owen likened early *Hyracotherium* fossils "to a hare in one passage and to something between a hog and a hyrax in another". A later name for the *Hyracotherium*, 'eohippus' ('dawn horse'), is also popular, though the earlier name takes precedence due to scientific naming conventions.

Hyracotherium

Hyracotherium lived in the Presian (early Eocene), about 52 mya (million years ago). It was an animal approximately the size of a fox (250-450 mm in height), with a relatively short head and neck and a springy, arched back. It had 44 low-crowned teeth, in the typical arrangement of an omnivorous, browsing mammal: 3 incisors, 1 canine, 4 premolars, and 3 molars on each side of the jaw. Its molars were uneven, dull, and bumpy, and used primarily for grinding foliage. The cusps of the molars were slightly connected in low crests. The *Hyracotherium* browsed on soft foliage and fruit, probably scampering between thickets in the mode of a modern muntjac; the *Hyracotherium* had a small brain, and possessed especially small frontal lobes.

Its limbs were decently long relative to its body, already showing the beginnings of adaptations for running. However, all of the major leg bones were unfused, leaving the legs flexible and rotatable. Its wrist and hock joints were low to the ground. The forelimbs had developed five toes, out of which only four were equipped with a small proto-hoof; the large fifth 'toe-thumb' was off the ground. The hind limbs had three out of the five toes equipped with small hooves, while the vestigial first and fifth toes did not touch the ground. Its feet were padded, much like a dog's, but with the small hooves on each toe in place of claws.

For a span of about 20 million years, the *Hyracotherium* thrived with few significant evolutionary changes. The most significant change was in the teeth, which began to adapt to the changing diet of *Hyracotheria*, as these early Equidae shifted from a mixed diet of fruits and foliage to one focused increasingly on browsing foods. During the Eocene, a *Hyracotherium* species (most likely *Hyracotherium vassacciense*) branched out into various new types of Equidae. Thousands of complete, fossilized skeletons of these animals have been found in the Eocene layers of North American strata, mainly in the Wind River basin in Wyoming. Similar fossils have also been discovered in Europe, such as *Propalaeotherium* (which is not considered ancestral to the modern horse).

Orohippus

Approximately 50 million years ago, in the early-to-middle Eocene, *Hyracotherium* smoothly transitioned into *Orohippus* over a gradual series of changes. Although its name means "mountain horse", *Orohippus* was not a true horse and did not live in the mountains. It resembled *Hyracotherium* in size, but had a slimmer body, an elongated head, slimmer forelimbs, and longer hind legs, all of which are characteristics of a good jumper. Although *Orohippus* was still pad-footed, the vestigial outer toes of *Hyracotherium* were not present in the *Orohippus*; there were four toes on each forelimb, and three on each hind leg.

The most dramatic change between *Hyracotherium* and *Orohippus* was in the teeth: the first of the premolar teeth were dwarfed, the last premolar shifted in shape and function into a molar, and the crests on the teeth became more pronounced. Both of these factors gave the teeth of *Orohippus* greater grinding ability, suggesting that *Orohippus* ate tougher plant material.

Epihippus

In the mid-Eocene, about 47 million years ago, *Epihippus*, a genus which continued the evolutionary trend of increasingly efficient grinding teeth, evolved from *Orohippus*. *Epihippus* had five grinding, low-crowned cheek teeth with well-formed crests. A late species of *Epihippus*, sometimes referred to as *Duchesnehippus intermedius*, had teeth similar to Oligocene equids, although slightly less developed. Whether *Duchesnehippus* was a subgenus of *Epihippus* or a distinct genus is disputed.

Mesohippus

In the late Eocene and the early stages of the Oligocene epoch (32-24 mya), the climate of North America became drier, and the earliest grasses began to evolve. The forests were yielding to flatlands, home to grasses and various kinds of brush. In a few areas these plains were covered in sand, creating the type of environment resembling the present-day prairies.

In response to the changing environment, the then-living species of Equidae also began to change. In the late Eocene, they began developing tougher teeth and becoming slightly larger and leggier, allowing for faster running speeds in open areas, and thus for evading predators in non-wooded areas. About 40 mya, *Mesohippus* ('middle horse') suddenly developed in response to strong new selective pressures to adapt, beginning with the species *Mesohippus celer* and soon followed by *Mesohippus westoni.*

In the early Oligocene, *Mesohippus* was one of the more widespread mammals in North America. It walked on three toes on each of its front and hind feet (the first and fifth toes remained, but were small and not used in walking). The third toe was stronger than the outer ones, and thus more weighted; the fourth front toe was diminished to a vestigial nub. Judging by its longer and slimmer limbs, *Mesohippus* was an agile animal.

Mesohippus was slightly larger than *Epihippus,* about 610 mm (24") at the shoulder. Its back was less arched, and its face, snout, and neck were somewhat longer. It had significantly larger cerebral hemispheres, and had a small, shallow depression on its skull called a *fossa,* which in modern horses is quite detailed. The fossa serves as a useful marker for identifying an equine fossil's species. *Mesohippus* had six grinding 'cheek teeth', with a single premolar in front—a trait all descendant Equidae would retain. *Mesohippus* also had the sharp tooth crests of *Epihippus,* improving its ability to grind down tough vegetation.

Miohippus

Around 36 million years ago, soon after the development of *Mesohippus, Miohippus* ('lesser horse') emerged, the earliest species being *Miohippus assiniboiensis.* Like *Mesohippus, Miohippus*'s evolution was relatively abrupt, though a few transitional fossils linking the two genera have been found. It was once believed that *Mesohippus* had anagenetically evolved into *Miohippus* by a gradual series of progressions, but new evidence has shown that *Miohippus*'s evolution was cladogenetic: a *Miohippus* population split off from the main *Mesohippus* genus, coexisted with *Mesohippus* for around 4 million years, and then over time came to replace *Mesohippus.*

Miohippus was significantly larger than its predecessors, and its ankle joints had subtly changed. Its facial fossa was larger and deeper, and it also began to show a variable extra crest in its upper cheek teeth, a trait that became a characteristic feature of equine teeth.

Miohippus ushered in a major new period of diversification in Equidae. While *Mesohippus* died out in the mid-Oligocene, *Miohippus* continued to thrive, and in the early Miocene (24-5.3 mya), it began to rapidly diversify and speciate. It branched out into two major groups, one of which adjusted to the life in forests once again, while the other remained suited to life on the prairies.

Miocene and Pliocene: True Equines

Kalobatippus

The forest-suited form was *Kalobatippus* (or *Miohippus intermedius,* depending on whether it was a new genus or species), whose second and fourth front toes were long, well-suited travel on the soft forest floors. *Kalobatippus* probably gave rise to *Anchitherium,* which travelled to Asia via the Bering Strait land bridge, and from there to Europe. In both North America and Eurasia, larger-bodied genera evolved from *Anchitherium; Sinohippus* in Eurasia and *Hypohippus* and *Megahippus* in North America. *Hypohippus* became extinct by the late Miocene.

Parahippus

The *Miohippus* population that remained on the steppes is believed to be ancestral to *Parahippus,* a North American animal about the size of a small pony, with a prolonged skull and a facial structure resembling the horses of today. Its third toe was stronger and larger, and carried the main weight of the body. Its four premolars resembled the molar teeth and the first were small and almost nonexistent. The incisive teeth of *Parahippus,* like those of its predecessors, had a crown as humans do; however, the top incisors had a trace of a shallow crease marking the beginning of the core/cup.

In the middle of the Miocene epoch, the grazer *Merychippus* flourished. *Merychippus* had wider molars than its predecessors, which are believed to have been used for crunching the hard grasses of the steppes. The hind legs, which were relatively short, had side toes equipped with small hooves, but they probably only touched the ground when running. *Merychippus* radiated into at least 19 additional grassland species.

Hipparion

Three lineages within Equidae are believed to be descended from the numerous varieties of *Merychippus: Hipparion, Protohippus* and *Pliohippus.* The most different from *Merychippus* was *Hipparion.* The main difference was in the structure of tooth enamel: in comparison with other Equidae, the inside, or tongue side, had a completely isolated parapet. A complete and well-preserved skeleton of the North American *Hipparion* shows an animal the size of a small pony. They were very slim, rather like antelopes, and were adapted to life on dry prairies. On its slim legs, *Hipparion* had three toes equipped with small hooves, but the side toes did not touch the ground.

In North America, *Hipparion* and its relatives (*Cormohipparion, Nannippus, Neohipparion,* and *Pseudhipparion*), proliferated into many kinds of equids, at least one of which managed to migrate to Asia and Europe during the Miocene epoch. (European *Hipparion* differs from American *Hipparion* in its smaller body size – the best-known discovery of these fossils was near Athens.)

Pliohippus arose from *Callippus* in the middle Miocene, around 12 mya. It was very similar in appearance to *Equus,* though it had two long extra toes on both sides of the hoof, externally barely visible as callused stubs. The long and slim limbs of *Pliohippus* reveal a quick-footed steppe animal.

Until recently, *Pliohippus* was believed to be the ancestor of present-day horses because of its many anatomical similarities. However, though

Pliohippus was clearly a close relative of *Equus*, its skull had deep facial *fossae*, whereas *Equus* had no *fossae* at all. Additionally, its teeth were strongly curved, unlike the very straight teeth of modern horses. Consequently, it is unlikely to be the ancestor of the modern horse; instead, it is a likely candidate for the ancestor of *Astrohippus*.

Dinohippus

Dinohippus was the most common species of Equidae in North America during the late Pliocene. It was originally thought that *Dinohippus* was monodactyl, but a 1981 fossil find in Nebraska shows that some were tridactyl.

Plesippus

Plesippus is often considered an intermediate stage between *Dinohippus* and the extant genus, *Equus*.

The famous fossils found near Hagerman, Idaho were originally thought to be a part of the genus *Plesippus*. Hagerman Fossil Beds (Idaho) is a Pliocene site, dating to about 3.5 mya. The fossilized remains were originally called *Plesippus shoshonensis*, but further study by paleontologists determined that fossils represented the oldest remains of the genus *Equus*. Their estimated average weight was 425 kg, roughly the size of an Arabian horse.

At the end of the Pliocene, the climate in North America began to cool significantly and most of the animals were forced to move south. One population of *Plesippus* moved across the Bering land bridge into Eurasia around 2.5 Mya.

Modern Horses

Equus

The genus *Equus*, which includes all extant equines, is believed to have evolved from *Dinohippus*, via the intermediate form *Plesippus*. One of the oldest species is *Equus simplicidens*, described as zebra-like with a donkey-shaped head. The oldest material to date is ~3.5 million years old from Idaho, USA. The genus appears to have spread quickly into the Old World, with the similarly aged *Equus livenzovensis* documented from western Europe and Russia.

Molecular phylogenies indicate that the most recent common ancestor of all modern equids (members of the genus *Equus*) lived ~5.6 (3.9-7.8) mya. The oldest divergencies are the Asian hemiones (subgenus *E. (Asinus))*, including the Kulan, Onager, and Kiang), followed by the African zebras (subgenera *E. (Dolichohippus)*, and *E. (Hippotigris)*). All other modern forms including the domesticated horse (and many fossil Pliocene and Pleistocene forms) belong to the subgenus *E. (Equus)* which diverged ~4.8 (3.2-6.5) million years ago.

Pleistocene horse fossils have been assigned to a multitude of species, with over 50 species of equines described from the Pleistocene of North

America alone, although the taxonomic validity of most of these has been called into question. Recent genetic work on fossils has found evidence for only three genetically divergent equid lineages in Pleistocene North and South America. These results suggest that all North American fossils of caballine-type horses (which also include the domesticated horse and Przewalski's Horse of Europe and Asia), as well as South American fossils traditionally placed in the subgenus *E. (Amerhippus)* belong to the same species: *E. ferus*. Remains attributed to a variety of species and lumped as New World stilt-legged horses (including *E. francisci*, *E. tau*, *E. quinni* and potentially N. American Pleistocene fossils previously attributed to *E. cf. hemiones*, and *E. (Asinus) cf. kiang*) likely all belong to a second species endemic to N. America, which despite a superficial resemblance to species in the subgenus *E. (Asinus)* (and hence occasionally referred to as North American Ass) is closely related to *E. ferus*. Surprisingly, the third species, endemic to S. America, and traditionally referred to as *Hippidion*, originally believed to be descended from Pliohippus, was shown to be a third species in the genus *Equus*, closely related to the New World stilt-legged horse. The temporal and regional variation in body size and morphological features within each lineage indicates extraordinary intraspecific plasticity. Such environment-driven adaptative changes would explain why the taxonomic diversity of Pleistocene equids has been overestimated on morphoanatomical grounds.

According to these results, it appears that the genus *Equus* evolved from a *Dinohippus*-like ancestor ~4-7 mya. It rapidly spread into the Old World and there diversified into the various species of asses and zebras. A North American lineage of the subgenus *E. (Equus)* evolved into the New World stilt-legged horse (NWSLH). Subsequently, populations of this species entered South America as part of the Great American Interchange shortly after the formation of the Isthmus of Panama and evolved into the form currently referred to as *'Hippidion'* ~2.5 million years ago. *'Hippidion'* is thus unrelated to the morphologically similar *Pliohippus*, which presumably went extinct during the Miocene. Both the NWSLH and *'Hippidium'* show adaptations to dry, barren ground, whereas the shortened legs of *"Hippidion"* may have been a response to sloped terrain. In contrast, the geographic origin of the closely related modern *E. ferus* is not resolved. However, genetic results on extant and fossil material of Pleistocene age indicate two clades, potentially subspecies, one of which had a holarctic distribution spanning from Europe through Asia and across North America and would become the founding stock of the modern domesticated horse. The other population appears to have been restricted to N. America. One or more N. American populations of *E. ferus* entered S. America ~1.0-1.5 million years ago, leading to the forms currently known as *'E. (Amerhippus)'*, which represent an extinct geographic variant or race of *E. ferus*, however.

Pleistocene Extinctions

Digs in western Canada have unearthed clear evidence that horses existed in North America until about 12,000 years ago. However, all Equidae in North America ultimately became extinct. The causes of this extinction (simultaneous with the extinctions of a variety of other American megafauna) have been a matter of debate. Given the suddenness of the event and the fact that these mammals had been flourishing for millions of years previously, something quite unusual must have happened. There are two main hypotheses. The first attributes extinction to climate change. For example, in Alaska, beginning approximately 12,500 years ago, the grasses characteristic of a steppe ecosystem gave way to shrub tundra, which was covered with unpalatable plants. Another hypothesis suggests extinction was linked to overexploitation of naive prey by newly arrived humans. Extinctions were roughly simultaneous with the end of the most recent glacial advance and the appearance of the big-game-hunting Clovis culture. Several studies have indicated that humans probably arrived in Alaska at the same time or shortly before the local extinction of horses. Additionally, it has been proposed that the steppe-tundra vegetation transition in Beringia may have been a consequence, rather than a cause, of the extinction of megafaunal grazers.

In Eurasia, horse fossils began occurring frequently again in archaeological sites in Kazakhstan and the southern Ukraine about 6,000 years ago. From then on, it is probable that domesticated horses as well as the knowledge of capturing, taming, and rearing horses spread relatively quickly, with wild mares from several wild populations being incorporated en route.

Return to the Americas

Horses only returned to the Americas with Christopher Columbus in 1493. These were Iberian horses first brought to Hispaniola and later to Panama, Mexico, Brazil, Peru, Argentina, and, in 1538, Florida. The first horses to return to the main continent were 16 specifically identified horses brought by Hernan Cortes. Subsequent explorers, such as Coronado and De Soto brought ever-larger numbers, some from Spain and other from breeding establishments set up by the Spanish in the Caribbean. Later, as Spanish missions were founded on the mainland, horses would eventually be lost or stolen, and proliferated into large herds of feral horses that became known as mustangs.

The indigenous peoples of the Americas did not have a specific word for horses, and came to refer to them in various languages as a type of dog or deer (in one case, 'elk-dog').

Toes

The ancestors of the horse came to walk only on the end of the third toe and both side toes. Skeletal remnants show obvious wear on the back of both sides of metacarpal and metatarsal bones, commonly called the 'splint bones'. They are the remnants of the second and the fourth toe. Modern horses retain the splint bones; it is often believed that they are a useless attachment, but they in fact play an important role in supporting the carpal joints (front knee) and even the tarsal joints (hock).

Teeth

Throughout the phylogenetic development, the teeth of the horse underwent significant changes. The type of the original omnivorous teeth with short, 'bumpy' molars, with which the prime members of the evolutionary line distinguished themselves, gradually changed into the teeth common to herbivorous mammals. They became long (as much as 100 mm), roughly cubical molars equipped with a flat grinding surface. In conjunction with the teeth, during the horse's evolution the elongation of the facial part of the skull is apparent, and can also be observed in the backward set eyeholes. In addition, the relatively short neck of the equine ancestors became longer with equal elongation of the legs. Finally, the size of the body grew as well.

The horse has been present in South Asia from at least the mid 2nd millennium BC, more than two millennia after its domestication in Central Asia. The earliest uncontroversial evidence of horse remains on the Indian Subcontinent date to the early Swat culture (ca. 1600 BC). There are claims of stray finds dating to earlier times, as early as the mid 3rd millennium, but these are not generally accepted. The topic is of some importance to the dating of Indo-Aryan migration to India.

Ashva (a Sanskrit word for a horse) is one of the significant animals finding references in several Hindu scriptures.

Rigveda

There are few clear references to actual horse riding in the Rigveda, most clearly in RV 5.61.2-3, describing the Maruts as riders:

- Where are your horses, where the reins? How came ye? how had ye the power? Rein was on nose and seat on back.
- The whip is laid upon the flank. The heroes stretch their thighs apart, like women when the babe is born.

According to researchers tribes also had horses. They point out that the Rigveda does not describe people riding horses in battle. This is in accord with the usual dating of the Rigveda to the late Bronze Age, when horses played a role as means of transport primarily as draught animals (while the introduction of cavalry dates to the early Iron Age, possibly an Iranian (specifically Parthian) innovation of ca. the 9th century BC).

RV 1.163.2 mythologically alludes to the introduction of the horse and horseriding:

- This Steed which Yama gave hath Trita harnessed, and him, the first of all, hath Indra mounted.
- His bridle the Gandharva grasped. O Vasus, from out the Sun ye fashioned forth the Courser.

Yajurveda

The Ashvamedha or horse sacrifice is a notable ritual of the Yajurveda.

Hayagriva

One of the famous avatars of Vishnu, Hayagriva, is depicted with a horse head. Hayagriva is worshipped as the God for Knowledge.

Horse Symbolism

The legend states that the first horse emerged from the depth of the ocean during the churning of the oceans. It was a horse with white colour and had two wings. It was known by the name of Uchchaihshravas. The legend continues that Indra, one of the gods of the Hindus, took away the mythical horse to his celestial abode, the svarga (heaven). Subsequently, Indra severed the wings of the horse and presented the same to the mankind. The wings were severed to ensure that the horse remain on the earth (prithvi) and does not fly back to Indra's suvarga.

According to researcher, Asva may not always denote the horse. Aurobindo argued that the words asva and asvavati symbolize energy. Asva or ratha was also interpreted to be sometimes the 'psycho-physical complex on which the Atman stands or in which it is seated'. In another symbolic interpretation based on RV 1.164.2 and Nirukta 4.4.27, asva may also sometimes symbolize the sun.

Paleolithic

Remains of the *Equus namadicus* have been found from Pleistocene levels in India. The *Equus namadicus* is closely related to the *Equus sivalensis*. The *Equus sivalensis* lived in the Himalayan foothills in prehistoric times and it is assumed that it was extinct during the last Ice Age.

Bronze Age

Remains of horses have been claimed to have been found in deposits at Mahagara near Allahabad (dated to c. 2265 BC to 1480 BC, described as *Equus ferus caballus* Linn), Hallur in Karnataka (c.1500 - 1300 BC, described as *Equus ferus caballus*), Mohenjo-Daro, Harappa ('small horse'), Lothal (e.g., a terracotta figurine and a molar horse tooth, dated to 2200 BC), Kalibangan, and Kuntasi (dated to 2300-1900 BC). Horse remains from the Harappan site Surkotada (dated to c. 2400-1700 BC) have been identified by researcher as *Equus ferus caballus*. The horse specialist later confirmed these conclusions and stated that the excavated tooth specimens could 'in all probability be considered remnants of true horses [i.e. *Equus ferus caballus*]'. Researcher stated that 'The occurrence of true horse (*Equus caballus* L.) was evidenced by the enamel pattern of the upper and lower cheek and teeth and by the size and form of incisors and phalanges (toe bones)'. However, archaeologists like Meadow (1997) disagree, on the grounds that the remains of the *Equus ferus caballus* horse are difficult to distinguish from other equid species like *Equus asinus* (donkeys) or *Equus hemionus* (onagers). An alleged clay model of a horse has been found in Mohenjo-Daro and an alleged horse figurine in Periano Ghundai in the Indus Valley.

Researcher remarked that the supply and import of horses has 'always' been a preoccupation of the Indians and that 'it is a structure of its history, then, that India has always been dependent upon western and central Asia for horses'. The paucity of horse remains could also be explained by India's climatic factors which lead to decay of horse bones. Horse bones may also be rare because horses were probably not eaten or used in burials by the Harappans.

It should however also be noted that other sites like the BMAC complex (which some consider nevertheless as Indo-Iranian) are at least as poor in horse remains as the Harappan sites. Note also that the horse only appears in Mesopotamia from ca. 1800 BC as ridden animal and when it acquires military significance with the invention of the chariot. Domestication of the horse before the 2nd millennium appears confined to its native habitat (the Great Steppe).

Researcher remarked that 'the significance of the horse ... has been much exaggerated' and Bryant holds that "using such negative evidence, by the same logic used to eliminate India as a candidate, ultimately any potential homeland can be disqualified due to lacking some fundamental Proto-Indo-European item or another. Renfrew's statement refers to his own Anatolian hypothesis which is criticized by mainstream scholarship on similar grounds.

In RV 1.162.18, the sacrificial horse is described as having 34 (2 × 17) ribs:

- The four-and-thirty ribs of the Swift Charger, kin to the Gods, the slayer's hatchet pierces.
- Cut ye with skill, so that the parts be flawless, and piece by piece declaring them dissect them.

Researcher speculates that the Rigvedic horse could therefore be the Indian Equus sivalensis (which may or may not have had 34 ribs; modern horses usually have 36, with occasional specimens of 34 or 38).

CHAPTER 3

Feral Horses

A feral horse is a free-roaming horse of domesticated ancestry. As such, a feral horse is not a wild animal in the sense of an animal without domesticated ancestors. However, some populations of feral horses are managed as wildlife, and these horses often are popularly called 'wild' horses. Feral horses are descended from domestic horses that strayed, escaped, or were deliberately released into the wild and remained to survive and reproduce there. Away from humans, over time, these animals' patterns of behaviour revert to behaviour more closely resembling that of wild horses. Some horses that live in a feral condition but may be occasionally handled or managed by humans, particularly if privately owned, are referred to as 'semi-feral'.

Feral horses live in groups called a *band, herd, harem,* or *mob.* Feral horse herds, like those of wild horses, are usually made up of small bands led by a dominant mare, containing additional mares, their foals, and immature horses of both sexes. There is usually one herd stallion, though occasionally a few less-dominant males may remain with the group. Horse 'herds' in the wild are best described as groups of several small bands who share a common territory. Bands are usually on the small side, as few as three to five animals, but sometimes over a dozen. The makeup of bands shifts over time as young animals are driven out of the band they were born into and join other bands, or as young stallions challenge older males for dominance. However, in a given closed ecosystem such as the isolated refuges in which most feral horses live today, to maintain genetic diversity the minimum size for a sustainable free-roaming horse or burro population is 150-200 animals.

Horses which live in an untamed state but have ancestors who have been domesticated are not true 'wild' horses; they are feral horses. The best known examples of feral horses are the 'wild' horses of the American west. When Europeans reintroduced the horse to the Americas, beginning with the arrival of the Conquistadors in the 15th century, some horses escaped and formed feral herds known today as Mustangs.

Australia has the largest population of feral horses in the world, with an excess of 400,000 feral horses. The Australian name equivalent to the 'Mustang' is the Brumby, feral descendants of horses brought to Australia by English settlers.

In Portugal, the free-ranging feral horse is known as Sorraia. There are also isolated populations of feral horses in a number of other places, including Sable Island off the coast of Nova Scotia, Assateague Island off the coast of Virginia and Maryland, and Vieques island off the coast of Puerto Rico. Some of these horses are said to be the descendants of horses who managed to swim to land when they were shipwrecked. Others may have been deliberately brought to various islands by settlers and either left to reproduce freely, or abandoned when assorted human settlements failed.

A modern feral horse population (*Janghali ghura*) is found in the Dibru-Saikhowa National Park and Biosphere reserve of Assam, in northern India, a herd of approximately 79 Feral horses descended from animals that escaped army camps during II World War.

Modern types of feral horses that have a significant percentage of their number living in a feral state, even though there may be some domesticated representatives, include the following types, landraces, and breeds:

- Banker horse, on the Outer Banks of North Carolina.
- Brumby, the feral horse of Australia.
- Chincoteague Pony, on Assateague Island off the coasts of Virginia and Maryland.
- Cumberland Island Horse, on Cumberland Island off the coast of southern Georgia.
- Danube Delta horse, in and around Letea Forest, between the Sulina and Chilia branches of Danube.
- Elegesi Qiyus Wild Horse (Cayuse), Canada; lives in the Nemaiah Valley, British Columbia.
- Kaimanawa horse, New Zealand.
- Kondudo horse, in the Kondudo region, Ethiopia; threatened with extinction.
- Misaki Pony, Japan.
- Mustang, legally protected by the Wild and Free-Roaming Horses and Burros Act of 1971 in the western United States.
- Namib desert horse, Namibia.
- Nokota horse.
- Sorraia, a feral horse native to Portugal and Spain.
- Sable Island Pony found in Nova Scotia.
- Welsh Pony, mostly domesticated, but a feral population of about 180 animals roams the Carneddau hills of North Wales. Other populations roam the eastern parts of the Brecon Beacons National Park.

Semi-feral Horses

In the United Kingdom, herds of free-roaming ponies live in apparently wild conditions in various areas, notably Dartmoor, Exmoor, and the New Forest. Similar horse and pony populations exist elsewhere on the European continent. These animals, however, are not truly feral, as all of them are privately owned, and roam out on the moors and forests under common grazing rights belonging to their owners. A proportion of them are halter-broken, and a smaller proportion broken to ride but simply turned out for a while for any of a number of reasons (for example a break in training to allow them to grow on, a break from working to allow them to breed under natural conditions, or retirement). In other cases, the animals may be government-owned and closely managed on controlled reserves.

- Camargue horse, in marshes of the Rhone delta, southern France
- Dartmoor pony, England; predominantly domesticated, also lives in semi-feral herds
- Exmoor pony, England; predominantly domesticated, also lives in semi-feral herds
- New Forest pony, predominantly domesticated, also lives in semi-feral herds in the area of Hampshire, England
- Konik, semi-feral horse of eastern Europe.
- Delft pony, feral herds first introduced by the Portuguese during colonial times to Delft island north of Sri Lanka.

Feral Population and its Impacts

Feral populations are usually controversial, with livestock producers often at odds with horse aficionados and other animal welfare advocates. Different habitats are impacted in different ways by feral horses. Where feral horses had wild ancestors indigenous to a region, a controlled population may have minimal environmental impact, particularly when their primary territory is one where they do not compete with domesticated livestock to any significant degree. However, in areas where they are an introduced species, such as Australia, or if population is allowed to exceed available range, there can be significant impacts on soil, vegetation and animals that are native species. If a feral population lives close to civilization, their behaviour can lead them to damage human-built livestock fencing and related structures. In some cases, where feral horses compete with domestic livestock, particularly on public lands where multiple uses are permitted, such as in the Western United States, there is considerable controversy over which species is responsible for degradation of rangeland, with commercial interests often advocating for the removal of feral horse population to allow more grazing for cattle or sheep, and advocates for feral horses recommending reduction in the numbers of domestic livestock allowed to graze on public lands.

There are certain populations that have considerable historic or sentimental value, such as the Chincoteague pony that lives on Assateague

Island, a national seashore with a delicate coastal ecosystem, or the Misaki pony of Japan that lives on a small refuge within the municipal boundaries Kushima. These populations manage to thrive with careful management that includes using the animals to promote tourism to support the local economy. Most sustained feral populations are managed by various forms of culling, which, depending on the nation and other local conditions, may include capturing excess animals for adoption or sale, or the often-controversial practice of simply shooting them. Fertility control is also sometimes used, though it is expensive and has to be repeated on a regular basis

BANKER HORSE

The Banker horse is a breed of feral horse (*Equus ferus caballus*) living on the islands of North Carolina's Outer Banks. It is small, hardy, and has a docile temperament. Descended from domesticated Spanish horses and possibly brought to the Americas in the 16th century, the ancestral foundation bloodstock may have become feral after surviving shipwrecks or being abandoned on the islands by one of the exploratory expeditions led by Lucas Vázquez de Ayllón or Sir Richard Grenville. Populations are found on Ocracoke Island, Shackleford Banks, Currituck Banks, and in the Rachel Carson Estuarine Sanctuary.

Although they can trample plants and ground-nesting animals, and are not considered to be indigenous to the islands, Bankers are allowed to remain because of their historical significance. They survive by grazing on marsh grasses, which supply them with water as well as food, supplemented by temporary freshwater pools.

To prevent overpopulation and inbreeding, and to protect their habitat from being overgrazed, the horses are managed by the National Park Service, the State of North Carolina, and several private organisations. The horses are monitored for diseases such as equine infectious anemia, an outbreak of which was discovered and subsequently eliminated on Shackleford in 1996. They are safeguarded from traffic on the North Carolina Highway 12. Island populations are limited by adoptions and by birth control. Bankers taken from the wild and trained have been used for trail riding, driving, and occasionally for mounted patrols.

Characteristics of Banker Horse

The typical Banker is relatively small, standing between 13.0 and 14.3 hands (52 and 59 inches, 132 and 150 cm) high at the withers and weighing 800 to 1,000 pounds (360 to 450 kg). The forehead is broad and the facial profile tends to be straight or slightly convex. The chest is deep and narrow and the back is short with a sloped croup and low-set tail. Legs have an oval-shaped cannon bone, a trait considered indicative of 'strong bone' or soundness. The callousities known as chestnuts are small, on some so tiny that they are barely detectable. Most Bankers have no chestnuts on the hind legs. The coat can be any colour, but is most often brown, bay, dun, or chestnut.

Bankers have long-strided gaits and many are able to pace and amble. They are easy keepers and are hardy, friendly, and docile.

Several of the Bankers' characteristics indicate that they share ancestry with other Colonial Spanish Horse breeds. The presence of the genetic marker 'Q-ac' suggests that the horses share common ancestry with two other breeds of Spanish descent, the Pryor Mountain Mustang and Paso Fino. These breeds diverged from one another 400 years ago. The breed shares skeletal traits of other Colonial Spanish horses: the wings of the atlas are lobed, rather than semi-circular; and the spine may be fused at the fifth and sixth lumbar vertebrae. No changes in function result from these spinal differences. The convex facial profile common to the breed also indicates Spanish ancestry.

Breed History

Since they are free-roaming, Bankers are often referred to as 'wild' horses; however, because they descend from domesticated ancestors, they are feral horses. It is thought that the Bankers arrived on the barrier islands during the 16th century. Several hypotheses have been advanced to explain the horses' origins, but none have yet been fully verified.

One theory is that ancestors of the Banker swam ashore from wrecked Spanish galleons. Ships returning to Spain from the Americas often took advantage of both the Gulf Stream and continental trade winds, on a route that brought them within 20 miles (32 km) of the Outer Banks. Hidden shoals claimed many victims, and earned this region the name of 'Graveyard of the Atlantic'. At least eight shipwrecks discovered in the area are of Spanish origin, dating between 1528 and 1564. These ships sank close enough to land for the horses to have made the shores. Alternatively, during hazardous weather, ships may have taken refuge close to shore, where the horses may have been turned loose. However, the presence of horses on Spanish treasure ships has not been confirmed—cargo space was primarily intended for transporting riches such as gold and silver.

Another conjecture is that the breed is descended from the 89 horses brought to the islands in 1526 by Spanish explorer Lucas Vázquez de Ayllón. His attempted colonization of San Miguel de Gualdape (near the Santee River in South Carolina) failed, forcing the colonists to move, possibly to North Carolina. Vázquez de Ayllón and about 450 of the original 600 colonists subsequently died, as a result of desertion, disease, and an early frost. Lacking effective leadership, the new settlement lasted for only two months; the survivors abandoned the colony and fled to Hispaniola, leaving their horses behind.

A similar theory is that Sir Richard Grenville brought horses to the islands in 1585, during an attempt to establish an English naval base. All five of the expedition's vessels ran aground at Wococon (present-day Ocracoke). Documents indicate that the ships carried various types of livestock obtained through trade in Hispaniola, including 'mares, kyne [cattle], buls, goates, swine [and] sheep'. While the smaller vessels were easily refloated, one of Grenville's larger ships, the *Tiger*, was nearly destroyed. Scholars believe that as the crew attempted to lighten the ship, they either unloaded the horses or forced them overboard, letting them swim to shore. In a letter to Sir Francis Walsingham that same year, Grenville suggested that livestock survived on the island after the grounding of his ships.

Life on the Barrier Islands

About 400 Bankers inhabit the long, narrow barrier islands of North Carolina's Outer Banks. These islands are offshore sediment deposits separated from the mainland by a body of water such as an estuary or sound. The islands can be up to 30 miles (48 km) from the shore; most are less than one mile (1.6 km) wide. Vegetation is sparse and consists mainly of coarse grasses and a few stunted trees. Each island in the chain is separated from the next by a tidal inlet.

The Bankers' small stature can be attributed, in part, to limited nutrients in their diet. They graze mostly on *Spartina* grasses, but will feed on other plants such as bulrush (*Typha latifolia*), sea oats, and even poison ivy. Horses living closer to human habitation, such as those on Currituck Banks, have sometimes grazed on residential lawns and landscaping. Domesticated Bankers raised on manufactured horse feed from an early age tend to exhibit slightly larger frames.

Water is a limiting resource for Bankers, as the islands are surrounded by salt water and have no freshwater springs or permanent ponds. The horses are dependent on ephemeral pools of rainwater and moisture in the vegetation they consume. Bankers will dig shallow holes, ranging from 2.5 to 4 feet (0.76 to 1.2 m) in depth, to reach fresh groundwater. Occasionally, they may resort to drinking seawater. This gives them a bloated appearance, a consequence of water retention caused by the body's effort to maintain osmotic balance.

Land Use Controversies

The National Park Service (NPS) is concerned about the impact of Bankers on the environmental health of North Carolina's barrier islands. Initially, the NPS believed that the non-native Bankers would completely consume the *Spartina alterniflora* grasses and the maritime forests, as both were thought to be essential to their survival. Research in 1987 provided information on the horses' diet that suggested otherwise. Half of their diet consisted of *Spartina*, while only 4 per cent of their nutrients came from the maritime forest. The study concluded that sufficient nutrients were replenished with each ocean tide to prevent a decline in vegetative growth from overgrazing. A 2004 study declared that the greatest impact on plant life was not from grazing but from the damage plants sustained when trampled by the horses' hooves. Bankers pose a threat to ground-nesting animals such as sea turtles and shorebirds. Feral horses interrupt nesting activities, and can crush the young.

Adoption and Management

As the Bankers are seen as a part of North Carolina's coastal heritage, they have been allowed to remain on the barrier islands. To cope with the expanding population, prevent inbreeding and attempt to minimize environmental damage, several organisations partner in managing the herds.

Ocracoke

Since 1959, Bankers on Ocracoke Island have been confined to fenced areas of approximately 180 acres (0.73 km^2; 0.28 sq mi). The areas protect the horses from the traffic of North Carolina Highway 12, as well as safeguarding the island from overgrazing. The NPS, the authority managing the Ocracoke herd, supplements the horses' diet with additional hay and grain. In 2006, as a precaution against inbreeding, two colts from the Shackleford herd were transported to Ocracoke.

Shackleford

Public Law 105-229, commonly referred to as the Shackleford Banks Wild Horses Protection Act, states that the Bankers on Shackleford Island are to be jointly managed by the National Park Service and another qualified nonprofit entity (currently the Foundation for Shackleford Horses). The herd is limited to 120-130 horses. Population management is achieved through adoption and by administering the contraceptive vaccine *Porcine zona pellucida* (PZP) to individual mares via dart. The island's horse population is monitored by freeze branding numbers onto each animal's left hindquarter. The identification of individuals allows the National Park Service to ensure correct gender ratios and to select which mares to inject with PZP.

Since 2000, adoptions of Bankers from Shackleford have been managed by the Foundation for Shackleford Horses. As of 2007, 56 horses had found new homes, 10 resided with another herd on Cedar Island, and two had been moved to the Ocracoke herd.

On November 12, 1996, the Shackleford horses were rounded up by the North Carolina Department of Agriculture's Veterinary Division and tested for equine infectious anemia (EIA). EIA is a potentially lethal disease, a lentivirus transmitted by bodily fluids and insects. Seventy-six of the 184 captured horses tested positive. Those that tested negative were allowed to remain on the island and those with the disease were transported to a temporary quarantine facility. Finding a permanent, isolated area for such a large number of Bankers was a challenging task for the Foundation; eight days later the state declared all proposed locations for the herd unsuitable. It ordered the euthanization of the 76 infected horses. Two more horses died in the process—one which was fatally injured during the roundup, and an uninfected foal that slipped into the quarantined herd to be with its mother.

Currituck Banks

As a consequence of Corolla's development in the 1980s, horses on Currituck Banks came into contact with humans more frequently. By 1989, eleven Bankers had been killed by cars on the newly constructed Highway 12. That same year, the Corolla Wild Horse Fund, a nonprofit organisation, was created to protect the horses from human interference. As a result of its efforts, a herd of 60 horses was moved to a more remote part of the island, where they were fenced into 1,800 acres (7.28 km^2; 2.81 sq mi) of combined federal and privately donated land. Corolla commissioners declared the site a feral horse sanctuary. The population is now managed by adopting out yearlings, both fillies and gelded colts.

Rachel Carson Site, North Carolina National Estuarine Research Reserve

A herd lives on the Rachel Carson component of the North Carolina National Estuarine Research Reserve, a series of five small islands and several salt marshes. There were no horses at the Sanctuary until the 1940s. It is unclear whether the Bankers swam over from nearby Shackleford or if they were left by residents who had used the islands to graze livestock. They are owned and managed by the State of North Carolina and regarded as a cultural resource.

No management action was taken until the late 1980s and early 1990s, when after years of flourishing population, the island's carrying capacity was exceeded. Malnourishment caused by overcrowding resulted in the deaths of several horses; the reserve's staff instituted a birth control programme to regulate the herd to about 40 animals.

Adopted Bankers are often used for pleasure riding and driving. As they have a calm disposition, they are used as children's mounts. The breed has also been used in several mounted patrols.

Before 1915, the United States Lifesaving Service used horses for beach watches and rescues. In addition to carrying park rangers on patrols, the horses hauled equipment to and from shipwreck sites. During World War II, the Coast Guard used them for patrols. In the 1980s Bankers were used for beach duty at Cape Hatteras National Seashore.

In 1955, ten horses were taken from the Ocracoke herd as a project for Boy Scout Troop 290. After taming and branding the horses, the scouts trained them for public service activities. The Bankers were ridden in parades and used as mounts during programmes to spray mosquito-ridden salt marshes.

BRUMBY

A Brumby is a free-roaming feral horse in Australia. Although found in many areas around the country, the best-known brumbies are found in the Australian Alps region in south-eastern Australia. Today, most of them are found in the Northern Territory, with the second largest population in Queensland. A group of Brumbies is known as a 'mob' or 'band'.

Brumbies are the descendants of escaped or lost horses, dating back in some cases to those belonging to the early European settlers, including the 'Capers' from South Africa, Timor Ponies from Indonesia, British pony and draught horse breeds, and a significant number of Thoroughbreds and Arabians.

Today they live in many places, including some National Parks. Occasionally they are mustered and domesticated for use as campdrafters, working stock horses on farms or stations, but also as trail horses, show horses, Pony Club mounts and pleasure horses. They are the subject of some controversy—regarded as a pest and threat to native ecosystems by environmentalists and the government, but also valued by others as part of Australia's heritage, with supporters working to prevent inhumane treatment or extermination, and rehoming Brumbies who have been captured.

Origin of the Term

The term *brumby* refers to a feral horse in Australia. Its first recorded use in print is in the *Australasian* magazine from Melbourne in 1880, which said that brumbies were the bush name in Queensland for 'wild' horses. In 1885, the *Once a Month* magazine suggested that *brumbies* was a New South Wales term, and the poet Banjo Paterson stated in the introduction for his poem *Brumby's Run* published in the Bulletin in 1894 that Brumby was the word for free-roaming horses. Its derivation is obscure, and may have come about from one or more of the following possibilities:

- Horses left behind by Sergeant James Brumby from his property at Mulgrave Place in New South Wales, when he left for Tasmania in 1804.
- An Aboriginal word *baroomby* meaning 'wild' in the language of the Pitjara Indigenous Australians on the Warrego and Nogoa Rivers in southern Queensland.
- A letter in 1896 to the Sydney Morning Herald also says that *baroombie* is the word for horse among the Aboriginal people of the Balonne, Nebine, Warrego and Bulloo Rivers.
- Baramba, which was the name of a creek and station in the Queensland district of Burnett, established in the 1840s and later abandoned, leaving many of the horses to escape into the wild.
- It has also been suggested that the name derives from the Irish word *bromach* or *bromaigh*.

Early Horse Imports

Horses first arrived in Australia in 1788 with the First Fleet of Irish and British settlers. They were imported for farm and utility work; recreational riding and racing were not major activities. By 1800, only about 200 horses are thought to have reached Australia. Horse racing became popular around 1810, resulting in an influx of Thoroughbred imports, mostly from England. Roughly 3,500 horses were living in Australia by 1820, and this number had grown to 160,000 by 1850, largely due to natural increase. The long journey by sea from England, Europe, and Asia meant that only the strongest horses survived the trip, making for a particularly healthy and strong Australian stock, which aided in their ability to flourish.

Origin of Feral Herds

Horses were likely confined primarily to the Sydney region until the early 19th century, when settlers first crossed the Blue Mountains and opened expansion inland. Horses were required for travel, and for cattle and sheep droving as the pastoral industry grew. The first report of an escaped horse is in 1804, and by the 1840s some horses had escaped from settled regions of Australia. It is likely that some escaped because fences were not properly installed, when fences existed at all, but it is believed that most Australian horses became feral because they were released into the wild and left to fend for themselves. This may have been the result of pastoralists abandoning their settlements, and thus their horses, due to the arid conditions and unfamiliar land that combined to make farming in Australia especially difficult. After World War I, the demand for horses by defence forces declined with the growth in mechanization, which led to a growth in the number of unwanted animals that were often set free. Throughout the 20th century, the replacement of horses with machines in farming led to further falls in demand, and therefore may have also contributed to increases in feral populations.

Currently, Australia has at least 400,000 horses roaming the continent. It is also estimated that, during periods of non-drought periods, the feral horse population increases at a rate of 20 per cent per year. Drought conditions and brushfires are natural threats. Despite population numbers, feral horses are generally considered to be a moderate pest. Where they are allowed to damage vegetation and cause erosion, the impact on the environment can be detrimental, and for that reason can be considered a serious environmental threat. However, because they also have cultural and potential economic value, the management of Brumbies presents a complex issue.

Brumbies roaming in the Australian Alps of south-eastern Australia are thought to be descendants of horses which were owned by the pastoralist and pioneer, Benjamin Boyd.

Pangare Brumbies

On the coast south of Geraldton, Western Australia the Brumbies there are known as 'Pangare Ponies', as they appear to carry the rare Pangaré gene. This colouring is commonly known as *mealy* and is seen mainly in a number of old breeds such as British Ponies, Timor Ponies, Haflingers and even Belgian Draught Horses. The gene causes lightening in parts of a horse's coat, resulting in a mealy coloured muzzle, forearms, flanks, and the belly. It is sometimes seen in chestnut horses with flaxen coloured manes and tails.

The Pangaré Brumbies appear have adapted well to their coastal environment, where they are consuming saltbush, which they do not appear to be damaging. The Department of Environment and Conservation and the Outback Heritage Horse Association of Western Australia (OHHAWA) are monitoring these particular Brumbies to ensure the careful management of these unusual feral horses.

Uses

Brumbies have been captured, fitted with GPS tracking collars, and used in extensive comparative research into the effect of terrain on the morphology and health of different horses' hooves. They have their paths of movement, diet, watering patterns, and mob structure tracked and recorded.

Captured Brumbies can be trained as stock horses and other saddle horses. Encouraging viewing of feral herds may also have potential as a tourist attraction. Brumbies are sometimes sold into the European horse meat market after their capture, and contribute millions of dollars to the Australian economy. Approximately 30 per cent of horses for meat export originates from the feral population. The hides and hair of these horses are also used and sold.

Wild Brumbies are used in Brumby training camps by organisations that promote positive interaction between troubled, high-risk youths. These camps usually last several weeks, allowing youths to train a wild Brumby to become a quiet, willing saddle horse while improving the youths' self esteem.

Wild Brumbies are also used in the Brumby catch and handle event in stockman's challenge competitions, where riders are required to catch a free running Brumby from their horse within a time limit of a few minutes. Sectional points are awarded for the stockman's challenge for care and skill in catching the Brumby and their ability to teach them to lead. These demanding challenges for riders are held in New South Wales at Dalgety, Tamworth and Murrurundi plus *The Man From Snowy River Challenge* in Corryong, Victoria. Several New South Wales show societies, including Walcha, Bellingen and Dorrigo hold special classes for registered Brumbies at their annual agricultural shows.

Impact of Environment

Horses were first described as pests in Australia in the 1860s. Their environmental impact may include soil loss, compaction, and erosion; trampling of vegetation; reduction in the vastness of plants; increased tree deaths by chewing on bark; damage to bog habitats and waterholes; spreading of invasive weeds; and various detrimental effects on population of native species. In some cases, when feral horses are startled, they may damage infrastructure, including troughs, pipes, and fences. However, Brumbies are also credited for help keeping tracks and trails clear for bush walkers and service vehicles in some areas.

In some habitats, hooves of free-roaming horses compact the soil, and when the soil is compacted, air spaces are minimized, leaving nowhere for water to collect. When this occurs, soil in areas where horses are prevalent has a water penetration resistance over 15 times higher than that in areas without horses. Trampling also causes soil erosion and damages vegetation, and because the soil cannot hold water, plant regrowth is hindered. Horse trampling also has the potential to damage waterways and bog habitats. Trampling near streams increases runoff, reducing the quality of the water and causing harm to the ecosystem of the waterway. Horse excrement tends to foul these waterways, as does the accumulation of carcasses that result when feral horses perish, adding to the negative environmental impact of this exotic species in Australia.

Alpine areas, such as those of Kosciuszko National Park, are at particular risk; low-growing alpine flora is highly vulnerable to trampling, and the short summers mean little time for plants to grow and recover from damage. The biodiversity there is high, with 853 species of plant, 21 of which are found nowhere else. Erosion in the limestone karst areas leads to runoff and silting. Sphagnum moss is an important component of highland bogs, and is trampled by horses seeking water.

Feral horses may also reduce the richness of plant species. Exposure of soil caused by trampling and vegetation removal via grazing, combined with increased nutrients being recycled by horse dung, favour weed species, which then invade the region and overtake native species, diminishing their diversity. The dispersal of weeds is aided by the attachment of seeds to the horses' manes and tails, and are also transferred via horse dung after consumption of weeds in one location and excrement in another. Although the effects of the weeds that actually germinate after transfer via dung is debated, the fact that a large number of weed species are dispersed via this method is of concern to those interested in the survival of native plant species in Australia. The effect on plants and plant habitats are more pronounced during droughts, when horses travel greater distances to find food and water. They consume the already threatened and limited vegetation, and their negative influences are more widespread. Feral horses may also chew the bark of trees, which may leave some trees vulnerable to external threats. This has occurred during drought, among eucalyptus species on the Red Range plateau. It appears as though feral horses may prefer these species.

Interaction with Other Animal Species

The changes in vegetation that result when feral horses overpopulate a region affects bird species by removing plants upon which they feed, as well as altering the habitat of the birds and their prey. Feral horse grazing is also linked to a decline in reptiles and amphibians due to habitat loss. In addition, the grazing and trampling near waterways influences aquatic fauna. In areas frequented by horses, crab densities are higher, increasing the propensity for predation on fish. As a result, fish densities decline as the removal of vegetation renders them more susceptible to predation.

In areas where horses are abundant, macropod populations are less prevalent. This is most likely due to the horses' consumption of vegetation upon which the macropods normally feed. When horses are removed, signs of the presence of various macropods, specifically the black-footed rock wallaby, increase. Thus, competition with horses may be the reason for the decline in macropod populations in certain areas.

Brumby populations also may have the potential to pass exotic diseases, such as equine influenza and African horse sickness to domestic horses. They also may carry tick fever, which can be passed to both horses and cattle. This can lead to high fatalities among domestic populations, causing many farmers to call for the management of feral horses.

Like all livestock, brumbies can carry the parasite *Cryptosporidium parvum*, which can result in serious gastroenteritis in people drinking contaminated drinking water.

Population Management

Although poor management of feral horses may pose an ecological and environmental threat in some parts of Australia, their management is made difficult by issues of feasibility and public concern. Currently, management attempts vary, as feral horses are considered pests in some states, such as South Australia, but not others, including Queensland. There is also controversy over removal of Brumbies from National Parks. The primary argument in favour of the removal of Brumbies is that they impact on fragile ecosystems and damage and destroy endangered native flora and fauna.

Public concern is a major issue in control efforts as many advocate for the protection of Brumbies, including the Aboriginal people, who believe feral horses belong to the country. Other horse interest groups resent the labelling of horses as 'feral' and are completely opposed to any measures that threaten their survival. While some Animal welfare groups such as the RSPCA reluctantly accept culling, other organisations such as Save the Brumbies oppose lethal culling techniques and attempt to organise relocation of the animals instead. It has been argued that relocation, which often involves hours of helicopter mustering, would be more traumatic for the horses.

Meanwhile, conservationist groups, such as the Australian Conservation Foundation, favour humane culling as a means of control because of the damage Brumby overpopulation can cause to native flora and fauna, but are also generally opposed to various means of extermination. This makes management a challenge for policymakers, though at present, the cost of allowing overpopulation of feral horses seems to outweigh other concerns.

Population Control Methods

The traditional method of removal, called brumby running, is reminiscent of Banjo Paterson's iconic poem, *The Man from Snowy River* where expert riders rope the Brumbies and remove them to a new location.

Options for population control include fertility control, ground and helicopter shooting, and mustering and trapping. None of the methods provide complete freedom from suffering for the horses, and the cost of each is very high. The costs include those that are economic, such as research, equipment purchases, and labour expenditures, as well as moral concerns over the welfare of the horses. As a result, more effective and efficient means of control have been called for.

Fertility control is a non-lethal method of population management that is usually viewed as the most humane treatment, and its use is supported by the RSPCA. While it appears as though these treatments are effective in the breeding season immediately following injection, the lasting effects are debated. Because it is costly and difficult to treat animals repeatedly, this method, despite being ideal, is not widely implemented.

Shooting by trained marksmen is considered to be the most practical method of control due to its effectiveness. The NSW Department of Primary Industries believe shooting is the preferred method of population control as it does not subject the horses to the stresses of mustering, yarding, and long-distance transportation, all of which are related to 'capture and removal' methods. Horses that are only initially wounded from shooting are tracked and dispatched if they are in accessible, open country. However, shooting of horses in in mountain ranges is not regarded as a humane means of control. Helicopter shootings allow for aerial reconnaissance of a large area to target the densest populations, and shooters may get close enough to the target animals to ensure termination. This method is considered the most effective and cost efficient means of control, but disapproval is high amongst those that believe it is inhumane. Organisations supporting Brumbies argue that aerial shooting is unnecessary and that alternative population control methods have not been given adequate trials, while government officials express concern about the need to control rapidly growing populations in order to avoid ecological problems associated with too many feral horses in certain areas.

Mustering is a labour intensive process that results in one of two major outcomes: slaughter for sale, or relocation. It may be assisted by feed-luring in which bales of hay are strategically placed to attract feral horses to a location where capture is feasible. Complicating this process is low demand for the captured horses, making it less desirable than fertility control or shooting, which reduce the population without having to find alternative locations for them.

Management in National Parks

Between 22 October and 24 October 2000, approximately 600 Brumbies were shot in the Guy Fawkes River National Park by the National Parks and Wildlife Service. As a result of the public outcry that followed the NSW Government established a Steering Committee to investigate alternative methods of control. Since the campaign began to remove horses from the national park, over 400 have been passively trapped and taken from the Park, and 200 of these have been re-homed.

A NSW National Parks and Wildlife Service cull during 2006 and 2007 in Kosciuszko National Park, where there were an estimated 1700 horses in 2005, resulted in a reduction of 64 horses.

The NSW National Parks and Wildlife Service commenced a plan in 2007 to reduce Brumby numbers by passive trapping in the Oxley Wild Rivers National Park. Over 60 brumbies captured in the Apsley River Gorge have now been re-homed.

In 2008 the third phase of an aerial culling of Brumbies took place, by shooting 700 horses from a helicopter, in Carnarvon Gorge in Carnarvon National Park, Queensland.

In Literature and Media

Brumbies, called 'wild bush horses', are mentioned in Banjo Paterson's poem *The Man from Snowy River*. This poem was expanded into the films *The Man from Snowy River* and *The Man from Snowy River II* — (US title: '*Return to Snowy River*' — UK title: '*The Untamed*') — also *The Man from Snowy River (TV series)* and *The Man from Snowy River: Arena Spectacular*.

Another Banjo Paterson poem, called *Brumby's Run*, describes a mob of brumbies running wild. Paterson was inspired to write the poem when he read of a N.S.W. Supreme Court Judge, who on hearing of Brumby horses, asked: 'Who is Brumby, and where is his Run?'

The popular Silver Brumby books by Elyne Mitchell were written for children and young adults. The stories describe the adventures of Thowra, a Brumby stallion. These stories were dramatised and made into a movie of the same name (also known as *The Silver Stallion: King of the Wild Brumbies*), starring Russell Crowe and Caroline Goodall.

The brumby was adopted as an emblem in 1996 by then newly formed ACT Brumbies, a Super 14 rugby union team based in Canberra, Australia.

CHINCOTEAGUE PONY

The Chincoteague Pony, also known as the Assateague horse, is a breed of pony that developed and lives in a feral condition on Assateague Island in the United States states of Virginia and Maryland. The breed was made famous by the *Misty of Chincoteague* series written by Marguerite Henry starting in 1947. While phenotypically horse-like, they are commonly called 'ponies'. This is due in part to their smaller stature, created by the poor habitat present on Assateague Island. Variation is found in their physical characteristics due to blood from different breeds being introduced at various points in their history. They can be any solid colour, and are often found in pinto patterns, which are a favourite with breed enthusiasts. Island Chincoteagues live on a diet of salt marsh plants and brush. This poor-quality and often scarce food combined with uncontrolled inbreeding created a propensity for conformation faults in the Chincoteague before outside blood was added beginning in the early 20th century.

Several legends are told regarding the origins of the Chincoteague, with the most popular being that they descend from survivors of wrecked Spanish galleons off the Virginia coast. It is more likely that they descend from stock released on the island by 17th century colonists looking to escape livestock laws and taxes on the mainland. In 1835, the practice of pony penning began, with settlers rounding up ponies and removing some of them to the mainland. In 1924 the first official 'Pony Penning Day' was held by the Chincoteague Volunteer Fire Company, where ponies were auctioned as a way to raise money for fire equipment. The annual event has continued in the same fashion almost uninterrupted to the present day.

Although popularly known as Chincoteague ponies, the feral ponies actually live on Assateague Island. Although the entire Island is owned by the federal government, Assateague is split by a fence at the Maryland/ Virginia state line, with a herd of around 150 ponies living on each side of the fence. The herds live on land managed by two different federal agencies with very different management strategies. Ponies from the Maryland herd, referred to in literature of the National Park Service as Assateague horses, live within Assateague Island National Seashore. They are generally treated as wild animals, given no more or less assistance than other species on the island, other than to be treated with contraceptives to prevent overpopulation. Conversely, the Virginia herd, referred to as Chincoteague ponies, lives within the Chincoteague National Wildlife Refuge but is owned by the Chincoteague Volunteer Fire Company. The Virginia ponies are treated to twice yearly veterinary inspections, which prepare them for life among the general equine population if they are sold at auction. While only around 300 ponies live on Assateague Island, around 1,000 more live off-island, having been purchased or bred by private breeders.

Characteristics

While phenotypically horses, the Chincoteague is most often referred to as a pony breed. Chincoteagues average around 13.2 hands (54 inches, 137 cm) in their feral state, but grow to at least 14.2 hands (58 inches, 147 cm) when domesticated and provided better nutrition.

They generally weigh around 850 pounds (390 kg). All solid colours are found in the breed, as are pinto patterns. Horses with pinto colouration tend to sell for the most money at the annual auction. Due to outside bloodlines being added to the Chincoteague herd, there is some variation in physical characteristics. In general, the breed tends to have a straight or slightly concave facial profile with a broad forehead and refined throatlatch and neck. The shoulders are well-angled, the ribs well-sprung, the chest broad and the back short with broad loins. The croup is rounded, with a thick, low-set tail. The breed's legs tend to be straight, with good, dense bone that makes them sound and sturdy. Domesticated Chincoteagues are considered intelligent and willing to please. They are viewed as easy to train, and are used as hunter, driving and trail ponies. In terms of health, they are generally hardy and easy keepers. In the late 19th century, one author praised their 'good manners and gentle disposition' while reporting the story of one pony who was ridden a distance of around 1,000 miles (1,600 km) in 34 days by a man with equipment, a load that weighed around 160 pounds (73 kg) – the pony weighed approximately 500 pounds (230 kg).

History

Legend states that Chincoteague ponies descend from Spanish horses shipwrecked off the Virginia coast on their way to Peru in the 16th century. Another story holds that they descend from horses left on the island by pirates. Both of these theories are unlikely, as no documentation has been found to show horses inhabiting the island this early, and no mention of horses already existing on the island was made by colonists on either the mainland or the island in the mid-to-late 1600s. Evidence points, however, to their ancestors actually being horses brought to the islands in the 17th century by mainland farmers. Livestock on the islands were not subject to taxes or fencing laws, and so many animals, including hogs, sheep, cattle and horses, were brought to the islands. While the National Park Service holds to the theory that the horses were brought to the island in the 17th century, the Chincoteague Volunteer Fire Company, which owns the ponies on the Virginia side of Assateague, argues that the Spanish shipwreck theory is correct. They argue that horses were too valuable in the 17th century to have been left to run wild on the island, and claim that there are two sunken Spanish galleons off the Virginia coast in support of their theory. The National Chincoteague Pony Association also promotes the shipwreck theory. In the early 1900s, they were described as having been on the islands since well before the American Revolution, and were described at that time as 'very diminutive, but many of them are of perfect symmetry and extraordinary powers of action and endurance'. In the early 1800s, Virginia governor Henry A. Wise released what one author called the 'earliest printed testimony' on the Chincoteague.

During the 1920s, before the herds were managed by various agencies, many conformation faults were found – the effects of uncontrolled inbreeding. Misshapen legs, narrow chests, poor bone and a lack of substance plagued the breed, with many stunted animals not growing above 12 hands (48 inches, 122 cm). This was partially due to the limited and poor-quality feed found on the islands, although this harsh habitat also allowed only the hardiest and most adaptable ponies to survive. Welsh and Shetland pony blood was added to upgrade the stock, and horses with pinto colouring were introduced to give the herd its common distinctive patterns and contribute to the more horse-like phenotype of the breed. Twenty Mustangs owned by the Bureau of Land Management were introduced in 1939. Arabian blood was added in the hopes of adding refinement and height to the breed, as well as increasing the length of their legs. Arabian stallions were used at two different points within the breed history: one was released with the herd, but did not survive, while another was bred to mares that had been removed from the island for breeding and then returned once in foal. The Chincoteague pony has a similar history to the lesser-known Shackleford Banker Horse, which comes from the Shackleford Banks off the coast of North Carolina. However, the Shackleford is a more isolated population, with no outside blood added to the island herd.

The Island itself has also undergone change. At one time, the island was connected to the lowest point of Fenwick Island. In August 1933, a hurricane created an inlet south of Ocean City, Maryland, separating the two landforms. After the storm, between 1933 and 1935, a permanent system of artificial jetties was built to preserve the inlet as a navigation channel. As a result of the jetties disrupting sand movement in the area, the island has drifted considerably westward, and the two landmasses are now over 1 kilometre (0.62 mi) apart.

Pony Penning

In 1835 the first written description of 'pony penning' appeared, though the practice of rounding up livestock on the island existed for many years before that. Initially, unclaimed animals were marked for ownership by groups of settlers. By 1885 the event had become a festival day, and two days of horse and sheep roundups were held on Assateague and Chincoteague Islands. While the sheep population diminished over time, the pony population grew. In 1909, the last Wednesday and Thursday of July were designated as the annual days for pony penning, still taking place on both Assateague and Chincoteague Islands. However, in the early 1920s, much of Assateague Island was purchased by a wealthy farmer, forcing many settlers to move to Chincoteague Island and necessitating a change in the pony penning format. By 1923, all parts of pony penning except for the actual roundup had moved to Chincoteague Island, with the ponies being transported by truck for the first two years before the annual swim was begun. By the early 1900s, Chincoteague Island had been established as a tourism and sport haven, and in 1922 a causeway was completed that connected the island to the Virginia mainland. After a pair of fires ravaged Chincoteague Island that same year, the Chincoteague Volunteer Fire Company was established. In 1924, the first official Pony Penning Day was held, where ponies were auctioned at $25-50 each to raise money for fire equipment. Pony Penning Day has been held annually ever since, with the exception of 1942 and 1943.

In the present day, up to 50,000 visitors gather on the last Wednesday in July to watch mounted riders bring the Virginia herd from Assateague and swim them across the channel to Chincoteague Island. The swim takes 5-10 minutes, with both the rider and the observers on hand to assist horses, especially foals, who may have a hard time with the crossing. Before the swim, the herd is evaluated and mares in the late stages of pregnancy and those with very young foals are removed from the herd to be trailered between the islands. During the swim, some lactating mares become affected with hypocalcemia, which is treated by on-site veterinarians. Larger foals are auctioned the next day and the majority of the herd, including any young foals, are returned to Assateague on Friday. As of 2009, the highest price paid for a pony was $11,700, while the average price was around $1,300. Some ponies are purchased under 'buy back' conditions, where the bidder donates the money to the fire department but allows the pony to be released back onto Assateague Island.

Breed Registry and Preservation

The National Chincoteague Pony Association was founded in 1985 and the Chincoteague Pony Association in 1994. The latter is open only to horses purchased from the annual auction, while the former maintains a breed registry and studbook that registers all ponies, including those from private breeders. Many ponies are registered with both associations. There are almost 1,000 Chincoteague ponies owned by private individuals off Chincoteague Island, spread throughout the US and Canada.

Management

All of Chincoteague Island lies within Virginia state lines, while Assateague Island is split between two states – a smaller northern portion in Maryland and the larger southern section within Virginia. Two separate herds of ponies live on Assateague Island, separated by a fence that runs along the Maryland-Virginia state border. Though descended from the same original stock, the Maryland feral ponies are called 'Assateague horses' and are maintained by the National Park Service. The Virginia feral ponies are called 'Chincoteague ponies' and are owned by Chincoteague Volunteer Fire Department. In 1943, the entire island was purchased by the federal government and divided into two protected areas, Assateague Island National Seashore in Maryland and Chincoteague National Wildlife Refuge in Virginia. The two herds lie under the jurisdiction of different governmental agencies, and different management strategies have been applied to each herd. The Maryland section of Assateague also contains Assateague State Park, state-owned land where the ponies are allowed to roam, although the state plays little or no part in their management.

The feral ponies in both herds separate themselves into small bands, with most consisting of a stallion, several mares and their foals. Ponies on Assateague have a diet that consists mainly of cordgrass, a coarse grass that grows in salt marshes, which makes up around 80 per cent of their food. This diet is supplemented by other vegetation such as rose hips, bayberry, greenbriar, American beach grass, seaweed and poison ivy. Chincoteague ponies require up to twice as much water as most horses require due to the saltiness of their diet. The increased amount of water that they drink contributes to many ponies appearing to be bloated or fat.

Maryland Herd

The Maryland herd, often called the Assateague herd, is owned and managed by the National Park Service. The Maryland herd is one of very few free-ranging wild horse populations left in the United States. This, combined with its presence on a relatively small and naturally confined area, has made it ideal for scientific study. Since the late 1970s, scientists have used the herd to conduct studies on feral horse behaviour, social structure, ecology, remote contraceptive delivery and pregnancy testing, and the effects of human intervention on other wild animal populations. There are few other wildlife populations of any species worldwide that have been studied in as much detail over as long a period as the Maryland herd of Chincoteague ponies.

Herd numbers grew from 28 to over 165 between 1968 and 1997 and overgrazing negatively impacted their living environment. To manage population numbers, long-term, non-hormonal contraceptives have been employed, proving 95 per cent effective over a seven-year field trial. The contraceptive, which began to be used at a management level in 1995 although it was used in smaller amounts as early as 1989, has also proven effective at improving the health and increasing the life expectancy of older mares through the removal of pregnancy and lactation-related stress. Since 1990, general herd health has improved, early mortality has decreased and older ponies are now found, with many over the age of 20 and some even over 25. No horse has ever been injured during the dart-administered treatments, although there is a 0.2 per cent rate of abscess at the injection site, which normally heals within two weeks. Each mare between two and four years old is given contraceptives, and treatment is then withdrawn until she produces a foal. Once she has produced enough foals to be well-represented genetically within the herd, she is placed on a yearly treatment plan until her death. After the introduction of the contraceptive, herd numbers continued to rise to a high of 175 in 2001 to 2005, but then dropped significantly to around 130 in 2009. In 2009, a study determined that mitochondrial DNA diversity in the herd was quite low, most likely due to their isolation, but that their nuclear genetic diversity remained at a level similar to that of breeds from the mainland.

Other than the contraceptive and treatment in emergencies, ponies from the Maryland herd are treated much like other wildlife, with no extra attention paid to them by Park Service employees. It is thought likely that the Maryland herd carries Equine Infectious Anemia (EIA); they are effectively quarantined, however, by allowing no riding or camping with privately owned horses along the mainland shore during the insect season which stretches from mid-May to October. Due to their treatment as wild animals, ponies from the Maryland herd can be aggressive, and there have been reports of them tearing down tents and biting, kicking and knocking down visitors. In 2010, after an increase in biting incidents, the National Park Service implemented new measures for educating visitors about the ponies. These measures included new safety information in brochures and recommended viewing distances between the visitors and the ponies. There is also some danger to the ponies from the visitors: ponies have become ill from being fed inappropriate human foods, and on average one Maryland pony a year is killed by a car. Since 1991 there has been a 'Pony Patrol', where volunteers on bikes patrol the island, educating visitors about the ponies.

The Virginia Herd

The Virginia herd, often called the Chincoteague herd, is owned and managed by the Chincoteague Volunteer Fire Company. The US Fish and

Wildlife Service (FWS) allows the ponies to live on Assateague under a special use grazing permit, allowing approximately 150 adult ponies in the Chincoteague National Wildlife Refuge.

Thirty to 45 foals are born into the Chincoteague herd each year. The annual Pony Pennings are used to maintain the herd size at around 150 animals. Since 1943, the FWS has been working on the island to protect and increase the wildfowl population, and their efforts have sometimes endangered the Chincoteague herd. Due to the placement of fences by the FWS, a reduced amount of land is available for grazing by the ponies. The fencing also prevents them from reaching the sea, where they often went to escape biting insects, including mosquitos. In 1962, several ponies were trapped in an enclosure by high water and died when they were carried out to sea during a storm. Unlike the Maryland herd, ponies on the Virginia side of the island are fenced off from roadways to prevent auto accidents and to discourage visitors from feeding the ponies.

In the late 20th century, some ponies previously sold at auction were returned to Assateague Island when population numbers threatened to drop below the targeted numbers due to large numbers of deaths from storms or other issues. Since 1990, the ponies from the Virginia herd have been swum to Chincoteague Island biannually for veterinary treatment, including deworming and vaccinations for diseases such as rabies, tetanus and Eastern and Western encephalitis. In addition, continual monitoring and basic first aid for any minor injuries is performed by a committee from the fire department. Such intervention is needed because many of the ponies will be brought into the general horse population through the auction and purchase by private buyers. During the veterinary visits, they are also tested for EIA.

In 1947, Marguerite Henry released the children's book *Misty of Chincoteague*, the first in a series of novels that made the Chincoteague breed internationally famous. The real Misty was foaled on Chincoteague Island in 1946 and was purchased as a weanling by Henry. In 1961, the publicity was increased even more when the film *Misty* was made, based on the book. The publicity generated by the books assisted the Chincoteague Fire Department and the breed in remaining viable into the 21st century.

While fictionalized, the books were based on a real horse and ranch on Chincoteague Island, and the Misty of Chincoteague Foundation was established in 1990 to preserve the Beebe Ranch and establish a museum with memorabilia from the series. Model horse company Breyer Animal Creations has created models of Misty and five of her descendants. As of 2001, there were around 40 surviving descendants of Misty worldwide.

KAIMANAWA HORSE

Kaimanawa horses are a population of feral horses in New Zealand that are descended from domestic horses released in the 19th and 20th centuries. They are known for their hardiness and quiet temperament. The

New Zealand government strictly controls the population to protect the habitat in which they live, which includes several endangered species of plants. The varying heritage gives the breed a wide range of heights, body patterns and colours. They are usually well-muscled, sure-footed and tough.

Horses were first reported in the Kaimanawa Range in 1876, although the first horses had been brought into New Zealand in 1814. The feral herds grew as horses escaped and were released from sheep stations and cavalry bases. Members of the herd were recaptured by locals for use as riding horses, as well as being caught for their meat, hair and hides. The herd declined as large scale farming and forestry operations encroached on their ranges, and only around 174 horses were known to exist by 1979. The Kaimanawa herd was protected by the New Zealand government in 1981, and there were 1,576 horses in the herd by 1994. A small, mostly unmanaged population also exists on the Aupouri Peninsula at the northern tip of the North Island. Roundups have been carried out annually since 1993 to manage the size of the herd, removing around 2,800 horses altogether. The Kaimanawa population is listed as a herd of special genetic value by the United Nations' Food and Agricultural Organisation, and several studies have been conducted on the herd dynamics and habits of the breed.

History

The first horses were introduced to New Zealand by Protestant missionary Reverend Samuel Marsden in December 1814, and wild horses were first reported in the Kaimanawa Range in central North Island of New Zealand in 1876. The Kaimanawa breed descended from domestic horses that were released in the late 19th century and early 20th century in the middle of the North Island around the Kaimanawa mountains. Between 1858 and 1875, Major George Gwavas Carlyon imported Exmoor ponies to Hawkes Bay and crossed them with local stock to produce the Carlyon pony. These Carlyon ponies were later crossed with two Welsh stallions, Kinarth Caesar and Comet, imported by Sir Donald McLean, and a breed known as the Comet resulted. At some point during the 1870s, McLean released a Comet stallion and several mares on the Kaingaroa Plains and the bloodline apparently became part of the wild Kaimanawa population. Other horses were added to the bloodline through escapes and releases from local sheep stations and from cavalry units at Waiouru that were threatened with a strangles epidemic. It is also thought that in the 1960s Nicholas Koreneff released an Arabian stallion into the Argo Valley region. Throughout the 19th and 20th centuries, horses were harvested from the feral herds and used as riding and stock horses, as well as being used for their meat, hair and hides. Originally there were many herds that roamed land owned by the British Crown and the native Maori, but many were eradicated with the intensification of large scale farming and forestry operations combined with increased mechanization that decreased the need for stock horses. Kaimanawa horses today have the highest amount of genetic similarity with the Thoroughbred and other Thoroughbred cross breeds.

Pressure from land development and an encroaching human population reduced the range and the number of the Kaimanawa horses, and in 1979 it was found that only about 174 horses remained. Starting in 1981, the Kaimanawa population, range size, and herd movements began to be officially measured, and a protected area was formed for the breed in the Waiouru Military Training Area. Legislative protection was similar to the kiwi and other native species. There was a rapid increase in the herd size following the protection of the breed, and 1,576 horses were known to exist in the area by 1994. There is also a small population of horses on the Aupouri Peninsula at the northern tip of the North Island, which is mostly unmanaged by the New Zealand government. In 2008, the Kaimanawa herds were the focus of a novel called *Kaimanawa Princess*, by Dianne Haworth.

Characteristics of Breed

Many characteristics of the Comet type are said to be shown in the Kaimanawa horses today, although the varied gene input has produced a wide range of sizes, colours, and body types among the wild horses. The Kaimanawa breed varies widely in general appearance, with heights ranging between 12.2 and 15 hands (50 and 60 inches, 127 and 152 cm) high. Any coat colour or pattern marking is acceptable. They are usually well-muscled. Their feral way of life has given them the ability to adapt quickly and live on very little, and they are usually sure-footed and tough. They have a medium sized head in good proportion to their body, with wide variation in shape due to the different conformation of their ancestors. Kaimanawa horses have a short, deep neck with a thick throat area, straight shoulders, a deep girth, and a short to medium back. The hindquarters vary from sloping to well-rounded. The legs are long and well-muscled, with strong hooves, and hind hooves that are generally smaller than the front ones. All horses are considered to age a year on the first of August, regardless of their actual foaling date.

Population Control and Study

Due to the increase in population after protective legislation was put into place, the Department of Conservation developed a management plan for the Kaimanawa herd in 1989 and 1990. A draft plan was made available to the public for comment in 1991, and the public made it clear that it objected to herd reduction through shooting from helicopters, and instead favoured the horses remaining alive after being removed from the herd. However, core animal welfare groups felt that shooting was the most humane option. Trial musters were conducted in 1993, 1994 and 1995, and were successful, although costly and with a limited demand for the captured horses.

In 1994, a working party was established to look at the management of the Kaimanawa herd. They aimed to decide which organisation was in charge of long term management, to ensure that the treatment of horses is humane, to preserve and control the best attributes of the herds, and to eliminate the impacts of the herds on other conservation priorities. Goals included ensuring the welfare of the horses, protecting natural ecosystems and features that the Kaimanawa herd may impact and keeping the herd at a sustainable level. Ecological objectives included ensuring that Kaimanawa horse does not adversely effect endangered, rare and biogeographically significant plants; ensuring that the herd does not further degrade the ecosystems in which it lives; and preventing the herd from spreading into the Kaimanawa Forest Park and the Tongariro National Park. Herd objectives included ensuring that the public was safe from roaming horses, while still allowing and improving public access to the herd and ensuring humane treatment of the horses; reducing conflict between the herd and other ecological values and land uses; and ensuring that the herd is contained to a population that is tolerated by the ecosystems in which they live while still maintaining a minimum effective population that is in general free ranging.

The Department of Conservation has since 1993 carried out annual culls and muster of Kaimanawas to keep the herd population around a target level of 500 horses. The target will be reduced to 300 horses in stages starting in 2009. These horses are either taken directly to slaughter or are placed at holding farms for later slaughter or adoption by private homes. A main reason for the strict population control is to protect the habitat in which they live. This habitat includes 16 plant species listed as endangered, which the Kaimanawa may endanger further through trampling and overgrazing. These plants include herbs, grasses, sedges, flowers and mistletoes; among these are *Deschampsia caespitosa* (a very rare tussock grass), *Peraxilla tetrapetala* (a vulnerable mistletoe) and *Libertia peregrinans* (a possibly locally extinct sand iris). The 2009 culling of the population removed 230 horses from the herd, the largest culling since the beginning of the programme, with homes found for 85 per cent of the horses removed. Conservation of these horses is an important matter to the public, and between 1990 and 2003 the New Zealand Minister for Conservation received more public comments on the Kaimanawa horse than on any other subject. In this period, more than 1,400 requests for information and letters were received, with public interest peaking in 1996 and 1997. This was due to a programme of population reduction by shooting scheduled to begin implementation in 1996; due to public opposition the shooting was cancelled and a large scale muster and adoption programme began in 1997. In 1997, around 1,069 horses were removed from the range and adopted, reducing the main herd to around 500, and reducing their range to around 25,000 ha from around 70,000. Since 1993, a total of around 2,800 horses have been removed from the range. Only one injury resulting in the death of a horse is known to have occurred.

The United Nations' Food and Agricultural Organisation lists the Kaimanawa horses as a herd of special genetic value that can be compared with other groups of feral horses such as New Forest ponies, Assateague ponies, wild Mustangs, and with free-living zebras. Kaimanawas are of special value because of their low rate of interaction with humans. This lack of interaction may result in a herd with more wild and fewer domestic characteristics, which is of special interest to researchers. Between 1994 and 1997, students from Massey University studied a population of around 400 Kaimanawa horses to learn their habits and herd dynamics. A 2000 study found that although sometimes there are more than two stallions in Kaimanawa horse herds, only the two stallions highest in the herd hierarchy mate with the herd females. This differs from other feral horse herds, some of which have only one stallion that mates with mares, while others have several stallions that sire foals.

MISAKI

The Misaki is a breed of pony that is native to Japan. Like other native horses of Japan, it is believed to have developed from horses brought to Japan from China, with the earliest imports dating back at least 2000 years.

The breed was first identified in the historical record in 1697 when the Akizuki family of the Takanabe Clan rounded up feral horses and developed a pool of breeding stock. Today, the Misaki is classified as an endangered but 'maintained' breed, with only about 100 living animals. This population has remained relatively stable for the past 20 years, up from a low of 53 individuals recorded in 1973.

The Misaki is one of eight breeds considered native to Japan, and lives as a feral horse in a natural setting in a designated National Monument on Cape Toi (also known as Toimisaki) that is located within the municipal boundaries of Kushima at the south end of Miyazaki Prefecture on the island of Kyushu. The Misaki ponies are a popular draw for tourists in the region and were designated a National Natural Treasure following the end of World War II.

The Misaki is of pony height, and stands between 12.2 and 13.2 hands high at the withers. However it has horse characteristics and proportions. Most individuals are coloured bay or black, with the occasional chestnut. White markings are rare.

MUSTANG HORSE

A Mustang is a free-roaming horse of the North American west that first descended from horses brought to the Americas by the Spanish. Mustangs are often referred to as wild horses, but there is intense debate over terminology. Because they are descended from once-domesticated horses, they can be classified as feral horses.

In 1971, the United States Congress recognized Mustangs as 'living symbols of the historic and pioneer spirit of the West, which continue to contribute to the diversity of life forms within the Nation and enrich the lives of the American people'. Today, Mustang herds vary in the degree to which they can be traced to original Iberian horses. Some contain a greater genetic mixture of ranch stock and more recent breed releases, while others are relatively unchanged from the original Iberian stock, most strongly represented in the most isolated populations.

Today, the Mustang population is managed and protected by the Bureau of Land Management. Controversy surrounds the sharing of land and resources by the free ranging Mustangs with the livestock of the ranching industry, and also with the methods with which the federal government manages the wild population numbers. An additional debate centres on the question if Mustangs—and horses in general—are a native species or an introduced, invasive species. Many methods of population management are used, including the adoption by private individuals of horses taken from the range.

Mustangs are often referred to as wild horses but, since all free-roaming horses now in the Americas descended from horses that were once domesticated, the more correct term is feral horses.

The English word 'mustang' comes from the Mexican Spanish word *mestengo,* derived from Spanish *mesteño,* meaning "stray livestock animal". The Spanish word in turn may possibly originate from the Latin expression *animalia mixta* (mixed beasts), referring to beasts of uncertain ownership, which were distributed in shepherd councils, known as *mestas* in medieval Spain. A *mestengo* was any animal distributed in those councils, and by extension any feral animal.

History

Today, the only true wild horse is the Przewalski's Horse, native to Mongolia. However, the horse family Equidae and the genus *Equus* evolved in North America. Studies using ancient DNA as well as DNA of recent individuals shows there once were two closely related horse species in North America, the 'wild horse' (*Equus ferus*) and the 'Stilt-legged Horse' which is taxonomically assigned to various names. Thus, primitive horses lived in North America in prehistoric times. However, the entire genus *Equus* in North America died out at the end of the last ice age around 10-12,000 years ago, possibly due to a changing climate or the impact of newly arrived human hunters. Thus at the beginning of the Columbian Exchange, there were no equids in the Americas at all. Horses first returned with the Conquistadors, beginning with Columbus, who imported horses from Spain to the West Indies on his second voyage in 1493. Domesticated horses came to the mainland with the arrival of Cortés in 1519.

The first Mustangs descended from Iberian horses brought to Mexico and Florida. Most of these horses were of Andalusian, Arabian and Barb ancestry. Some of these horses escaped or were stolen by Native Americans, and rapidly spread throughout western North America.

Native Americans quickly adopted the horse as a primary means of transportation. Horses replaced the dog as a travois puller and greatly improved success in battles, trade, and hunts, particularly bison hunts.

Starting in the colonial era and continuing with the westward expansion of the 1800s, horses belonging to explorers, traders and settlers that escaped or were purposely released joined the gene pool of Spanish-descended herds. It was also common practice for western ranchers to release their horses to locate forage for themselves in the winter and then recapture them, as well as any additional Mustangs, in the spring. Some ranchers also attempted to 'improve' wild herds by shooting the dominant stallions and replacing them with pedigreed animals.

By 1900 North America had an estimated two million free-roaming horses. Since 1900, the Mustang population has been reduced drastically. Mustangs were viewed as a resource that could be captured and used or sold (especially for military use) or slaughtered for food, especially pet food. The controversial practice of mustanging was dramatized in the John Huston film *The Misfits,* and the abuses linked to certain capture methods, including hunting from airplanes and poisoning, led to the first federal wild free-roaming horse protection law in 1959. This statute, known as the 'Wild Horse Annie Act', prohibited the use of motor vehicles for hunting wild horses and burros. Protection was increased further by the Wild and Free-Roaming Horses and Burros Act of 1971.

The 1971 Act provided for protection of certain previously established herds of horses and burros. Today, the Bureau of Land Management is the primary authority that oversees the protection and management of Mustang herds on public lands, while the United States Forest Service administers additional wild horse or burro territories.

Ancestry

Native American people readily integrated use of the horse into their cultures. Among the most capable horse-breeding native tribes of North America were the Comanche, the Shoshoni, and the Nez Perce. The last in particular became master horse breeders, and developed one of the first distinctly American breeds: the Appaloosa. Most other tribes did not practice extensive amounts of selective breeding, though they sought out desirable horses through capture, trade and theft, and quickly traded away or otherwise eliminated those with undesirable traits.

In some modern mustang herds there is clear evidence of other domesticated horse breeds having become intermixed with feral herds. Some herds show the signs of the introduction of Thoroughbred or other light racehorse-types into herds, a process that also led in part to the creation of the American Quarter Horse. Other herds show signs of the intermixing of heavy draft horse breeds turned loose in an attempt to create work horses. Other, more isolated herds, retain a strong influence of original Spanish stock.

Some breeders of domestic horses consider the Mustang herds of the west to be inbred and of inferior quality. However, supporters of the Mustang argue that the animals are merely small due to their harsh living conditions and that natural selection has eliminated many traits that lead to weakness or inferiority. Some mustang supporters also maintain that some 'inbreeding' actually concentrates the traits of hardiness and durability, making the mustang a valuable genetic resource. Regardless of these debates, the Mustang of the modern west has several different breeding populations today which are genetically isolated from one another and thus have distinct traits traceable to particular herds. These herds vary in the degree to which they can be traced to original Iberian horses. Some contain a greater genetic mixture of ranch stock and more recent breed releases, others are relatively unchanged from the original Iberian stock.

Two researchers have advanced an argument that Mustangs should be legally classified as 'wild' rather than 'feral'. They argue that, due to the presence of *Equus ferus ferus* on the North American continent till the end of the Pleistocene era, horses were once native animals and should still be considered as native animals, and therefore defined as 'wild', and not viewed as an exotic species that draws resources and attention away from true native species.

Mustangs Today

Today, free-roaming horses are protected under United States law, but have disappeared from several states where there were once established populations. A few hundred free-roaming horses survive in Alberta and British Columbia. The BLM considers roughly 26,000 individuals a manageable number, but the feral Mustang population in February 2010 was 33,700 horses and 4,700 burros. More than half of all Mustangs in North America are found in Nevada (which features the horses on its State Quarter in commemoration of this), with other significant populations in Montana, Wyoming and Oregon. Another 34,000 horses are in holding facilities.

Land Use Controversies

Controversy surrounds the presence of feral Mustang herds. Supporters argue that Mustangs are part of the natural heritage of the American West, whose history predates modern land use practices, and thus the animals have an inherent right of inhabitation. However, other people remain vehemently opposed to their presence, arguing that the animals degrade rangeland and compete with livestock and wild species for forage.

The debate as to what degree Mustangs and cattle compete for forage is multifaceted. One group of opponents, primarily cattle and sheep ranchers and those who depend on the livestock industry, argue essentially that feral horses degrade rangeland and compete with private livestock for public land forage. The environmentalist community is split over the position of the Mustang within the North American ecosystem. This debate centres on the potential classification of Mustangs as either an introduced species such as cattle, or as a reintroduced native species due to the prehistoric presence of horses in North America, albeit with a gap of thousands of years between their extinction and reintroduction from European stock.

Researchers note that most current Mustang herds live in arid areas which cattle cannot fully utilize due to the lack of water sources. Horses are better adapted by evolution to such climates; they may range nine times as far from water sources as cattle, traveling as much as 50 miles a day. This allows them to utilize areas not grazed by cattle. In addition, horses are 'hindgut fermenters', meaning that they digest nutrients by means of the cecum rather than by a multi-chambered stomach. In practical effect, horses can obtain adequate nutrition from poorer forage than can cattle, surviving in areas where cattle will starve.

Management and Adoption

The Bureau of Land Management (BLM) is tasked with protecting, managing, and controlling wild horses and burros under the authority of the 1971 Wild Free-Roaming Horses and Burros Act to ensure that healthy herds thrive on healthy rangelands and as multiple-use mission under the 1976 Federal Land Policy and Management Act. Under the 1971 Act, shooting or poisoning Mustangs in the wild is illegal, and doing so can be prosecuted as a criminal felony.

Healthy adult Mustangs have few natural predators aside from mountain lions, and to a lesser extent, grizzly bears and wolves. The mountain lion is well-known for predation on feral horses, and the larger members of the species may hunt both horses and moose. They are very effective predators that kill by either leaping onto an animal or chasing it down in a sprint, then grabbing the prey with their front claws and biting the neck, either at the windpipe or the spine.

Where there is natural balance of predators and prey, Mustang numbers tend to stay in balance. However, in many areas, natural predators have been eliminated from the ecosystem. Without some form of population control, Mustang herd sizes can multiply rapidly, doubling as fast as every four years. To maintain population balance, (or, some argue, to make room for cattle) one of the BLM's key responsibilities under the 1971 law is to determine an appropriate management level (AML) of wild horses and burros in areas of public rangelands dedicated specifically for them.

Control of the population to within AML is achieved through a capture programme. There are strict guidelines for techniques used to round up Mustangs. One method uses a tamed horse, called a 'Judas horse', which has been trained to lead wild horses into a pen or corral. Once the Mustangs are herded into an area near the holding pen, the Judas horse is released. Its job is then to move to the head of the herd and lead them into a confined area.

Most horses that are captured are offered for adoption to individuals or groups willing and able to provide humane, long-term care after payment of an adoption fee of at least $125. In order to prevent the later sale of mustangs as horse meat, adopted mustangs are still protected under the Act, and cannot be sold in the first year except when certain very specific criteria are met. As of 2010, nearly 225,000 Mustangs have been adopted.

Because there is a much larger pool of captured horses than of prospective adoptive owners, a number of efforts have been made to reduce the number of horses in holding facilities. At present, there are about 34,000 Mustangs in holding facilities and long-term grassland pastures. The BLM has publicly considered euthanasia as a possible solution to overpopulation. In January 2005, a controversial amendment was attached to an appropriation bill before the United States Congress by former Senator Conrad Burns, dubbed the 'Burns rider'. This modified the adoption programme to allow the sale (with the result usually being slaughter) of captured horses that are 'more than 10 years of age', or that were 'offered unsuccessfully for adoption at least three times'. In 2009, Secretary of the Interior Ken Salazar proposed the creation of federal wild horse preserves in the midwest, where non-reproducing animals would be kept. Another approach to placing excess animals has been advanced by Madeleine Pickens, wife of oil magnate T. Boone Pickens, who seeks to create a private sanctuary in northern Nevada. There are also increased efforts to assist with finding appropriate adoption homes. One example is a promotional competition that gives trainers 100 days to gentle and train 100 mustangs, which are then adopted through an auction.

NAMIB DESERT HORSE

The Namib Desert Horse is a rare horse found in the Namib Desert, of Namibia, Africa. It is most likely the only feral herd of horses residing in Africa. Today, approximately 150 horses now live in 350 square kilometres of the Namib desert. The origin of these animals is unclear, though several theories have been put forward. Genetic tests have been performed, although none to date have completely verified their origin.

History

Horses are not native to Sub-Saharan Africa. The first horses in sub-Saharan Africa were brought by the Dutch to the area of the Cape of Good Hope in the 17th century. There are several theories on how the Namib Desert Horse originated: One theory says that a ship with horses on board was run aground; the strongest horses were able to swim ashore to the mouth of the Orange River and up to the Garub Plains, where the modern herds live today.

There is also a theory that Namib Desert Horses are descendents of the horses of the German Schutztruppe brought in during the 19th century. Others say they are from Farm Duwisib (south of Maltahöhe), owned by Baron Hansheinrich von Wolf. Other sources suggest they came from imports in the 20th century, between 1904 and the beginning of World War I, when the Germans brought 30,000 horses into the area. Others suggest that some of these horses' forebears escaped from the South African cavalry during I World War.

Research in the archives of pre-1914 horse breeding operations found at Windhoek, combined with blood-typing studies suggests that the animals descended from a gene pool of high-quality riding animals, as opposed to work horses. A study released in 2005 suggests two likely source of these horses' forebears. The first source was a stud farm near Kubub, owned by Emil Kreplin, once mayor of Lüderitz from 1909-to 1914. In this period, Kreplin bred both work horses and race horses. Photo albums from the stud show animals with distinctive characteristics still seen in the Namib Desert Horse of today. In addition, during World War I, at one point, the South African military was advancing against the Schutztruppe, then located in the Namib near Aus, when the pilot of a German biplane dropped bombs onto the South African camp near Garub. In the process, some ordinance landed among a herd of 1,700 grazing horses. These escaped army animals may have joined stock animals lost from Kreplin's stud farm during the turmoil of the war. Horses in the area would likely have congregated together at the few existing watering places in the Aus Mountains and Garub.

Regardless of origins, after 100 years there were only 200 horses left in the deserts, but those that survived had adapted to the conditions of the South Namib Desert.

The Namib desert horses were originally forced to compete with domesticated livestock turned loose by farmers onto the same ground where the horses grazed. Due in part to this competition for limited forage, the horses nearly became extinct. However, they were saved in part due to the efforts of Jan Coetzer, employee of Consolidated Diamond Mine (CDM or DBCM), mining in a certain part of Sperrgebiet. Coetzer was fond of horses and made sure they always had water at the Garub windmill, put there as a permanent water tank by CDM. Later, the horses' habitat was made part of Namib-Naukluft Park in the late 1980s. The park was headed by Chris Eyre, head of the Nature Conservation.

Characteristics

The Namib Desert Horses are athletic, muscular, clean limbed, and are very strong boned. They are short backed with oblique shoulders and good withers. The horses have the appearance of well bred riding horses in head, skin, and coat.

The Namib desert horse must eat while on the move. When grazing, they only stay in one spot for a short time. They must cover considerable distances, as much as 15 to 20 kilometres (9 to 12 mi) between the few existing water sources and the best grazing sources. Due to scarcity of water, the Namib desert horse sometimes has to go without water for as long as thirty hours in summer and has been known to go close to 72 hours without water during the winter. As a consequence, Namib Desert Horses are considered very hardy. Due to the distances they must travel and the scarcity of water, selection pressure is severe, and weak animals do not survive.

The most common colour of the Namib desert horse is bay, although there are a few chestnut horses. There are occasional individuals with dorsal striping but no zebra stripes. No other colours have been recorded.

Genetics

Genetic testing results published in 2001 indicated that Namib Desert Horses are one of the most isolated horse populations in the world, with the second-lowest genetic variation of all horse populations that have been studied to date. In part, this is due to their small founding population, and generally small modern population, made smaller during periods of drought.

On Cothran's *Family Tree of Horse breeds*, they fall in the Arabian group, nearest the Shagya Arabian, a horse breed from Hungary that had been imported into colonial German South-West Africa. However, though the horses have a genetic similarity to Arabian-type horses, they do not closely resemble them in outward appearance. Further, in blood typing studies done in the 1990s, a new variant was noted. Its absence from the blood samples of all other horse breeds indicates the presence of a mutation that probably occurred after the horses became established in the desert.

Daily Life

The Namib desert horse usually live in herds of up to ten animals, consisting of one or, occasionally, two stallions with a few mares and foals. These are the breeding groups. There are also 'bachelor' groups. The breeding groups are led by a mare. The lead mare decides when to go, stop, choose another grazing spot, and when to go to a water source.

There are few natural predators in the area, other than the Hyena, which poses a threat primarily to foals. When a foal is threatened, it is usually the mare that is the mother of the foal who defends her young. The stallion will deal with threats to the entire herd, though in many cases, the stallion primarily keeps bachelor animals away. There are few serious fights, most are for show.

NOKOTA HORSE

The Nokota horse is a feral and semi-feral horse breed located in the badlands of southwestern North Dakota in the United States. The breed developed in the 19th century from foundation bloodstock consisting of ranch-bred horses produced from local Indian horses mixed with Spanish horses, Thoroughbreds, harness horses and related breeds. The Nokota was almost wiped out during the early 20th century when ranchers, in cooperation with state and federal agencies, worked together to reduce competition for livestock grazing. However, when Theodore Roosevelt National Park was created in the 1940s, a few bands were inadvertently trapped inside, and thus were preserved. Today, the park conducts regular thinning of the herd to keep numbers between 70 and 110, and the excess horses are sold off. In the late 1970s, brothers Leo and Frank Kuntz began purchasing the horses with the aim of preserving the breed, and in 1999 started the Nokota Horse Conservancy, later beginning a breed registry through the same organisation. Later, a separate breed registry was begun by another organisation in Minnesota.

Characteristics of Breed

The Nokota horse has an angular frame, is commonly blue roan in colour, and often exhibits an ambling gait called the "Indian shuffle". The breed is generally separated into two sections, the traditional and the ranch type, which differ slightly in conformation and height. They are used in many events, including endurance riding, western riding and English disciplines.

The Nokota horse has an angular frame with prominent withers, a sloped croup, and a low set tail. Members of the breed are often blue roan, which is a colour rare in other breeds, although black and gray are also common. Other, less common, colours include red roan, bay, chestnut, dun, grullo and palomino. Pinto patterns such as overo and sabino occur occasionally. There are two general types of the Nokota horse. The first is the traditional Nokota, known by the registry as the National Park Traditional. They tend to be smaller, more refined, and closer in type to the Colonial Spanish Horse, and generally stand between 14 and 14.3 hands (56 and 59 inches, 142 and 150 cm) high.

The second type is known as the ranch-type or National Park Ranch, more closely resemble early 'foundation type' Quarter Horses, and generally stand from 14.2 to 17 hands (58 to 68 inches, 147 to 173 cm). Members of the breed often exhibit an ambling gait, once known as the 'Indian shuffle'. Nokota horses are described as versatile and intelligent. Members of the breed have been used in endurance racing and western riding, and a few have been used in events such as fox hunting, dressage, three day eventing and show jumping. The Nokota derives its name from the Nokota Indian tribe that inhabited North and South Dakota.

History

The Nokota horse developed in the southwestern corner of North Dakota, in the Little Missouri River Badlands. Feral horses were first encountered by ranchers in the 19th century, and horses from domestic herds mingled with the original feral herds. Ranchers often crossbred local Indian ponies, Spanish horses from the southwest, and various draft, harness, Thoroughbred and stock horses to make hardy, useful ranch horses. Theodore Roosevelt, who ranched in the Little Missouri area between 1883 and 1886, wrote:

> In a great many—indeed in most—localities there are wild horses to be found, which, although invariably of domestic descent, being either themselves runaways from some ranch or Indian outfit, or else claiming such for their sires and dams, yet are quite as wild as the antelope on whose domain they have intruded.

In 1884, the HT Ranch, located near Medora, North Dakota, bought 60 mares from a Sioux Indian herd of 250 originally confiscated from Sitting Bull and sold at Fort Buford, North Dakota in 1881. Some of these mares were bred to the Thoroughbred racing stallion Lexington, also owned by the HT Ranch.

By the early 20th century, the feral horse herds became the target of local ranchers looking to limit grazing competition for their livestock. Many horses were rounded up, and either used as ranch horses, sold for slaughter or shot. From the 1930s through the 1950s, federal and state agencies worked with ranchers to remove horses from western North Dakota. However, when Theodore Roosevelt National Park was established in the 1940s, during construction, a few bands of horses were accidentally enclosed within the Park fence, and by 1960 these bands were the last remaining feral horses in North Dakota. Nonetheless, the Park fought to eliminate these horses, and in the 1970s won exemption from federal laws that covered other free roaming horse and burro management actions.

In the late 1970s, growing public opposition to the removal of feral horses prompted management strategy changes, and today the herds within the Theodore Roosevelt National Park are managed for the purposes of historical demonstration. However, the Park added outside bloodlines in the 1980s with the aim of modifying the appearance of the Nokota. The dominant herd stallions were removed and replaced with two feral stallions from Bureau of Land Management Mustang herds, a crossbred Shire stallion, a Quarter Horse stallion and an Arabian stallion. At the same time that the stallion replacements took place, a large number of horses from the park were rounded up and sold at auction. At these auctions, concerned about the welfare of the Nokota horse, Leo and Frank Kuntz purchased a large number of the horses. After researching the history of the breed, the Kuntzs stated that they had found evidence that the horses in the park were probably related to the remaining horses from the band of 250 Sitting Bull horses, who had been range-bred by the Marquis de Mores, who founded the town of Medora. However, the Nokota Horse Association today says that there is no evidence that this is the case.

1990s to Today

In 1999, the Kuntz brothers founded the Nokota Horse Conservancy to protect and conserve the Nokota horse. In 1993, the Nokota was declared the Honorary State Equine of the state of North Dakota. In 1994, researchers conducted a study of the horses in the park and on the Kuntz's ranch, and discovered that none of the horses in the park, and only about 20 on the ranch, had characteristics consistent with the Colonial Spanish Horse. Since then, the horses on the Kuntz ranch have been bred to maintain and improve their Spanish characteristics. The Nokota Horse Conservancy currently tracks around 1,000 living and dead horses, and Nokota horses can be found in Pennsylvania, Minnesota, Montana and Oregon, as well as North Dakota.

Theodore Roosevelt National Park has continued thinning the herd, with several roundups conducted throughout the 1990s and first decade of the 21st century. In 2000, the last horse to be considered of 'traditional' Nokota type was removed from the wild. The National Park Service currently maintains a herd of 70 to 110 horses. In 2006, the breed was chosen to be the beneficiary of Breyer Animal Creations' annual "Benefit Horse" Campaign for the following year; a Breyer model was created, manufactured, and marketed in 2007, with a portion of the proceeds going to the Nokota Horse Conservancy.

The Nokota Horse Registry is the breed registry, organized by the Nokota Horse Conservancy. There was briefly a second registry: a Minnesota-based organisation called the Nokota Horse Association. In October 2009, the two registries disputed which had the right to the Nokota breed name, with the Association claiming that they own the legal trademark to the name. The Registry sued, contending that they created the name and had a longer history with the breed. A US District Court ordered that the Association cease registering horses until the matter was settled, and the association disappeared from public view soon after.

SORRAIA

The Sorraia is a rare breed of horse indigenous to the portion of the Iberian peninsula known today as Portugal. The Sorraia is known for its primitive features, including a convex profile and dun colouring with primitive markings. Concerning its origins, a theory has been advanced by some authors that the Sorraia is a descendant of primitive horses belonging to the naturally occurring wild fauna of Southern Iberia. Studies are currently ongoing to discover the relationship between the Sorraia and various wild horse types, as well as its relationship with other breeds from the Iberian Peninsula and Northern Africa.

Members of the breed are small, but hardy and well-adapted to harsh conditions. They were occasionally captured and used by native farmers for centuries, and a remnant population of these nearly extinct horses was discovered by a Portuguese zoologist in the early 20th century. Today, the Sorraia has become the focus of preservation efforts, with European scientists leading the way and enthusiasts from several countries forming projects and establishing herds to assist in the re-establishment of this breed from its current endangered status.

Characteristics

The Sorraia breed stands between 14.1 and 14.3 hands high [57 to 59 inches (145 to 150 cm)], although some individuals are as small as 12.3 hands high [51 inches (130 cm)]. The head tends to be large, the profile convex, and the ears long. The neck is slender and long, the withers high, and the croup slightly sloping. The legs are strong, with long pasterns and well-proportioned hooves. These horses have good endurance and are easy keepers, thriving on relatively little fodder. They have a reputation for being independent of temperament, but tractable.

On adult horses, the lay of the hair can create the appearance of stripes or 'barring' on the neck and chest. Also due to the lay of the hair, newborn foals can appear to have stripes all over, reminiscent of zebra stripes. The breed standard refers to this as 'hair stroke'.

Sorraia are generally dun or a dun variation called grullo.

Dun colouring includes primitive markings such as a black dorsal stripe, black tipped ears, horizontal striping on the legs and a dark muzzle area. The dark muzzle area is in contrast to some other dun-coloured horse breeds, who have light-coloured muzzle areas and underbellies, possibly due to the presence of pangare genetics. Sorraia horses have bi-coloured manes and tails with lighter coloured hairs that fringe the outside of the longer growing black hair. This is a characteristic shared with other predominantly dun-coloured breeds, such as the Fjord horse. Purebred Sorraia occasionally have white markings, although they are rare and undesired by the breed's studbook.

Taxonomy and Evolution

The relationship between the Sorraia and other breeds remains largely undetermined, as is its relationship to the wild horse subspecies, the Tarpan and the Przewalski's Horse. The Sorraia originally developed in the southern part of the Iberian peninsula. d'Andrade hypothesized that the Sorraia would be the ancestor of the Southern Iberian breeds. Morphologically, scientists place the Sorraia as closely related to the Gallego and the Asturcon, but genetic studies using mitochondrial DNA show that the Sorraia forms a cluster that is largely separated from most Iberian breeds. Some evidence links this cluster with Konik and domestic Mongolian horses. At the same time, one of the maternal lineages is shared with the Lusitano. Genetic evidence has not supported an hypothesis that the Sorraia is related to the Barb horse, an African breed introduced to Iberia by the Moors.

Multiple researchers have suggested that the Sorraia might be a descendant of the Tarpan based on shared morphological features, principally the typical colour of its coat. Other authors simply state that the Sorraia has 'evident primitive characteristics', although they do not refer to a specific ancestor. However, there have been no genetic studies comparing the Sorraia with the Tarpan, and similarity of external morphology is an unreliable measure of relatedness.

Genetic studies to date have been inconclusive about the closest relative of the Sorraia. On one hand, studies using mitochondrial DNA showed a relationship with the Przewalski's Horse, in that Przewalski's Horse has a unique haplotype (A2) not found in domestic horses, which differs by just one single nucleotide from one of the major Sorraia haplotypes. In comparison, genetic distances within the domestic horse are as large as 11 nucleotide differences. However, this relationship with the Przewalski's Horse was contradicted in another study using microsatellite data that showed that the genetic distance between the Prewalski's Horse and the Sorraia was the largest. Such conflicting results can arise when a population passes through a genetic bottleneck, and evidence suggests that the Sorraia, among other rare breeds, has recently passed through a bottleneck, effectively obscuring the position of this breed in the family tree of the domestic horse. Thus, the morphological, physiological, and cultural characteristics of the Sorraia are the subject of continued study to better understand the relationship between various Iberian horse breeds and wild horse subspecies.

History

Although it is known that the Sorraia developed in the southern part of the Iberian peninsula, the breed was isolated and unknown to science until the 20th century. Despite the lack of documentation, attempts have been made to reconstruct its history. Paleolithic parietal art images in the region depict equines with a distinct likeness to the Sorraia, with similar zebra-like markings. Analysis of mtDNA has been performed on Mustangs in the western United States that show similar mtDNA patterns between some Mustangs and the Sorraia breed. Spanish conquistadors took Iberian horses, some of whom closely resembled the modern-day Sorraia, to the Americas in their conquests, probably as pack animals. Similarities between the Sorraia and several North and South American breeds are shown in the dun and grullo colouring and various physical characteristics. This evidence suggests that the Sorraia, their ancestors, or other horses with similar features, may have had a long history in the Iberian region and a role in the creation of American breeds.

Otherwise, the Sorraia breed was lost to history until 1920, when Portuguese zoologist and paleontologist Dr. Ruy d'Andrade first encountered the Sorraia horse during a hunting trip in the Portuguese lowlands. This remnant herd of primitive horses had continued to live a wild existence in these lowlands, which were rather inaccessible and had been used as a hunting preserve by Portuguese royalty until the early 1900s. At the time of d'Andrade's initial meeting the breed, the horses were ill-regarded by native farmers, although they were considered hardy native fauna that lived off of the uncultivated lands and salt marshes in the local river valleys. For centuries, peasant farmers of the area would occasionally capture the horses and use them for agricultural work, including threshing grain and herding bulls.

In the 1920s and 1930s, as mechanization became more prevalent, both wild and domesticated breeding stock diminished to almost nothing, and d'Andrade, along with his son Fernando, encouraged the conservation of the breed. In 1937, d'Andrade began a small herd of his own with five stallions and seven mares from horses obtained near Coruche, Portugal. All Sorraias currently in captivity descend from these original horses obtained by d'Andrade, and it is believed that the remnant wild herds of the breed died out soon after. These horses were kept in a habitat similar to their native one. In 1975, two other farms took up the Sorraia's cause and acquired small herds to help with conservation. In 1976, three stallions and three mares were imported to Germany from Portugal to begin a sub-population there. In March 2004, a small breeding herd of Sorraia horses was released on the estate of a private land owner who dedicated a portion of his property so that these horses could live completely wild, as did their ancestors. The refuge created for them is in the Vale de Zebro region of south western Portugal, one of places so named because this is where the Sorraia's predecessors dwelt.

Two Sorraia stallions were imported to the United States in the early 21st century. In 2006, another Sorraia stallion was imported to Canada where a Sorraia Mustang Preserve has been established on Manitoulin Island in Ontario Unrelated to existing preservation efforts which work in conjunction with the Sorraia Mustang Studbook, another project by a consortium of breeders in the United States is attempting to establish a separate network and studbook. These breeders have gathered Spanish Mustangs that through mtDNA testing show a genetic relationship with the Sorraia and are breeding them according to both genotype and phenotype in an attempt to help preserve what they are calling the 'American Sorraia'.

Today, the breed is nearly extinct, with fewer than 200 horses existing as of 2007, including around 80 breeding mares. The Food and Agriculture Organisation considers it to be maintaining critical risk status. The first studbook was published in 2004, dedicated to maintaining a written record of the bloodlines of the Sorraia. Sorraias are present mainly in Portugal, with a small population in Germany. While not bred for a specific use, the Sorraia horses are versatile and have been used in herding bulls, dressage riding and light harness.

Researcher gave the breed their name of 'Sorraia'. D'Andrade took the name from the Sorraia River in Portugal. The breed had previously been known by the local Portuguese as 'zebro' or 'zebra', due to their markings. In the time of Christopher Columbus, the Sorraia was also known as the Marismeño, but the Sorraia and the Marismeño have evolved into two different breeds over time. Today, the name Marismeño refers to a population of semiferal horses living in Doñana Natural Park in Spain.

SABLE ISLAND PONY

The Sable Island Pony, also known as the Sable Island Horse, is a type of feral horse found on Sable Island, an island off the coast of Nova Scotia, Canada. The first horses were brought to the island for pasture in the late eighteenth century, and additional horses were later transported to improve the herd's breeding stock. The horses are protected by law in their feral state. The horses live only at Sable Island and at the Shubenacadie Wildlife Park in nearby Shubenacadie. The latter herd is descended from horses removed from the island in the 1950s.

History

The first horses on Sable Island were brought to the island during the late 18th century. Many people believe that they arrived on the island from shipwrecks, but they were intentionally taken there for breeding and pasture.

The first recorded horses were brought by a Boston clergyman, the Reverend Andrew Le Mercier in 1737; mariners stole other horses and took them to the island to graze and multiply.

The present-day horses are thought to have descended mostly from horses seized by the British from the Acadians during the Expulsion of the Acadians. The Boston merchant and shipowner Thomas Hancock purchased the horses and transported them to the island in 1760. Although often referred to as ponies due to their small size, they have a horse phenotype.

After the government of Nova Scotia established a lifesaving station on Sable Island in 1801, workers trained some of the horses to haul supplies and rescue equipment. Lifesaving staff brought additional horses to the island to improve the herd's breeding stock. They recorded the importation of the stallion, Jolly, taken there in 1801.

Although the horses live in a challenging and isolated environment, they maintain a stable and healthy herd. Its numbers vary, but it averages between 200 and 350 horses. The Sable Island horses have been protected since 1961 by regulations of the Canada Shipping Act prohibiting removing or interfering with them. In 2008, the Nova Scotia Legislature declared the Sable Island Horse as one of the provincial symbols, making them the official horse of Nova Scotia.

Aside from the island, Sable Island Horses live only at the Shubenacadie Wildlife Park in Shubenacadie, Nova Scotia. It maintains descendants of Sable Island Ponies removed from the island in the 1950s by the Canadian Department of Transport. The Nova Scotia Museum has a study and specimen collection of the Sable Island horses through a Research Associate. A complete skeleton of Sable Island Pony is displayed in the Mammals Gallery at the Nova Scotia Museum of Natural History in Halifax.

Characteristics of Breed

The horses that remain on Sable Island are feral. In the past, people trained the horses exported to the mainland. They reported the horses as excellent, tough and enduring, and able to travel with ease on any terrain. The present-day horses are very hardy and thrive in an inhospitable environment. As the herds are not managed, the horses exhibit a range of characteristics. In general, they have nice heads with a straight or convex profile, and are short, stocky and muscular in frame. Tails are low-set and shaggy. Their coats are mostly dark colours, but some do have white markings. About half are bays, with the rest evenly distributed among chestnut, black and palomino. There are no grays. Males average about 360 kilograms; females about 300 kilograms.

WELSH PONY AND COB

The Welsh Pony and Cob are closely related horse breeds including both pony and cob types, which originated in Wales in the United Kingdom.

The breed society for the Welsh breeds has four sections, primarily distinguished by height, but also by variations in type:

- The Welsh Mountain Pony (Section A);
- The Welsh Pony (Section B);
- The Welsh Pony of Cob Type (Section C); and
- The Welsh Cob (Section D).

Welsh ponies and cobs are known for their good temperament, hardiness, and free-moving gaits.

Native ponies existed in Wales prior to 1600 BC, and a Welsh-type cob was known as early as the Middle Ages. They were influenced by the Arabian horse, and possibly also by the Thoroughbred and the Hackney horse. In 1901, the first stud book for the Welsh breeds was established in the United Kingdom, and in 1907 another registry was established in the United States. Interest in the breed declined during the Great Depression, but revived in the 1950s.Throughout their history, the Welsh breeds have had many uses, including as a cavalry horse, a pit pony, and as a working animal on farms.

Today, the modern Welsh Pony and Cob breeds are used for many equestrian competitive disciplines, including showing, jumping and driving, as well as for pleasure riding, trekking and trail riding The smaller types are popular children's ponies. The Welsh also crosses well with many other breeds and has influenced the development of many British and American horse and pony breeds.

History

Evidence suggests that a native Welsh-type of pony existed before 1600 BC. The original Welsh Mountain Pony is thought to have evolved from the prehistoric Celtic pony. Welsh ponies were primarily developed in Wales and their ancestors existed in the British Isles prior to the arrival of the Roman Empire. Bands of ponies roamed in a semi-feral state, climbing mountains, leaping ravines, and running over rough moorland terrain.

They developed into a hardy breed due to the harsh climate, limited shelter and sparse food sources of their native country. At some point in their development, the Welsh breeds had some Arabian blood added, although this did not take away the physical characteristics that make the breed unique.

The Welsh Cob existed as a type as early as the Middle Ages, and mentions of such animals can be found in medieval Welsh literature. During this time period they were known for their speed, jumping ability and carrying capacity. Before the introduction of large, 'coldblood' draft horse breeds, they were used for farm work and timbering. In 1485 the Welsh Militia, riding local animals presumed to be ancestors of the modern Welsh Cob, assisted Henry Tudor in gaining the English throne. During the 15th century, similar small horses were also used as rounceys, leading war horses known as destriers.

The characteristics of the breeds as they are known today are thought to have been established by the late 15th century, after the Crusaders returned to England with Arabian stallions obtained from the Middle East. In the 16th century, King Henry VIII, thinking to improve the breeds of horses, particularly war horses, ordered the destruction of all stallions under 15 hands and all mares under 13 hands in the Breed of Horses Act 1535. The laws for swingeing culls of 'under-height' horses were partially repealed by a decree by Queen Elizabeth I in 1566 on the basis that the poor lands could not support the weight of the horses desired by Henry VIII because of "their rottenness ... [they] are not able to breed beare and bring forth such great breeds of stoned horses as by the statute of 32 Henry VIII is expressed, without peril of miring and perishing of them", and (fortunately for the future of Britain's mountain and moorland pony breeds) many ponies in their native environments, including the Welsh breeds, therefore escaped the slaughter.

On the upland farms of Wales, Welsh ponies and cobs would often have to do everything from ploughing a field to carrying a farmer to market or driving a family to services on Sunday. When coal mining became important to the economy of England, many Welsh ponies were harnessed for use in mines, above and below ground.

In the 18th century and 19th century, more Arabian blood was added by stallions who were turned out in the Welsh hills. Other breeds have also been added, including the Thoroughbred, Hackney, Norfolk Roadster, and the Yorkshire Coach Horse. Before the car was developed, the speediest mode of transportation in Wales was the Welsh Cob. Tradesmen, doctors and other businessmen often selected ponies by trotting them the 35 uphill miles from Cardiff to Dowlais. The best ponies could complete this feat in under three hours, never breaking gait. Formal breeding stock licensing was introduced in 1918, but before this, breeding stock was selected by trotting tests like these.

In 1901 English and Welsh breeders established a breed registry, called the Welsh Pony and Cob Society, and the first stud book was published in 1902. It was decided that the Welsh Stud Book should be separated into sections divided by type and height. Welsh Ponies were originally only classified as Section A, but in 1931, with the rising demand for riding ponies for children, Section B was added. In the first stud books, the Section B was the Welsh Pony of Cob Type, and the Welsh Cob was Section C and Section D. The upper height limit for Section D Cobs was removed in 1907 and in 1931 Sections C and D were combined as simply Section C. The current standards of Cobs as Sections C and D were finalized in 1949. Until the mid 20th century, the British War Office considered the Welsh Cob so valuable that they paid premiums to the best stallions. After World War II, only three stallions were registered with Section C, but numbers have since recovered.

Welsh ponies adapted easily to the terrain and climate variations they encountered when exported to Canada and the United States. They were first exported to the United States as early as 1880s, and large numbers of animals were exported between 1884 and 1910. The United States registry, also named the Welsh Pony and Cob Society, was incorporated in 1906., and by 1913 a total of 574 ponies had been registered. During the Great Depression, interest in the breed declined, but made a comeback in the 1950s. The population continued to grow, 2,881 ponies had been registered by the end of 1957, and annual studbooks began to be published. All Welsh ponies and cobs in the United States today descend from ponies registered with the UK registry, and over 34,000 have been registered with the US registry as of 2009.

Foundation Lines

The stallion Dyoll Starlight was credited with being the foundation sire of the modern breed, and was a combination of Welsh and Arab breeding. From his line came an influential stallion of the Section B type: Tan-y-Bwlch Berwyn. This stallion was sired by a Barb and out of a mare from the Dyoll Starlight line. Influential stallions on the Section C and D bloodlines include: Trotting Comet, foaled in 1840 from a long line of trotting horses; True Briton, foaled in 1930, by a trotting sire and out of an Arabian mare; Cymro Llwyd, foaled in 1850, by an Arabian stallion and out of a trotting mare; and Alonzo the Brave, foaled in 1866, tracing his ancestry through the Hackney breed to the Darley Arabian.

Characteristics of Breed

All sections of Welsh ponies and Welsh cobs have small heads with large eyes, sloped shoulders, short backs and strong hindquarters. The forelegs are straight and the cannon bone short. The tail is high-set. The breed ranges from 11 hands (44 inches, 112 cm) for the smallest ponies to over 16 hands (64 inches, 163 cm) for the tallest cobs. They may be any solid colour, but not piebald, skewbald, (US: pinto) or leopard-spotted. Black, chestnut and bay are the most common, but there are also duns, palominos, and greys.

Their movement is bold and free and characteristically fast, especially at the trot, with great power coming from the hocks. Their trot has been favourably compared to that of the Standardbred horse. They are reputed to be trustworthy, of a good disposition with even temperaments and friendly characters, but spirited and with great endurance, and are known for their stamina, soundness, and high level of intelligence, which usually makes them easy to train.

The Sections

Section A

The Section A Welsh Pony is also known as the Welsh Mountain pony. Both the Section A and Section B ponies are more refined than those in Section

C and D. They are characterized from the cob types by a large eye, small head (often with a dished face from the Arabian influence), high set on tail, and refined leg conformation, but retaining good bone and correctness.

Section B

The Welsh Mountain Pony (Section A) may not exceed 12.2 hands (50 inches, 127 cm) in the US or 12 hands (48 inches, 122 cm) in the United Kingdom.

The Welsh Pony of Riding Type (Section B) is the second division within the Welsh pony registry. The Section B Welsh Pony is a larger, riding-type pony. The Section B combines the hardiness and substance of the Section A with elegant movement and athletic ability.

Section B ponies are taller than Section A with a maximum height of 13.2 hands (54 inches, 137 cm) in the UK and 14.2 hands (58 inches, 147 cm) in the U.S. They are known for elegant movement and athletic ability while still retaining the substance and hardiness of the foundation stock, the Section A Welsh pony. They have no lower height limit.

Section B ponies also generally have a slightly lighter build, as a result of Thoroughbred and Hackney blood. Section B ponies resemble the Section A pony, but are of a more refined 'riding type'. However, they should not be light of bone; they should resemble their Mountain Pony ancestors for quality of bone. In addition to the desirable characteristics of the Type A pony, Type B ponies have a free-flowing movement. They should have a muscular neck, arching from withers to poll, and have a deep, wide chest. Section B ponies are more commonly used as children's ponies and as pony hunter-jumpers.

Section C

The Welsh Pony of Cob Type (Section C) may not exceed 13.2 hands (54 inches, 137 cm) high. They are known for their strength, hardiness and gentle nature. Unlike the Welsh pony (Section B), it is heavier and more coblike and compact. They have a moderate amount of feathering on their legs.

The Welsh Pony of Cob Type first resulted from a crossbreeding between the Welsh mountain pony (Section A) and the Welsh Cob (Section D). Today, some Section C ponies are still produced from this cross. In the past the WPCS also accepted Section C ponies with Section B blood but that is no longer the case. There were also crosses with Iberian horses, which led to the development of the Powys horse, which was also a foundation for this type. Other breeds also influenced the Section C, including the Norfolk Trotter, the Hackney and Yorkshire Coach Horse.

The Welsh Pony of Cob Type is shown in jumping events and in harness, notably in competitive driving.

Section D Cob

The Welsh Cob (Section D) is the largest size within the Welsh Pony and Cob breed registries. They must be taller than 13.2 hands (54 inches, 137 cm), with no upper height limit. They are used as riding animals for both adults and children, and are also used for driving. They are known for their hardiness and gentle nature.

Though they are the tallest and stockiest of the Welsh sections, the head remains full of pony character, with large eyes, and neat ears. The legs may be relatively short, also akin to pony proportions. Mature stallions have somewhat cresty necks, those of mares are generally leaner. Like the section C, they have powerful, extravagant action. Grey colouring is rarer in the section D cob than other types of Welsh ponies, but bold white markings are common.

Today, the Section D is best known for use in harness driving, but they are also shown under saddle and in hand. Like other Welsh ponies, Cobs are also exhibited over fences as hunters and jumpers. The Welsh also crosses well with many other breeds and has influenced the Pony of the Americas and the British Riding Pony. Many are also crossbred with Thoroughbreds, and other horse breeds. The Welsh Pony has contributed to the founding of several other horse and pony breeds. The Morgan horse is one such breed, being in part descended from Welsh Cobs left behind by British forces after the end of the Revolutionary War. They are crossed with Arabians to produce riding horses, and with Thoroughbreds to produce jumpers, hunters and eventers. Mares have also been used to breed polo ponies that were agile and nimble. The Welsh Pony was used to create the Welara, a popular crossbred of the Welsh and the Arabian horse, which created a separate breed registry in America in 1981.

The Welsh Pony has been put to many uses. Historically, they were used for postal routes and in coal mines. The British War Office used the Welsh Cob to pull heavy guns and equipment through terrain where motorized vehicles could not, and also used them for mounted infantry. Today, they are used as riding and driving ponies for both children and adults. They have proven their ability at driving in Fédération Équestre Internationale (FEI) level competition, and they have been used for dressage. They also compete against one another in breed show competition as hunters, eventers, and western pleasure horses. The abilities of the Welsh pony were showcased in 2008 when the first champion Large Pony Hunter to be made into a model Breyer horse was a gray Welsh pony gelding.

Trivia

A life-sized statue of a Welsh cob stallion, created by sculptor David Mayer, was erected in the town of Aberaeron in 2005, and was donated to the town by the Aberaeron Festival of Welsh Ponies and Cobs to denote the area as Welsh Cob country.

A small semi-feral population of about 180 animals roams the Carneddau mountains in Snowdonia.

CHAPTER 4

Horse Breed

Horse breed is a broad term with no clear consensus as to definition, but most commonly refers to selectively bred populations of domesticated horses, often with pedigrees recorded in a breed registry. However, the term is sometimes used in a very broad sense to define landrace animals, or naturally selected horses of a common phenotype located within a limited geographic region. Depending on definition, hundreds of 'breeds' exist today, developed for many different uses. Horse breeds are loosely divided into three categories based on general temperament: spirited 'hot bloods' with speed and endurance; 'cold bloods', such as draft horses and some ponies, suitable for slow, heavy work; and 'warmbloods', developed from crosses between hot bloods and cold bloods, often focusing on creating breeds for specific riding purposes, particularly in Europe.

Horse breeds are groups of horses with distinctive characteristics that are transmitted consistently to their offspring, such as conformation, colour, performance ability, or disposition. These inherited traits are usually the result of a combination of natural crosses and artificial selection methods aimed at producing horses for specific tasks. Certain breeds are known for certain talents. For example, Standardbreds are known for their speed in harness racing. Some breeds have been developed through centuries of crossings with other breeds, while others, such as Tennessee Walking Horses and Morgans, developed from a single sire from which all current breed members descend. There are more than 300 horse breeds in the world today.

Origin of Breeds

Modern horse breeds developed in response to a need for 'form to function', the necessity to develop certain physical characteristics in order to perform a certain type of work. Thus, powerful but refined breeds such as the Andalusian or the Lusitano developed in the Iberian peninsula as riding horses that also had a great aptitude for dressage, while heavy draft horses such as the Clydesdale and the Shire developed out of a need to perform demanding farm work and pull heavy wagons. Ponies of all breeds originally developed mainly from the need for a working animal that could fulfill specific local draft and transportation needs while surviving in harsh environments. However, by the 20th century, many pony breeds had Arabian and other blood added to make a more refined pony suitable for riding. Other horse breeds developed specifically for light agricultural work, heavy and light carriage and road work, various equestrian disciplines, or simply as pets.

Purebred Registries

Horses have been selectively bred since their domestication. Today, there are over 300 breeds of horses in the world. However, the concept of purebred bloodstock and a controlled, written breed registry only became of significant importance in modern times. Today, the standards for defining and registration of different breeds vary. Sometimes purebred horses are called Thoroughbreds, which is incorrect; 'Thoroughbred' is a specific breed of horse, while a 'purebred' is a horse (or any other animal) with a defined pedigree recognized by a breed registry.

An early example of people who practiced selective horse breeding were the Bedouin, who had a reputation for careful breeding practices, keeping extensive pedigrees of their Arabian horses and placing great value upon pure bloodlines. Though these pedigrees were originally transmitted via an oral tradition, written pedigrees of Arabian horses can be found that date to the 14th century. In the same period of the early Renaissance, the Carthusian monks of southern Spain bred horses and kept meticulous pedigrees of the best bloodstock; the lineage survives to this day in the Andalusian horse. One of the earliest formal registries was General Stud Book for Thoroughbreds, which began in 1791 and traced back to the Arabian stallions imported to England from the Middle East that became the foundation stallions for the breed.

Some breed registries have a closed stud book, where registration is based on pedigree, and no outside animals can gain admittance. For example, a registered Thoroughbred or Arabian must have two registered parents of the same breed. Other breeds have a partially closed stud book but still allow certain infusions from other breeds. For example, the modern Appaloosa must have at least one Appaloosa parent, but may also have a Quarter Horse, Thoroughbred, or Arabian parent so long as the offspring exhibits appropriate colour characteristics. The Quarter Horse normally requires both parents to be registered Quarter Horses, but allows 'Appendix' registration of horses with one Thoroughbred parent, and the horse may earn its way to full registration by completing certain performance requirements.

Others, such as most of the warmblood breeds used in sport horse disciplines, have open stud books to varying degrees. While pedigree is considered, outside bloodlines are admitted to the registry if the horses meet the set standard for the registry. These registries usually require a studbook selection process involving judging of an individual animal's quality, performance, and conformation before registration is finalized. A few 'registries', particularly some colour breed registries, are very open and will allow membership of all horses that meet limited criteria, such as coat colour and species, regardless of pedigree or conformation.

Breed registries also differ as to their acceptance or rejection of breeding technology. For example, all Jockey Club Thoroughbred registries require that a registered Thoroughbred be a product of a natural mating, so called 'live cover'. A foal born of two Thoroughbred parents, but by means of artificial insemination or embryo transfer, cannot be registered in the Thoroughbred studbook. On the other hand, since the advent of DNA testing to verify parentage, most breed registries now allow artificial insemination (AI), embryo transfer (ET), or both. The high value of stallions has helped with the acceptance of these techniques because they allow a stallion to breed more mares with each 'collection', and greatly reduce the risk of injury during mating. Cloning of horses is highly controversial, and at the present time most mainstream breed registries will not accept cloned horses, though several cloned horses and mules have been produced.

Hybrids

Horses can crossbreed with other equine species to produce hybrids. These hybrid types are not breeds, but they resemble breeds in that crosses between certain horse breeds and other equine species produce characteristic offspring. The most common hybrid is the mule, a cross between a 'jack' (male donkey) and a mare. A related hybrid, the hinny, is a cross between a stallion and a jenny (female donkey). Most other hybrids involve the zebra (see Zebroid). With rare exceptions, most equine hybrids are sterile and cannot reproduce. A notable exception is hybrid crosses between horses and *Equus ferus przewalskii*, commonly known as Przewalski's horse.

HORSE BREEDING

Horse breeding is reproduction in horses, and particularly the human-directed process of selective breeding of animals, particularly purebred horses of a given breed. Planned matings can be used to produce specifically desired characteristics in domesticated horses. Furthermore, modern breeding management and technologies can increase the rate of conception, a healthy pregnancy, and successful foaling.

The male parent of a horse, a stallion, is commonly known as the *sire* and the female parent, the mare, is called the *dam*. Both are genetically important, as each parent provides half of the genetic makeup of the ensuing offspring, called a foal. (Contrary to popular misuse, the word 'colt' refers to a young male horse only; 'filly' is a young female.) Though many horse owners may simply breed a family mare to a local stallion in order to produce a companion animal, most professional breeders use selective breeding to produce individuals of a given phenotype, or breed. Alternatively, a breeder could, using individuals of differing phenotypes, create a new breed with specific characteristics.

A horse is 'bred' where it is foaled (born). Thus a foal conceived in England but foaled in the United States is regarded as being bred in the US. In some cases, most notably in the Thoroughbred breeding industry, American-bred horses may also be described by the state in which they are foaled. Some breeds denote the country, or state, where conception took place as the origin of the foal.

Similarly, the 'breeder', is the person who owned or leased the mare at the time of foaling. That individual may not have had anything to do with the mating of the mare. It's important to review each breed registry's rules to determine which applies to any specific foal.

In the horse breeding industry, the term 'half-brother' or 'half-sister' only describes horses which have the same dam, but different sires. Horses with the same sire but different dams are simply said to be 'by the same sire', and no sibling relationship is implied. 'Full' (or 'own') siblings have both the same dam and the same sire. The terms paternal half-sibling, and maternal half-sibling are also often used. Three-quarter siblings are horses out of the same dam, and are by sires that are either half-brothers (i.e. same dam) or who are by the same sire.

Thoroughbreds and Arabians are also classified through the 'distaff' or direct female line, known as their 'family' or 'tail female' line, tracing back to their taproot foundation bloodstock or the beginning of their respective stud books. The female line of descent always appears at the bottom of a tabulated pedigree and is therefore often known as the *bottom line.*

'Linebreeding' technically is the duplication of fourth generation or more distant ancestors. However, the term is often used more loosely, describing horses with duplication of ancestors closer than the fourth generation. It also is sometimes used as a euphemism for the practice of inbreeding, a practice that is generally frowned upon by horse breeders, though used by some in an attempt to fix certain traits.

The Estrous Cycle of the Mare

The estrous cycle (also spelled oestrous) controls when a mare is sexually receptive toward a stallion, and helps to physically prepare the mare for conception. It generally occurs during the spring and summer months, although some mares may be sexually receptive into the late fall, and is controlled by the photoperiod (length of the day), the cycle first triggered when the days begin to lengthen. The estrous cycle lasts about 19-22 days, with the average being 21 days. As the days shorten, the mare returns to a period when she is not sexually receptive, known as anestrus. Anestrus - occurring in the majority of, but not all, mares - prevents the mare from conceiving in the winter months, as that would result in her foaling during the harshest part of the year, a time when it would be most difficult for the foal to survive.

This cycle contains two phases:

1. *Estrus, or Follicular, phase:* 5-7 days in length, when the mare is sexually receptive to a stallion. Estrogen is secreted by the follicle. Ovulation occurs in the final 24-48 hours of estrus.
2. *Diestrus, or Luteal, phase:* 14-15 days in length, the mare is not sexually receptive to the stallion. The corpus luteum secretes progesterone.

Depending on breed, on average, 16 per cent of mares have double ovulations, allowing them to twin, this does not affect the length of time of estrus or diestrus.

Effects on the Reproductive System during the Estrous Cycle

Changes in hormone levels can have great effects on the physical characteristics of the reproductive organs of the mare, thereby preparing, or preventing, her from conceiving.

- **Uterus:** It increased levels of estrogen during estrus cause edema within the uterus, making it feel heavier, and the uterus loses its tone. This edema decreases following ovulation, and the muscular tone increases. High levels of progesterone do not cause edema within the uterus. The uterus becomes flaccid during anestrus.
- **Cervix:** The cervix starts to relax right before estrus occurs, with maximal relaxation around the time of ovulation. The secretions of the cervix increase. High progesterone levels (during diestrus) cause the cervix to close and become toned.
- **Vagina**: The portion of the vagina near the cervix becomes engorged with blood right before estrus. The vagina becomes relaxed and secretions increase.
- **Vulva**: It relaxes right before estrus begins. Becomes dry, and closes more tightly, during diestrus.

Hormones Involved in the Estrous Cycle

The cycle is controlled by several hormones which regulate the estrous cycle, the mare's behaviour, and the reproductive system of the mare. The cycle begins when the increased day length causes the pineal gland to reduce the levels of melatonin, thereby allowing the hypothalamus to secrete GnRH.

- **GnRH (Gonadotropin releasing hormone)**: It secreted by the hypothalamus, causes the pituitary to release of 2 gonadotrophins: LH and FSH.
- **LH (Luteinizing Hormone)**: Its levels are highest 2 days following ovulation, then slowly decrease over 4-5 days, dipping to their lowest levels 5-16 days after ovulation. Stimulates the follicle to mature, which then in turn secretes estrogen. Unlike most mammals, the mare does not have an increase of LH right before ovulation.
- **FSH (Follicle-stimulating Hormone)**: Follicle-stimulating hormone secreted by the pituitary, causes the ovarian follicle to develop. Levels of FSH rise slightly at the end of estrus, but have their highest peak

about 10 days before the next ovulation. FSH is inhibited by inhibin at the same time LH and estrogen levels rise, which prevents immature follicles from continuing their growth. Mares may however have multiple FSH waves during a single estrous cycle, and diestrus follicles resulting from a diestrus FSH wave are not uncommon, particularly in the height of the natural breeding season.

- **Estrogen**: Estrogen secreted by the developing follicle, it causes the pituitary gland to secrete more LH (therefore, these 2 hormones are in a positive feedback loop). Additionally, it causes behavioural changes in the mare, making her more receptive toward the stallion, and causes physical changes in the cervix, uterus, and vagina to prepare the mare for conception. Estrogen peaks 1-2 days before ovulation, and decreases within 2 days following ovulation.
- **Inhibin**: Inhibin secreted by the developed follicle right before ovulation, 'turns off' FSH, which is no longer needed now that the follicle is larger.
- **Progesterone**: Progesterone prevents conception and decreases sexual receptibility of the mare to the stallion. Progesterone is therefore lowest during the estrus phase, and increases during diestrus. It decreases 12-15 days after ovulation, when the corpus luteum begins to decrease in size.
- **Prostaglandin**: Prostaglandin secreted by the endrometrium 13-15 days following ovulation, causes luteolysis and prevents the corpus luteum from secreting progesterone
- **eCG - equine chorionic gonadotropin - (also called PMSG (pregnant mare serum gonadotropin)**: Chorionic gonadotropins secreted if the mare conceives. First secreted by the endometrial cups around the 36th day of gestation, peaking around day 60, and decreasing after about 120 days of gestation. Also help to stimulate the growth of the fetal gonads.
- **Prolactin**: Stimulates lactation.
- **Oxytocin**: It stimulates the uterus to contract.

Breeding and Gestation

While horses in the wild mate and foal in mid to late spring, in the case of horses domestically bred for competitive purposes, especially horse racing and various futurities, it is desirable that they be born as close to January 1 in the northern hemisphere or August 1 in the southern hemisphere as possible, so as to be at an advantage in size and maturity when competing against other horses in the same age group. When an early foal is desired, barn managers will put the mare 'under lights' by keeping the barn lights on in the winter to simulate a longer day, thus bringing the mare into estrus sooner than she would in nature. Mares signal estrus and ovulation by urination in the presence of a stallion, raising the tail and revealing the vulva. A stallion, approaching with a high head, will usually nicker, nip and nudge the mare, as well as sniff her urine to determine her readiness for mating.

Once fertilized, the oocyte (egg) remains in the oviduct for approximately 5.5 more days, and then descends into the uterus. The initial single cell combination is already dividing and by the time of entry into the uterus, the egg might have already reached the blastocyst stage.

The gestation period lasts for about eleven months, or about 340 days (normal average range 320-370 days). During the early days of pregnancy, the conceptus is mobile, moving about in the uterus until about day 16 when 'fixation' occurs. Shortly after fixation, the embryo proper (so called up to about 35 days) will become visible on trans-rectal ultrasound (about day 21) and a heartbeat should be visible by about day 23. After the formation of the endometrial cups and early placentation is initiated (35-40 days of gestation) the terminology changes, and the embryo is referred to as a fetus. True implantation - invasion into the endometrium of any sort - does not occur until about day 35 of pregnancy with the formation of the endometrial cups, and true placentation (formation of the placenta) is not initiated until about day 40-45 and not completed until about 140 days of pregnancy. The fetus gender can be determined by day 70 of the gestation using ultrasound. Halfway through gestation the fetus is the size of between a rabbit and a beagle. The most dramatic fetal development occurs in the last 3 months of pregnancy when 60 per cent of fetal growth occurs.

Care of the Pregnant Mare

Domestic mares receive specific care and nutrition to ensure that they and their foals are healthy. Mares are given vaccinations against diseases such as the Rhinopneumonitis (EHV-1) virus (which can cause abortions) as well as vaccines for other conditions that may occur in a given region of the world. Pre-foaling vaccines are recommended 4-6 weeks prior to foaling to maximize the immunoglobulin content of the colostrum in the first milk. Deworming the mare a few weeks prior to foaling is also important, as the mare is the primary source of parasites for the foal.

Mares can be used for riding or driving during most of their pregnancy, and it's healthy for them to have exercise. But only moderate exercise, especially when they become heavy in foal. Exercise in excessively high temperatures has been suggested as being detrimental to pregnancy maintenance during the embryonic period - it should however be noted that ambient temperatures encountered during the research were in the region of 100 degrees F and the same results may not be encountered in regions with lower ambient temperatures.

During the last 3-4 months of gestation, rapid growth of the fetus increases the pregnant mare's nutritional requirements. Energy requirements during these last few months, and during the first few months of lactation are similar to those of a horse in full training. Trace minerals such as Copper are extremely important, particularly during the tenth month of pregnancy, for proper skeletal formation. Many feeds designed for pregnant and lactating mares provide the careful balance required of increased protein, increased calories through extra fat as well as vitamins and minerals. During the first several months of pregnancy, the nutritional requirements do not increase significantly since the rate of growth of the fetus is very slow. However, during this time, the mare should be provided supplemental vitamins and minerals, particularly if forage quality is questionable. Overfeeding the pregnant mare, particularly during early gestation, should be avoided, as excess weight may contribute to difficulties foaling or fetal/foal related problems.

Foaling

Mares due to foal are usually separated from other horses, both for the benefit of the mare and the safety of the soon-to-be-delivered foal. In addition, separation allows the mare to be monitored more closely by humans for any problems that may occur while giving birth. In the northern hemisphere a special foaling stall that is large and clutter free is frequently used, particularly by major breeding farms. Originally, this was due in part to a need for protection from the harsh winter climate present when mares foal early in the year, but even in moderate climates, such as Florida, foaling stalls are still common because they allow closer monitoring of mares. Smaller breeders often use a small pen with a large shed for foaling, or they may remove a wall between two box stalls in a small barn to make a large stall. In the milder climates seen in much of the southern hemisphere, most mares foal outside, often in a paddock built specifically for foaling, especially on the larger stud farms. Many stud farms worldwide employ technology to alert human managers when the mare is about to foal, including webcams, closed-circuit television, or assorted types of devices that alert a handler via a remote alarm when a mare lies down in a position to foal.

On the other hand, some breeders, particularly those in remote areas or with extremely large numbers of horses, may allow mares to foal out in a field amongst a herd, but may also see higher rates of foal and mare mortality in doing so.

Most mares foal at night or early in the morning, and prefer to give birth alone when possible. Labor is rapid, often no more than 30 minutes, and from the time the feet of the foal appear to full delivery is often only about 15 to 20 minutes. Once the foal is born, the mare will lick the newborn foal to clean it and help blood circulation. In a very short time, the foal will attempt to stand and get milk from its mother. A foal should stand and nurse within the first hour of life.

To create a bond with her foal, the mare licks and nuzzles the foal, enabling her to distinguish hers from others. Some mares are aggressive when protecting their foals, and may attack other horses or unfamiliar humans that come near their newborns.

After birth, a foal's navel is dipped in antiseptic to prevent infection, it is sometimes given an enema to help clear the meconium from its digestive tract, and the newborn is monitored to ensure that it stands and nurses without difficulty. While most horse births happen without complications, many owners have first aid supplies prepared and a veterinarian on call in case of a birthing emergency. People who supervise foaling should also watch the mare to be sure that she passes the placenta in a timely fashion, and that it is complete with no fragments remaining in the uterus, where retained fetal membranes could cause a serious inflammatory condition (endometritis) and/or infection. If the placenta is not removed from the stall after it is passed, a mare will often eat it, an instinct from the wild, where blood would attract predators.

Foal Care

Foals develop rapidly, and within a few hours a wild foal can travel with the herd. In domestic breeding, the foal and dam are usually separated from the herd for a while, but within a few weeks are typically pastured with the other horses. A foal will begin to eat hay, grass and grain alongside the mare at about 4 weeks old; by 10-12 weeks the foal requires more nutrition than the mare's milk can supply. Foals are typically weaned at 4-8 months of age, although in the wild a foal may nurse for a year.

Development of Breeds

Beyond the appearance and conformation of a specific type of horse, breeders aspire to improve physical performance abilities. This concept, known as matching 'form to function', has led to the development of not only different breeds, but also families or bloodlines within breeds that are specialists for excelling at specific tasks.

For example, the Arabian horse of the desert naturally developed speed and endurance to travel long distances and survive in a harsh environment, and domestication by humans added a trainable disposition to the animal's natural abilities. In the meantime, in northern Europe, the locally adapted heavy horse with a thick, warm coat was domesticated and put to work as a farm animal that could pull a plow or wagon. This animal was later adapted through selective breeding to create a strong but ridable animal suitable for the heavily-armored knight in warfare.

Then, centuries later, when people in Europe wanted faster horses than could be produced from local horses through simple selective breeding, they imported Arabians and other oriental horses to breed as an outcross to the heavier, local animals. This led to the development of breeds such as the Thoroughbred, a horse taller than the Arabian and faster over the distances of a few miles required of a European race horse or light cavalry horse. Another cross between oriental and European horses produced the Andalusian, a horse developed in Spain that was powerfully built, but extremely nimble and capable of the quick bursts of speed over short distances necessary for certain types of combat as well as for tasks such as bullfighting.

Later, the people who settled the Americas needed a hardy horse that was capable of working with cattle. Thus, Arabians and Thoroughbreds were crossed on Spanish horses, both domesticated animals descended from those brought over by the Conquistadors, and feral horses such as the Mustangs, descended from the Spanish horse, but adapted by natural selection to the ecology and climate of the west. These crosses ultimately produced new breeds such as the American quarter horse and the Criollo of Argentina.

In modern times, these breeds themselves have since been selectively bred to further specialize at certain tasks. One example of this is the American quarter horse. Once a general-purpose working ranch horse, different bloodlines now specialize in different events. For example, larger, heavier animals with a very steady attitude are bred to give competitors an advantage in events such as team roping, where a horse has to start and stop quickly, but also must calmly hold a full-grown steer at the end of a rope. On the other hand, for an event known as cutting, where the horse must separate a cow from a herd and prevent it from rejoining the group, the best horses are smaller, quick, alert, athletic and highly trainable. They must learn quickly, have conformation that allows quick stops and fast, low turns, and the best competitors have a certain amount of independent mental ability to anticipate and counter the movement of a cow, popularly known as 'cow sense'.

Another example is the Thoroughbred. While most representatives of this breed are bred for horse racing, there are also specialized bloodlines suitable as show hunters or show jumpers. The hunter must have a tall, smooth build that allows it to trot and canter smoothly and efficiently. Instead of speed, value is placed on appearance and upon giving the equestrian a comfortable ride, with natural jumping ability that shows bascule and good form.

A show jumper, however, is bred less for overall form and more for power over tall fences, along with speed, scope, and agility. This favours a horse with a good galloping stride, powerful hindquarters that can change speed or direction easily, plus a good shoulder angle and length of neck. A jumper has a more powerful build than either the hunter or the racehorse.

History of Horse Breeding

The history of horse breeding goes back millennia. Though the precise date is in dispute, humans could have domesticated the horse as far back as approximately 4500 BCE. However, evidence of planned breeding has a more blurry history.

One of the earliest people known to document the breedings of their horses were the Bedouin of the Middle East, the breeders of the Arabian horse. While it is difficult to determine how far back the Bedouin passed on pedigree information via an oral tradition, there were written pedigrees of Arabian horses by A.D. 1330. The Akhal-Teke of West-Central Asia is another breed with roots in ancient times that was also bred specifically for war and racing. The nomads of the Mongolian steppes bred horses for several thousand years as well.

The types of horse bred varied with culture and with the times. The uses to which a horse was put also determined its qualities, including smooth amblers for riding, fast horses for carrying messengers, heavy horses for plowing and pulling heavy wagons, ponies for hauling cars of ore from mines, packhorses, carriage horses and many others.

Medieval Europe bred large horses specifically for war, called destriers. These horses were the ancestors of the great heavy horses of today, and their size was preferred not simply because of the weight of the armor, but also because a large horse provided more power for the knight's lance. Weighing almost twice as much as a normal riding horse, the destrier was a powerful weapon in battle.

On the other hand, during this same time, lighter horses were bred in northern Africa and the Middle East by Muslim warriors, who preferred a faster, more agile horse. The lighter horse suited the raids and battles of the Bedouins, allowing them to outmaneuver rather than overpower the enemy. When Muslim warriors and European knights collided in warfare, the heavy knights were frequently outmaneuvered. The Europeans, however, soon made up for the lack of speed of their native breeds by incorporating genetic traits from captured oriental horses such as the Arabian, Barb to their stables. This cross-breeding led both to a nimbler war horse, such as today's Percheron, but also to created a type of horse known as a Courser, a predecessor to the Thoroughbred, which was used as a message horse.

During the Renaissance, horses were bred not only for war, but for haute ecole riding, derived from the most athletic movements required of a war horse, and popular among the elite nobility of the time. Breeds such as the Lipizzan were developed from Spanish-bred horses for this purpose, and also became the preferred mounts of cavalry officers, who were derived mostly from the ranks of the nobility. It was during this time that gunpowder was developed, and so the light cavalry horse, a faster and quicker war horse, was bred for a 'shoot and run' tactic rather than the close hand-to-hand fighting seen in the Middle Ages.

After Charles II retook the British throne in 1660, horse racing, which had been banned by Cromwell, was revived. The Thoroughbred was developed 40 years later, bred to be the ultimate racehorse, through the lines of 3 foundation Arabian stallions.

In the 18th century, James Burnett, Lord Monboddo noted the importance of selecting appropriate parentage to achieve desired outcomes of successive generations. Monboddo worked more broadly in the abstract thought of species relationships and evolution of species. The Thoroughbred breeding hub in Lexington, Kentucky was developed in the late 18th century, and became a mainstay in American racehorse breeding.

The 17th and 18th centuries saw more of a need for fine carriage horses in Europe, bringing in the dawn of the warmblood. The warmblood breeds have been exceptionally good at adapting to changing times, and from their carriage horse beginnings they easily transitioned during the 20th century into a sport horse type. Today's warmblood breeds, although still used for competitive driving, are more often seen competing in the show jumping or dressage arenas.

The Thoroughbred continues to dominate the horseracing world, although its lines have been more recently used to improve warmblood breeds and to develop sport horses.

The predecessor of the American Quarter Horse was developed in the 18th century, mainly for quarter racing (racing ¼ of a mile). The breed was later adapted for work in the west, and 'cow sense' was particularly bred for as their use for herding cattle increased. However, because there was also a need for animals suitable for sprint racing, the modern Quarter Horse has two distinct types: the sleeker racing type and the stock horse type. The racing type most resembles the finer-boned ancestors of the first racing Quarter Horses, and the type is still used for ¼-mile races. The stock horse type, used in western events, is bred for a shorter stride, docile temperament, and cow sense.

The need for horses for heavy draft and carriage work continued until the industrial revolution and the advent of the automobile and the tractor. After this time, draft and carriage horse numbers dropped significantly, though light riding horses remained popular for recreational pursuits. Draft horses today are used on a few small farms, but today are seen mainly for pulling and plowing competitions rather than farm work. Heavy harness horses are now used as an outcross with lighter breeds, such as the Thoroughbred, to produce the modern warmblood breeds popular in Olympic and sport horse disciplines.

Deciding to Breed a Horse

Breeding a horse is an endeavor where the owner, particularly of the mare, will usually need to invest considerable time and money. For this reason, a horse owner needs to consider several factors, including:

- Does the proposed breeding animal have valuable genetic qualities to pass on?
- Is the proposed breeding animal in good physical health, fertile, and able to withstand the vigors of reproduction?
- For what purpose will the foal be used?
- Is there a market for the foal in the event that the owner does not wish to keep the foal for its entire life?
- What is the anticipated economic benefit, if any, to the owner of the ensuing foal?
- What is the anticipated economic benefit, if any, to the owner(s) of the sire and dam or the foal?

- Does the owner of the mare have the expertise to properly manage the mare through gestation and parturition?
- Does the owner of the potential foal have the expertise to properly manage and train a young animal once it is born?

There are value judgements involved in considering whether an animal is suitable breeding stock, hotly debated by breeders. Additional personal beliefs may come into play when considering a suitable level of care for the mare and ensuing foal, the potential market or use for the foal, and other tangible and intangible benefits to the owner.

If the breeding endeavor is intended to make a profit, there are additional market factors to consider, which may vary considerably from year to year, from breed to breed, and by region of the world. In many cases, the low end of the market is saturated with horses, and the law of supply and demand thus allows little or no profit to be made from breeding unregistered animals or animals of poor quality, even if registered.

The minimum cost of breeding for a mare owner includes the stud fee, and the cost of proper nutrition, management and veterinary care of the mare throughout gestation, parturition, and care of both mare and foal up to the time of weaning. Veterinary expenses may be higher if specialized reproductive technologies are used or health complications occur.

Making a profit in horse breeding is often difficult. While some owners of only a few horses may keep a foal for purely personal enjoyment, many individuals breed horses in hopes of making some money in the process.

A general rule of thumb is that a foal intended for sale should be worth three times the cost of the stud fee if it were sold at the moment of birth. From birth forward, the costs of care and training are added to the value of the foal, with a sale price going up accordingly. If the foal wins awards in some form of competition, that may also enhance the price.

On the other hand, without careful thought, foals bred without a potential market for them may wind up being sold at a loss, and in a worst-case scenario, sold for 'salvage' value—a euphemism for sale to slaughter as horsemeat.

Therefore, a mare owner must consider their reasons for breeding, asking hard questions of themselves as to whether their motivations are based on either emotion or profit and how realistic those motivations may be.

Choosing Breeding Stock

The stallion should be chosen to complement the mare, with the goal of producing a foal that has the best qualities of both animals, yet avoids having the weaker qualities of either parent. Generally, the stallion should have proven himself in the discipline or sport the mare owner wishes for the 'career' of the ensuing foal. Mares should also have a competition record showing that they also have suitable traits, though this does not happen as often.

Some breeders consider the quality of the sire to be more important than the quality of the dam. However, other breeders maintain that the mare is the most important parent. Because stallions can produce far more offspring than mares, a single stallion can have a greater overall impact on a breed. However, the mare may have a greater influence on an individual foal because its physical characteristics influence the developing foal in the womb and the foal also learns habits from its dam when young. Foals may also learn the 'language of intimidation and submission' from their dam, and this imprinting may affect the foal's status and rank within the herd. Many times, a mature horse will achieve status in a herd similar to that of its dam; the offspring of dominant mares become dominant themselves.

A purebred horse is usually worth more than a horse of mixed breeding, though this matters more in some disciplines than others. The breed of the horse is sometimes secondary when breeding for a sport horse, but some disciplines may prefer a certain breed or a specific phenotype of horse. Sometimes, purebred bloodlines are an absolute requirement: For example most Racehorses in the world must be recorded with a breed registry in order to race.

Bloodlines are often considered, as some bloodlines are known to cross well with others. If the parents have not yet proven themselves by competition or by producing quality offspring, the bloodlines of the horse are often a good indicator of quality and possible strengths and weaknesses. Some bloodlines are known not only for their athletic ability, but could also carry a conformational or genetic defect, poor temperament, or for a medical problem. Some bloodlines are also fashionable or otherwise marketable, which is an important consideration should the mare owner wish to sell the foal.

Horse breeders also consider conformation, size and temperament. All of these traits are heritable, and will determine if the foal will be a success in its chosen discipline. The offspring, or "get", of a stallion are often excellent indicators of his ability to pass on his characteristics, and the particular traits he actually passes on. Some stallions are fantastic performers but never produce offspring of comparable quality. Others sire fillies of great abilities but not colts. At times, a horse of mediocre ability sires foals of outstanding quality.

Mare owners also look into the question of if the stallion is fertile and has successfully 'settled' (i.e. impregnated) mares. A stallion may not be able to breed naturally, or old age may decrease his performance. Mare care boarding fees and semen collection fees can be a major cost.

Costs Related to Breeding

Breeding a horse can be an expensive endeavor, whether breeding a backyard competition horse or the next Olympic medalist. Costs may include:

- The stud and booking fee.

- Fees for collecting, handling, and transporting semen (if AI is used and semen is shipped).
- Mare exams: to determine if she is healthy enough to breed, to determine when she ovulates, and (if AI is used) to inseminate her.
- Mare transport, care, and board if the mare is bred live cover at the stallion's residence.
- Veterinary bills to keep the pregnant mare healthy while in foal.
- Possible veterinary bills during pregnancy or foaling should something go wrong.
- Veterinary bills for the foal for its first exam a few days following foaling.

Stud fees are determined by the quality of the stallion, his performance record, the performance record of his get (offspring), as well as the sport and general market that the animal is standing for.

The highest stud fees are generally for racing Thoroughbreds, which may charge from two to three thousand dollars for a breeding to a new or unproven stallion, to several hundred thousand dollars for a breeding to a proven producer of stakes winners. Stallions in other disciplines often have stud fees that begin in the range of $1000 to $3000, with top contenders who produce champions in certain disciplines able to command as much as $20,000 for one breeding. The lowest stud fees to breed to a grade horse or an animal of low-quality pedigree may only be $100-$200, but there are trade-offs: the horse will probably be unproven, and likely to produce lower-quality offspring than a horse with a stud fee that is in the typical range for quality breeding stock.

As a stallion's career, either performance or breeding, improves, his stud fee tends to increase in proportion. If one or two offspring are especially successful, winning several stakes races or an Olympic medal, the stud fee will generally greatly increase. Younger, unproven stallions will generally have a lower stud fee earlier on in their careers.

To help decrease the risk of financial loss should the mare die or abort the foal while pregnant, many studs have a live foal guarantee (LFG) - also known as 'no foal, free return' or 'NFFR' - allowing the owner to have a free breeding to their stallion the next year. However, this is not offered for every breeding.

There are two general ways to 'cover' or breed the mare:

1. **Live cover**: The mare is brought to the stallion's residence and is covered 'live' in the breeding shed. She may also be turned out in a pasture with the stallion for several days to breed naturally ('pasture bred'). The former situation is often preferred, as it provides a more controlled environment, allowing the breeder to ensure that the mare was covered, and places the handlers in a position to remove the horses from one another should one attempt to kick or bite the other.

2. **Artificial Insemination (AI):** The mare is inseminated by a veterinarian or an equine reproduction manager, using either fresh, cooled or frozen semen.

After the mare is bred or artificially inseminated, she is checked using ultrasound 14-16 days later to see if she 'took', and is pregnant. A second check is usually performed at 28 days. If the mare is not pregnant, she may be bred again during her next cycle.

It is considered safe to breed a mare to a stallion of much larger size. Because of the mare's type of placenta and its attachment and blood supply, the foal will be limited in its growth within the uterus to the size of the mare's uterus, but will grow to its genetic potential after it is born. Test breedings have been done with draft horse stallions bred to small mares with no increase in the number of difficult births.

Live Cover

When breeding live cover, the mare is usually boarded at the stud. She is 'teased' several times with a stallion that will not breed to her, usually with the stallion being presented to the mare over a barrier. Her reaction to the teaser, whether hostile or passive, is noted. A mare that is in heat will generally tolerate a teaser (although this is not always the case), and may present herself to him, holding her tail to the side. A veterinarian may also determine if the mare is ready to be bred, by ultrasound or palpating daily to determine if ovulation has occurred.

When it has been determined that the mare is ready, both the mare and intended stud will be cleaned. The mare will then be presented to the stallion, usually with one handler controlling the mare and one or more handlers in charge of the stallion. Multiple handlers are preferred, as the mare and stallion can be easily separated should there be any trouble.

The Jockey Club, the organisation that oversees the Thoroughbred industry in the United States, requires all registered foals to be bred through live cover. Artificial insemination, listed below, is not permitted. Similar rules apply in other countries.

By contrast, the U.S. standardbred industry allows registered foals to be bred by live cover, or by artificial insemination (AI) with fresh or frozen (not dried) semen. No other artificial fertility treatment is allowed. In addition, foals bred via AI of frozen semen may only be registered if the stallion's sperm was collected during his lifetime, and used no later than the calendar year of his death or castration.

Artificial Insemination

Artificial insemination (AI) has several advantages over live cover, and has a very similar conception rate:

- The mare and stallion never have to come in contact with each other, which therefore reduces breeding accidents, such as the mare kicking the stallion.

- AI opens up the world to international breeding, as semen may be shipped across continents to mares that would otherwise be unable to breed to a particular stallion.
- A mare also does not have to travel to the stallion, so the process is less stressful on her, and if she already has a foal, the foal does not have to travel.
- AI allows more mares to be bred from one stallion, as the ejaculate may be split between mares.
- AI reduces the chance of spreading sexually transmitted diseases between mare and stallion.
- AI allows mares or stallions with health issues, such as sore hocks which may prevent a stallion from mounting, to continue to breed.
- Frozen semen may be stored and used to breed mares even after the stallion is dead, allowing his lines to continue. However, the semen of some stallions does not freeze well. Some breed registries may not permit the registration of foals resulting from the use of frozen semen after the stallion's death, although other large registries accept such usage and provide registrations. The overall trend is toward permitting use of frozen semen after the death of the stallion.

A stallion is usually trained to mount a phantom (or dummy) mare, although a live mare may be used, and he is most commonly collected using an artificial vagina (AV) which is heated to simulate the vagina of the mare. The AV has a filter and collection area at one end to capture the semen, which can then be processed in a lab. The semen may be chilled or frozen and shipped to the mare owner or used to breed mares "on-farm". When the mare is in heat, the person inseminating introduces the semen directly into her uterus using a syringe and pipette.

Advanced Reproductive Techniques

Often an owner does not want to take a valuable competition mare out of training to carry a foal. This presents a problem, as the mare will usually be quite old by the time she is retired from her competitive career, at which time it is more difficult to impregnate her. Other times, a mare may have physical problems that prevent or discourage breeding. However, there are now several options for breeding these mares. These options also allow a mare to produce multiple foals each breeding season, instead of the usual one. Therefore, mares may have an even greater value for breeding.

Embryo Transfer

This relatively new method involves flushing out the mare's fertilized embryo a few days following insemination, and transferring to a surrogate mare, which has been synchronized to be in the same phase of the estrous cycle as the donor mare.

Gamete Intrafallopian Transfer (GIFT)

The mare's ovum and the stallion's sperm are deposited in the oviduct of a surrogate dam. This technique is very useful for subfertile stallions, as fewer sperm are needed, so a stallion with a low sperm count can still successfully breed.

Egg Transfer

An oocyte is removed from the mare's follicle and transferred into the oviduct of the recipient mare, who is then bred. This is best for mares with physical problems, such as an obstructed oviduct, that prevent breeding.

Horse Breeds

A breed is defined generally as a viable true-breeding population, and its members are called 'purebreds'. In most cases, bloodlines of horse breeds are recorded with a breed registry. However, in horses, the concept is somewhat flexible, as open stud books are created for fairly new types of horse that are not yet fully true-breeding. Registries also are considered the authority as to whether a given breed is listed as a 'horse' or a 'pony'. There are also a number of 'colour breed', sport horse, and gaited horse registries for horses with various phenotypes or other traits, which admit any animal fitting a given set of physical characteristics, even if there is little or no evidence of the trait being a true-breeding characteristic. Other recording entities or specialty organisations may recognize horses from multiple breeds, thus, for the purposes of this article, such animals are classified as a 'type' rather than a 'breed'.

Horses are members of *Equus ferus caballus* that generally mature to be 14.2 hands (58 inches (150 cm)) or taller, but many breed registries do accept animals under this height and classify them as 'horses', as horse characteristics include factors other than height. For the purposes of this page, if a breed registry or stud book classifies the breed as a horse, it is listed here as a horse, even if some representatives are pony-sized or have some pony characteristics.

Abaco Barb, Barb (horse)	American quarter horse
Abtenauer	American saddlebred
Abyssinian horse	American warmblood
Aegidienberger	Andalusian horse *some bloodlines also called* Pura Raza Española (PRE) or Pure Spanish-bred
Akhal-Teke	Andravida horse
Albanian horse	Anglo-Arabian
Altai horse	Anglo-Arabo-Sardo, Sardinian Anglo-Arab
Altèr Real, Lusitano	Anglo-Kabarda
American cream draft	Anglo-Norman horse
American Indian horse	Appaloosa
American paint horse	

'Appendix', American Quarter Horse
AraAppaloosa, *also called* Ara-Appaloosa, Arappaloosa or Araloosa
Arabian horse
Ardennes horse, or Ardennais
Arenberg-Nordkirchen
Argentine Criollo, Criollo horse
Asturcón Australian Brumby, Brumby
Australian draught horse
Australian stock horse
Austrian warmblood
Auxois
Avelignese, haflinger (horse)
Azerbaijan horse
Azteca horse
Baise horse, *also known as* Guangxi
Balearic horse
Balikun horse
Baluchi horse
Ban'ei
Banker horse
Barb (horse)
Bardigiano
Bashkir Curly
Basque mountain horse
Bavarian warmblood
Belgian (horse)
Belgian Warmblood (includes Belgian Half-blood)
Black Forest Horse, *also called* Black Forest cold blood *or* Schwarzwälder Kaltblut
Blazer horse
Boulonnais horse
Brabant, Belgian (horse)
Brandenburger
Brazilian Sport Horse (Brasileiro de Hipismo)
Breton horse, or Trait Breton
Brumby
Budyonny (horse) or Budenny
Burguete horse
Byelorussian Harness
Calabrese horse
Camargue (horse)
Camarillo white horse
Campolina
Canadian horse
Canadian Pacer
Carolina Marsh Tacky
Carthusian horse, Andalusian horse
Caspian horse
Castilian horse
Catria horse
Cavallo Romano della Maremma Laziale
Chickasaw horse, Florida Cracker horse
Chilean Corralero
Chilean horse
Choctaw horse
Cleveland Bay
Clydesdale (horse)
Colonial Spanish horse
Colorado Ranger
Coldblood trotter
Comtois horse
Costa Rican Saddle horse
Cretan horse, Messara
Criollo horse, *also spelled* Crioulo
Cuban Criollo horse
Curly horse
Czech warm blood
Daliboz
Danish warmblood
Danube Delta horse
Dole Gudbrandsdal, *also called* Dole, or Dølahest

Don, Russian Don
Draft Trotter, *also called* Light Dole, Dole trotter
Dutch harness horse
Dutch heavy draft
Dutch warmblood
East Bulgarian
East Friesian horse, Ostfriesen and Alt-Oldenburger
Estonian draft
Estonian horse
Falabella
Faroese or Faroe horse, Faroe pony in pony section
Finnhorse, or Finnish Horse
Fleuve
Fjord horse *also called* Norwegian Fjord horse
Florida cracker horse
Fouta or Foutanké
Frederiksborg horse
Freiberger
French trotter
Friesian cross (includes Friesian Sport Horses) Friesian horse
Friesian Sporthorse (a type of Friesian cross)
Furioso-North Star
Galiceno or Galiceño
Galician Pony (Caballo de pura raza Gallega)
Gelderland horse
Georgian Grande horse
German Warmblood or ZfDP
Giara horse
Gidran
Groningen horse
Gypsy Vanner horse, *sometimes called* 'Gypsy horse', 'Vanner horse', 'Gypsy Cob' or 'Coloured Cob'
Hackney (horse)
Haflinger (horse)
Hanoverian horse
Heck horse
Heihe horse
Hirzai
Hispano-Bretón
Hispano horse *also known as* Hispano-Arabe or Spanish Anglo-Arab
Holsteiner horse
Hungarian Warmblood
Icelandic horse
Indian Half-Bred
Iomud Irish Draught, *also spelled* Irish Draft
Irish Sport Horse *sometimes called* Irish hunter
Italian heavy draft
Italian trotter
Jaca navarra
Jutland horse
Kabarda horse, *also known as* Kabardian *or* Kabardin
Kaimanawa horses
Karabair
Karabakh horse *also known as* Azer At
Karossier *see* Ostfriesen and Alt-Oldenburger
Kathiawari
Kentucky Mountain Saddle horse
Kiger Mustang
Kinsky horse
Kisber Felver
Kladruber
Knabstrupper
Konik
Kustanair
Latvian horse

Lipizzan or Lipizzaner
Lithuanian heavy draught
Lokai
Losino horse
Lusitano
Lyngshest, Nordlandshest/ Lyngshest
M'Bayar, Fouta
Malapolski
Mallorquín
Mangalarga
Mangalarga Marchador
Maremmano
Marismeño horse
Marsh Tacky, Carolina Marsh Tacky
Marwari horse
Mecklenburger
Menorquín
Mérens horse
Messara
Mezohegyesi sport-horse (sportló), *or* Mezohegyes felver, Hungarian Warmblood
Metis Trotter, Russian Trotter
Miniature horse
Misaki
Missouri fox Trotter
Monchina
Mongolian horse
Monterufolino
Morab Morgan horse
Moyle horse
Murakoz horse, Muräkozi, or Muraközi ló (Hungary)
Murgese
Mustang (horse)
Namib Desert horse
Nangchen horse
National show horse
Nez Perce horse
Nokota horse
Noma
Nonius horse
Nordlandshest/Lyngshest
Noriker horse, *also called* Pinzgauer
Normandy Cob Anglo-Norman horse
Norsk Kaldblodstraver (Norwegian coldblood trotter), Coldblood trotter
North Swedish horse
Norwegian Fjord, Fjord horse
Novokirghiz
Oberlander horse
Oldenburg horse, *also spelled* Oldenburgh, Oldenburger
Orlov trotter
Ostfriesen and Alt-Oldenburger paint, American paint horse
Pampa horse
Paso Fino
Pentro horse
Percheron
Persano horse
Peruvian Paso, *sometimes called* Peruvian stepping horse
Pintabian
Pleven horse
Poitevin horse *also called* Mulassier
Pottok
Pryor mountain mustang
Przewalski's Horse, *also known as* Takhi, Mongolian Wild Horse *or* Asian Wild Horse. (Species, not a 'breed' but listed here for convenience)
Purosangue Orientale
Qatgani
Quarab
Quarter horse, American quarter horse
Racking horse
Retuerta horse

Rhenish-German Cold-Blood *also known as* Rhineland Heavy Draft
Rhinelander horse
Riwoche horse
Rocky mountain horse
Romanian Sporthorse
Rottaler, heavy warmblood
Russian Don
Russian heavy draft
Russian Trotter
Saddlebred, American Saddlebred
Salerno (horse breed)
Samolaco horse
San Fratello horse
Sarcidano horse
Sardinian Anglo-Arab, *also known as* Sardinian horse
Sella Italiano
Selle Français
Shagya Arabian
Shire horse
Siciliano indigeno
Sorraia
Sokolsky horse
Soviet heavy draft
Spanish Jennet horse, modern, *not to be confused with* the historic Jennet or Spanish Jennet
Spanish Mustang
Spanish-Norman horse
Spanish Tarpan, Sorraia
Spotted Saddle horse standardbred horse
Suffolk Punch
Svensk Kallblodstravare (Swedish coldblood trotter), Coldblood trotter
Swedish Ardennes
Swedish Warmblood
Swiss Warmblood
Taishuh
Tawleed
Tchernomor, Budyonny horse
Tennessee walking horse
Tersk horse
Thoroughbred
Tinker horse, Gypsy Vanner horse
Tiger horse
Tolfetano
Tori (horse)
Trait Du Nord
Trakehner
Tuigpaard, Dutch harness horse
Ukrainian riding horse
Unmol horse
Uzunyayla Ventasso horse (Cavallo Del Ventasso)
Virginia highlander
Vlaamperd
Vladimir heavy draft
Vyatka
Waler horse, *also known as* Waler or Australian Waler
Walkaloosa
Warmblood
Westphalian horse
Wielkopolski
Württemberger or Württemberg
Xilingol horse
Yakutian horse
Yili horse
Yonaguni horse
Zweibrücker

Ponies are usually classified as members of *Equus caballus* that mature at less than 14.2 hands. However, some pony breeds may occasionally have individuals who mature over 14.2 but retain all other breed characteristics. There are also some breeds that now frequently mature over 14.2 hands due to modern nutrition and management, yet retain the historic classification 'pony'. For the purposes of this list, if a breed registry classifies the breed as a 'pony', it is listed here as such, even if some individuals have horse characteristics.

American Shetland, Shetland pony
American Walking Pony
Anadolu pony *also called* Anadolu Ati
Ariegeois pony Mérens horse in horse section
Assateague pony, Chincoteague pony
Asturian pony, Asturcon in horse section
Australian pony
Australian Riding pony
Bali pony
Bashkir pony
Basque pony, pottok
Basuto pony, *also spelled* Basotho pony
Batak Pony
Bhutia Pony, *also* Bhotia, Bhote ghoda, Bhutan, Bhutani, Bhutua Indian Country bred
Boer pony
Bosnian pony
British riding pony
British spotted pony Burmese pony
Carpathian pony, Hucul pony
Canadian rustic pony
Caspian pony
Chincoteague pony
Chinese Guoxia
Coffin Bay pony
Connemara pony
Czechoslovakian small riding pony
Dales pony
Danish sport pony
Dartmoor pony
Deli pony
Deutsches reitpony German riding pony
Dülmen pony
Eriskay pony
Esperia Pony
Exmoor pony
Falabella, Falabella
Faroe pony
Fell Pony
Flores pony, timor pony French saddle pony
Galician pony
Garrano
Gayoe
German riding Pony, *also called* Deutsche Reitpony *or* Weser-Ems Pony
Gotland pony
Guizhou pony
Guangxi, baise horse
Guo-xìa pony, Chinese Guoxia
Hackney pony
Highland pony, Garron
Hokkaido pony
Hucul pony
Hunter pony
Icelandic pony, Icelandic horse in horse section
Indian Country Bred
Java pony
Kazakh pony
Kerry bog pony
Landais pony
Lijiang pony
Lundy pony
Manipuri pony
Merens pony
Miniature horse

Misaki	Shetland pony
Miyako pony	Skogsruss, Gotland pony
Narym pony	Spiti pony
New forest pony	Sumba and Sumbawa pony
Newfoundland pony	Tibetan pony Timor pony
Noma pony	Tokara pony
Nooitgedacht pony	Virginia highlander
Northlands pony	Vyatka (horse)
Ob pony *also called* priob pony	Welara
Peneia pony petiso Argentino	Welsh pony
Pindos pony	Welsh mountain pony, Welsh pony
Poney Mousseye	Welsh pony, Welsh pony
Pony of the Americas	Welsh pony of cob type, Welsh pony
Pottok	Western Sudan pony
Quarter pony	Yakut pony
Riding pony	Yonaguni
Sable Island pony	Zaniskari pony
Sandalwood pony	Žemaitukas, *also known as* Zemaituka,
Sardinian pony	Zhumd, Zhemaichu, or Zhmudka

There are some registries that accept horses (and sometimes ponies and mules) of almost any breed or type for registration. Colour is either the only criterion for registration or the primary criterion. These are called 'colour breeds', because unlike 'true' horse breeds, there are few other physical requirements, nor is the stud book limited in any fashion. As a general rule, the colour also does not always breed on (in some cases due to genetic impossibility), and offspring without the stated colour are usually not eligible for recording with the colour breed registry. The best-known colour breed registries are for the following colours:

- Buckskin (horse)
- Palomino

White (horse). Some of these animals are registered in the United States with the American creme and white horse registry, which was once called an 'Albino' registry until it was understood that true albino does not exist in horses.

There are breeds that have colour that usually breeds 'true' as well as distinctive physical characteristics and a limited stud book. These horses are true breeds that have a preferred colour, not colour breeds, and include the Friesian horse, the Cleveland Bay, the Appaloosa, and the American Paint Horse.

Types of Horse

Types of horse A 'type' of horse is not a breed but is simply a term used to describe a group of breeds that are similar in appearance (phenotype) or use. A type usually has no breed registry, and often encompasses several breeds. However, in some nations, particularly in Europe, there is a recording method or means of studbook selection for certain types to allow them to be licensed for breeding. Horses of a given type may be registered as one of several different recognized breeds, or a term may include horses that are of no particular pedigree but meet a certain standard of appearance or use.

Modern Types

- AQPS ('Autre Que Pur-Sang'), French designation for riding horses 'other than Thoroughbred', usually referring to the Anglo-Arabian, Selle Francais and other Thoroughbred crosses. There is a registry for AQPS horses in France.
- Baroque horse, *includes* heavily muscled, powerful, yet agile Classical dressage breeds such as the Lipizzaner, Friesian, Andalusian, and Lusitano.
- Canadian Cutting Horse - any cutting horse in Canada, most of American Quarter Horse bloodlines
- Cob (horse)
- Colonial Spanish Horse, the original Jennet-type horse brought to North America, now with a number of modern descendants with various breed names.
- Feral horse, a horse living in the wild, but descended from once-domesticated ancestors. Most 'wild' horses today are actually feral. The only true wild (never domesticated) horse in the world today is the Przewalski's horse.
- Gaited horse, term used to describe any of a number of breeds with an intermediate speed four-beat ambling gait, including the Tennessee Walker, Paso Fino, and many others.
- Galloway, a term used in Australia to collectively refer to show horses over 14 hands but under 15 hands.
- German Warmblood or ZfDP, collective term for any of the various warmblood horses of Germany, of which some may be registered with the nation-wide German Horse Breeding Society (ZfDP).
- Grade horse, a term used to describe a horse of unknown or mixed breed parentage.
- Hack, a basic riding horse, particularly in the UK, also includes Show hack horses used in competition.
- Heavy warmblood, heavy carriage and riding horses, predecessors to the modern warmbloods, several old-style breeds still in existence today.
- Hunter, a type of jumping horse, either a show hunter or a field hunter.

- Hunter pony, a show hunter or show jumping animal under 14.2 hands, may be actually of a horse or pony breed, height determines category of competition.
- Iberian horse, encompassing horse and pony breeds developed in the Iberian peninsula, including the Andalusian, Lusitano and others.
- Mountain and moorland or 'M & M' is a general term which covers several breeds of pony native to the British Isles.
- New Zealand Warmblood, a developing warmblood type based on Hanoverian and KWPF breeding.
- Oriental horse, referring to the "hot-blooded" breeds descended from the Oriental prototype under the 'four foundations' theory.
- Polo pony, a horse used in the sport of polo, not actually a pony, usually a full-sized horse, often a thoroughbred.
- Riding Pony, a term used in the United Kingdom to describe certain types of show ponies.
- Sport horse or Sporthorse, includes any breeds suitable for use in assorted international competitive disciplines governed by the FEI.
- Stock horse, heavily-muscled riding horses of several different breeds, suitable for working cattle. Not to be confused with the breed Australian Stock Horse.
- Warmblood, a group of Sport horse breeds developed for modern Dressage and other Olympic disciplines, *including* the Dutch Warmblood Hanoverian (horse), Swedish Warmblood, Westphalian (horse), etc.
- Windsor Grey, the gray carriage horses of British Royalty.

Archaic Types

Prior to approximately the 13th century, few pedigrees were written down, and horses were classified by physical type or use. Thus, many terms for Horses in the Middle Ages did not describe breeds as we know them today, but rather described appearance or purpose. These terms included:

- Courser (horse)
- Courser (horse)
- Destrier or 'Great Horse'
- Hobby, Irish Hobby
- Jennet, sometimes called Spanish Jennet
- Palfrey
- Rouncey
- Steppe horse, refers to various domesticated horse and wild horse species, particularly those from Siberia and other parts of western Asia

Extinct Species and Breeds

These horses and ponies either were a recognized, distinct breed of horse that no longer exists as such, or varieties of *Equus ferus caballus* that have become extinct at some point since domestication of the horse. This section does not include any species within evolution of the horse prior to modern *Equus caballus*.

Early Prototypes

Before the availability of DNA techniques to resolve the questions related to the domestication of the horse, various hypothesis were proposed. One classification was based on body types and conformation, suggesting the presence of four basic prototypes that had adapted to their environment prior to domestication. More recent studies suggest that all domesticated horses originated from a single wild species and that different body types were entirely a result of selective breeding after domestication, or possibly landrace adaptation. The original domesticated animal has sometimes been called the 'Tarpan subtype', due to its probable external resemblance to the Tarpan, though the Tarpan that survived into modern times was a separate subspecies and not able to be domesticated.

The other prototypes are:

- The 'Warmblood subspecies' or 'Forest Horse' (once proposed as *Equus ferus silvaticus*, also called the Diluvial Horse), with a later variety once proposed as *Equus ferus germanicus*. This prototype may have contributed to the development of the warmblood horses of northern Europe, as well as older 'heavy horses' such as the Ardennais.
- The 'Draft' subspecies, a small, sturdy, heavyset animal with a heavy hair coat, arising in northern Europe, adapted to cold, damp climates, somewhat resembling today's Fjord horse and even the Shetland pony.
- The 'Oriental' subspecies, (once proposed as *Equus agilis*) a taller, slim, refined and agile animal arising in western Asia, adapted to hot, dry climates, thought to be the progenitor of the modern Arabian horse and Akhal-Teke.

Extinct Breeds

These were human-developed breeds, now no longer in existence.

- Chapman horse, Cleveland Bay, into which it developed
- Ferghana horse
- Galloway pony
- Karacabey (horse)
- Irish Hobby
- Jennet, or Spanish Jennet
- Mazury (horse) Narragansett Pacer
- Neapolitan horse
- Nisean horse
- Norfolk Trotter, *also called* the Norfolk Roadster, Yorkshire Trotter or Yorkshire Roadster

- Öland horse
- Old English Black horse Pozan
- Tundra Horse, the probable ancestor of the Yakutian horse.
- Turkoman Horse *also known as* Turkemene. The Akhal-Teke may be a direct descendant.
- Yorkshire coach horse.

CHAPTER 5

Wild Horse

The wild horse (*Equus ferus*) is a species of the genus *Equus*, which includes as subspecies the domesticated horse as well as the undomesticated Tarpan and Przewalski's Horse. The Tarpan became extinct in the 19th century, and Przewalski's Horse was saved from the brink of extinction and reintroduced successfully to the wild. The possible ancestor of the domestic horse was the Tarpan, which roamed the steppes of Eurasia at the time of domestication. However, other subspecies of *Equus ferus* may have existed and could have been the stock from which domesticated horses are descended. Since the extinction of the Tarpan, attempts have been made to reconstruct the phenotype of the Tarpan, resulting in horse breeds such as the Konik and Heck horse. However, the genetic makeup and foundation bloodstock of those breeds is substantially derived from domesticated horses, and therefore these breeds possess domesticated traits.

The term 'wild horse' is also used colloquially to refer to free roaming herds of feral horses such as the Mustang in the United States, the Brumby in Australia, and many others. These feral horses are untamed members of the domestic horse subspecies (*Equus ferus caballus*), and should not be confused with the two truly 'wild' horse subspecies.

Subspecies and their History

E.ferus had several subspecies. Three survived into modern times:

- The Domestic horse (*Equus ferus caballus*)
- The Tarpan or Eurasian Wild Horse (*Equus ferus ferus*), once native to Europe and western Asia. The Tarpan became effectively extinct in the late 19th century, and the last specimen died in captivity in a Ukraine zoo in 1918 or 1919.
- Przewalski's Horse (*Equus ferus przewalskii*), also known as the Mongolian Wild Horse or Takhi, native to Central Asia and the Gobi Desert.

The latter two are the only never-domesticated 'wild' groups that survived into historic times. However, other subspecies of *Equus ferus* may have existed and could have been the stock from which domesticated horses are descended.

Przewalski's Horse

Przewalski's Horse occupied the eastern Eurasian steppes, perhaps from the Urals to Mongolia, although the ancient border between Tarpan and Przewalski distributions has not been clearly defined. Przewalski's Horse was limited to Dzungaria and western Mongolia in the same period, became extinct in the wild during the 1960s, but was re-introduced in the late 1980s to two preserves in Mongolia. Although researchers such as Marija Gimbutas theorized that the horses of the Chalcolithic period were Przewalski's, more recent genetic studies indicate that Przewalski's Horse is not an ancestor to modern domesticated horses.

Przewalski's Horse is still found today, though it is an endangered species and for a time was considered extinct in the wild. Roughly 1500 Przewalski's Horses are protected in zoos around the world. A small breeding population has been reintroduced in Mongolia. As of 2005, a cooperative venture between the Zoological Society of London and Mongolian Scientists has resulted in a free-ranging population of 248 animals in the wild.

Przewalski's Horse has some biological differences from the domestic horse; unlike domesticated horses and the Tarpan, which both have 64 chromosomes, Przewalski's Horse has 66 chromosomes due to a Robertsonian translocation. However, the offspring of Przewalski and domestic horses are fertile, possessing 65 chromosomes.

Taxonomy and Evolution

The horse family Equidae and the genus *Equus* evolved in North America, before the species moved into the Eastern Hemisphere. Studies using ancient DNA as well as DNA of recent individuals, shows the presence of two closely related horse species in North America, the Wild Horse and the 'New World stilt-legged horse'; the latter is taxonomically assigned to various names. Currently, three subspecies that lived during recorded human history are recognized. One subspecies is the widespread domestic horse (*Equus ferus caballus*), as well as two wild subspecies, the recently-extinct Tarpan (*Equus ferus ferus*) and the endangered Przewalski's Horse (*Equus ferus przewalskii*). Genetically, the pre-domestication horse, *Equus ferus ferus*, and domesticated horse, *Equus ferus caballus*, form a single homogeneous group (clade) and are genetically indistinguishable from each other. The genetic variation within this clade shows only a limited regional variation, with a notable exception of Przewalski's Horse. Przewalski's Horse has several unique genetic differences that distinguishes it from the other subspecies, including 66 instead of 64 chromosomes, unique Y-chromosome gene haplotypes, and unique mtDNA haplotypes. Besides genetic differences, osteological evidence from across the Eurasian wild horse range, based on cranial and metacarpal differences, indicates the presence of only two subspecies in post-glacial times, the Tarpan and Przewalski's Horse.

Scientific Naming

At present, the domesticated and wild horses are considered a single species, with the valid scientific name for the horse species being *Equus ferus*. The wild Tarpan subspecies is *Equus ferus ferus*, Przewalski's Horse is *Equus ferus przewalskii*, and the domesticated horse is *Equus ferus caballus*. The rules for the scientific naming of animal species are determined in the International Code of Zoological Nomenclature, which stipulates that the oldest available valid scientific name is used to name the species. Previously, when taxonomists considered domesticated and wild horse two subspecies of the same species, the valid scientific name was *Equus caballus* Linnaeus 1758 , with the subspecies labeled *Equus caballus caballus* (domesticated horse), *Equus caballus ferus* Boddaert, 1785 (tarpan) and *Equus caballus przewalskii* Poliakov, 1881 (Przewalski's Horse). However, in 2003, the International Commission on Zoological Nomenclature decided that the scientific names of the wild species have priority over the scientific names of domesticated species, therefore mandating the use of *Equus ferus* for the horse, independent of the position of the domesticated horse. Horses that live in an untamed state but have ancestors who have been domesticated are not truly "wild" horses; they are feral horses. For example, when Europeans reintroduced the horse to the Americas beginning in the late 15th century, some horses escaped and formed feral herds, the best-known being the Mustang. The Australian equivalent to the Mustang is the Brumby, descended from horses strayed or let loose in Australia by English settlers. There are isolated populations of feral horses in a number of places, including Portugal, Scotland, and a number of barrier islands along the Atlantic coast of North America from Sable Island off Nova Scotia, to the Shackleford Banks of North Carolina. While these are often referred to as 'wild' horses, they are not truly 'wild' in the biological sense of having no domesticated ancestors.

In 1995, British and French explorers discovered a new population of horses in the Riwoche Valley of Tibet, unknown to the rest of the world, but apparently used by the local Khamba people. It was speculated that the horse might be a relict population of wild horses, but testing did not reveal genetic differences with domesticated horses, which is in line with news reports indicating that they are used as pack and riding animals by the local villagers. These horses only stand 12 hands (48 inches, 122 cm) tall and are said to resemble the images known as 'horse No. 2' depicted in cave paintings alongside images of Przewalski's horse.

CHAPTER 6

Draft Horse

A draft horse (US), draught horse (UK) or dray horse (from the Old English *dragan* meaning to draw or haul; compare Dutch *dragen* meaning to carry), less often called a heavy horse, is a large horse bred for hard, heavy tasks such as ploughing and farm labour. There are a number of different breeds, with varying characteristics but all share common traits of strength, patience and a docile temperament which made them indispensable to generations of pre-industrial farmers. Draft horses and draft crossbreds are versatile breeds used today for a multitude of purposes, including farming, show, logging, recreation, and other uses. They are also commonly used for crossbreeding, especially to light riding breeds such as the Thoroughbred for the purpose of creating sport horses. While most draft horses are used for driving, they can be ridden and some of the lighter draft breeds are capable performers under saddle.

Characteristics

Draft horses are recognizable by their tall stature and extremely muscular build. In general, they tend to have a more upright shoulder, producing more upright movement and conformation that is well-suited for pulling. They tend to have short backs with very powerful hindquarters, again best suited for the purpose of pulling. Additionally, the draft breeds usually have heavy bone, and a good deal of feathering on their lower legs. Many have a straight profile or 'Roman nose' (a convex profile). Draft breeds range from approximately 16 to 19 hands high and from 1,400 to 2,000 lb (640 to 910 kg).

Draft horses crossbred on light riding horses adds height and weight to the ensuing offspring, and may increase the power and 'scope' of the animal's movement.

History

Draft horses may have originated with primitive ancestors such as the Forest Horse and the 'draft subtype', wild subspecies that may have descendants as diverse as the large Shire horse and the small but sturdy Shetland pony. These wild prototypes were adapted by natural selection to the cold, damp climates of northern Europe.

Humans domesticated horses and needed them to perform a variety of duties. One type of horse-powered work was the hauling of heavy loads, plowing fields, and other tasks that required pulling ability. A heavy, calm, patient, well-muscled animal was desired for this work. Conversely, a light, more energetic horse was needed for riding and rapid transport. Thus, to the extent possible, a certain amount of selective breeding was used to develop different types of horse for different types of work.

While it is a common misunderstanding that the Destrier that carried the armoured knight of the Middle Ages had the size and conformation of a modern draft horse, and some of these Medieval war horses may have provided some bloodlines for some of the modern draft breeds, the reality was that the high-spirited, quick-moving Destrier was closer to the size, build, and temperament of a modern Andalusian or Friesian. There also were working farm horses of more phlegmatic temperaments used for pulling military wagons or performing ordinary farm work also provided bloodlines of the modern draft horse. Records indicate that even medieval drafts were not as large as those today. Of the modern draft breeds, the Percheron probably has the closest ties to the medieval war horse.

By the 19th century, horses weighing more than 1600 pounds that also moved at a quick pace were in demand. Tall stature, muscular backs, and powerful hindquarters made the draft horse a source of 'horsepower' for farming, hauling freight and moving passengers, particularly before railroads came on the scene. Even in the 20th century, draft horses were used for practical work, including over half a million used during World War I to support the military effort.

In the late 19th century and early 20th century, thousands of draft horses were imported from Western Europe into the United States. Percherons came from France, Belgians from Belgium, Shires from England, Clydesdales from Scotland. Many American draft registries were founded in the late 19th century. The Percheron, with 40,000 broodmares registered as of 1915, was America's most numerous draft breed at the turn of the 20th century. A breed developed exclusively in the U.S. was the American Cream Draft, which had a stud book established by the 1930s.

Beginning in the late 19th century, and with increasing mechanization in the 20th century, especially following World War I in the USA and after World War II in Europe, the popularity of the internal combustion engine, and particularly the tractor, reduced the need for the draft horse. Many were sold to slaughter for horsemeat and a number of breeds went into significant decline.

Today draft horses are most often seen at shows, pulling competition and entered in competitions called 'heavy horse' trials, or as exhibition animals pulling large wagons. However, they are still seen on some smaller farms in the USA and Europe. They are particularly popular with groups such as Amish and Mennonite farmers, as well as those individuals who wish to farm with a renewable source of power. Crossbred draft horses also played a significant role in the development of a number of warmblood breeds, popular today in international FEI competition up to the Olympic Equestrian level.

Mackinac Island

In America's Upper Midwest, Mackinac Island banned the personal motorized vehicle in order to protect the draft horses in the late 19th century and again in the 1920s. Today, the ban is still in effect and Belgians, Percherons, Hackneys and other large breeds continue to serve the community and the tourists who visit each season. Everything is moved by drays and people get around on horse drawn taxis, elaborate private carriages and also by bicycle.

Feeding, caring for and shoeing a 2,000 lb (910 kg) purebred draft is costly. The draft horse's metabolism is often similar to that of ponies in that Draft horses have lower needs per bodyweight than light horse breeds, but because of their size, most are fed a significant amount of feed and hay per day. A grain feeding of only .3 per cent of body weight is all drafts need. Drafts not subjected to extreme energy demands can do well on good quality grass.

World Record

The Shire horse holds the record for the world's biggest horse; Sampson, foaled in 1846 in Bedfordshire, England, stood 21.2½ hands high (i.e. 7 ft 2½in or approx 2.2 m at his withers, and weighed approx 3,300 lb (1,500 kg) or over 1.5 tons.

Breeds

A number of horse breeds are used as draft horses, with the popularity of a given breed often closely linked to geographic location.

Harness Horse

The terms harness horse and light harness horse refer to horses of a lighter build, such as traditional carriage horses and show horses, and are not terms generally used to denote 'heavy' or draught horses. Harness horse breeds include Heavy warmblood breeds such as the Oldenburg and Cleveland Bay, as well as lighter breeds such as the Hackney, and in some disciplines, such as combined driving, light riding breeds such as the Thoroughbred or Morgan may be seen.

CHAPTER 7

Foal

A foal is an equine, particularly a horse, that is one year old or younger. More specific terms are colt for a male foal and filly for a female foal, but these terms are used until the horse is age three or four. When the foal is nursing from its dam (mother), it may also be called a *suckling*. After the young horse has been weaned from its dam, it may be called a *weanling*.

After a horse is one year old, it is no longer a foal, and is called a *yearling*. There are no special age-related terms for young horses older than yearlings. When young horses reach breeding maturity, the terms change: a filly over the age of three (four in horse racing) is called a mare and a colt over the age of three is called a stallion. A castrated male horse is called a gelding, regardless of age, though colloquially the term 'gelding colt' is sometimes used until a young gelding is three or four years old. (There is no specific term for a spayed female horse, they are simply 'spayed mares'.)

Horses that mature at a small size are called ponies and are occasionally confused with foals. However, body proportions are very different. An adult pony can be ridden and put to work, while a foal, regardless of size, is too young to be ridden or used as a working animal. Foals, whether they grow up to be horse or pony-sized, can be distinguished from adult horses by their extremely long legs and small, slim bodies. Their heads and eyes also exhibit juvenile characteristics. Although ponies exhibit some neoteny with the wide foreheads and small size, their body proportions are similar to that of an adult horse. Pony foals are proportionally smaller than adults, but like horse foals, are slimmer and proportionally longer-legged than their adult parents.

Early Development

Foals are born after a gestation period of approximately 11 months. Birth takes place quickly, consistent with the status of a horse as a prey animal, and more often at night than during the day. Foals are born with an ability to quickly escape from predators; normally a foal will stand up and nurse within the first hour after it is born, can trot and canter within hours, and most can gallop by the next day. A newborn foal's legs are almost as long (90%) as those of an adult horse.

Healthy foals grow quickly and can put on up to three pounds or over a kilo a day. A sound diet improves growth and leads to a healthier adult animal, although genetics also plays a part. In the first weeks of life the foal gets everything it needs from the mare's milk. Like a human infant, it receives nourishment and antibodies from the colostrum in milk that is produced within the first few hours or days following parturition. The mare needs additional water to help her produce milk for the foal and may benefit from supplementary nutrition.

A foal may start to eat solids from ten days of age, after eight to ten weeks it will need more nutrition than the mare's milk can supply; supplementary feeding is required by then. It is important when adding solid food to the foal's diet to not overfeed the foal or feed an improperly balanced diet. This can trigger one of several possible growth disorders that can cause lifelong soundness problems. On the other hand, insufficient nutrition to mare or foal can cause stunted growth and other health problems for the foal as it gets older.

Meaning and Maturity

It is typical for foals under human management to be weaned between four and six months of age, though under natural conditions, they may nurse for longer, occasionally until the following year when the mare foals again. A foal that has been weaned but is less than one year old is called a weanling.

Mare's milk is not a significant source of nutrients for the foal after about four months, though it does no harm to a healthy mare for a foal to nurse a month or two longer and may be of some psychological benefit to the foal. A mare that is both nursing and pregnant will have increased nutritional demands made upon her in the last months of pregnancy, and therefore most domesticated foals are weaned some time in the autumn in the Northern Hemisphere.

Weanlings are not capable of reproduction. Puberty occurs in most horses during their yearling year. Therefore, some young horses are capable of reproduction prior to full physical maturity, though it is not common. Two year olds sometimes are deliberately bred, though doing so, particularly with fillies, may put undesirable stress on their still-growing bodies. As a general rule, breeding young horses prior to the age of three is considered undesirable.

Early Training

In spite of rapid growth, a foal is too young to be ridden or driven. However, foals usually receive very basic horse training in the form of being taught to accept being led by humans, called halter-breaking. They may also learn to accept horse grooming, hoof trimming by a farrier, having hair trimmed with electric clippers, and to become familiar with things it will have to do throughout life, such as loading into a horse trailer or wearing a horse blanket. One of the most important aspects of working with foals is to remember that horses in general have excellent memories, so a foal must not be taught anything as a young horse that would be undesirable for it to do as a full-grown animal.

There is tremendous debate over the proper age to begin training a foal. Some advocate beginning to accustom a foal to human handling from the moment of birth, using a process termed imprinting or 'imprint training'. Others feel that imprint training of a foal interferes with the mare and foal bond and prefer to wait until the foal is a few days old, but do begin training within the first week to month of life. Yet other horse breeding operations wait until weaning, theorizing that a foal is more willing to bond to a human as a companion at the time it is separated from its mother. Regardless of theory, most modern horse breeding operations consider it wise to give a foal basic training while it is still young, and consider it far safer than trying to tame a semi-feral adult-sized horse.

Horses are not fully mature until the age of four or five, but most are started as working animals much younger, though care must be taken not to over-stress the 'soft' bones of younger animals. Yearlings are generally too young to be ridden at all, though many race horses are put under saddle as 'long' yearlings, in autumn. Physiologically young horses are still not truly mature as two-year olds, though some breeders and most race horse trainers do start young horses in a cart or under saddle at that age. The most common age for young horses to begin training under saddle is the age of three. A few breeds and disciplines wait until the animal is four.

YEARLING

A yearling is a young horse of either sex that is between one and two years old. Yearlings are comparable in development to a very early adolescent, they are not fully mature physically, and while they may be in the earliest stages of sexual maturity, they are considered too young to be breeding stock.

In addition, the word colt may also be used to describe a male horse, and the term filly is used to describe a female horse. Both 'colt' and 'filly' describe not only yearlings, but any other young horse under the age of four.

Development of Training

Generally, the training of yearlings consists of basic gentling on the ground; most are too young to be ridden or driven. Yearlings are often full of energy and quite unpredictable. Even though they are not fully mature, they are heavier and stronger than a human and require knowledgeable handling. Many colts who are not going to be used as breeding stallions are gelded at this age—in part to improve their behaviour.

Under ideal conditions, a yearling will have already been trained as a suckling or weanling foal to lead, to have its hooves handled, to be groomed, clipped, blanketed and loaded into a horse trailer. If these tasks have not been accomplished, the yearling year is a time they are often done, in part to get the horse used to human handling before it reaches its full adult strength.

Other than basic gentling, training and management of yearlings has many areas of dispute, mainly because some yearlings look very mature and strong, even though they do not yet have the skeletal structure to support hard work. Yearlings grow at different rates and some horse breeds mature faster than others. For example, some people teach longeing or roundpenning to yearlings, others avoid it, arguing that work in small circles stresses the joints of the young horse, which are still 'soft', and not fully developed. Thoroughbred and American Quarter Horse race horses are often 'backed', or put under saddle, during the autumn of their yearling year, after the age of 18 months, though the riders are generally very light in weight and the young horses are not actually raced at this age. Likewise, some draft horse breeds and yearling Standardbreds are introduced to a harness and the concept of pulling an object, though they are not asked to handle any significant amount of weight. Conversely, breeds such as the Lipizzan do not even consider putting a young horse under saddle until it is four years.

Some breeding farms tend to leave yearlings alone to grow in pastures and natural settings, others keep them stabled and condition them intensively for show or sale. For business purposes, the yearling year is considered a good time for breeders to sell young horses. One of the most famous horse auctions in the world is the Keeneland yearling sale in Kentucky, where young Thoroughbred yearlings are put up for sale to the highest bidder, generally selling for prices in the five and six figures, but sometimes bringing prices in the millions.

The world of halter exhibition is another area of controversy. Because larger, more mature yearlings place better in halter (or in-hand) classes at horse shows, and hence sell sooner and for better prices, there is a temptation to over-feed young horses and provide supplemental products, such as steroids, to promote rapid growth. Such practices may have long-term health implications for the future athletic career of the young animal and may put it at risk for growth disorders.

CHAPTER

8

Domestication of the Horse

There are a number of hypotheses on many of the key issues regarding the domestication of the horse. Although horses appeared in Paleolithic cave art as early as 30,000 BCE, these were truly wild horses and were probably hunted for meat. How and when horses became domesticated is disputed. The clearest evidence of early use of the horse as a means of transport is from chariot burials dated c. 2000 BCE. However, an increasing amount of evidence supports the hypothesis that horses were domesticated in the Eurasian Steppes (Dereivka centreed in Ukraine) approximately 4000-3500 BCE. Recent discoveries on Botai culture suggest that Botai culture settlements in the Akmola Province of Kazakhstan are the location of the earliest domestication of the horse.

The date of the domestication of the horse depends to some degree upon the definition of 'domestication'. Some zoologists define 'domestication' as human control over breeding, which can be detected in ancient skeletal samples by changes in the size and variability of ancient horse populations. Other researchers look at broader evidence, including skeletal and dental evidence of working activity; weapons, art, and spiritual artifacts; and lifestyle patterns of human cultures. There is also evidence that horses were kept as meat animals prior to being trained as working animals.

Attempts to date domestication by genetic study or analysis of physical remains rests on the assumption that there was a separation of the genotypes of domesticated and the wild populations. Such a separation appears to have taken place, but dates based on such methods can only produce an estimate of the latest possible date for domestication without excluding the possibility of an unknown period of earlier gene-flow between wild and domestic populations (which will occur naturally as long as the domesticated population is kept within the habitat of the wild population). Further, all modern horse populations retain the ability to revert to a feral state, and all feral horses are of domestic types; that is, they descend from ancestors that escaped from captivity.

Whether one adopts the narrower zoological definition of domestication or the broader cultural definition that rests on an array of zoological and archaeological evidence affects the time frame chosen for domestication of the horse. The date of 4000 BCE is based on evidence that includes the appearance of dental pathologies associated with bitting, changes in butchering practices, changes in human economies and settlement patterns, the depiction of horses as symbols of power in artifacts, and the appearance of horse bones in human graves. On the other hand, measurable changes in size and increases in variability associated with domestication occurred later, about 2500-2000 BCE, as seen in horse remains found at the site of Csepel-Haros in Hungary, a settlement of the Bell Beaker culture.

Regardless of the specific date of domestication, use of horses spread rapidly across Eurasia for transportation, agricultural work and warfare. Horses and mules in agriculture used a breastplate type harness or a yoke more suitable for oxen, which was not as efficient at utilizing the full strength of the animals as the later-invented padded horse collar that arose several millennia later in western Europe.

Predecessors to the Domestic Horse

A 2005 study analyzed the mitochondrial DNA (mtDNA) of a worldwide range of equids, from 53,000 year old fossils to contemporary horses. Their analysis placed all equids into a single clade, or group with a single common ancestor, consisting of three genetically divergent species: Hippidion, the New World stilt-legged horse, and the true horse. The true horse, which ranged from western Europe to eastern Beringia, included prehistoric horses and the Przewalski's Horse, as well as what is now the modern domestic horse, belonged to a single Holarctic species. A more detailed analysis of the true horses grouped them into two major clades. One of these clades, which seemed to have been restricted to North America, is now extinct. The other clade was broadly distributed from North America to central Europe, north and south of Pleistocene ice sheets. It became extinct in Beringia around 14,200 years ago, and in the rest of the Americas around 10,000 years ago. This clade survived in Eurasia, however, and it is from these horses which all domestic horses appear to have descended. These horses showed little phylogeographic structure, probably reflecting their high degree of mobility and adaptability.

Therefore, the domestic horse today is classified as *Equus ferus caballus.* No genetic originals of native wild horses currently exist, other than the never-domesticated Przewalski's Horse. But genetic evidence suggests that modern Przewalski's horses are descended from a distinct regional gene pool in the eastern part of the Eurasian steppes, not from the same genetic group that gave rise to modern domesticated horses. Nevertheless, evidence such as the cave paintings of Lascaux suggests that the ancient wild horses that some researchers now label the 'Tarpan subtype' probably resembled Przewalski horses in their general appearance: big heads, dun colouration (either the tan-coloured 'zebra dun' or 'blue dun', sometimes called grullo), thick necks, stiff upright manes, and relatively short, stout legs.

The horses of the Ice Age were hunted for meat in Europe and across the Eurasian steppes and in North America by early modern humans. Numerous kill sites exist and many cave paintings in Europe indicate what they looked like. Many of these Ice Age subspecies died out during the rapid climate changes associated with the end of the last Ice Age or were hunted out by humans, particularly in North America, where the horse became completely extinct.

Classification based on body types and conformation, absent the availability of DNA for research, once suggested that that there were roughly four basic wild prototypes, thought to have developed with adaptations to their environment prior to domestication. There were competing theories, some argued that the four prototypes were separate species or subspecies, while others suggested that the prototypes were physically different manifestations of the same species. However, more recent study indicates that there was only one wild species and all different body types were entirely a result of selective breeding or landrace adaptation after domestication. Either way, the most common theories of prototypes from which all modern breeds are thought to have developed suggests than in addition to the so-called Tarpan subtype, there were the following base prototypes:

- The 'Warmblood subspecies' or 'Forest Horse' (once proposed as *Equus ferus silvaticus*, also called the Diluvial Horse), which evolved into a later variety sometimes called *Equus ferus germanicus*. This prototype may have contributed to the development of the warmblood horses of northern Europe, as well as older 'heavy horses' such as the Ardennais.
- The 'Draft' subspecies, a small, sturdy, heavyset animal with a heavy hair coat, arising in northern Europe, adapted to cold, damp climates, somewhat resembling today's draft horse and even the Shetland pony.
- The 'Oriental' subspecies, (once proposed as *Equus agilis*) a taller, slim, refined and agile animal arising in western Asia, adapted to hot, dry climates, thought to be the progenitor of the modern Arabian horse and Akhal-Teke.

Only two never-domesticated 'wild' groups survived into historic times, Przewalski's horse (*Equus ferus przewalski*), and the Tarpan (*Equus ferus ferus*). The Tarpan became extinct in the late 19th century and Przewalski's horse is endangered; it became extinct in the wild during the 1960s, but was re-introduced in the late 1980s to two preserves in Mongolia. Although researchers such as Marija Gimbutas theorized that the horses of the

Chalcolithic period were Przewalski's, more recent genetic studies indicate that Przewalski's horse is not an ancestor to modern domesticated horses. Other subspecies of *Equus ferus,* appear to have existed and could have been the stock from which domesticated horses are descended.

Genetic Evidence

The domestication of stallions and mares can be analyzed separately by looking at those portions of the DNA that are passed on exclusively along the maternal (mitochondrial DNA or mtDNA) or paternal line (Y-chromosome or Y-DNA). DNA studies indicate that there may have been multiple domestication events for mares, as the number of female lines required to account for the genetic diversity of the modern horse suggests a minimum of 77 different ancestral mares, divided into 17 distinct lineages. On the other hand, genetic evidence with regard to the domestication of stallions points at a single domestication event for a limited number of stallions combined with repeated restocking of wild females into the domesticated herds.

Genes located on the Y-chromosome are inherited only from sire to its male offspring and these lines show a very reduced degree of genetic variation (aka genetic homogeneity) in modern domestic horses than expected based on the overall genetic variation in the remaining genetic material. This indicates that a relatively few stallions were domesticated, and that it is unlikely that many male offspring originating from unions between wild stallions and domestic mares were included in early domesticated breeding stock.

Genes located in the mitochondrial DNA are passed on along the maternal line from the mother to her offspring. Multiple analyses of the mitochondrial DNA obtained from modern horses as well as from horse bones and tooth from archaeological and palaeological finds consistency shows an increased genetic diversity in the mitochondrial DNA compared to the remaining DNA, showing that a large number of mares has been included into the breeding stock of the domesticated horse. Variation in the mitochondrial DNA is used to determine so-called haplogroups. A haplogroup is a group of closely related haplotypes that share the same common ancestor. In horses, seven main haplogroups are recognized (A-G), each with several subgroups. Several haplogroups are unequal distributed around the world, indicating the addition of local wild mares to the domesticated stock. One of these haplotypes (Lusitano group C) is exclusively found on in Iberian Peninsula, leading to a hypothesis that the Iberian peninsula or North Africa was an independent origin for domestication of the horse. However, until there is additional analysis of nuclear DNA and a better understanding of the genetic structure of the earliest domestic herds, this question cannot be answered.

Even though horse domestication was widespread in a short period of time, it is still possible that domestication began with a single culture, which passed on techniques and breeding stock. It is possible that the two 'wild' subspecies remained when all other groups of once 'wild' horses died out because all others had been, perhaps, more suitable for taming by humans and the selective breeding that gave rise to the modern domestic horse.

Archaeological Evidence

Evidence for the domestication of the horse comes from three kinds of sources:

1. changes in the skeletons and teeth of ancient horses;
2. changes in the geographic distribution of ancient horses, particularly the introduction of horses into regions where no wild horses had existed; and
3. archaeological sites containing artifacts, images, or evidence of changes in human behaviour connected with horses.

Archaeological evidence includes horse remains interred in human graves; changes in the ages and sexes of the horses killed by humans; the appearance of horse corrals; equipment such as bits or other types of horse tack; horses themselves interred with equipment intended for use by horses, such as chariots; and depictions of horses used for riding, driving, draught work, or symbols of human power.

Few of these categories, taken alone, provide irrefutable evidence of domestication, but combined add up to a persuasive argument.

Horses Interred with Chariots

The least ancient, but most persuasive evidence of domestication comes from sites where horse leg bones and skulls, probably originally attached to hides, were interred with the remains of chariots in at least 16 graves of the Sintashta and Petrovka cultures. These were located in the steppes southeast of the Ural Mountains, between the upper Ural and upper Tobol Rivers, a region today divided between southern Russia and northern Kazakhstan. Petrovka was a little later than and probably grew out of Sintashta, and the two complexes together spanned about 2100-1700 BCE in calibrated or true years calibration methods. A few of these graves contained the remains of as many as eight sacrificed horses placed in, above, and beside the grave.

In all of the dated chariot graves, the heads and hooves of a pair of horses were placed in a grave that once contained a chariot. Evidence of chariots in these graves was inferred from the impressions of two spoked wheels set in grave floors 1.2-1.6 m apart; in most cases the rest of the vehicle left no trace. In addition a pair of disk-shaped antler 'cheekpieces', an ancient predecessor to a modern bit shank or bit ring, were placed in pairs beside each horse head-and-hoof sacrifice. The inner faces of the disks had protruding prongs or studs that would have pressed against the horse's lips when the reins were pulled on the opposite side. Studded cheekpieces were a new and fairly severe kind of control device that appeared simultaneously with chariots.

All of the dated chariot graves contained wheel impressions, horse bones, weapons (arrow and javelin points, axes, daggers, or stone mace-heads), human skeletal remains, and cheekpieces. Because they were buried in teams of two with chariots and studded cheekpieces, the evidence is extremely persuasive that these steppe horses of 2100-1700 BCE were domesticated. Shortly after the period of these burials, the expansion of the domestic horse throughout Europe was little short of explosive. In the space of possibly 500 years, there is evidence of horse-drawn chariots in Greece, Egypt, and Mesopotamia. By another 500 years, the horse-drawn chariot had spread to China.

Skeletal Indicators of Domestication

Some researchers do not consider an animal to be 'domesticated' until it exhibits physical changes consistent with selective breeding, or at least having been born and raised entirely in captivity. Until that point, they classify captive animals as merely 'tamed'. Those who hold to this theory of domestication point to a change in skeletal measurements was detected among horse bones recovered from middens dated about 2500 BCE in eastern Hungary in Bell-Beaker sites, and in later Bronze Age sites in the Russian steppes, Spain, and eastern Europe. Horse bones from these contexts exhibited an increase in variability, thought to reflect the survival under human care of both larger and smaller individuals than appeared in the wild; and a decrease in average size, thought to reflect penning and restriction in diet. Horse populations that showed this combination of skeletal changes probably were domesticated. Most evidence suggests that horses were increasingly controlled by humans after about 2500 BCE. However, more recently there have been skeletal remains found at a site in Kazakhstan which display the smaller, more slender limbs characteristic of corralled animals, dated to 3500 BCE.

Botai Culture

Some of the most intriguing evidence of early domestication comes from the Botai culture, found in northern Kazakhstan. The Botai culture was a culture of foragers who seem to have adopted horseback riding in order to hunt the abundant wild horses of northern Kazakhstan between 3500-3000 BCE. Botai sites had no cattle or sheep bones; the only domesticated animals, in addition to horses, were dogs. Botai settlements in this period contained between 50-150 pit houses. Garbage deposits contained tens to hundreds of thousands of discarded animal bones, 65 per cent to 99 per cent of which had come from horses. Also, there has been evidence found of horse milking at these sites, with horse milk fats soaked into pottery shards dating to 3500 BCE. Earlier hunter-gatherers who lived in the same region had not hunted wild horses with such success, and lived for millennia in smaller, more shifting settlements, often containing less than 200 wild animal bones.

Entire herds of horses were slaughtered by the Botai hunters, apparently in hunting drives. The adoption of horseback riding might explain the appearance of specialized horse-hunting techniques and larger, more permanent settlements. Domesticated horses could have been adopted from neighboring herding societies in the steppes west of the Ural Mountains, where the Khvalynsk culture had herds of cattle and sheep, and perhaps had domesticated horses, as early as 4800 BCE.

Other researchers have argued that all of the Botai horses were wild, and that the horse-hunters of Botai hunted wild horses on foot. As evidence, they note that Zoologists have found no skeletal changes in the Botai horses that indicate domestication. And because they were hunted for food, the majority of the horse remains found in Botai-culture settlements indeed probably were wild. On the other hand, any domesticated riding horses were probably the same size as their wild cousins and cannot now be distinguished by bone measurements. They also note that the age structure of the horses slaughtered at Botai represents a natural demographic profile for hunted animals, not the pattern expected if they were domesticated and selected for slaughter. However, these arguments were published prior to the discovery of a corral at Krasnyi Yar and mats of horse-dung at two other Botai sites.

Bit Wear

The presence of bit wear suggest that a horse was ridden or driven, and the earliest of such evidence from a site in Kazakhstan dates to 3500 BCE. Because horses can be ridden and controlled without bits by using a noseband or a hackamore, and such tools are used even today, the absence of bit wear on horse teeth is not conclusive evidence against domestication, but such materials do not produce significant physiological changes nor are they apt to be preserved for millennia.

The regular use of a bit to control a horse can create wear facets or bevels on the anterior corners of the lower second premolars. The corners of the horse's mouth normally keep the bit on the 'bars' of the mouth, an interdental space where there are no teeth, forward of the premolars. The bit must be manipulated by a human or the horse must move it with its tongue for it to touch the teeth. Wear can be caused by the bit abrading the front corners of the premolars if the horse grasps and releases the bit between its teeth; other wear can be created by the bit striking the vertical front edge of the lower premolars, due to very strong pressure from a human handler.

Modern experiments showed that even organic bits of rope or leather can create significant wear facets, and also showed that facets 3 mm deep or more do not appear on the premolars of wild horses. However, other researchers disputed both conclusions.

Wear facets of 3 mm or more also were found on seven horse premolars in two sites of the Botai, Botai and Kozhai 1, dated about 3500-3000 BCE. The Botai culture premolars are the earliest reported multiple examples of this dental pathology in any archaeological site, and preceded any skeletal change indicators by 1000 years. While wear facets more than 3 mm deep were discovered on the lower second premolars of a single stallion from Dereivka in Ukraine, an Eneolithic settlement dated about 4000 BCE, dental material from one of the worn teeth later produced a radiocarbon date of 700-200 BCE, indicating that this stallion was actually deposited in a pit dug into the older Eneolithic site during the Iron Age.

Dung and Corrals

Soil scientists working with Sandra Olsen of the Carnegie Museum of Natural History at the Chalcolithic (also called Eneolithic, or 'Copper Age') settlements of Botai and Krasnyi Yar in northern Kazakhstan found layers of horse dung, discarded in unused house pits in both settlements. The collection and disposal of horse dung suggests that horses were confined in corrals or stables. An actual corral, dated to 3000-3500 BCE was identified at Krasnyi Yar by a pattern of post holes for a circular fence, with the soils inside the fence yielding ten times more phosphorus than the soils outside. The phosphorus could represent the remains of manure.

Geographic Expansion

The appearance of horse remains in human settlements in regions where they had not previously been present is another indicator of domestication. Although images of horses appear as early as the Upper Paleolithic period in places such as the caves of Lascaux, France, suggesting that wild horses lived in regions outside of Eurasia prior to domestication and may have even been hunted by early humans, concentration of remains suggests animals being deliberately captured and contained, an indicator of domestication, at least for food, if not necessarily use as a working animal.

Around 3500-3000 BCE horse bones began to appear more frequently in archaeological sites beyond their centre of distribution in the Eurasian steppes and were seen in central Europe, the middle and lower Danube valley, and the North Caucasus and Transcaucasia. Evidence of horses in these areas had been rare before, and as numbers increased, larger animals also began to appear in horse remains. This expansion in range was contemporary with the Botai culture, where there are indications that horses were corralled and ridden. This does not necessarily mean that horses were first domesticated in the steppes, but the horse-hunters of the steppes certainly pursued wild horses more than in any other region. This geographic expansion is interpreted by many zoologists as an early phase in the spread of domesticated horses.

European wild horses were hunted for up to 10 per cent of the animal bones in a handful of Mesolithic and Neolithic settlements scattered across Spain, France, and the marshlands of northern Germany, but in many other parts of Europe, including Greece, the Balkans, the British Isles, and much of central Europe, horse bones do not occur or occur very rarely in Mesolithic, Neolithic or Chalcolithic sites. In contrast, wild horse bones regularly exceeded 40 per cent of the identified animal bones in Mesolithic and Neolithic camps in the Eurasian steppes, west of the Ural Mountains.

Horse bones were rare or absent in Neolithic and Chalcolithic kitchen garbage in western Turkey, Mesopotamia, most of Iran, South and Central Asia, and much of Europe. While horse bones have been identified in Neolithic sites in central Turkey, all equids together totaled less than 3 per cent of the animal bones. Within this three per cent, horses were less than 10 per cent, with 90 per cent or more of the equids represented by onagers (*Equus hemionus*) or another ass-like equid that later became extinct, *Equus Hydruntinus.* Onagers were the most common native wild equids of the Near East. They were hunted in Syria, Anatolia, Mesopotamia, Iran, and Central Asia; and domesticated asses (Equus asinus) were imported into Mesopotamia, probably from Egypt, but wild horses apparently did not live there.

Other Evidence of Geographic Expansion

Later, images of horses, identified by their short ears, flowing manes, and tails that bushed out at the dock, began to appear in artistic media in Mesopotamia during the Akkadian period, 2300-2100 BCE. The word for 'horse', literally translated as *ass of the mountains,* first appeared in Sumerian documents during the Third Dynasty of Ur, about 2100-2000 BCE. The kings of the Third Dynasty of Ur apparently fed horses to lions for royal entertainment, perhaps indicating that horses were still regarded as more exotic than useful, but King Shulgi, about 2050 BCE, compared himself to 'a horse of the highway that swishes its tail', and one image from his reign showed a man apparently riding a horse at full gallop. Horses were imported into Mesopotamia and the lowland Near East in larger numbers after 2000 BCE in connection with the beginning of chariot warfare.

A further expansion, into the lowland Near East and northwestern China, also happened around 2000 BCE, again apparently in conjunction with the chariot. Although 'Equus' bones of uncertain species are found in some Late Neolithic sites in China dated before 2000 BCE, 'Equus caballus' or 'Equus ferus' bones first appeared in multiple sites and in significant numbers in sites of the Qijia and Siba cultures, 2000-1600 BCE, in Gansu and the northwestern provinces of China. The Qijia culture was in contact with cultures of the Eurasian steppes, as shown through similarities between Qijia and Late Bronze Age steppe metallurgy, so it was probably through these contacts that domesticated horses first became frequent in northwestern China.

Horses Images As Symbols of Power

About 4200-4000 BCE, more than 500 years before the geographic expansion evidenced by the presence of horse bones, new kinds of graves, named after a grave at Suvorovo, appeared north of the Danube delta in the coastal steppes of Ukraine near Izmail. Suvorovo graves were similar to and probably derived from earlier funeral traditions in the steppes around the Dnieper River. Some Suvorovo graves contained polished stone mace-heads shaped like horse heads and horse tooth beads. Earlier steppe graves also had contained polished stone mace-heads, some of them carved in the shape of animal heads. Settlements in the steppes contemporary with Suvorovo, such as Sredni Stog II and Dereivka on the Dnieper River, contained 12 per cent-52 per cent horse bones.

When Suvorovo graves appeared in the Danube delta grasslands, horse-head maces also appeared in some of the indigenous farming towns of the Tripolye and Gumelnitsa cultures in present-day Romania and Moldova, near the Suvorovo graves. These agricultural cultures had not previously used polished-stone maces, and horse bones were rare or absent in their settlement sites. Probably their horse-head maces came from the Suvorovo immigrants. The Suvorovo people in turn acquired many copper ornaments from the Tripolye and Gumelnitsa towns. After this episode of contact and trade, but still during the period 4200-4000 BCE, about 600 agricultural towns in the Balkans and the lower Danube valley, some of which had been occupied for 2000 years, were abandoned. Copper mining ceased in the Balkan copper mines, and the cultural traditions associated with the agricultural towns were terminated in the Balkans and the lower Danube valley. This collapse of 'Old Europe' has been attributed to the immigration of mounted Indo-European warriors. The collapse could have been caused by intensified warfare, for which there is some evidence; and warfare could have been worsened by mounted raiding; and the horse-head maces have been interpreted as indicating the introduction of domesticated horses and riding just before the collapse.

However, mounted raiding is just one possible explanation for this complex event. Environmental deterioration, ecological degradation from millennia of farming, and the exhaustion of easily mined oxide copper ores also are cited as causal factors.

Artifacts

Perforated antler objects discovered at Dereivka and other sites contemporary with Suvorovo have been identified as cheekpieces or 'psalia' for horse bits. This identification is no longer widely accepted, as the objects in question have not been found associated with horse bones, and could have had a variety of other functions. However, through studies of microscopic wear, it has been extablished that many of the bone tools at Botai were used to smooth rawhide thongs, and rawhide thongs might have been used to manufacture of rawhide cords and ropes, useful for horse tack. Similar bone thong-smoothers are known from many other steppe settlements, but it cannot be known how the thongs were used. The oldest artifacts clearly identified as horse tack—bits, bridles, cheekpieces, or any other kind of horse gear—are the antler disk-shaped cheekpieces associated with the invention of the chariot, at the Sintashta-Petrovka sites.

Horses Interred in Human Graves

The oldest possible archaeological indicator of a changed relationship between horses and humans is the appearance about 4800-4400 BCE of horse bones and carved images of horses in Chalcolithic graves of the early Khvalynsk culture and the Samara culture in the middle Volga region of Russia. At the Khvalynsk cemetery near the town of Khvalynsk, 158 graves of this period were excavated. Of these, 26 graves contained parts of sacrificed domestic animals, and additional sacrifices occurred in ritual deposits on the original ground surface above the graves. Ten graves contained parts of lower horse legs; two of these also contained the bones of domesticated cattle and sheep. At least 52 domesticated sheep or goats, 23 domesticated cattle, and 11 horses were sacrificed at Khvalynsk. The inclusion of horses with cattle and sheep and the exclusion of obviously wild animals together suggest that horses were categorized symbolically with domesticated animals.

At S'yezzhe, a contemporary cemetery of the Samara culture, parts of two horses were placed above a group of human graves. The pair of horses here was represented by the head and hooves, probably originally attached to hides. The same ritual—using the hide with the head and lower leg bones as a symbol for the whole animal—was used for many domesticated cattle and sheep sacrifices at Khvalynsk. Horse images carved from bone were placed in the above-ground ochre deposit at S'yezzhe and occurred at several other sites of the same period in the middle and lower Volga region. Together these archaeological clues suggest that horses had a symbolic importance in the Khvalynsk and Samara cultures that they had lacked earlier, and that they were associated with humans, domesticated cattle, and domesticated sheep. Thus, the earliest phase in the domestication of the horse might have begun during the period 4800-4400 BCE.

Methods of Domestication

Equidae died out in the Western Hemisphere at the end of the last Ice Age. A question raised is why and how horses avoided this fate on the Eurasian continent. It has been theorized that domestication saved the species. While the environmental conditions for equine survival in Europe were somewhat more favourable in Eurasia than in the Americas, the same stressors that led to extinction for the Mammoth did have an impact on horses. Thus, some time after 8000 BCE, the approximate date of extinction in the Americas, humans in Eurasia may have begun to keep horses as a livestock food source, and by keeping them in captivity, may have helped to preserve the species. Horses also fit the six core criteria for livestock domestication, and thus, it could be argued, 'chose' to live in close proximity to humans.

One model of horse domestication starts with individual foals being kept as pets while the adult horses were slaughtered for meat. Foals are relatively small and easy to handle. Horses behave as herd animals and need companionship to thrive. Both historic and modern data shows that foals can and will bond to humans and other domestic animals to meet their social needs. Thus domestication may have started with young horses being repeatedly made into pets over time, preceding the great discovery that these pets could be ridden or otherwise put to work.

However, there is a dispute over what *domesticated* means. One theory suggests that domestication must include physiological changes associated with being selectively bred in captivity, and not merely 'tamed'. It has been noted that traditional peoples worldwide (both hunter-gatherers and horticulturists) routinely tame individuals from wild species, typically by hand-rearing infants whose parents have been killed, and these animals are not necessarily 'domesticated'.

On the other hand, some researchers look to examples from historical times in order to hypothesize how domestication occurred. For example, while Native American cultures captured and rode horses from the 16th century on, most tribes did not exert significant control over their breeding, thus their horses developed a genotype and phenotype adapted to the uses and climatological conditions in which they were kept, making them more of a landrace than a planned breed as defined by modern standards, but nonetheless 'domesticated'.

Driving *Versus* Riding

A difficult question is if domesticated horses were first ridden or driven. While the most unequivocal evidence shows horses first being used to pull chariots in warfare, there is strong, though indirect, evidence for riding occurring first, particularly by the Botai. Bit wear may correlate to riding, though, as the modern hackamore demonstrates, horses can be ridden without a bit by using rope and other evanescent materials to make equipment that fastens around the nose. So the absence of unequivocal evidence of early riding in the record does not settle the question.

Thus, on one hand, logic suggests that horses would have been ridden long before they were driven. But it is also far more difficult to gather evidence of this, as the materials required for riding—simple hackamores or blankets—would not survive as artifacts, and other than tooth wear from a bit, the skeletal changes in an animal that was ridden would not necessarily be particularly noticeable. Direct evidence of horses being driven is much stronger.

On the other hand, others argue that evidence of bit wear does not necessarily correlate to riding. Some theorists speculate that a horse could have been controlled from the ground by placing a bit in the mouth, connected to a lead rope, and leading the animal while pulling a primitive wagon or plow. Since oxen were usually relegated to this duty in Mesopotamia, it is possible that early plows might have been attempted with the horse, and a bit may indeed have been significant as part of agrarian development rather than as warfare technology.

Horses in Ancient Warfare

While riding may have been practiced during the 4th and 3rd millennia BCE, and the disappearance of 'Old European' settlements may be related to attacks by horseback-mounted warriors, the clearest impact by horses on ancient warfare was by pulling chariots, introduced c. 2000 BCE.

Horses in the Bronze Age were relatively small by modern standards, which led some theorists to believe the ancient horses were too small to be ridden and so must have been driven. Herodotus' description of the Sigynnae, a steppe people who bred horses too small to ride but extremely efficient at drawing chariots, illustrates this stage. However, as horses remained generally smaller than modern equines well into the Middle Ages, this theory is highly questionable.

The Iron Age in Mesopotamia saw the rise of mounted cavalry as a tool of war, as evidenced by the notable successes of mounted archer tactics used by various invading equestrian nomads such as the Parthians. Over time, the chariot gradually become obsolete.

The horse of the Iron Age was still relatively small, perhaps 12.2 to 14.2 hands high (1.27 to 1.47 metres, measured at the withers.) This was shorter overall average height than modern riding horses, which range from 14.2 to 17.2 hh (1.47 to 1.78 metres). However, small horses were used successfully as light cavalry for many centuries. For example, Fell ponies, believed to be descended from Roman cavalry horses, are comfortably able to carry fully grown adults (although with rather limited ground clearance) at an average height of 13.2 hands (1.37 m). Likewise, the Arabian horse is noted for a short back and dense bone, and the successes of the Muslims against the heavy mounted knights of Europe demonstrated that a 14.2 hand horse (1.47 m) can easily carry a full-grown human adult into battle.

Mounted warriors such as the Scythians, Huns and Vandals of late Roman antiquity, the Mongols who invaded eastern Europe in the 7th century through 14th centuries CE, the Muslim warriors of the 8th through 14th centuries CE, and the American Indians in the 16th through 19th centuries each demonstrated effective forms of light cavalry.

CHAPTER 9

Horse Training

Horse training refers to a variety of practices that teach horses to perform certain behaviours when asked to do so by humans. Horses are trained to be manageable by humans for everyday care as well as for equestrian activities from horse racing to therapeutic horseback riding for people with disabilities.

Historically, horses were trained for warfare, farm work, sport and transport. Today, most horse training is geared toward making horses useful for a variety of recreational and sporting equestrian pursuits. Horses are also trained for specialized jobs from movie stunt work to police and crowd control activities, circus entertainment, and equine-assisted psychotherapy.

There is tremendous controversy over various methods of horse training and even some of the words used to describe these methods. Some techniques are considered cruel, other methods are considered gentler and more humane.

Basic Goals of Training

The range of training techniques and training goals is large, but basic animal training concepts apply to all forms of horse training. The initial goal of most types of training is to create a horse that is safe for humans to handle (under most circumstances) and able to perform a useful task for the benefit of humans

A few specific considerations and some basic knowledge of horse behaviour helps a horse trainer be effective no matter what school or discipline is chosen:

- *Safety is paramount:* Horses are much larger and stronger than humans, so must be taught behaviour that will not injure people.
- Horses, like other animals, differ in brain structure from humans and thus do not have the same type of thinking and reasoning ability as human beings. Thus, the human has the responsibility to think about how to use the psychology of the horse to lead the animal into an understanding of the goals of the human trainer.

- Horses are social herd animals and, when properly handled, can learn to follow and respect a human leader.
- Horses, as prey animals, have an inborn fight or flight instinct that has to be adapted to human needs. Horses need to be taught to rely upon humans to determine when fear or flight is an appropriate response to new stimuli and not to react by instinct alone.
- Like most animals, a young horse will more easily adapt to human expectations than an older one, so human handling of the horse from a very early age is generally advised.

Training of Foals and Younger Horses

Most young domesticated horses are handled at birth or within the first few days of life, though some are only handled for the first time when they are weaned from their mothers, or *dams.* Advocates of handling foals from birth sometimes use the concept of imprinting to introduce a foal within its first few days and weeks of life to many of the activities they will see throughout their lives. Within a few hours of birth, a foal being imprinted will have a human touch it all over, pick up its feet, and introduce it to human touch and voice.

Others may leave a foal alone for its first few hours or days, arguing that it is more important to allow the foal to bond with its dam. However, even people who do not advocate imprinting often still place value on handling a foal a great deal while it is still nursing and too small to easily overpower a human. By doing so, the foal ideally will learn that humans will not harm it, but also that humans must be respected.

While a foal is far too young to be ridden, it is still able to learn skills it will need later in life. By the end of a foal's first year, it should be *halter-broke,* meaning that it allows a halter placed upon its head and has been taught to be led by a human at a walk and trot, to stop on command and to stand tied. The young horse needs to be calm for basic grooming, as well as veterinary care such as vaccinations and de-worming. A foal needs regular hoof care and can be taught to stand while having its feet picked up and trimmed by a farrier. Ideally a young horse should learn all the basic skills it will need throughout its life, including: being caught from a field, loaded into a horse trailer, and not to fear flapping or noisy objects. It also can be exposed to the noise and commotion of ordinary human activity, including seeing motor vehicles, hearing radios, and so on. More advanced skills sometimes taught in the first year include learning to accept blankets placed on it, to be trimmed with electric clippers, and to be given a bath with water from a hose. The foal may learn basic voice commands for starting and stopping, and sometimes will learn to square its feet up for showing in in-hand or conformation classes. If these tasks are completed, the young horse will have no fear of things placed on its back, around its belly or in its mouth.

Some people, whether through philosophy or simply due to being pressed for time, do not handle foals significantly while they are still nursing, but wait until the foal is weaned from its dam to begin halter breaking and the other tasks of training a horse in its first year.

The argument for gentling and halter-breaking at weaning is that the young horse, in crisis from being separated from its dam, will more readily bond with a human at weaning than at a later point in its life. Sometimes the tasks of basic gentling are not completed within the first year but continue when the horse is a yearling. Yearlings are larger and more unpredictable than weanlings, plus often are easily distracted, in part due to the first signs of sexual maturity. However, they also are still highly impressionable, and though very quick and agile, are not at their full adult strength.

Rarer, but not uncommon even in the modern world, is the practice of leaving young horses completely unhandled until they are old enough to be ridden, usually between the age of two and four, and completing all ground training as well as training for riding at the same time. However, waiting until a horse is full grown to begin training is often far riskier for humans and requires considerably more skill to avoid injury.

Ground Training

After a young horse is taught to lead and other basic skills, various tasks can be introduced to the horse as it matures while it is still too young to be ridden. Some schools of training do a great deal of work with young horses during their yearling and two-year-old years to prepare them for riding, others merely reinforce the basic lessons taught to the horse as a foal and simply keep the horse accustomed to the presence of humans. Many times, a young horse did not have all necessary basic skills described above taught to it as a foal and its 'adolescent' years are spent learning or re-learning basic lessons.

Several ground training techniques are commonly introduced to a young horse some time after it is a year old, but prior to being ridden. All horses usually have some or all of this ground work done prior to being ridden, though the time spent can range from hours to months. While a foal or yearling can be introduced to a small amount of ground work, a young horse's bones and joints are quite soft and fragile. So, to prevent joint and cartilage injury, intense work, particularly intense work in a confined circle (such as advanced roundpenning or longeing), should wait until the horse is at least two years old. Common ground training techniques include:

- *Liberty* work, sometimes called *free longeing, round pen work* or *roundpenning,* but regardless of terminology, is the process of working a loose horse in a small area (usually a round pen 40-60 feet/15-20 metres in diametre) with the handler holding only a long whip or a rope lariat, teaching the horse to respond to the voice and body language of the handler as he or she asks the horse to move faster or slower, to change direction, and to stop.

- *Longeing* (Lungeing- UK), pronounced 'lungeing', the training of a young horse to move in circles at the end of a long rope or line, usually about 25 to 30 feet long.
- *Desensitization,* sometimes called *Sacking out,* the process of introducing a horse to flapping objects such as blankets, teaching the horse to allow itself to be touched by an object and not to fear things that people move about a horse.
- Introduction to a saddle and bridle or harness, without actually getting on the horse or hooking up a cart.
- *Ground driving,* also called long-lining, teaching a young horse to move forward with a person walking behind it, a precursor to both harness driving and having reins used by a mounted rider.
- *Bitting,* the process of accustoming a horse to a bit and bridle, sometimes with the addition of side reins that attach to a saddle, harness, or surcingle (a wide leather or nylon band that goes around the horse's barrel) and accustom the horse to the feel of pressure on the bit.

A horse is not ready to be ridden until it is accustomed to all the equipment that it needs to wear and is responsive to basic voice, and usually rein, commands to start, stop, turn and change gaits.

For some disciplines, ground work is also used to develop specific types of muscling as well as to instill certain behaviours. When ground work incorporates both mental and muscular development, it may take considerably longer for the horse to be ready to be ridden, but advocates of these methods maintain that the additional time on the ground allows the horse to advance more quickly or with better manners once under saddle.

Riding the Young Horse or Backing

The age that horses are first ridden, or 'backed' (UK) varies considerably by breed and discipline. Many Thoroughbred race horses have small, light riders on their backs as early as the fall of their yearling year. Most stock horse breeds, such as the American Quarter Horse, are ridden at the age of two. Most horses used in harness have a cart first put behind them at age two, and even some horses not ridden until age three will be trained to pull a light cart at two, in order to learn better discipline and to help develop stronger muscles with less stress. The vast majority of horses across disciplines and throughout the world are first put under saddle at the age of three. However, some slower-maturing breeds, such as the Lipizzan, are not ridden until the age of four.

The act of getting on a horse for the first time goes by many names, including *backing, breaking, mounting,* and simply *riding.* There are many techniques for introducing the young horse to a rider or to a harness and cart for driving, but the end goal of all methods is to have the horse calmly and quietly allow a rider on its back or behind it in a cart and to respond to basic commands to go forward, change gaits and speed, stop, turn and back up.

Ideally, a young horse will have no fear of humans and view being ridden as simply one more new lesson. A properly handled young horse that had adequate ground work will seldom buck, rear, or run away when it is ridden, even for the very first time.

Horses that have never been taught to be ridden can learn at any age, though it may take somewhat longer to teach an older horse. An older horse that is used to humans but has no prior bad habits is easier to put under saddle than is a completely feral horse caught "wild" off the open range as an adult. However, an adult feral horse will be easier to train than a domesticated animal that has previously learned to treat humans with disrespect.

Once basic skills under saddle are mastered, the horse is usually ready to go on to more specialized training for a particular disciplines or set of disciplines.

Training for a Specific Discipline

There are many horse training philosophies and techniques and details are far too extensive to describe in a single article. Also, horses have different conformation, athletic potential, temperaments and personalities, all of which may influence what techniques are used.

CHAPTER 10

Horse Behaviour

Horse behaviour is best understood from the perspective that horses are prey animals with a well-developed fight-or-flight instinct. Their first response to a threat is to flee, although they are known to stand their ground and defend themselves or their offspring in cases where flight is untenable, such as when a foal would be threatened.

Nonetheless, because their physiology is also suited to a number of work- and entertainment-related tasks, humans domesticated horses thousands of years ago, and they have served humans ever since. Through selective breeding, some breeds of horses have been bred to be quite docile, particularly certain large draft horses. On the other hand, most light horse riding breeds were developed for speed, agility, alertness and endurance; building on natural qualities that extended from their wild ancestors.

The instincts of horses can be used to human advantage to create a bond between human and horse. These techniques vary, but are part of the art of horse training.

Horse as Herd Animals

Horses are highly social herd animals that prefer to live in a group. Like all creatures, equine social behaviour developed to help the species survive.

There also is a linear dominance hierarchy in any herd. They will establish a 'pecking order' for the purpose of determining which herd member directs the behaviour of others, eats and drinks first, and so on. This behaviour pattern also applies to their interrelationship with humans. A horse that respects the human as a 'herd member' who is higher in the social order will behave in a more appropriate manner towards all humans than a horse that has been allowed to engage in dominant behaviour over humans.

Horses are able to form companionship attachments not only to their own species, but with other animals, including humans. In fact, many domesticated horses will become anxious, flighty and hard to manage if they are isolated. Horses kept in near-complete isolation, particularly in a closed stable where they cannot see other animals may require a stable companion such as a cat, goat or even a small pony or donkey to provide company and reduce stress.

When anxiety over separation occurs while a horse is being handled by a human, the horse is described as 'herd-bound'. However, through proper training, horses learn to be comfortable away from other horses, often because they learn to trust a human handler, essentially ranking humans as a dominant member of a 'herd'.

Herd Behaviour in the Wild

Feral and wild horse herds are usually made up of several separate small bands who share a given territory. Bands are organized on a 'harem model' in that they usually consist of one adult male and a group of females. Each band is led by a mare who is dominant in the hierarchy, called the 'dominant mare', the 'lead mare' or the 'boss mare'. The band contains additional mares, their foals, and immature horses of both sexes. There is usually a single 'herd' or 'lead' stallion, though occasionally a few less-dominant males may remain on the fringes of the group.

Bands are usually on the small side, as few as 3 to 35 animals. The makeup of bands shifts over time as young animals are driven out of the band they were born into and join other bands, or as young stallions challenge older males for dominance.

However, in a given closed ecosystem such as the isolated refuges in which most wild horses live today, to maintain genetic diversity the minimum size for a sustainable wild horse or burro population is 150-200 animals.

Hierarchical Structure

Survival dictates that the herd members ultimately cooperate and stick together. As with many animals that live in large groups, establishment of a stable hierarchical system or 'pecking order' is important to smooth group functioning. This is often, but not always, a completely linear system. Situations arise where horse A may be dominant over horse B who is dominant over horse C, yet in certain circumstances horse C could be dominant over horse A in competition for a particular resource. Dominance depends on a variety of factors, including an individual's need for a particular resource at a given time. It is therefore variable throughout the lifetime of the herd or individual animal. Some horses may be dominant over all resources and some may indeed be submissive over all resources.

Contention for dominance can be risky since one well-placed kick to a leg could cripple another horse to such an extent that it would be defenseless, exposed, and possibly unable to get to food or water. Therefore, once this system of dominance and submission is generally established aggressive behaviour is minimal between herd members, though higher-ranked animals often will assume a role of exercising control and moderating aggressive behaviour in the herd.

In times of stress, whether from predators or extreme weather, the centre of the herd is the safest because it offers the most protection from the elements and is further away from predators than any other part. Because of this, 'punishment' of misbehaving members is sometimes delivered in the form of expulsion from the herd—temporarily or sometimes permanently.

Most young horses in the wild are allowed to stay with the herd until sometime in their yearling or 2-year old year, when they reach full sexual maturity. Studies of wild herds have shown that the herd stallion will usually drive out both young colts and fillies. Experts who study wild horses theorize that this may be an instinct that prevents inbreeding, so that the herd stallion does not mate with his own female offspring. The fillies usually join another band in fairly short order, and the colts driven out from various herds usually join together for safety in small 'bachelor' groups until those who are able establish dominance over an older stallion in another herd.

Role of the Lead Mare

Contrary to traditional portrayals of the herd stallion as the 'ruler' of a 'harem' of females, the actual leader of a wild or feral herd is the alpha or dominant mare, commonly known as the 'boss mare' or 'lead mare'. She is usually one of the more mature animals, responsible for the overall safety of the herd, familiar with the terrain and resources available. She takes the lead when the herd travels, determines the best route, when to move from one place to another, and claims the right to drink first from watering holes and stake out the best location for grazing.

Role of Stallion

The edge of the herd is the domain of the herd stallion, who must fight off both predators and other males. When the herd travels, the stallion brings up the rear, watching for predators and driving straggling herd members on, keeping the group together. During mating season, stallions tend to act more aggressively, in order to keep the mares from straying off. However, most of the time, the stallion is fairly relaxed, spending much of his time "guarding" the herd not by herding the mares around, but by scent-marking manure piles and urination spots in order to make clear his position as herd stallion.

By living on the periphery of the herd, exposed to weather, predators, and challenges from other stallions, the herd stallion endures a somewhat vulnerable existence. He is exposed to more risks than any other herd member and can be replaced by a stronger successor at any time. Interestingly, a herd stallion will occasionally tolerate one young stallion to live at the edge of the herd, possibly as a sort of designated successor, even though the young horse will eventually gain mastery over the older stallion and claim the herd.

Ratio of Stallions and Mares

Biologically, and depending on the physical environment available to a herd in the wild, there is only a need for one stallion for every 10 to 20 mares, though most bands are smaller than this. Domesticated stallions, with careful human management, often 'cover' more mares in a year than is possible in the wild. .

Traditionally, Thoroughbred stud farms limited stallions to breeding between 40 and 60 mares a year. Today, by carefully breeding mares only when at the peak of their Estrous cycle, a few thoroughbred stallions have 'covered' over 200 mares per year. With use of technologies such as artificial insemination one stallion could sire thousands of offspring annually, though in actual practice, economic considerations usually limit the number of foals produced.

Domesticated Stallion Behaviour

Some horse breeders keep horses in semi-natural conditions, allowing a single stallion to run with a group of mares. This is referred to as 'pasture breeding'. Young stallions who are not of breeding age live in a separate 'bachelor herd'. While this has advantages of less intensive labor for human caretakers, and full time turnout may be psychologically healthy for the horses, pasture breeding presents a risk of injury to valuable breeding stock, both stallions and mares, particularly when unfamiliar animals are added to the herd. It also raises questions of when or if a mare is bred, and may also raise questions as to parentage of ensuing foals. Thus, keeping stallions in a natural herd is not particularly common, especially on breeding farms standing multiple stallions to outside mares. It is more often seen on farms with closed herds; only one or a few stallions with a stable mare herd and few, if any, outside mares.

More often, mature domesticated stallions are commonly kept by themselves in a stable or small paddock with a strong, high fence that prevents escape. When stallions are stabled in such a way that they can both see each other and touch nose to nose, such as through bars or a grill, they will often challenge one another and sometimes attempt to fight. For this reason, stallions are often kept from sight and touch of other stallions, due to risk of injury and disruption to the rest of the stable, even if several are kept in the same barn. If they have access to paddocks, there often is a corridor between the paddocks so the stallions cannot touch one another, and in some cases, stallions are let out for exercise at different times of day so they do not see or hear one another.

To avoid stable vices associated with isolation, some stallions, though not all, do well when stabled with a non-horse companion, such as a gelded donkey or a goat. (The Godolphin Arabian was said to be particularly fond of a barn cat). While many domesticated stallions become too aggressive to tolerate the close presence of any other male horse without fighting, some tolerate a gelding as a companion, particularly one that has a very calm, unflappable temperament. One example of this was the racehorse Seabiscuit, who lived with a gelding companion named 'Pumpkin'. Other stallions may tolerate the close presence of an immature and thus less dominant stallion.

While stallions and mares often compete together at horse shows and in horse races, stallions generally must be kept away from close contact with mares, both to avoid unintentional or unplanned matings, but also to minimize their instincts to fight one another for dominance when in the presence of mares. When horses are lined up for placing at shows, handlers keep stallions at least a horse's length from any other animal and do not allow their horses to touch noses with any other animals. Stallions can be taught to ignore any mares or other stallions that are in close proximity while they are working.

However, stallions do live peacefully in bachelor herds in the wild and in natural management settings. For example, the stallions in the New Forest region of the United Kingdom live in stallion-only bachelor herds on their winter grazing. Stallions are still herd animals, and when managed as domesticated animals, some farms assert that carefully managed social contact benefits stallions. Well-tempered stallions who will be kept together for a long period of time may be stabled in closer proximity, though this method of stabling is generally used only by experienced stable managers. An example of this are the stallions of the Spanish Riding School, who travel, train and are stabled close together. In these settings, more dominant animals are kept apart by stabling a young or less dominant stallion in the stall between them. However, sometimes a stallion raised in isolation from other horses cannot be stabled in this fashion at all due to aggressive behaviour.

Dominance in Domesticated Herds

Because domestication of the horse usually requires stallions to be isolated from other horses, either mares or geldings may become dominant in a domestic herd. Usually dominance in these cases is a matter of age and, to some extent, temperament. It is common for older animals to be dominant, though old and weak animals may lose their rank in the herd. There are also studies suggesting that a foal will 'inherit' or perhaps imprint dominance behaviour from its dam, and at maturity seek to obtain the same rank in a later herd that its mother held when the horse was young.

In recent studies of domesticated horses, new evidence indicates that horses appear to benefit from a strong female presence in the herd. Groupings of all geldings, or herds where a gelding is dominant over the rest of the herd (for example, if the mares in the herd are quite young or of low status), may be more anxious as a group and less relaxed than those where a mare is dominant.

Communication

Horses communicate in various ways, including vocalizations such as nickering, squealing or whinnying; touch, through mutual grooming or nuzzling; smell; and body language. Body language is probably the predominant means of communication. Horses use a combination of ear position, neck and head height, movement, and foot stomping or tail swishing to communicate. Discipline is maintained in a horse herd first through body language and gestures, then, if needed, through physical contact such as biting, kicking, nudging, or other means of forcing a misbehaving herd member to move. In most cases, the animal that successfully causes another to move is dominant, whether it uses only body language or adds physical reinforcement.

Horses can interpret the body language of other creatures, including humans, who they view as predators. If socialized to human contact, horses usually respond to humans as a non-threatening predator. Humans do not always understand this, however, and may behave in a way, particularly if using aggressive discipline, that resembles an attacking predator and triggers the horse's fight-or-flight response. On the other hand, some humans exhibit fear of a horse, and a horse may interpret this behaviour as human submission to the authority of the horse, placing the human in a subordinate role in the horse's mind. This may lead the horse to behave in a more dominant and aggressive fashion. Human handlers are more successful if they learn to properly interpret a horse's body language and temper their own responses accordingly. Some methods of horse training explicitly instruct horse handlers to behave in ways that the horse will interpret as the behaviour of a trusted leader in a herd and thus more willingly comply with commands from a human handler. Other methods encourage operant conditioning to teach the horse to respond in a desired way to human body language, but also teach handlers to recognize the meaning of horse body language.

Horses are not particularly vocal, but do have four basic vocalizations: the neigh or whinny, the nicker, the squeal and the snort. They may also make sighing, grunting or groaning noises at times.

Ear position is often one of the most obvious behaviours that humans notice when interpreting horse body language. In general, a horse will direct the pinna of an ear toward the source of input it is also looking at. Horses have a narrow range of binocular vision, and thus a horse with both ears forward is generally concentrating on something in front of it. Similarly, when a horse turns both ears forward, the degree of tension in the horse's pinna suggests if the animal is calmly attentive to its surroundings or tensely observing a potential danger. However, because horses have strong monocular vision, it is possible for a horse to position one ear forward and one ear back, indicative of similar divided visual attention. This behaviour is often observed in horses while working with humans, where they need to simultaneously focus attention on both their handler and their surroundings. A horse may turn the pinna back when also seeing something coming up behind it.

Due to the nature of a horse's vision, head position may indicate where the animal is focusing attention. To focus on a distant object, a horse will raise its head. To focus on an object close by, and especially on the ground, the horse will lower its nose and carry its head in a near-vertical position. Eyes rolled to the point that the white of the eye is visible often indicates fear or anger.

Ear position, head height, and body language may change to reflect emotional status as well. For example, the clearest signal a horse sends is when both ears are flattened tightly back against the head, sometimes with eyes rolled so that the white of the eye shows, often indicative of pain or anger, frequently foreshadowing aggressive behaviour that will soon follow. Sometimes ears laid back, especially when accompanied by a strongly swishing tail or stomping or pawing with the feet are signals used by the horse to express discomfort, irritation, impatience, or anxiety. However, horses with ears slightly turned back but in a loose position, may be drowsing, bored, fatigued, or simply relaxed. When a horse raises its head and neck, the animal is alert and often tense. A lowered head and neck may be a sign of relaxation, but depending on other behaviours may also indicate fatigue or illness.

Tail motion may also be a form of communication. Slight tail swishing is often a tool to dislodge biting insects or other skin irritants. However, aggressive tail-swishing may indicate either irritation, pain or anger. The tail tucked tightly against the body may indicate discomfort due to cold or, in some cases, pain. The horse may demonstrate tension or excitement by raising its tail, but also by flaring its nostrils, snorting, and intently focusing its eyes and ears on the source of concern.

The horse does not use its mouth to communicate to the degree that it uses its ears and tail, but a few mouth gestures have meaning beyond that of eating, grooming, or biting at an irritation. Bared teeth, as noted above, are an expression of anger and an imminent attempt to bite.

Horses, particularly foals, sometimes indicate appeasement of a more aggressive herd member by extending their necks and clacking their teeth. Horses making a chewing motion with no food in the mouth do so as a soothing mechanism, possibly linked to a release of tension, though some horse trainers view it as an expression of submission. Horses will sometimes extend their upper lip when scratched in a particularly good spot, and if their mouth touches something at the time, their lip and teeth may move in a mutual grooming gesture. A very relaxed or sleeping horse may have a loose lower lip and chin that may extend further out than the upper lip. The curled lip flehmen response, noted above, most often is seen in stallions, but is usually a response to the smell of another horse's urine, and may be exhibited by horses of any sex. Horses also have assorted mouth motions that are a response to a bit or the rider's hands, some indicating relaxation and acceptance, others indicating tension or resistance.

Horses and Humans

Horses are creatures of habit and have excellent memories, which make consistent training extremely important to the horse. Untrained young horses, even with top bloodlines, can be bought for relatively little money compared to those with training. Once a horse is started under saddle and demonstrates that it is trainable, ridable and has some athletic talent for its work, the price easily triples.

Humans are usually viewed by wild horses as potential predators. However, horses are also innately curious and may investigate any creature that is interesting but not threatening.

Any domesticated horse with some experience of humans usually views people as generally harmless objects of curiosity worth at least minor notice, especially if they know that humans may bring food or treats. Rarely will any domestic horse become truly vicious unless it has been spoiled or abused by humans, though many stallions have a great deal of naturally aggressive, dominant behaviour that requires that they be managed only by knowledgeable handlers. However, any horse is a large animal that retains some wild instincts, so can react unpredictably by running, biting, striking, or kicking. Thus humans must always be alert around horses because they can accidentally harm people.

The ability of humans to work in cooperation with the horse is based on both the natural curiosity of the horse and the strong social bonds that horses have with each other. Horses do not like to be separated from their herd, because to be alone is to be exposed to predators on all sides. Also, in a herd, less dominant horses tend to gravitate toward the most mature and confident members. Therefore, many horse training principles are based upon having the horse accept a human as the dominant herd member. Ideally this is not done by force, but by the horse developing trust in the ability of the human and confidence that the human will be a responsible 'herd leader'.

Horses are also adapted to covering large amounts of territory and must have a certain boldness to do so. A horse that is afraid more than necessary will expend energy needlessly and then may not be able to escape when a threat is real. Thus, horses have an ability to check out the unusual and not immediately flee from something that is merely different.

This willingness to consider new things can also be used by a human trainer to adapt the horse's behaviour to an extraordinary range of activities that are well outside the range of instinctive horse behaviour, including acts considered naturally dangerous by the average horse such as bullfighting, jumping off cliffs, diving into water, jumping through a ring of fire, or walking into a modern television studio, complete with enclosed space, bright lights, and tremendous noise.

People who train horses first have to educate them that some normal herd behaviour is inappropriate around humans. For example, biting and 'shadow boxing' (rearing, striking) that is common play among young horses, colts in particular, could be injurious or fatal to people. Other instinctive traits, such as running away when frightened, bucking off anything that lands on a horse's back (like a mountain lion or other predator), or never entering a small enclosed area, also have to be overcome before the horse is useful to humans.

Even when trained, most horses will still test boundaries, at least mildly, and some horses with dominant personalities will openly challenge a weak or inexperienced handler. For example, if handled with incompetence or abuse, a horse may ignore its training and attempt to nip, bite, kick, refuse to be led, or try other ways to challenge human dominance. Without consistent handling, some horses, especially young ones, will revert to their untrained ways. However, due to their good memory, horses with solid training from trustworthy handlers often retain what they have learned, even after a gap of many years.

Sleep Patterns

Horses are able to sleep both standing up and lying down. They are able to doze and enter light sleep while standing, an adaptation from life as a prey animal in the wild. Lying down makes an animal more vulnerable to predators. Horses are able to sleep standing up because a 'stay apparatus' in their legs allows them to relax their muscles and doze without collapsing. In the front legs, their equine forelimb anatomy automatically engages the stay apparatus when their muscles relax. The horse engages the stay apparatus in the hind legs by shifting its hip position to lock the patella in place. At the stifle joint, a "hook" structure situated on the inside bottom end of the femur cups the patella and the medial patella ligament, preventing the leg from bending.

Unlike humans, horses do not need a solid, unbroken period of sleep time. They obtain needed sleep by means of many short periods of rest. This is to be expected of a prey animal, one that needs to be ready on a moment's notice to flee from predators.

Horses may spend anywhere from four to fifteen hours a day in standing rest, and from a few minutes to several hours lying down. However, not all this time is the horse actually asleep; total sleep time in a day may range from several minutes to a couple of hours. Horses require approximately two and a half hours of sleep, on average, in a 24-hour period. Most of this sleep occurs in many short intervals of about 15 minutes each.

Horses must lie down to reach REM sleep. They only have to lie down for an hour or two every few days to meet their minimum REM sleep requirements. However, if a horse is never allowed to lie down, after several days it will become sleep-deprived, and in rare cases may suddenly collapse as it involuntarily slips into REM sleep while still standing. This condition differs from narcolepsy, though horses may also suffer from that disorder.

Horses sleep better when in groups because some animals will sleep while others stand guard to watch for predators. A horse kept entirely alone may not sleep well because its instincts are to keep a constant eye out for danger.

Eating Pattern

Horses have a strong grazing instinct, preferring to spend most hours of the day eating forage. Horses and other Equids evolved as grazing animals, adapted to eating small amounts of the same kind of food all day long. In the wild, the horse adapted to eating prairie grasses in semi-arid regions and traveling significant distances each day in order to obtain adequate nutrition. Thus, they are 'trickle eaters', meaning they have to have an almost constant supply of food to keep their digestive system working properly. Horses can become anxious or stressed if there are long periods of time between meals. When stabled, they do best when they are fed on a regular schedule; they are creatures of habit and easily upset by changes in routine. When horses are in a herd, their behaviour is hierarchical; the higher-ranked animals in the herd eat and drink first. Low-status animals, who eat last, may not get enough food, and if there is little available feed, higher-ranking horses may keep lower-ranking ones from eating at all.

CHAPTER 11

Horse Care

There are many aspects to horse care. Horses, ponies, mules, donkeys and other domesticated equids require attention from humans for optimal health and long life.

Living Environment

Worldwide, horses and other equids usually live outside with access to shelter from the elements. In some cases, animals are kept in a barn or stable, or may have access to a shed or shelter. Horses require both shelter from wind and precipitation, as well as room to exercise and run. They must have access to clean fresh water at all times, and access to adequate forage such as grass or hay. In the winter, horses grow a heavy hair coat to keep warm and usually stay warm if well-fed and allowed access to shelter. But if kept artificially clipped for show, or if under stress from age, sickness or injury, a horse blanket may need to be added to protect the horse from cold weather. In the summer, access to shade is well-advised. For horse owners who do not own their own land, fields and barns can be rented from a private land owner or space for an individual horse may be rented from a boarding farm. Unless an animal can be fully maintained on pasture with a natural open water source, horses must be fed daily. As horses evolved as continuous grazers, it is better to feed small amounts of grain throughout the day than to feed a large amount of grain at one time. If a horse cannot be fed by its owner every day, it is usually kept at a boarding stable, where the staff will care for the horse for a fee. As equines are herd animals, most have better mental behaviour when in proximity to other equine company. However, this is not always possible, and it has been known for companionship bonds to develop between horses and cats, goats and other species. There are exceptions. Some horses, particularly stallions may need to live on their own as they may fight with other animals. Horses that are not on full-time turnout in a field or pasture normally require some form of regular exercise, whether it is being ridden, longed or turned out for free time. However, if a horse is ill or injured it may need to be confined to a stable, usually in a box stall.

Pastures

If a horse is kept in a pasture, the amount of land needed for basic maintenance varies with climate, an animal needs more land for grazing in a dry climate than in a moist one. However, an average of between one and 3 acres (12,000 m^2) of land per horse will provide adequate forage in much of the world, though feed may have to be supplemented in winter or during periods of drought. To lower the risk of laminitis, horses also may need to be removed from lush, rapidly changing grass for short periods in the spring and fall (autumn), when the grass is particularly high in non-structural carbohydrates such as fructans. If the terrain does not provide natural shelter in the form of heavy trees or other windbreaks, an artificial shelter must be provided; a horse's insulating hair coat works less efficiently when wet or when subjected to wind, horses that cannot get away from wind and precipitation put unnecessary energy into maintaining core body warmth and may become susceptible to illness. Some horses are turned out in a natural setting during the winter or when retired from work. However, even in these cases, animals need to be checked frequently for evidence of injury, parasites, sickness or weight loss. Horses cannot live for more than a few days without water. Therefore even in a natural, semi-feral setting, a check every day is recommended; a stream or irrigation source can dry up, ponds may become stagnant or develop toxic blue-green algae, a fence can break and allow escape, poisonous plants can take root and grow; windstorms, precipitation, or even human vandalism can create unsafe conditions.

Pens and Fences

Horses evolved to live on prairie grasslands and to cover long distances unfettered by artificial barriers. Therefore, when fenced in, accident potential must be considered. Horses will put their heads and legs through fences in an attempt to reach forage on the other side. They may run into fences if chased by another animal, or even when running at play if the fence (such as a wire fence) is not particularly visible. The smaller the area, the more visible and substantial a fence needs to be. For exercise alone, a pen, run, corral or 'dry lot' without forage can be much smaller than a pasture, and this is a common way that many horses are managed; kept in a barn with a turnout run, or in a dry lot with a shelter, feeding hay, allowing either no pasture access, or grazing for only a few hours per day. Outdoor turnout pens range greatly in size, but 12 feet (4 m) by 20 to 30 feet (9 m) is a bare minimum for a horse that does not get ridden daily. To gallop for short stretches, a horse needs a 'run' of at least 50 to 100 feet (30 m). When kept in a dry lot, a barn or shelter is a must. If kept in a small pen, a horse needs to be worked regularly or turned out in a larger area for free exercise.

Fences in pens must be sturdy. In close quarters, a horse may contact the fence frequently. Wire is very dangerous in any small pen. Pens are often made of metal pipe, or wood. Larger pens are sometimes enclosed in closely woven mesh, sometimes called 'no climb' fencing. However, if a wire mesh is used in a small pen, the openings must be too small for a horse hoof to pass through.

Types of Fencing

Over vast areas, barbed wire is often seen in some parts of the world, but it is the most dangerous fencing material that can be used around horses, even in a large pasture. If a horse is caught in barbed wire, it can quickly become severely hurt, often leaving lasting scars or even permanent injuries. Horse management books and periodicals are nearly universal in stating that barbed wire should never be used to contain horses. However, this advice is widely ignored, particularly in the western United States. Various types of smooth wire fencing, particularly when supported by a strand of electric fence, can be used to enclose a large pasture of several acres, and is one of the least expensive fencing options. A wire fence should have at least four, preferably five strands to provide adequate security. However, even without sharp barbs, wire has the highest potential for horses to become tangled in the fence and injured. If used, it must be properly installed and kept tight through regular maintenance. Visibility is also an issue; a horse galloping in an unfamiliar pasture may not see a wire fence until it is too late to stop.

Woven mesh wire is safer but more expensive than strands of smooth wire. It is more difficult to install, and has some visibility issues, but horses are less likely to become tangled in it or be injured if they run into it. Adding a top rail of wood or synthetic material increases visibility of the fence and prevents it from being bent by horses reaching over it. A strand of electric fence may also keep horses from pushing on a mesh fence. Mesh fencing needs to be heavy-gauge wire, woven, not welded, and the squares of the mesh should be too small for a horse to put a foot through. 'Field fence' or 'no-climb' fence are safer designs than more widely woven 'sheep fence'.

Chain link fence is occasionally seen, but horses can bend chain link almost as easily as a thinner-gauge wire, so the additional expense is often not justified by any gain over good-quality woven wire.

Electric fence comes in many styles of wire, rope and webbing, and is particularly useful for internal division of pastures. It carries only a mild charge that causes a noticeable shock, but no permanent injury to animals or people. It is relatively inexpensive and is easy to install, but if electricity fails, it is easily broken. It is excellent both as a temporary fence and, in single strands, as a top or middle barrier to keep horses away from conventional fencing. There is some danger that horses can become tangled in an electric fence, though because the materials are finer, it usually breaks, stopping the current, though injuries are still possible. Because electricity can fail, it should not be the sole fencing used on property boundaries, particularly next to roads, though a strand on top may be used to keep a horse from leaning over a fence made of other materials. Nor should it be used alone in small pens where horses may accidentally bump into it on a regular basis. However, small single-horse enclosures are sometimes seen at endurance riding competition, where temporary fencing must be set up in remote areas. In residential areas, warning signs should be posted on any boundary fences with electrified sections to keep people from touching the fence and accidentally being shocked. Wood is the 'classic' form of horse fencing, either painted planks or natural round rails. It is one of the safest materials for containing horses. Wood or a synthetic material with similar properties is the best option for small paddocks, pens and corrals. It can be used to fence pastures and has some ability to give or break if a horse collides with it. However, wood is expensive, high maintenance and not completely without safety concerns; boards can splinter, nails can stick out and cause lacerations. Wood-like synthetics are even more expensive, but are often safer and lower maintenance.

Cable of various sorts is sometimes used for horse fencing, and, especially if combined with a top rail or pipe or wood, can be reasonably safe. However, if cable is not kept tight, like wire, horses can be tangled in it. However, it not only cannot break but unlike wire, it also cannot easily be cut by humans. Its advantage over wire is that it poses less of a risk of entanglement. It is often less expensive than wood or pipe, has some give if a horse runs into it, and requires relatively little maintenance. Metal pipe is often used for fences instead of wood and if properly installed, can be fairly safe in the right circumstances. Pipe is often the most expensive fencing option, but is low maintenance and is very strong. Pipe will generally not give or break if it is run into or if the horse puts a foot through it, which can itself be a potential injury risk; horse owners debate the relative merits and dangers of pipe versus wood for horse fencing. Usually pipe is most suitable for very small areas such as pens where a horse may often bump or test the fence, but will not be at risk of colliding with the fence at full speed.

Solid wall masonry fences, typically either brick or fieldstone, are a type of horse fencing with an ancient tradition. Advantages of stone fences are high visibility, durability, strength and safety. Horses cannot get caught or tangled in them, put legs through, and if a horse runs into one, the impact is spread over much of the body, rather than concentrated on a single spot. They will last for decades with only minor repairs. The major disadvantage is the cost: the materials are expensive, fences require skilled labor for proper construction, and take longer to build.

Barns and Stables

Horses are sometimes kept indoors in buildings called either barns or stables. The terms are often used interchangeably; a barn is the more general term for a rural building that houses livestock, the term stable is more often used in urban areas and can be used as a noun to refer to the building that houses horses or the collection of horses themselves, or as a verb to describe the act of keeping horses in a stable. These buildings are usually unheated and well-ventilated; horses may develop respiratory problems when kept in damp or stuffy conditions. Most horse barns have a number of box stalls inside, that allow many horses to be safely stabled together in separate quarters. There are also separate areas or even rooms for feed, equipment and tack storage and, in some large stables, there may be additional facilities such as a veterinary treatment area or a washing area in the building. Barns may be designed to hold one horse in the backyard of a family home, or be a commercial operation capable of holding dozens of animals.

The standard dimensions for a box stall (called a 'box' in the UK, and a 'stall' in the USA) vary from 10' by 12' to 14' by 14', depending on local cultural traditions, the breed of horse, gender, and any special needs. Mares with foals often are kept in double stalls. Stallions, kept alone with less access to turnout, are also often given larger quarters. Ponies sometimes are kept in smaller box stalls, and warmbloods or draft horses may need larger ones. Horses kept in stables need daily exercise and may develop stable vices if they are not given work or turnout. Box stalls usually contain a layer of absorbent bedding such as straw or wood shavings and need to be cleaned daily; a horse generates approximately 15 pounds (6.8 kg) of manure and several gallons of urine each day. There are health risks to the horse if forced to stand all day in its own waste. However, stables are built as much for the convenience of humans as horses; most healthy horses are equally, if not more, comfortable in a field or paddock with a simple three-sided shed that protects them from the elements.

In some parts of the world, horses that are worked daily are kept in tie stalls, usually about 5 to 6 feet (2 m) wide and 8 to 10 feet (3 m) long. As the name implies, a horse is tied, usually to a ring in front of a hay manger, and cannot turn around in a tie stall. But if the stall is wide enough, it can lay down. Tie stalls were used extensively prior to the 20th century, and barns with tie stalls are still seen in some regions, particularly in poorer countries, at older fairgrounds and agricultural exposition facilities, but are not used as often in modern barns.

Feeding

A horse or pony needs approximately 1.5 per cent to 2.5 per cent of its body weight in food per day, depending on its age and level of work. This may include forages such as grass or hay and concentrates such as grain or commercially prepared pelleted feeds. Like people, some horses are 'easy keepers' and prone to obesity, while others are 'hard keepers' and need a great deal of food just to maintain a slim build. The average riding horse weighs roughly 1,000 pounds (450 kg), but the weight of a horse can be more closely estimated using a weight tape, which can be purchased from a feed store or tack shop.

Best practice is to feed horses two or three times daily, unless they are on full time pasture. Fresh, clean water should be provided free choice at all times, unless there is a specific reason to limit water intake for a short period of time.

A horse that is not ridden daily or subjected to other stressors can maintain adequate nutrition on pasture or hay alone, with adequate water (10-12 gallons per day minimum) and free access to a salt block or loose salt. However, horses and ponies in regular work often need a ration of both forage and concentrates.

Horses that are fed improperly may develop colic or laminitis, particularly if fed spoiled feed, subjected to excessive feed, or an abrupt change of feed. Young horses who are improperly fed may develop growth disorders due to an imbalance of nutrients. Young horses may also develop osteochondrosis if they are overfed.

Grooming

Horses groomed regularly have healthier and more attractive coats. Many horse management handbooks recommend grooming a horse daily, though for the average modern horse owner, this is not always possible. However, a horse should always be groomed before being ridden to avoid chafing and rubbing of dirt and other material, which can cause sores on the animal and also grind dirt into horse tack. Grooming also allows the horse handler to check for injuries and is a good way to gain the trust of the animal.

Proper basic grooming of a horse is a multi-step process involving several simple tools:

- *Curry, curry comb, or currycomb:* Usually a round tool with short teeth made of plastic or stiff rubber, used to loosen dirt, hair, and other detritus, plus stimulate the skin to produce natural oils.
- *Dandy brush:* A stiff-bristled, 'dandy' brush is used to remove the dirt, hair and other material stirred up by the curry. The best quality dandy brushes are made of stiff natural bristles such as rice stems, plastic-bristled dandy brushes are more common.
- *Body brush:* A soft-bristled 'body' brush removes finer particles and dust. Some natural body brushes are made of boar bristles, like human hairbrushes, others are made of soft synthetic fibres.
- *Grooming rag or towel:* A terrycloth towel or other type of cloth. Sometimes called a 'stable rubber'.
- *Mane brush or comb:* Horses with short, pulled manes have their manes combed with a wide-toothed plastic or metal comb. Horse tails and long manes many be finger-combed or are brushed with either a dandy brush, body brush, or a suitable human hairbrush.
- *Hoof pick:* All four feet of the horse need to be cleaned out and inspected for signs of injury or infection.

- In special weather conditions, a metal shedding blade with short, dull teeth is used to remove loose winter hair. Metal grooming tools used on sheep and show cattle may also be too harsh to use on a horse.
- In the summer, fly spray is often applied to the horse after grooming.
- *Sweat or Water Scraper:* A metal or plastic tool to remove excess liquid from a horse's coat.
- Sometimes, though not always, horses are clipped with scissors or, preferably, electric clippers. The most common areas are a short 'bridle path' just behind the ears, where a few inches of mane is removed to help the bridle lay more neatly; and the fetlocks, where extra hair can collect undesired amounts of mud and dirt. For horse show and exhibition purposes, additional clipping may be done.

Beyond the basic equipment, there are literally thousands of grooming tools on the market, from multiple designs on the basic brushes, available in many colours, to specialized tools for braiding manes, polishing hooves and clipping loose hair. There are also grooming products for horses ranging from moisturizing hair dressings to glitter gel and hoof polish.

Horses can be bathed by being wet down with a garden hose, but they do not require bathing and many horses live their entire lives without a bath. Either horse or human shampoo may be safely used on a horse, if thoroughly rinsed out, and cream rinses or hair conditioners, similar to those used by humans, are often used on show horses. Too-frequent shampooing can strip the hair coat of natural oils and cause it to dry out. A well-groomed, clean horse can be kept clean by wearing a horse blanket or horse sheet.

A horse show class that considers quality of grooming for as much as 40 per cent of the total score is called showmanship.

Shoeing and Hoof Care

The hooves of a horse or pony are cleaned by being picked out with a hoof pick to remove any stones, mud and dirt and to check that the shoes (if worn) are in good condition. Keeping feet clean and dry wherever possible helps prevent both lameness as well as hoof diseases such as thrush (a hoof fungus). The feet should be cleaned every time the horse is ridden, and if the horse is not ridden, it is still best practice to check and clean feet frequently. Daily cleaning is recommended in many management books, but in practical terms, a weekly hoof check of healthy horses at rest is often sufficient during good weather.

Use of hoof oils, dressings, or other topical treatments varies by region, climate, and the needs of the individual horse. Many horses have healthy feet their entire lives without need for any type of hoof dressing. While some horses may have circumstances where a topical hoof treatment is of benefit, improper use of dressings can also create hoof problems, or make a situation worse instead of better. Thus, there is no universal set of guidelines suitable for all horses in all parts of the world. Farriers and veterinarians in a horse owner's local area can provide advice on the use and misuse of topical hoof dressings, offering suggestions tailored for the needs of the individual horse.

Horses and ponies require routine hoof care by a professional farrier every 6 to 8 weeks, depending on the animal, the work it performs and, in some areas, weather conditions. Hooves usually grow faster in the spring and fall than in summer or winter. They also appear to grow faster in warm, moist weather than in cold or dry weather. In damp climates, the hooves tend to spread out more and wear down less than in dry climates, though more lush, growing forage may also be a factor. Thus, a horse kept in a climate such as that of Ireland may need to have its feet trimmed more frequently than a horse kept in a drier climate such as Arizona, in the southwestern United States.

All domesticated horses need regular hoof trims, regardless of use. Horses in the wild do not need hoof trims because they travel as much as 50 miles (80 km) a day in dry or semi-arid grassland in search of forage, a process that wears their feet naturally. Domestic horses in light use are not subjected to such severe living conditions and hence their feet grow faster than they can be worn down. Without regular trimming, their feet can get too long, eventually splitting, chipping and cracking, which can lead to lameness.

On the other hand, horses subjected to hard work may need horseshoes for additional protection. Some advocates of the barefoot horse movement maintain that proper management may reduce or eliminate the need for shoes, or propose hoof boots as an alternative. Certain activities, such as horse racing and police horse work, create unnatural levels of stress and will wear down hooves faster than they would in nature. Thus, some types of working horses almost always require some form of hoof protection.

The cost of farrier work varies widely, depending on the part of the world, the type of horse to be trimmed or shod, and any special issues with the horse's foot that may require more complex care. The cost of a trim is roughly half to one-third that of the cost of a set of shoes, and professional farriers are typically paid at a level commeasurate with other skilled labourers in an area, such as plumbers or electricians, though farriers charge by the horse rather than by the hour.

In the United Kingdom, it is illegal for anyone else other than a registered farrier to shoe or trim a horse's feet. The farrier should have any one of the following qualifications, the FWCF being the most highly skilled:

- DipWCF (Diploma of the Worshipful Company of Farriers)
- AWCF (Associateship of the Worshipful Company of Farriers)
- FWCF (Fellowship of the Worshipful Company of Farriers)

In the USA, there are no legal restrictions on who may do farrier work. However, there are professional organisations, such as the American Farrier's Association (AFA), that maintain a voluntary certification programme. Levels of certification in the AFA include:

- CF (Certified Farrier),
- CTF (Certified Tradesman Farrier),
- CJF (Certified Journeyman Farrier)

For each level of certification, farriers must pass written exams (addressing anatomy, physiology, and biomechanics), forging exams (modifications to keg shoes and building shoes from barstock), and live shoeing exams. Once a farrier has completed the highest level of certification (the CJF), he or she can also pursue Specialty Endorsements, such as the TE (Therapeutic Endorsement).

Bandaging and Leg Care

The legs of a horse require routine observation for lacerations or swelling. Everyday care involves brushing the legs with a brush to remove dirt and mud. A currycomb is generally not used below the knees. It is common to have excess hair trimmed from the fetlock to prevent excess accumulation of mud and moisture that may lead to skin problems. Many riders wrap the horse's legs with protective boots or bandages to prevent injury while working or exercising. After a ride, it is common for a rider or groom to hose off the legs of a horse to remove dirt and to ease any minor inflammation to the tendons and ligaments. Liniment may also be applied as a preventative measure to minimize stiffness and ease any minor strain or swelling. If the horse has been overworked, injured, or is to be transported, a standing bandage or shipping boot may be placed on the horse's legs for protection, to hold a wound dressing, or to provide support.

Wrapping legs requires care and skill. A too loose bandage will fall off, potentially tangling in the horse's legs, causing panic or injury. A too tight bandage may cause injury to tendons, ligaments and possible circulation problems. Commercial boots for riding or shipping are simpler to apply as they attach with a hook and loop fastening, or, less often, with adjustable buckles. Leg bandages require more attention. A bandage is usually applied over a protective padding of roll cotton or a premade quilted pad. The bandage is started on the outside of the leg, in the middle of the cannon bone, then wrapped down to either the fetlock or the hoof, depending on the purpose for which it is used, then back up to just under the knee, then back to the centre of the cannon just above the starting point, ending on the outside of the leg. Most of the time, a left leg is wrapped in a counter-clockwise direction, and a right leg wrapped in a clockwise direction, starting on the outside, moving front to back. Legs may be bandaged with either disposable stretchable wrap that sticks to itself, or with washable fleece or cotton wraps that are reusable and fasten at the ends with a hook and loop closure. Bandages may also be taped with medical tape to help them stay on.

Veterinary Care

There are many disorders that affect horses, including colic, laminitis, and internal parasites. Horses also can develop various infectious diseases that can be prevented by routine vaccination. It is sensible to register a horse or pony with a local equine veterinarian, in case of emergency. The veterinary practice will keep a record of the owner's details and where the horse or pony is kept, and any medical details. It is considered best practice for a horse to have an annual checkup, usually in the spring. Some practitioners recommend biannual checkups, in the spring and fall.

Vaccinations and Travel Requirements

Horses and ponies need annual vaccinations to protect against any number of sicknesses, though the precise vaccines required varies depending on the part of the world where the horse lives and the uses to which the animal is put. In most nations, equine influenza and tetanus shots are commonly given, and in many places, various forms of Equine Encephalitis are a concern, including West Nile Virus. Many additional vaccines may be needed, depending on local conditions.

As a general rule, a horse or pony that has never had a particular vaccination will be given an initial vaccination and then a booster a few weeks later, then normally once a year after that. Animals kept in a public boarding facility, those shipped for breeding and those frequently on the show circuit often require more vaccinations than horses that are not exposed to outside animals and who do not travel.

Some type of veterinary certificate or proof of vaccination is often required for horses to travel or compete, especially when crossing state, provincial, or international boundaries.

In the USA, a certificate stating that the horse has a negative 'Coggins' test must be in the vehicle carrying the horse when crossing state lines. This certificate, authorized by a veterinarian, certifies that the horse has been tested with a recent period of time and does not have an incurable disease called equine infectious anemia (EIA).

First-aid Kit

A well-stocked equine (and human) first-aid kit should be kept in a place where it is easily accessed. Any used or out-of-date items should be replaced as soon as possible. However, other than for minor injuries, a veterinarian should be consulted before treating a sick or injured animal.

The basic items any equine first-aid kit should include are:

- Tools and diagnostic equipment
  - Rectal thermometre
  - Petroleum jelly (to use as lubrication for thermometre)
  - Stethoscope (for listening to heartbeat, respiration and, in the case of suspected colic, gut sounds) Pulse and respiration can be determined without a stethoscope. Gut sounds can be heard by putting one's ear to the horse's side, but doing so increases the risk of being kicked by the horse.

  - Sharp, clean scissors, reserved for first aid kit only
  - Wire cutters (for freeing a tangled horse) or equivalent such as a fencing tool or lineman's pliers; though these objects are often kept in a well-organized barn, an extra set in a first-aid kit is helpful for major emergencies.
  - Flashlight and extra batteries (for nighttime emergencies or to add a light source in a shadowed area).
  - Twitch, a device for holding the animal still during minor treatment.
- Cleaning supplies.
  - Clean bucket, reserved for first-aid kit only, for washing out wounds.
  - Clean sponge, reserved for first-aid kit only.
  - Gauze (for cleaning wounds).
  - Cotton balls or sheet cotton for absorbing liquids, particularly good for dipping into liquid products and then squeezing or dabbing the liquid onto a wound. (Cotton used to clean a wound may leave fibres in the injury; gauze is a better product if the wound must be touched).
  - Hypodermic syringe (without needle), for cleaning wounds. (Using the syringe to wash out a wound is preferable to cleaning it with cotton or gauze.) An old syringe, if cleaned first, works fine for this.
  - Sterile saline solution, which is used to clean wounds. Contact lens solution may be used for this purpose.
  - Latex/medical gloves, unused.
  - Clean towels and rags.
  - Disposable rags or paper towels.
- Bandages and other forms of protection.
  - Absorbent padding, such as roll cotton or a set of cotton leg wraps (keep a clean set sealed in a plastic bag).
  - Gauze to be used as wound dressing underneath bandages.
  - Sterile wound dressing, such as telfa pads; large sizes of those intended for humans work well.
  - Leg Bandages – stable bandages or rolls of self-adhering vet wrap.
  - Adhesive tape for keeping bandages in place.
  - Poultice boot, for hoof injuries. (A hoof boot can be used for this purpose, though a medical boot is usually easier to put on and take off).
  - Over-the-counter medications.
  - Medical grade antibacterial soap.
  - Wound ointment for minor scrapes.

- Antiseptic/Disinfectant, such as Betadine, diluted iodine solution, or hydrogen peroxide.
- Epsom salts for drawing out infection and treating pain.
- Poultice dressing. Disposable diapers (nappies) or sanitary napkins may also be cut and used as a poultice as they draw moisture out of wounds. Kaolin clay may also be used as a poultice.

• Veterinary medications – in most locations, these are prescription medications and can only be obtained through a licensed Veterinarian. They should generally not be administered without prior consultation with a veterinarian, either over the telephone or by specific advance instruction.
  - Phenylbutazone ('Bute') paste for pain relief.
  - Flunixin Meglumine ('Banamine', 'Finadyne') granules or paste for colic treatment.
  - Acepromazine ('Ace') or similar tranquilizer pill, paste, or pre-filled injector.
  - Epinephrine (adrenaline) auto-injectors for emergency treatment of a horse that goes into anaphylactic shock when stung by a bee, wasp or other insect.

• Other.
  - Veterinarian's and farrier's telephone and emergency numbers.
  - A paper and pencil, for recording symptoms, pulse, respiration and veterinary instructions.
  - A Veterinary Emergency Handbook, giving basic instructions, in the event that a veterinarian cannot be reached immediately.
  - Suitable box/container for all of the above, to keep materials and equipment clean and tidy.

Parasite Management

All equines have a parasite burden, and therefore treatment is periodically needed throughout life. Some steps to reduce parasite infection include regularly removing droppings from the animal's stall, shed or field; breaking up droppings in fields by harrowing or disking; minimizing crowding in fields; periodically leaving a field empty for several weeks; or placing animals other than equines on the field for a period of time, particularly ruminants, which do not host the same species of parasites as equines. If botflies are active, frequent application of fly spray may repel insects. A small pumice stone or specialized bot egg knife can also scrape off any bot eggs that were laid on the hairs of the horse.

However, internal parasites cannot be completely eliminated. Therefore, most modern horse owners commonly give anthelmintic drugs (wormers) to their horses to manage parasite populations.

Methods of Worming

There are two common methods of worming. *Purge wormers* that kill parasites with a single strong dose, are given periodically, usually every 8-12 weeks, depending on local conditions and veterinary recommendations. *Continuous wormers,* also known as "daily" wormers, are given in the horse's feed each day, in small doses, and kill worms as they infect the horse. Neither of these methods is perfect; purge wormers are effective for rapidly killing all parasites, but are gone from the horses' body in a few days, and then the horse may start to be re-infected. Continuous wormers are a mild low dose and may be easier on the horse, but may not be effective in quickly killing worms in a heavily-infected horse and may contribute to drug resistance. Neither type will kill all types of worms, so horses normally require a purge worming with a different drug on a rotating basis, at least 2 or 3 times per year. Many horse owners also rotate between the different chemical classes of wormers to combat the tendency of parasites to develop resistance to a given class of drugs. If a treatment doesn't kill at least 95 per cent of a worm species, that species is classed as 'resistant' to the drug. However, frequent rotation of several types of wormers is not recommended, as it can often lead to multiple species of worms becoming resistant to multiple types of medication.

Another way of combating drug resistance is to worm less frequently, by having manure samples tested for the presence of parasite eggs and then worming only when the count gets high enough with a wormer specific for the type of worm eggs found. This strategy is now recommended by most veterinarians and parasitologists, as it reduces the probability of resistance. However, this method is not entirely reliable, as the parasite load varies somewhat with the seasons, and some parasites (such as bots) may not show up in a fecal egg count at all.

Wormers come in several forms, including pastes, gels, powders, and granules or pellets. Powders and granules normally come in single-dose packaging, and the wormer is normally mixed in with the horse's feed. Pastes and gels normally come in a plastic syringe which is inserted in the side of the horse's mouth and used to administer the wormer onto the back of the horse's tongue. A wormer syringe has a plastic ring on the plunger that is turned to adjust the dosage for the horse's weight.

Risks of Worming

Modern anthelmintics are generally effective against worms. However, if a horse is heavily infested with parasites, wormers must be given carefully. If worms become overpopulated in a horse's digestive tract, they will often form dormant cysts embedded in the intestinal epithelium. A decrease in the active population of worms, as in the case of worming, can cause a massive activation of these cysts. In other situations, a heavily-infested horse's body may be overwhelmed by the toxins released by a heavy load of dead parasites after worming with a powerful drug. There have been documented cases of horses, particularly if also undernourished, ill, or otherwise weakened, to become sick or even die. Thus, in heavily-infested animals, a veterinarian may recommend worming with a mild class of drugs, such as Panacur or a low-dose daily wormer. for the first month or so, followed by periodic purge wormer treatments.

Drug resistance is a growing concern for many horse owners. Parasite resistance has been observed to ivermectin, moxidectin, benzimidazoles, tetrapyrimidines, and piperazine. Development of new drugs takes many years, leading to the concern that worms could out-evolve the drugs currently available to treat them. As a result, most veterinarians now recommend worming based on actual fecal egg counts and actual infestation to minimize the development of resistant worm populations.

Types of parasites found in equines:

- *Ascarids*, also known as *roundworms*
- *Pinworms*, sometimes known as *seatworms*
- *Tapeworms*
- *Strongyles* – large and small, sometimes known as *Redworm.*
- *Bots* – fly larvae – bot eggs are laid on a horse's coat, and when accidentally ingested through the horse licking its coat, the larvae hatch in the tongue, migrate down the esophagus and mature in the stomach.

Ringworm in horses is not actually a worm but a contagious fungal skin disease and is normally treated using an anti-fungal wash.

There are several different brands of wormer, using different types of active chemical – which in turn kill different types of parasites. It is sometimes necessary to use a specific wormer at a certain time of year, depending on the life cycle of the parasites involved. Many horse owners *rotate* wormers during the year, using different brands or formulations with different active chemicals, to combat drug-resistant parasites.

Dental Care

A horse's teeth grow continuously throughout its life and can develop uneven wear patterns. Most common are sharp edges on the sides of the molars which may cause problems when eating or being ridden. For this reason a horse or pony needs to have its teeth checked by a veterinarian or qualified equine dentist at least once a year. If there are problems, any points, unevenness or rough areas can be ground down with a rasp until they are smooth. This process is known as 'floating'.

Basic floating can be accomplished by the practitioner pulling the end of horse's tongue out the side of the mouth, having an assistant hold the tongue while the teeth are rasped. The horse will not bite its own tongue, and will often tolerate the floating process if held closely and kept in a confined area where it cannot move. When complex dental work is required or if a horse strenuously objects to the procedure, sedation is used.

A horse can also suffer from an equine malocclusion where there is a misalignment between the upper and lower jaws. This can lead to a number of dental problems.

Alternative Medicine in Horses

Folk remedies and assorted 'natural' treatments are sometimes used to care for horses. These treatments are controversial. Some remedies are supported by scientific studies that suggest that they are effective, others have no scientific basis and in fact may actually be harmful. The most common treatments are called nutraceuticals, assorted supplements that support the natural systems of the horse and which may have some scientific basis for efficacy, even if not fully supported or yet to be approved as either a drug or a feed supplement. The most popular of these are joint supplements such as glucosamine, chondroitin, and MSM.

Examples of folk remedies that are not effective include the feeding of chewing tobacco or diatomaceous earth to horses as a wormer. Neither of these has been proven to work in any empirical study. Other natural remedies, whether useful or not, may show up in drug testing, particularly any herbs derived from the Capsicum or valerian families.

Sometimes natural remedies are all that is available in certain remote areas. Examples include horses in certain tropical nations who have sprained tendons or ligaments are treated with rachette (Nopalea cochenillifera), castor bean leaves (*Ricinus communis*), aloes (*Aloe vera*) or leaves of wonder of the world (*Kalanchoe pinnata*). Natural remedies are also used to treat exercise induced pulmonary haemorrhage (EIPH) with lungwort (*Pulmonaria officinalis*). Other plants used in combination with conventional medications included liquorice (*Glycyrrhiza glabra*) root, aerial parts of mullein (*Verbascum thapsus*) or mallow (*Althea*), and comfrey (*Symphytum officinalis*) root.

Guidelines for General Horse Care

- Even routine horse care is a significant and ongoing expense. In fact, the cost of purchasing a horse is often much less than the cost of maintaining one for a year. Make sure you are realistic about your ability to afford quality care before you adopt an equine companion.
- *Horses need a regular supply of food:* In most cases, they need to have hay or pasture throughout the day, with additional grain feedings twice a day. An average-size horse will eat about 20 lbs. of food a day and drink at least eight gallons of water. Because their stomachs are relatively small and their digestive systems surprisingly delicate, horses need to nibble or graze throughout the day, rather than have one or two meals a day.
- *Horses need regular hoof care:* Plan to hire a farrier (blacksmith) every six to eight weeks for routine hoof trimming or shoeing.
- *Horses need regular veterinary care:* At least once a year, your horse will need to be vaccinated against tetanus and other diseases. The

veterinarian will also provide routine dental care. Keep in mind that medical emergencies, which are always an unfortunate possibility, can cost several thousand dollars to treat.

- Since horses are constantly exposed to intestinal worms from the ground they graze on, they must be dewormed every six to eight weeks. Carrying a heavy burden of worms can cause serious illness or death in equines, so regular and timely treatment is crucial to your horse's health.
- Horses need constant access to a dry, safe, comfortable shelter to protect them from rain, wind, and snow. In warm and sunny weather, the shelter you supply will provide your companion with much needed shade. At a minimum, you should have a well-constructed, three-sided shed into which your horse can retreat at all times. You will need to remove manure from the stall or shelter every day.
- *Horses need exercise:* To supplement the exercise your horse will get when you ride him, he should have a paddock or pasture in which to relax and stroll. No horse should spend all day confined in a stall, except on a veterinarian's recommendation. The pasture should be bordered by safe, sturdy fencing that will keep the horse safe and secure. Barbed wire is not an acceptable fencing material—it has been the cause of many serious injuries.

CHAPTER 12

Horse Grooming

Horse grooming is hygienic care given to a horse, or a process by which the horse's physical appearance is enhanced for horse shows or other types of competition.

Reasons for Grooming

Horsemen agree that grooming is an important part of horse care, and proper grooming is essential for horses that are used in competition. Most recommend grooming a horse daily, although this is not always possible. However, regular grooming helps to ensure the horse is healthy and comfortable. At a minimum, horses are generally groomed before being worked, and are usually groomed and cleaned up after a workout as well.

The main reasons for daily grooming include:

- improved health of the skin and coat;
- decreases the chance of various health problems such as thrush, scratches, and other skin problems;
- cleans the horse, so chafing does not occur under areas of tack;
- gives the groom a chance to check the horse's health, such as looking for cuts, heat, swelling, lameness, a change in temperament (such as depression) which could indicate the horse is sick, and look to see if the horse has loose or missing horseshoes.
- helps to form a relationship between horse and handler, which can carry over to other handling duties and riding.

Horse showmanship is a horse show class that considers quality of grooming for as much as 40 per cent of the total score.

Tools Used for Grooming

There are several tools that are commonly used when grooming a horse. Proper use and technique helps to ensure the horse remains comfortable during the grooming process, and allows for greater ease in cleaning the animal.

- **Curry** or **Curry comb**: A tool made of rubber or plastic with short 'teeth' on one side, that slides onto the hand of the groom. It is usually the first tool used in daily grooming. The horse is rubbed or 'curried' to help loosen dirt, hair, and other detritus, plus stimulate the skin to produce natural oils. The curry comb is usually used in a circular motion to work loose embedded material. Curries are generally too harsh to be used on the legs or head, though varieties made of softer rubber are available.
- **Metal curry comb** or **Fitch curry comb**: The metal curry comb is not designed to use directly on a horse's coat as the metal teeth can damage the skin and hair. It is a curry comb made of several rows of short metal teeth, with a handle. They are primarily designed for use on show cattle, but are frequently used to clean horse grooming brushes by moving the brush across the metal curry comb teeth every few strokes.
- **Dandy brush** or **Hard-bristled brush**: A stiff-bristled brush is used to remove the dirt, hair and other material stirred up by the curry. Brushes are used in the direction of the horse's hair coat growth, usually in short strokes from front to back, except at the flanks, where the hair grows in a different pattern. The best quality dandy brushes are made of stiff natural bristles such as rice stems, though they wear out quickly. Plastic-bristled dandy brushes are more common. Dandy brushes can usually be used on the legs, but many horses object to a stiff brush being used on the head. Some dandy brushes do double duty as a Water Brush, when moistened in water and used to wet down the hair coat, mane or tail. Such use may include creating quarter marks for show.
- **Body brush** or **Soft brush**: A soft-bristled brush removes finer particles and dust, adds a shine to the coat and is soothing to the horse. A body brush, particularly a smaller design called a Face brush, can be used on the head, being careful to avoid the horse's eyes. Some natural body brushes are made of horsehair, goat hair or boar bristles, like human hairbrushes, others are made of soft synthetic fibres. The body brush is generally the last brush used on the horse.
- **Grooming rag or towel**, also called a Stable rubber: A linen or terrycloth towel or similar type of cloth, or sheepskin mitt, can be used to give a final polish to a horse's coat and is also used after riding to help remove sweat.
- **Mane brush or comb:** Horses with short, pulled manes have their manes combed with a wide-toothed plastic or metal comb. Tails and long manes are brushed with either a dandy brush or a suitable human hairbrush. Extremely long show-quality manes and tails are often picked out by hand to avoid breaking the hairs. A short-toothed Pulling comb is used to pull the mane to shorten and thin it in preparation for braiding.

- **Hoof pick**: A hooked tool, usually of metal, used to clean the hooves of a horse. Some designs include a small, very stiff brush for removing additional mud or dirt. All four feet of the horse need to be cleaned out before and after riding.
  A combination shedding blade/sweat scraper.
- **Shedding blade**: In special weather conditions, a metal shedding blade with short, dull teeth is used to remove loose winter hair. A shedding blade is also useful for removing caked-on mud. However, grooming tools with metal teeth can split and dull the horse's hair coat and may irritate the skin, so must be used with appropriate care. Likewise, metal grooming tools used on sheep and show cattle may also be too harsh to use on a horse.
- **Sweat scraper**: Several styles of sweat scraper exist to remove sweat after exertion or water after bathing. One is a simple curved and fluted metal or plastic wand, about 18 inches (46 cm) long. Another design is an arc of plastic or rubber attached to a handle, sometimes with two curved blades (one rubber, one metal or plastic) attached back to back. A third design is a flexible curved blade with teeth on one side to use as a shedding blade, and smooth on the other, for use as a sweat scraper.
- **Fly spray**: In the summer, fly spray is often applied to the horse after grooming. Care must be taken to avoid the eyes and mucous membranes.
- **Bot knife**: It used to remove botfly eggs from the horse, which are usually laid on the legs or shoulder. Bot eggs are yellow and roughly the size of a grain of sand, they are clearly visible on dark hair, harder to spot on white hair. A bot knife generally has a blunt end and curved blade and is used to 'shave' off the egs. A bot brick is a small pumice stone or block of dense styrofoam that will pick up eggs when rubbed on the hair.
- **Scissors**: Used to trim long hairs growing under the jaw and the fetlocks, as well as trimming the bridle path or banging the tail.
- **Clippers:** In order to remove a horse's winter coat to allow him to work more comfortably and dry faster in the colder months, larger electric clippers are used. Small clippers are also useful for trimming ears, jawlines and legs. Hand-operated clippers are still available but not often used, since electric clippers are so much more efficient.
- **Sponges**: Small sponges can be used to clean the eyes, nose, lips and, using a separate sponge dedicated to the task, beneath the dock and around the genitals. Larger sponges can be used to wet down and clean the body and legs.

The Hoof

Hoof care is especially important when caring for the horse. Although many horses are quite healthy without daily brushing, lack of hoofcare can result in various problems, which if unattended, can result in short or long-term soundness issues for the horse. Hooves need to be trimmed after four to ten weeks otherwise, they will grow too long and cause discomfort.

Cleaning the Feet

The most basic form of hoofcare is cleaning, or *picking out* the feet. A hoof pick is used to remove mud, manure, and rocks from the sole of the hoof. Removal of mud and manure helps to prevent thrush, a common hoof ailment which in very severe cases may cause lameness, and the removal of rocks helps to prevent stone bruises. In the winter, hoof picking also provides the chance to remove packs of snow from the horse's hooves, which can cause uncomfortable 'snowballs'. Additionally, when the hoof is cleaned, it can be visually inspected for problems such as puncture wounds due to a nail (which has the potential to be very serious if left untreated).

All crevices of the hoof are cleaned, particularly between the frog and the bars, as those areas are most likely to trap rocks or other debris, and also are the most common area to develop thrush. It is best to work the hoof pick from heel to toe, so to avoid accidentally jabbing the horse's leg, the frog of the hoof, or the person using the pick. When picking the feet, the groom stands at the horse's side, facing the tail of the horse, then slides his or her hand down the horse's leg. If the horse was not trained to pick up its foot when a person runs their hand to the fetlock and lifts lightly, most horses will pick up their feet if the tendons behind their cannon bone are squeezed. Some horses, particularly draft breeds, may be trained to pick up their feet to pressure on their fetlock.

Most horse management guidelines recommend picking the feet daily, and in many cases, the feet are picked twice in one day, both before and after a ride.

Dressings and Polish

Hoof dressing is a liquid substance used on the hooves to improve their moisture content, which in turn helps prevent hoof cracks, lost shoes, tender feet, and other common hoof problems. Polish for hooves is used for show purposes and is either based on formulas similar to either wax-based shoe polish or to enamelized human nail polish.

For many disciplines, the hooves are painted with either clear or black hoof polish as a finishing touch. Clear polish is generally used in dressage, show hunters, jumpers, and eventing, as well as most breed shows, other than some stock horse breeds. Black polish is seen in the western disciplines, especially western pleasure, but some breeds, notably the Appaloosa, ban any polish that alters the natural hoof colour. Gaited breeds have varying rules, some allowing black polish, others limiting its use. Whether clear or coloured, polish is applied purely for aesthetic reasons, as a finishing touch.

Bathing

Horses can be bathed by being wet down with a garden hose or by being sponged off with water from a bucket. Horses do not require bathing and many horses live their entire lives without a bath. However, horses are often hosed off with water after a heavy workout as part of the cooling down process, and are often given baths prior to a horse show to remove every possible speck of dirt. They must be trained to accept bathing, as a hose and running water are unfamiliar objects and initially may frighten a horse. A hose is usually used for bathing. Start near the legs, being careful to point the hose at a downward angle. When spraying the body, be sure to angle the hose so that water doesn't hit the horse in the face. Either horse or human shampoo may be safely used on a horse, if thoroughly rinsed out, and cream rinses or hair conditioners, similar to those used by humans, are often used on show horses. Too-frequent shampooing can strip the hair coat of natural oils and cause it to dry out. Though horses in heavy work, such as racehorses, may be rinsed off after their daily workout, it is generally not advisable to shampoo a horse more than once a week, even in the show season. A well-groomed, clean horse can be kept clean by wearing a horse blanket or horse sheet.

Clipping

Many horses have hair trimmed or removed, especially for show. Different disciplines have *very* different standards. The standards for breed competitions are also highly variable, and deviation from the acceptable grooming method may not be permitted at breed shows. It is often best to check the rules, and to ask a horseman experienced in your discipline or breed of choice, before performing any type of trimming or clipping to a show horse. Severely 'incorrect' clipping is often considered a great faux pas in the horse world.

Trimming

Clipping style is quite variable by breed, region and discipline. While some clipping has its origins in practical purposes, much clipping today is very much based on the showing style for which a particular horse is used. The most common areas clipped include:

- **Bridle path:** It is a section of mane, just behind the ears, is frequently clipped or shaved off. For practical purposes, this allows the bridle to lie comfortably on the across the poll, makes it slightly easier to bridle the horse, as the mane and forelock are separated and easier to keep out of the way. The length of the bridle path varies by breed and region of the world: for example, the American Saddlebred and the Arabian are commonly shown in the United States with bridle paths that are several inches long, while other breeds (such as the Friesian horse) are not permitted to have any bridle path. In the UK and continental Europe, bridle paths are generally rather short if clipped at all, though there is variation depending on breed.
- **Face:** There is little real need to clip the face, it is done primarily for aesthetic reasons. The most practical location to clip is under the jaw, to

create a more refined appearance and remove excess hair that may interfere with the cavesson and throatlatch of the bridle. The whiskers of the muzzle are commonly shaved in the United States, though not as often in Europe. Some also clip the feelers above and below the eyes. Clipping the whiskers of the muzzle or eyes is a topic of minor controversy, as they are thought to help prevent injury because the horse can 'feel' when it is approaching an object.

- **Ears:** The hair on the pinnae (ears) of the horse may be clipped, sometimes both inside and out. The practice of clipping the inside of the ears is also controversial, as the hairs inside the ear protect the inner ear from dirt and insects. When the ears are trimmed on the inside, a fly mask with ear protection is often put on the horse to replace its natural protection.
- **Legs:** The fetlocks can collect undesired amounts of mud, dirt, and burrs and may be trimmed for practical reasons. The back of the lower cannon is also commonly clipped, also to remove long hairs. For a truly polished look, the coronary band is clipped to shorten the small straggling hairs that grow along the edges of the hoof. Leg clipping is done for most light riding horses. However, there are several breeds, particularly draft horse breeds, that consider lower leg feathering to be a breed trait and do not permit the clipping of the fetlocks or 'feather' on the lower legs.

Body Clipping

In addition to basic trimming, many horses are 'body clipped' in the winter months, to remove their winter coat. This can serve a practical purpose, as it keeps the horse more comfortable during work, and helps it cool down faster. It can also serve an aesthetic purpose, as most horsemen agree a horse looks finer and more show-worthy with a shorter coat. Additionally, grooming is usually easier and less time-consuming when the hair is shortened.

Before one makes the decision to body clip a horse, one must be sure to consider the fact that they are removing the horse's natural defences against the cold. They must therefore be able to provide blanketing, and in some cases, stabling, for the horse if the temperature drops, or if there is a cold rain or snow. This will increase the amount of work needed to keep the horse, as the groom must change the blankets as needed, but it is essential to keep the horse comfortable and healthy.

Types of body clips include:

- **Body clip** or **Full body clip:** the horse's entire body is clipped, including the head and legs. This is the most common body clip in the USA, used in many disciplines. It provides the most "natural" clip, resembling a horse's normal summer coat, plus it is a relatively straightforward clip for a groom to complete. However, it provides the least amount of natural protection for the horse.

- **Hunter clip:** The entire horse is clipped, except for the legs and a patch of hair under the saddle. This clip traces back to the hunt field, and is still used there today, as it provides extra protection to the back of the horse (essential during several hours of hunting) as well as to the lower legs (which may be cut by brambles), but still allows the horse to stay cool while galloping.
- **Blanket clip:** Long hair is left in a blanket-shaped area on the horse. The shoulders and neck are clipped, the legs are left unclipped.
- **Trace clip:** It varies, but generally the horse is clipped from under its throat, down along the jugular groove, and then clipped half-way up the shoulder and belly. Variations include clipping higher along the neck, shoulder, and belly, and clipping a strip off the side of the hindquarter, to the buttock. Additionally, many clip a strip half-way up the cheek to the muzzle. The back and legs are left unclipped. The clip is named after the traces of the carriage, as it follows a similar pattern. The amount of hair removed is based on the work the horse is in, the amount it sweats during work, and the areas where it sweats the most. It is most commonly seen used by eventers.
- **Chaser Clip:** Hair is removed from a line below the poll to the stifle, legs are left on. This is a popular clip for steeplechasers as it keeps the horses' back warm but also allows for hard work.
- **Strip clip** or **Belly clip**: Hair is clipped along the jugular groove, chest and under the barrel. This is a minimal clip, and many horses with this clip do not need extra care beyond regular blanketing.

The Mane

The modern horse usually has its mane groomed to fit a particular breed, style, or practical purpose. For informal pleasure riding, the mane is simply detangled with a brush or wide-toothed comb and any foreign material removed.

The mane may be kept in a long, relatively natural state, which is required for show by some breeds, particularly those used in Saddle seat style English riding competition. A long mane may be placed into five to seven long, relatively thick braids between shows to keep it in good condition, to help it grow, and to minimize debris and dirt from entering. Breeds mandated to show with a long mane keep a long mane in almost all disciplines, even those where show etiquette normally requires thinning or pulling.

In some breeds or disciplines, particularly many Western and hunt seat competitions, the mane is thinned and shortened for competition purposes. The most common method of shortening and thinning the mane is by pulling it. Originally a thinned mane was considered easier to keep free of dirt, burrs, and out of the way of the rider, thus worth the time and upkeep of regular thinning. Today, its purpose is primarily for tradition and to make it lay down flat and easier to braid or band.

Horses shown in hunter, jumper, dressage, eventing and related hunt seat and show hack disciplines usually have their manes not only shortened and thinned, but placed into many individual braids for show. Heavier breeds of horses, particularly draft horses, may have their manes french braided instead of being pulled, thinned and placed in individual braids. Breeds required to show with long manes may also french braid the mane if an animal is cross-entered in both a breed and a hunter/jumper discipline.

The mane may also be 'roached' or 'hogged', meaning that it is completely shaved off. This is most commonly seen in polo ponies, Australian Stock Horses and roping horses, to keep the mane out of the rider's way, and to prevent the mallet or rope from becoming entangled.

Tail

Basic tail grooming begins with simply brushing out foreign material, snarls, and tangles, sometimes with the aid of a detangling product. Horses used in exhibition or competition may have far more extensive grooming. However, the tail's main purpose is fly protection, and certain types of show grooming can inhibit the use of this natural defense.

In show grooming, the dock of the tail (the flesh-covered part of the tail where the hair is rooted) and the 'skirt' (the hair below the tip of the dock) may be styled in a wide variety of ways: The tail may be kept natural and encouraged to grow as long as possible, and sometimes even has additional hair artificially attached. Other times, it may be clipped, thinned, or even cut very short. A few breeds are shown with docked tails.

A 'natural' tail is not clipped nor braided when the horse is presented in the ring. The tail may be encouraged to grow as long as possible, often by keeping the skirt of the tail in a long braid when not in competition, usually also folded up and covered by a wrap to keep it clean. The shorter hairs of the dock are allowed to hang loose so that the horse can still swat flies. 'Natural' tails can also be thinned and shaped by pulling hairs at the sides of the dock, or by pulling the longest hairs in the skirt of the tail, to make the tail shorter and less full, though retaining a natural shape.

Tail hairs are also cut. 'Clipping' the tail usually refers to trimming the sides of the dock, to a point about halfway down the dock. *Banging* the tail involves cutting the bottom of the tail straight at the bottom. In modern competition, this is usually done well below the hocks. On the other hand, Tail extensions, also known as 'false tails', or 'tail wigs', are false hairpieces which are braided or tied into the tail to make it longer or fuller.

Braiding the dock of the tail in a French braid with the skirt left loose is commonly seen in hunter competition and hunt seat equitation. In polo, draft horse showing and on Lipizzan horses that perform the capriole, the entire tail, dock and skirt, is generally braided and the braid is folded or rolled into a knot, with or without added ribbons and other decorative elements.

In inclement weather, many other show disciplines will allow competitors to put up the skirt of the tail into a similar type of stylized knot known as a *mud tail.*

In the draft horse and some harness breeds the tail is cut very short to keep it from being tangled in a harness. The term 'docked' or 'docking' may simply mean cutting the hair of the tail skirt very short, just past the end of the natural dock of the tail. However, it can also refer to partial tail amputation. This type of docking is banned in some places, and either type of docking can make it difficult for a horse to effectively swat flies. Another controversial practice, tail setting, involves placing the dock of the tail in a device that causes it to be carried at all times in an arched position desired for show. The set is used when the horses are stalled, and removed during performances. It stretches the muscles to keep the tail in position, and is not used after the horse is retired from competition. Sometimes the process is sped up by the controversial practice of nicking or cutting the check ligament that normally pulls the tail downward. This practice is generally only used for a few breeds, such as the American Saddlebred.

Other Show Grooming Products and Supplies

Highlighter

Highlighter is a gel, ointment or oil used to add shine and thus accentuate certain parts of the horse's face. Less often, it is placed on the bridle path, crest, knees, hocks, mane and tail. It is commonly used in the United States by certain breeds such as stock and gaited breeds, but is frowned upon in the Hunter disciplines. Other nations often do not use such products on show animals at all. In a few disciplines, such products are banned. Most breeds that allow highlighting require such it to be clear, without dye or colour.

Neck Sweats

Neck sweats are wraps, usually of neoprene, placed on the neck or jowl of the horse to cause it to sweat. This is a short-term method that will temporarily reduce a thick jowl or cresty neck, to make it appear finer in appearance. This tool is used both by breeds prone to heavy necks who benefit from some slimming, but also by breeds with refined necks to create a more extreme refinement, often called a 'hooky' neck.

Coat Treatments

A number of products, usually in spray form, have been developed to add extra gloss, smoothness or shine to a coat. Some sprays are oil-based, but because they attract dust, more common coat enhancement sprays are oil-free, often called 'silicone' sprays, that leave the hair coat very smooth and slick. Most are applied to the horse after it has been bathed and dried, though are occasionally used on a horse that has not been bathed to add a quick gloss for short-term purposes.

CHAPTER 13

Horse Hoof

A horse hoof is a structure surrounding the distal phalanx of the 3rd digit (digit III of the basic pentadactyl limb of vertebrates, evolved into a single weight-bearing digit in equids) of each of the four limbs of Equus species, which is covered by complex soft tissue and keratinised (cornified) structures. Since a single digit must bear the full proportion of the animal's weight that is borne by that limb, the hoof is of vital importance to the horse. The phrase 'no hoof, no horse' underlines how much the health and the strength of the hoof is crucial for horse soundness.

Both wild and feral equid hooves have enormous strength and resilience, allowing any gait on any ground. A common example of the feral horse type is the Mustang. The Mustang is, in part, descended from the Iberian horses brought to the Americas by the Spanish, but most herds also have ancestry from other breeds. Therefore, the famous Mustang hoof strength is in part a result of natural selection and environment. Thus, it is proposed that other domestic breeds could develop similar hooves if raised under similar conditions.

The recent barefoot movement claims that such a strength can be almost completely restored to domesticated horses, when appropriate trimming and living conditions are applied, to such an extent that horseshoes are no longer necessary in almost any horse. If true, it would undermine the belief that 'the horseshoe is a necessary evil'.

The barefoot management system has not, however, gained a foothold among serious equine professionals, due to the increased strain placed on the hoof in sports, such as eventing and endurance riding.

Anatomy

The hoof is made up by an outer part, the hoof capsule (composed of various cornified specialised structures) and an inner, living part, containing soft tissues and bone. The cornified material of the hoof capsule is different in structure and properties in different parts. Dorsally, it covers, protects and supports P3 (also known as the coffin bone, pedal bone, PIII). Palmarly/plantarly, it covers and protects specialised soft tissues (tendons, ligaments, fibro-fatty and/or fibrocartilaginous tissues and cartilage). The upper, almost circular limit of the hoof capsule is the coronet (coronary band), having an angle to the ground of roughly similar magnitude in each pair of feet (i.e. fronts and backs). These angles may differ slightly from one horse to another, but not markedly. The walls originate from the coronet band. Walls are longer in the dorsal portion of the hoof (toe), intermediate in length in the lateral portion (quarter) and very short in palmar/plantar portion (heel). Heels are separated by an elastic, resilient structure named the 'frog'. In the palmar/plantar part of the foot, above the heels and the frog, there are two oval bulges named the 'bulbs'.

When viewed from the lower surface, the hoof wall's free margin encircles most of the hoof. The triangular frog occupies the centre area. Lateral to the frog are two grooves, deeper in their posterior portion, named 'collateral grooves'. At the heels, the palmar/plantar portion of the walls bend inward sharply, following the external surface of collateral grooves to form the bars. The lower surface of the hoof, from the outer walls and the inner frog and bars, is covered by an exfoliating keratinised material, called the 'sole'.

Just below the coronet, the walls are covered for about an inch by a cornified, opaque 'periople' material. In the palmar/plantar part of the hoof, the periople is thicker and more rubbery over the heels, and it merges with frog material. Not all horses have the same amount of periople. Dry feet tend to lack this substance, which can be substituted with a hoof dressing.

The Walls

The walls are considered as a protective shield covering the sensitive internal hoof tissues (like the exoskeleton of arthropods), as a structure devoted to dissipating the energy of concussion, and as a surface to provide grip on different terrains. They are elastic and very tough, and vary in thickness from 6 to 12 mm. The walls are composed of three distinct layers: the pigmented layer, the water line and the white line.

The *pigmented layer* is generated by the coronet, and its colour is just like that of the coronet skin from which it is derived. If the coronet skin has any dark patch, the walls show a parallel pigmented line, from the coronet to the ground, showing the wall's growth direction. This layer has predominately protective role, and is not as resistant to ground contact, where it can break and flake away.

The *water line* is built up by the coronet and by the wall's corium (the living tissue immediately beneath the walls). Its thickness increases proportionally to the distance from the coronet and, in the lower third of the walls, is thicker than the pigmented layer. It is very resistant to contact to the ground, and it serves mainly a support function.

The *white line* is the inner layer of the wall. It is softer and fibrous in structure and light in colour; white in a freshly trimmed hoof, yellowish or gray after exposure to air and dirt. From the underside of the healthy hoof, it is seen as a thin line joining the sole and the walls. The white line grows out from the laminar connections. Any visible derangement of the white line indicates some important derangement of laminar connections that fix the walls to the underlying P3 bone. Since the white line is softer than both the walls and the sole, it wears fast where it appears on the surface; it appears as a subtle groove between the sole and the walls, often with some debris or sand inside.

The three layers of the wall merge in a single mass and they grow downwards together. If the wall does not wear naturally, from sufficient movement on abrasive terrains, then it will protrude from the solar surface. It then becomes prone to breakage, and the healthy hoof will self-trim, by breaking or chipping off.

When a horseshoe is applied, it is fixed to the wall. Nails are driven in, oblique to the walls. They enter the wall at the outside edge of the white line and they emerge at the wall's surface, about 15 to 20 mm from the base of the wall.

The wall is anatomically analogous to the human finger or toe nail.

The Frog

The frog is a V shaped structure that extends forwards across about two-thirds of the sole. Its thickness grows from the front to the back and, at the back, it merges with the heel periople. In its midline, it has a central groove (sulcus), that extends up between the bulbs.

It is dark gray-blackish in colour and of a rubbery consistency, suggesting its role as shock absorber and grip tool on hard, smooth ground. Actually, the frog acts like a pump to move the blood back to the heart, a great distance from the relatively thin leg to the main organ of the circulatory system.

In the stabled horse, the frog does not wear, but degrades, due to bacterial and fungal activity, to an irregular, soft, slashed surface. In the free-roaming horse, it hardens into a callous consistency with a near-smooth surface.

It is anatomically analogous to the human fingertip.

The Sole

The sole has a whitish-yellowish, sometimes grayish colour. It covers the whole space from the perimetre of the wall to the bars and the frog, on the underside of the hoof. Its deep layer has a compact, waxy character and it is called 'live sole'. Its surface is variable in character as a result of ground contact. If there is no contact, as in shod hooves or when the walls are too long or the movement poor, the lower surface of the sole has a crumbly consistency, and it is easily abraded by scratching it with a hoofpick.

Conversely, it has a very hard consistency, with a smooth, bright surface, when there is a consistent, active contact with the ground. The front portion beneath the front of the pedal bone is called the 'sole callus'.

A stone bruise affects the sole of the horse's foot. It is often caused by a horse treading on a stone or sharp type of object, landings from high jumps and excessive exposure to snow. A major symptom is lameness.

The Bars

Bars are the inward folds of the wall, originating from the heels at an abrupt angle. The strong structure built up by the extremity of the heel and of the bar is named the 'heel buttress'. The sole between the heel walls and the bars is named the 'seat of corn', and it is a very important landmark used by natural hoof trimmers to evaluate the correct heel height. The bars have a three-layer structure, just like the walls. When overgrown, they bend outwards and cover the lower surface of the sole.

Internal Structure

The third phalanx (coffin bone; pedal bone; P3;) is completely (or almost completely) covered by the hoof capsule. It has a crescent shape and a lower cup-like concavity. Its external surface mirrors the wall's shape. The corium, a dermo-epidermal, highly vascularized layer between the wall and the coffin bone, has a parallel, laminar shape, and is named the laminae. Laminar connection has a key role in the strength and the health of the hoof. Beneath the rear part of the sole, there is the digital cushion, which separates the frog and the bulb from underlying tendons, joints and bones, providing cushioning protection. In foals and yearlings, the digital cushion is composed of fibro-fatty, soft tissue. In the adult horse, it hardens into a fibro cartilagineous tissue when sufficient, consistent concussion stimulates the back of the hoof. Normal transformation of the digital cushion into fibrocartilagineous tissue is now considered a key goal, both for prevention of, and for rehabilitation of recovering cases of navicular syndrome . The flexor tendon lays deeper, just along the posterior surface of the small pastern bone (PII) and navicular bone, and it connects with posterior surface of P3; the navicular functions as a pulley.

Hoof Mechanism

The horse hoof is not at all a rigid structure. It is elastic and flexible. Just squeezing the heels by hand will demonstrate that. When loaded, the hoof physiologically changes its shape. In part, this is a result of solar concavity, which has a variable depth, in the region of 1–1.5 cm. In part, it is a result of the arched shape of the lateral lower profile of the walls and sole, so that when an unloaded hoof touches a firm ground surface, there is only contact at toe and heels (active contact). A loaded hoof has a much greater area of ground contact (passive contact), covering the lower wall edge, most of the sole, bars and frog. Active contact areas can be seen as slightly protruding spots in the walls and in the callused sole.

The shape changes in a loaded hoof are complex. The plantar arch flattens, the solar concavity decreases in depth and heels spread. The hoof diametre increases to a 'dilated' configuration and P3 drops marginally into the hoof capsule. There is some recent evidence that a depression takes place in this phase, with blood pooling ('diastolic phase') mainly into the wall corium. When unloaded, the hoof restores its 'contracted' configuration, the pressure rises and the blood is squeezed out ('systolic phase'). There is a secondary pumping action, with the flexion of the foot, as it is raised.

The hoof mechanism ensures an effective blood circulation into the hoof, and it aids general circulation, too.

Time-related Changes of the Hoof

Hooves have to be considered as a plastic structure and their time-related, very complex changes can be considered in the short term (days/weeks), in the medium term (the horse's lifespan) and in the long term (the evolution of equids).

Hoof Changes in the Short Term

Just like the cornified layer of epidermis and of any mammalian nail, the hoof capsule is created only from epidermis, the outer living layer of the skin. From a microscopic point of view, epidermis is a multi-layered, specialised cornifying epithelium. It overlays the dermis, and it is separated from it by a basal lamina. It has no blood vessels and living cells acquire their oxygen and nutrients by fluid exchanges and molecular diffusion, from underlying dermis, flowing into microscopical spaces among individual cells. Products of metabolism are cleared by a reverse of this process. Epidermis growth take place by mitotic activity in its deepest layer, into the basal layer, with slow outward migration and maturation of cells. As these cells approach the surface, special proteins accumulate into their cytoplasm, then the cells die and 'dry', into microscopic, tightly-connected individual layers, composed mainly of keratin. The resulting 'dead' superficial layer serves a protective function, saving underlying living tissues from injury, from dehydration and from fungal and bacterial attack. The constant thickness of the cornified layer results most commonly from regular superficial exfoliation. When a specialised cornified structure has a particular toughness, as in nails and hair, little or no exfoliation occurs and the cornified structures must slowly migrate away from their original position.

Thus, the specialised cornified structures of the hoof are the wall, the sole, the frog and periople. The wall does not exfoliate at all; it is constantly growing downward (about 1 cm per month), and self-trims by wearing or chipping by ground contact, in wild and feral horses. Solar, frog and periople material grow outwards and exfoliate at the surface by ground contact and wearing. In the domesticated horse, movement and typical ground hardness are insufficient to allow self-trimming, so humans have to care for them, trimming the walls and the frog, and scraping off the dead sole.

Hoof Changes in the Medium Term

Front and hind hooves are identical in the foal, but differ visibly in the adult horse. This is good evidence of medium-term plasticity of the whole hoof shape, as a result of variation in its use. Slow changes in hoof shape occur under any consistent change in the horse's movement pattern and under a wide variety of pathological conditions. They can be seen now as a clear example of a complex adaptive system, a frequent feature of living beings and structures.

Self-adapting capabilities of the hooves show their maximal effectiveness in wild equids (but domesticated horses show this too, to a lesser extent), as shown by the perfect soundness of feral horses, such as Mustangs, in a wide variety of environments.

Hoof Changes in the Long Term

Equid hooves are the result of the 55-million-year evolution of the horse. Wild and domesticated *Equus* species share a very similar hoof shape and function. The present-day conformation of the hoof is a result of a progressive evolutionary loss of digits I, II, IV and V of the basal pentadactyl limb, with changes in bones, joints and hoof capsule. The resulting conformation allows a heavy, strong body to move with high speed on any ground, and most efficiently on open, hard, flat areas like prairies and deserts (i.e., 'cursorial specialisation').

Natural Hoof Care

Natural hoof care is the practice of keeping horses so that their hooves are worn down naturally and so do not suffer overgrowth, splitting and other disorders. Horseshoes are not used but domesticated horses may still require trimming, exercise and other measures to maintain a natural shape and degree of wear.

Within the natural hoof care philosophy, the term Barefoot horses refers to horses which are kept barefoot full time, as opposed to horses who are fitted with horse shoes. The hooves of barefoot horses are trimmed with special consideration to a barefoot lifestyle. The barefoot horse movement advocates a generalized use of barefoot horses, both in non-competitive and competitive riding, often coupled with a more natural approach to horse care. Keeping horses barefoot is seen in many parts of the world, including South America, Mongolia and other industrialized and non-industrialized cultures.

History

Horses were used for work and pleasure by man for thousands of years prior to the invention of horse shoes. Some of the oldest writings about the care of hooves are found in the works of Xenophon, a fourth century BC Greek cavalry commander, who wrote "naturally sound hooves get spoiled in most stalls," and included the instruction that their hooves should be toughened by putting a cobblestone area in their paddock, (a practice still in use today). The Ancient Greeks did not shoe their horses and Xenophon wrote of measures to strengthen horses' feet in his classic work on horsemanship:

> "To secure the best type of stable-yard, and with a view to strengthening the horse's feet, I would suggest to take and throw down loosely four or five waggon loads of pebbles, each as large as can be grasped in the hand, and about a pound in weight; the whole to be fenced round with a skirting of iron to prevent scattering. The mere standing on these will come to precisely the same thing as if for a certain portion of the day the horse were, off and on, stepping along a stony road; whilst being curried or when fidgeted by flies he will be forced to use his hoofs just as much as if he were walking. Nor is it the hoofs merely, but a surface so strewn with stones will tend to harden the frog of the foot also".

More recently, Jaime Jackson, who studied wild and domestic horse hooves, promoted the modern variant of natural hoof care.

Benefits of Barefooting

While horses have been used without shoes throughout history, the benefits of keeping horses barefoot has recently enjoyed increased popularity. Not only does the horse benefit with a healthier hoof in some cases, it can be less expensive to keep a horse barefoot, and many owners have learned to trim their horses' hooves themselves. As the health and movement benefits of barefooting have become more apparent in horses that have completed transition, horses are being competed barefoot in various sports (including dressage, show jumping, flat racing, steeplechase racing, trail riding and endurance riding).

Barefoot Trim

There are several styles of barefoot trim in use today, including the Wildhorse Trim, the 4-Point Trim, the Strasser Trim, among others. Some types, such as the 4-Point Trim can be used alone, or with shoes. Barefoot trims are marketed to the public as something different from the 'pasture' or 'field' trim farriers are trained to provide, taking into consideration hoof health and bony column angles, though each branded type of barefoot trim has its individual differences and there is no standardization or agreement between various barefoot advocacy groups. In contrast to 'farrier trims' which have served the needs of domestic horses for millennia, barefoot trims are marketed as though they are something different, designed by nature itself to maintain a healthy, sound hoof without the use of shoes, and aim to emulate the way in which hooves are maintained naturally in wild horse herds, like the assorted feral horse herds such as the American.

Mustang in the western United States, or the Australian Brumby, as well as of wild zebras and other wild equine populations. It has been observed in wild conditions, the hoof tends to make contact with the ground on four points, and the hoof wall does not contact the ground at all. This is another difference between the barefoot trim and the pasture trim, where the hoof wall was left long and in contact with the ground. Like wild horse populations, barefoot domestic horses can develop callouses on the soles of the hooves, allowing them to travel over all types of terrain without discomfort.

Important to the success of the barefoot trim is consideration for the domestic horse's environment and use and the effects this has on hoof balance, shape, and the comfort of the horse. Included in the objectives are:

1. shortening the hoof wall and heel to the outer edge of the concave sole for best hoof conformation; and
2. applying a rounded bevel ('mustang roll') to the bottom edge of the wall to allow for a correct breakover (the moment when the foot unloads and tips forward as it begins to lift off the ground) and to prevent chipping and flaring of the wall.

There is some research, but no scientific double blind studies, which indicates removing horseshoes and using barefoot trimming techniques can reduce or in some cases eliminate founder (laminitis) in horses and navicular syndrome.

Impact of Horseshoes

Removable iron horseshoes known as 'hipposandals' may have been invented by the Roman legions. Nailed-on shoes were certainly used in Europe by the Middle Ages.

Horses were shod with nailed-on horseshoes from the Middle Ages to the present, though well trained farriers also performed barefoot trimming for horses that did not require the additional protection of shoes. It has become standard practice to shoe most horses in active competition or work. However, there is a growing movement to eliminate shoes on working horses. Advocates of barefooting point out many benefits to keeping horses barefoot and present studies showing that improper shoeing can cause or exacerbate certain hoof ailments in the horse.

Damage from improperly fitted and applied horse shoes can be seen in a gradual distortion of hoof shape, along with other ailments. Hoof soles are often sensitive when going barefoot after a long period of having been shod.

It can take weeks to months to a year or more, depending o the horse's prior condition, before a horse is sound and usable on bare feet. During this transition period, the horse can be fitted with hoof boots which protect the soles of the feet until the horse has time to heal and build up callouses, though hoof boots, especially when not properly fitted and used, can cause hoof damage as well.

Hoof Health

The two things which can directly affect the health of the hoof are diet and exercise. Observers of wild horse populations note that the equine hoof stays in notably better condition when horses are in a herd situation and are free to move around 24 hours a day, as wild horses do, permitting good circulation inside the hoof. It is recommended that horses be allowed to walk at least 5 miles per day for optimum hoof health. The terrain should be varied, including gravel or hard surfaces and a water feature where the hooves can be wet occasionally.

Diet is very important too, as changes in feed can directly affect hoof health, most notably seen in cases of laminitis. Even some lots of hay may be high enough in sugar to cause laminitis. A healthy diet for horses currently with or prone to laminitis is based on free access to hay that has been tested for carbohydrate content and found to be less than 10 per cent WSC + starch, some mineral supplementation, with no grain. Feeds and forage with high levels of sugar (carbohydrates) correlate with higher risk of clinical or subclinical laminitis and with other hoof ailments.

Modern research by individuals such as Jaime Jackson and Tia Nelson have studied feral horses to observe the way in which their natural foraging and roaming affected their hooves. They noticed that the hooves of these horses had a different configuration from domestic horses kept in soft pasture, having shorter toes and thicker, stronger hoof walls.

Controversies Over the Barefoot Movement

The issue of which is better for the horse, shoes or barefoot, is the subject of some controversy. Opponents of the barefoot movement argue that domesticated horses are routinely put through abnormal levels of activity, stress, and strain, and their hooves undergo excessive wear and shock. Stable-kept horses are not exposed to the same environment as wild horses, which can affect their hoof quality.

Additionally, humans sometimes favour certain traits over hoof quality (such as speed), and will breed horses with poor hoof quality if they are exceptional athletes. This can lead to overall decreased hoof quality within a breed and in riding horses in general. Advocates of traditional hoof care suggest that shoeing is needed to protect the hoof from unnatural destruction, and that the horseshoe and its various incarnations has been necessary to maintain the horse's usability under extreme and unnatural conditions.

Horseshoe

A horseshoe is a U-shaped item made of metal or of modern synthetic materials, nailed or glued to the hooves of horses and some other draught animals. Like a shoe on a human, it is used to protect the animal's feet from wear and tear. Professional horseshoers, also called farriers or blacksmiths (more commonly used in the UK), attach horseshoes on the palmar surface of the hoof, usually by nailing through the insensitive hoof wall, which is anatomically similar to the human toenail, though much larger and thicker.

Horseshoes are available in a wide variety of materials and styles, developed for different types of horse and for the work they do. The most common materials are steel and aluminum, but specialized shoes may include use of rubber, plastic, magnesium, titanium, or copper.

Steel tends to be preferred in sports where a strong, long-wearing shoe is needed, such as polo, eventing, show jumping, and western riding events. Aluminum shoes are lighter, making them common in horse racing, where a lighter shoe is desired; and often facilitate certain types of desired movement, and so are favoured in the discipline of dressage. Some horseshoes have 'caulkins', 'caulks', or 'calks': protrusions at the toe and/or heels of the shoe, to provide additional traction.

When kept as a talisman, a horseshoe is said to bring good luck. Many believe that to hang it with the ends pointing upwards is good luck as it acts as a storage container of sorts for any good luck that happens to be floating by, whereas to hang it with the ends pointing down, is bad luck as all the good luck will fall out. Others believe that the shoe should be hung the other way, as it will then release its luck to the people around it. A stylized variation of the horseshoe is used for a popular throwing game, horseshoes.

Since the early history of domestication of the horse, it was noted that working animals were exposed to many conditions that created breakage or excessive hoof wear. Ancient people recognized the need for the walls (and sometimes the sole) of domestic horses' hooves to have additional protection over and above any natural hardness.

An early form of hoof protection was seen in ancient Asia, where horses' hooves were wrapped in rawhide, leather or other materials for both therapeutic purposes and protection from wear.

The nailed shoe was a relatively late invention. The ancient Greek horse trainer Xenophon mentioned nothing about horseshoes in his treatise on the care of military cavalry, nor did the *Digesta Artis Veterinariae* by Vegetius Renatus, written in AD 480, mention nailed-on shoes, though he accurately enumerated everything connected with an army forge in the time. There are early literary references in the Koran, circa AD 632, to 'war-horses... which strike fire, by dashing their hoofs against the stones...' which, if taken literally, is an effect that could be obtained only by shod horses, as barefoot hooves striking stone do not create sparks.

Because iron was a valuable commodity, and any worn out items were generally melted down and reused, it is difficult to locate clear archaeological evidence of the earliest horseshoes. From archaeological finds in Great Britain, it appears that the Romans attempted to protect their horses' feet with a strap-on, solid-bottomed 'hipposandal' that has a slight resemblance to the modern hoof boot.

Though the ancients were sufficiently impressed by the damage done to horses hoofs to devise certain forms of covering for them (in the shape of socks or sandals), the practice of nailing iron plates or rim-shoes to the hoof does not appear to have been introduced earlier than the 2nd century B.C., and was not commonly known till the close of the 5th century A.D., or in regular use till the middle ages. The evidence for the earlier date depends on the doubtful interpretations of designs on coins.

There is very little evidence of nailed-on shoes prior to AD 500 or 600, though there is speculation that the Gauls were the first to nail on metal horseshoes.

The nailed iron horseshoe first appeared in the archaeological record in Europe about 5th century A.D. when a horseshoe, complete with nails, was found in the tomb of the Frankish King Childeric I at Tournai, Belgium. The earliest clear written record of iron horseshoes is a reference to 'crescent figured irons and their nails' in AD.

Around 1000 AD, cast bronze horseshoes with nail holes became common in Europe. Common was a design with a scalloped outer rim and six nail holes. The 13th and 14th centuries brought the widespread manufacturing of iron horseshoes. By the time of the Crusades (1096-1270), horseshoes were widespread and frequently mentioned in various written sources. In that period, due to the value of iron, horseshoes were even accepted in lieu of coin to pay taxes.

By the 13th century, shoes were forged in large quantities and could be bought ready-made. Hot shoeing, the process of shaping a heated horseshoe immediately before placing it on the horse, became common in the 16th century. From the need for horseshoes, the craft of blacksmithing became 'one of the great staple crafts of medieval and modern times and contributed to the development of metallurgy'.

In 1835, the first U.S. patent for a horseshoe manufacturing machine capable of making up to sixty horseshoes per hour was issued to Henry Burden.

In the mid 19th century Canada, marsh horseshoes kept horses from sinking into the soft intertidal mud during dike-building. In a common design, a metal horseshoe holds a flat wooden shoe in place.

Physical Stresses Requiring Horseshoes

- **Abnormal stress:** Horses' hooves can become quite worn out when subjected to the added weight and stress of a rider, pack load, cart, or wagon.

  These bar shoes are commonly used in corrective shoeing, to help support the heels.
- **Corrective shoeing:** The shape, weight, and thickness of a horseshoe can significantly affect the horse's gait. Farriers may forge custom shoes to help horses with bone or musculature problems in their legs, or fit commercially available remedial shoes.
- **Traction:** Traction devices such as borium for ice, horse shoe studs for muddy or slick conditions, calks, carbide-tipped road nails and rims are useful for performance horses such as eventers, show jumpers, polo ponies, and other horses that perform at high speeds, over changing terrain, or in less-than-ideal footing.

- **Gait Manipulation:** Some breeds such as the Saddlebred, Tennessee Walking Horse, and other gaited horses are judged on their high-stepping movement. Special shoeing can help enhance their natural movement.

Horseshoeing Theories and Debates

Horseshoes have always been viewed as an aid to assist horses' hooves when subjected to the various unnatural conditions brought about by domestication, whether due to work conditions or stabling and management. Countless generations of domestic horses bred for size, colour, speed, and many other traits with little regard for hoof quality and soundness make some breeds more dependent on horseshoes than feral horses such as mustangs, which develop strong hooves as a matter of natural selection.

Nonetheless, domestic horses do not always require shoes. There is near-universal agreement among farriers that when possible, a barefoot hoof, at least for part of every year, is a healthy option for most horses.

However, other farriers are equally adamant that horseshoes have their place and can help prevent excess or abnormal hoof wear and injury to the foot. Many farriers agree that some horses may even be able to go without shoes year-round, using temporary protection such as hoof boots for short-term use.

Recently, there has been a renewed debate over the traditional role of horseshoes. Observations of feral horses and barefoot domestic horses in natural boarding situations (including being kept on roomy pasture, not in stalls) have provided additional evidence that domesticated horses can grow hooves as healthy as those of feral horses and may not need shoes as often as many people think. Proponents of this idea, also known as the barefoot horse movement, argue that with proper care, horses may never need shoes at any time once they have been properly transitioned. Thus, the debate of when, where, why and whether to use horseshoes is a hot topic today.

Process of Shoeing

Shoeing, when performed correctly, causes no pain to the animal. Farriers trim the insensitive part of the hoof, which is the same area into which they drive the nails. This is analogous to a manicure on a human fingernail, only on a much larger scale.

Before beginning to shoe, the farrier removes the old shoe using *pincers* (shoe pullers) and trims the hoof wall to the desired length with *nippers*, a sharp pliers-like tool, and the sole and frog of the hoof with a *hoof knife*. Shoes do not allow the hoof to wear down as it naturally would in the wild, and it can then become too long.

The coffin bone inside the hoof should line up straight with both bones in the pastern. If the excess hoof is not trimmed, the bones will become misaligned, which would place stress on the legs of the animal.

Shoes are then measured to the foot and bent to the correct shape using a *hammer and anvil*, and other modifications, such as taps for shoe studs, are added. Farriers may either cold shoe, in which he bends the metal shoe without heating it, or hot shoe, in which he places the metal in a forge before bending it.

Hot shoeing can be more time-consuming, and requires the farrier to have access to a forge, however it usually provides a better fit, as the mark made on the hoof from the hot shoe can show how even it lies. It also allows the farrier to make more modifications to the shoe, such as drawing toe- and quarter-clips. The farrier must take care not to hold the hot shoe against the hoof too long, as the heat can damage the hoof.

Hot shoes are placed in water to cool them off. The farrier then nails the shoes on, by driving the nails into the hoof wall at the white line of the hoof. The nails are shaped in such a way that they bend outward as they are driven in, avoiding the sensitive inner part of the foot, so that they emerge on the sides of the hoof. When the nail has been completely driven, the farrier cuts off the sharp points and uses a *clincher* (a form of tongs made especially for this purpose) or a clinching block with hammer to bend the rest of the nail so it is almost flush with the hoof wall. This prevents the nail from getting caught on anything, but also helps to hold the nail (and therefore the shoe) in place.

The farrier then uses a *rasp* (large file), to smooth the edge where it meets the shoe and eliminate any sharp edges left from cutting off the nails.

Shoeing Mistakes

Mistakes are sometimes made by even a skilled farrier, especially if the horse does not stand still. This may sometimes result in a nail coming too close to the sensitive part of the hoof (putting pressure on it), or a nail that is driven slightly into the sensitive hoof, called 'quicking' or nail pricking. This occurs when a nail penetrates the wall and hits the sensitive internal structures of the foot.

Quicking results in bleeding and pain and the horse may show signs of lameness or may become lame in following days. Whenever it happens, the farrier must remove the offending nail. Usually a horse that is quicked will react immediately, though some cases where the nail is close to sensitive structures may not cause immediate problems. These mistakes are made occasionally by anyone who shoes horses, and in most cases is not an indication that the farrier is unskilled. It happens most commonly when horses move around while being shod, but also may occur if the hoof wall is particularly thin (common in Thoroughbreds), or if the hoof wall is brittle or damaged. It may also occur with an inexperienced or unskilled horseshoer who misdrives a nail, uses a shoe that is too small, or has not fitted the shoe to the shape of the horse's hoof. Occasionally, manufacturing defects in nails or shoes may also cause a misdriven nail that quicks a horse.

However, the term 'farrier' implies a professional horseshoer with skill, education, and training. Some people who shoe horses are untrained or unskilled, and likely to do more harm than good for the horse. People who do not understand the horse's foot will not trim the hoof correctly. This can cause serious problems for the animal, resulting in chronic lameness and damage to the hoof wall. Poor trimming will usually place the hoof at an incorrect angle, leave the foot laterally unbalanced and may cut too much off certain areas of the hoof wall, or trim too much of the frog or sole. Some horseshoers will rasp the hoof down to fit an improperly shaped or too-small size of shoe, which is damaging to the movement of the horse and can damage the hoof itself if trimmed or rasped too short. A poor horseshoer can also make mistakes in the shoeing process itself, not only quicking a horse, but also putting shoe on crooked, using the wrong type of shoe for the job at hand, shaping the shoe improperly, or setting it on too far forward or back.

CHAPTER 14

Horse Teeth

Horses' teeth are often used to estimate the animal's age, hence the sayings 'long in the tooth', 'straight from the horse's mouth' and 'Don't look a gift horse in the mouth'.

Types of Teeth

At five years of age a horse has between 36 and 44 teeth. All horses have:

- Twelve premolars and twelve molars commonly known as cheek teeth or jaw teeth.
- Twelve incisors, or front teeth.

Additionally, a horse may have:

- Four or five canine teeth (tushes, tusks) between the molars and incisors. Generally all male horses have four canines. However, few female horses (less than 28%) have canines, and those that do usually have only one or two, which many times are only partially erupted.
- Between zero and four wolf teeth, which are vestigial premolars and *not* canines as the name may suggest. About 13-32 per cent of all horses also are born with wolf teeth, with most of those having only one or two. They are equally common in male and female horses and much more likely to be on the upper jaw. If present these can cause problems in the bitting of the horse as they can interfere with the horse's bit contact, and may also make it difficult to rasp the second premolar. Therefore, wolf teeth are commonly removed.

Continuous Eruption and Loss

A horse's incisors, premolars, and molars, once fully developed, continue to erupt as the grinding surface is worn down through chewing. A young adult horse will have teeth which are 4.5-5 inches long, but the majority of the crown remaining below the gumline in the dental socket.

The rest of the tooth will slowly emerge from the jaw, erupting about 1/8″ each year, as the horse ages. When the animal reaches old age, the crowns of the teeth are very short and the teeth are often lost altogether. Very old horses, if lacking molars, may need to have their fodder ground up and soaked in water to create a soft mush for them to eat in order to obtain adequate nutrition. Commercially prepared hay pellets and Hay cubes can be moistened for this purpose. Beet pulp may also be a suitable feed.

Contrary to popular belief, the bit of a bridle is not held between the horse's teeth, but lies in the 'interdental space'. This space lacks teeth, providing an area for the bit to rest without forcing the jaws open, and occurs between the cheek teeth and the incisors (or canines, should the horse have them).

However, if the bridle is adjusted so that the bit rests too low, or (more commonly) too high, it may push against the teeth and cause discomfort.

Sometimes, a 'bit seat' is filed in the first cheek tooth. A veterinarian rounds the surface, so that, when the bit is pulled, the flesh of the cheek is not pushed into the sharp edge of the tooth. Although this practice is disputed, and most agree that an extreme bit seat can indeed be harmful, many veterinarians believe it makes riding more comfortable for the horse.

It is possible to age a horse using signs of the tooth eruption and wear. However, this is not an exact science, and become increasingly difficult after the horse is 'aged'. Horses are individuals, and two horses of the same age may have different wear patterns.

There are 24 deciduous teeth (also known as milk, temporary, or baby teeth). These come out in pairs, and are pushed out later by the permanent teeth. The number of permanent teeth may vary, depending on whether the horse has wolf teeth or canines. Most mares have 36, and most male horses have 40.

By age five, all permanent teeth have usually erupted. The horse is then said to have a 'full' mouth.

However, individual horses vary, and some breeds and types of horse are known to have differing eruption timelines. These include:

- **Shetland ponies:** The middle and corner incisor (both deciduous and permanent) usually erupt later than the average horse.
- **Draft horses and miniature horses:** The permanent middle and corner incisors usually erupt later than average.

Estimating Age Using Wear Patterns

After five years, the age of a horse can only be conjectured by study of the wear patterns on the incisors, shape, the angle at which the incisors meet, and other factors. The wear of teeth may also be affected by diet, natural abnormalities, and cribbing.

- **Cups:** are hollow and rectangular or oval in shape, appearing on the tables of the permanent incisors, that wear away over time. In general, cups are worn away on the lower central incisors by age 6, the lower intermediates by age 7, and corners at age 8. The cups of the upper central incisors are worn away by 9 years of age, the upper intermediate incisors by 10, and the corners by 11. When all the cups are gone, the horse is referred to as 'smooth mouthed'. In the past, dishonest dealers would 'bishop' the teeth of old horses, usually by burning an indentation into the teeth, to imitate cups: but this practice was detectable by the absence of the white edge of enamel which always surrounds the real cup, by the shape of the teeth, and other marks of age about the animal.

- **Pulp mark/Dental star:** After some wear has occurred on the teeth, the central pulp cavity is exposed, and the tooth is marked by a 'dental star' or 'pulp mark' that is smaller than the incisor cups. These begin as a dark line in front of the dental cup, which grows in size and becomes more oval in shape as the cups are worn away. Dental stars are usually first visible at age 6, on the animal's lower central incisors, and very visible by age 8. They appear on the lower intermediates by age 9, and on the other incisors between the ages of 10-12 years.
- **Hook/Notch:** A hook appears on the upper corner incisor around age 7, and disappears by age 8. It reappears around age 13, again disappearing about 1 year later.
- **Galvayne's Groove:** The Galvayne's groove occurs on the upper corner incisor, producing a vertical line, and is helpful in approximating the age of older horses. It generally first appears at age 10, reaches half-way down the tooth by age 15, is completely down the tooth at age 20. It then begins to disappear, usually half-way gone by age 25, and completely gone by age 30.
- **Lower jaw shape:** Older horses may appear to have a lean, shallow lower jaw, as the roots of the teeth have begun to disappear. Younger horses may seem to have a lumpy jaw, due to the presence of permanent teeth within the jaw.
- **Angle and Shape of the incisors:** As the horse ages, the angle of the incisors generally becomes more acute, slanting forward. The incisors gradually change their form as the horse ages, becoming round, oval, and then triangular.

Like humans, horses can develop a variety of dental problems, some which may be very serious and require surgery. To head off any potential issues an annual exam is recommended and especially if the horse exhibits any signs of feeding problems. Abnormal teeth not only affect the horse's comfort while chewing,but may also manifest themselves as disobediences or other performance issues while the animal is ridden. Tooth issues may have an impact on how the horse uses its entire body. Treatment can be performed by an equine veterinarian, ideally one that specializes in horse's teeth check their animals' teeth regularly. In some nations, non-veterinarian specialists in equine dentistry may also perform equine tooth care services.

Problems due to Wear Patterns

Many dental problems in horses are related to the fact that their teeth erupt continuously throughout their life. Horses are evolved to graze nearly continuously, often on rough forage in semi-arid climates. Their teeth are designed to wear against the tooth above or below as the horse chews, thus preventing excess growth. The upper jaw is wider than the lower one. Sharp edges occur on the outside of the upper molars and the inside of the lower molars, as they are unopposed by an opposite grinding surface.

There are many times when tooth wear is not even, and the horse may develop sharp edges on their teeth that reduce chewing efficiency of the teeth, interfere with jaw motion, and in extreme cases can cut the tongue or cheek, making eating and riding painful.

In the wild, natural foodstuffs may have allowed teeth to wear more evenly. Because many modern horses often graze on lusher, softer forage than their ancestors, and are also frequently fed grain or other concentrated feed, it is possible some natural wear may be reduced in the domestic horse. On the other hand, this same uneven wear in the wild may have at times contributed to a shorter lifespan. Modern wild horses live an estimated 20 years at most, while a domesticated horse, depending on breed and management, quite often lives 25 to 30 years. Thus, because domesticated animals also live longer, they may simply have more time to develop dental issues that their wild forebears never faced.

Sharp enamel points usually develop on the outside of the upper cheekteeth (grinders) and the inside of the lower cheekteeth. 'Hooks' also commonly occur on the front of the first upper cheekteeth or at the posterior end of the last lower molars.

A *step mouth* occurs when one cheek tooth grows longer than the others in that jaw. This is usually because the tooth opposing that particular one, located in the opposite jaw, was missing or broken, and therefore could not wear down its opponent.

A *wave mouth* occurs when at least two of the cheek teeth are higher than the others, so that, when viewed from the side, the grinding surfaces produce a wave-like pattern rather than a straight line. This can lead to periodontal disease and excessive wear of some of the teeth, eventually leading to some discomfort or trouble with mastication.

A *shear mouth* occurs when the grinding surfaces of the cheek teeth are severely sloped on each individual tooth (so the inner side of the teeth are much higher or lower than the outer side of the teeth). This may result in an angle at 60-75 degrees, opposed to the normal 15-degree angle seen on most horses. Again, the chewing motion is severely affected.

Bite Problems

Horses may also experience an overbite/brachygnathism (parrot mouth), or an underbite/prognathism (sow mouth, monkey mouth). These may affect how the incisors wear. In severe cases, the horse's ability to graze may be affected. Horses also sometimes suffer from equine malocclusion where there is a misalignment between their upper and lower jaws.

The curvature of the incisors may also vary from the normal, straight bite. The curvature may be dorsal or ventral . These curvatures may be the result of an incisor malocclusion (e.g. ventral=overbite/dorsal=underbite). The curvature may also be diagonal, stemming from a wear pattern,offset incisors, or pain in the cheek teeth (rather than the incisors), which causes the horse to chew in one direction over the other.

Other common problems include abscessed, loose, infected, or cracked teeth, retained deciduous teeth, and plaque build up. Wolf teeth may also cause problems, and are many times removed, as are retained caps.

Signs of possible dental problems:

- Reluctance to eat, does not finish food, or eats slowly.
- Dull coat, weight loss, and ioss of condition.
- Quidding (horse drops partially chewed food while chewing), or chewing with the mouth open.
- Turning of head to the side while chewing.
- Excessive salivation while eating, blood in saliva.
- Foul smell from mouth or nose.
- Draining of abscess from the jaw.
- Discharge from one nostril.
- Undigested feed in manure.
- Colic.
- Excessive salivation.
- Facial swelling.

Additionally, many problems under saddle can be tooth-related, such as:

- Head tossing
- Difficulty in picking up the canter or in performing flying changes
- Tilting of the head while riding or difficulty in bending
- Refusal to collect
- Bucking
- Difficulty in getting the horse 'on-the-bit' (especially if the horse tends to go behind the bit)
- Gaping the mouth

For many performance-related problems, it is often best to check the teeth to rule out that factor.

Prevention of Dental Problems

To help prevent dental problems, it is recommended to get a horse's teeth checked by a veterinarian or equine dental technician every 6 months. However, regular checks may be needed more often for individuals, especially if the horse is very young or very old. Additionally, the horse's teeth should be checked if it is having major performance problems or showing any of the above signs of a dental problem.

Many horses require floating (or rasping) of teeth once every 12 months, although this, too, is variable and dependent on the individual horse. In young horses, twenty four teeth are deciduous or 'caps'. These are the first three premolars of each arcade (not including wolf teeth) and all incisors. Caps are pushed out by the new permanent teeth, starting late in a horse's two year old year. Caps will eventually shed on their own, but may cause discomfort when still loose, requiring extraction. The first four or five years of a horse's life are when the most growth-related changes occur and hence frequent checkups may prevent problems from developing. Equine teeth get harder as the horse gets older and may not have rapid changes during the prime adult years of life, but as horses become aged, particularly from the late teens on, additional changes in incisor angle and other molar growth patterns often necessitate frequent care. Once a horse is in its late 20s or early 30s, molar loss becomes a concern. Floating involves a veterinarian wearing down the surface of the teeth, usually to remove sharp points or to balance out the mouth. However, the veterinarian must be careful not to take off too much of the surface, or there will not be enough roughened area on the tooth to allow it to properly tear apart food. Additionally, too much work on a tooth can cause thermal damage (which could lead to having to extract the tooth), or expose the sensitive interior of the tooth (pulp). A person without a veterinary degree who performs this service is called a *horse floater* or equine dental technician.

In Popular Culture

The common folk saying 'don't look a gift horse in the mouth' is taken from the era when gifting horses was common. The teeth of a horse are a good indication of the age of the animal, and it was considered rude to inspect the teeth of a gifted animal as you would one that you were purchasing. The saying is used in reference to being an ungrateful gift receiver.

CHAPTER 15

Horse Show

A Horse show is a judged exhibition of horses and ponies. Many different horse breeds and equestrian disciplines hold competitions worldwide, from local to the international levels. Most horse shows run from one to three days, sometimes longer for major, all-breed events or national and international championships in a given discipline or breed. Most shows consist of a series of different performances, called *classes,* wherein a group of horses with similar training or characteristics compete against one another for awards and, often, prize money.

International Organizations and Competition

There are ten international disciplines run under rules established by the *Fédération équestre internationale* (FEI):

- Combined driving
- Dressage
- Endurance riding
- Eventing
- Horseball
- Paraequestrianism (Paralympic equestrian sport for athletes with disabilities)
- Reining
- Show jumping
- Tent pegging
- Vaulting.

The rules of the FEI govern competitions open to riders from all nations, including the Olympic games and the World Equestrian Games.

At the other end of the competition spectrum, Pony Club is an international movement that teaches young people riding skills suitable for eventing and other English riding competition.

To help develop positive experience and good sportsmanship, Pony Clubs also sponsor horse shows open only to young people under the age of 18 and their horses. Various nations also have their own programmes for developing young equestrians, such as the 4-H programme in the United States.

Horse Shows within Various Countries

Australia

Horse shows in Australia are governed by Equestrian Australia.

Canada

The governing body for Equestrian activities in Canada is Equine Canada (EC).

United Kingdom

In the United Kingdom there is a distinct difference between 'horse competitions' such as dressage or eventing and horse shows. Horse shows provide an opportunity for riders and owners to exhibit their animals without taking part in any of the Olympic disciplines. Classes are divided into ridden and in-hand sections and there are many different classes for different horses and ponies. For example, there are classes for Mountain and moorland pony breeds, show hunters, show hacks, equitation, and various show pony classes. Many clubs hold riding club classes, where a horse or pony must perform a short 'show' (solo performance) and jump a single fence that varies in height from 2 feet to 3 feet 3 inches. Most shows also include show jumping and working hunter sections.

The British Horse Society oversees many shows at national, regional and local level as does the Pony Club, the British Show Pony Society and the British Show Horse Association. Breed societies, particularly those that look after the Welsh pony and the Arabian horse also organise their own shows. At local, unaffiliated level, riding clubs across Britain organise regular shows, which are often staffed by volunteers. The newly formed Showing Council is working towards officially overseeing all horse shows (non-FEI disciplines).

The Olympic equestrian disciplines are overseen by the British Equestrian Federation. However, there are several subdivisions within the federation. Dressage competitions are held separately from regular horse shows, and are overseen by British Dressage. Show jumping competitions are overseen by the British Showjumping Association (BSJA), while one day and three day eventing are overseen by British Eventing.

U.S.A.

The United States Equestrian Federation is the American national body for equestrian sport and as such is also the recognized entity overseeing the Olympic-level United States Equestrian Team. It also organizes and sponsors horse shows for many horse breeds who wish to utilize the drug testing, judge certification and standardize rulemaking process of the USEF. In addition, it sanctions events in disciplines and lower-level competitive areas that are not internationally recognized, such as show hunter and equitation. Other US organisations such as the National Cutting Horse Association , United States Eventing Association (USEA) and United States Dressage Federation (USDF) organize competitions for specific disciplines, such as Cutting, and some breed organisations such as the American Quarter Horse Association sanction their own breed-specific shows.

Horse shows in the United States take several forms: Some are restricted to a particular breed, others are 'open' or 'all-breed' horse shows, which offer both classes open to all breeds as well as breed-specific classes for many different breeds. In the last few decades, American "open" horse shows have tended to become specialized by discipline into hunter-jumper or 'sport horse' shows, dressage shows, and shows featuring English or Western riding events. However, there are still some multi-day, all-breed events that feature multiple breeds and disciplines.

Structure

There are a range of competitive equestrian events available and specific offerings range widely by nation and even by region within a given country. However, in North America, most horse shows provide the following range of classes:

- The English riding classes fall into two primary styles, hunt seat and saddle seat. 'Hunt type' or sport horse classes include dressage, show jumping and show hunters, Eventing (also called horse trials), and English pleasure or Hunter Under Saddle, also known as a 'flat' class, where the event is judged on presentation, manners and rideability of the horse). 'Saddle seat' or 'Saddle type' classes are all on the flat and are mostly variations on English Pleasure, though the high action 'Park' style classes differ because they emphasize brilliant trotting action. Equitation classes judge the form and ability of the rider.

Show jumping, eventing and dressage are sometimes called 'Olympic' events, because they are the equestrian sports included in the Olympic Games.

Western or Stock horse competition includes working cattle events, such as cutting, team penning and working cow horse in the USA, and campdrafting in Australia. They also include 'dry' classes (without cattle) that include western pleasure, reining and equitation.

There are also specialized classes for draft horse showing, and a number of events for horses and ponies driven in harness, including Fine Harness classes for Saddle Seat-type horses, Roadster classes that use equipment similar to that of harness racing, and the FEI-sanctioned sport of combined driving. Miniature horses also have their own shows, with a number of specialized classes.

Most horse shows offer Halter classes, also called 'breeding', 'conformation', or 'In-hand' classes. In these classes the horse is led without a saddle, not ridden, and its conformation and gaits are judged. To train young equestrians in halter showing techniques, horse showmanship classes (also called Showmanship in hand or youth showmanship), are offered. They are the halter equivalent of equitation, in that the handler, not the horse, is judged on his or her abilities.

Classes may be broken down by the age of horse or rider, by the number of first place ribbons earned by horse or rider, and by size or breed of horse (or pony). In addition, there is a near-infinite range of regional or specialty classes that may be offered. Various types of costume classes are frequently offered; sidesaddle classes are common; a 'leadline' or 'walk-trot' division may be offered for small children or very inexperienced riders; and assorted 'freestyle' classes, where a horse and rider perform a routine set to music, are also popular.

Rodeos and horse pulling competitions are not technically horse shows, but they are competitive equestrian events, often with a great deal of prize money. Equestrian vaulting is not usually seen at ordinary horse shows, even though it is an FEI-recognized equestrian sport. Games, such as Gymkhana or O-Mok-See competition are usually held separately from ordinary horse shows, though a few of these 'speed' events may be thrown in as 'fun classes', particularly at 4-H, Pony Club, and other small shows.

Awards

Prize Money

Prize money is sometimes awarded, particularly at larger competitions. The sum varies by the placing of the rider, the prestige of the show, and the difficulty of the class. Horse Shows do not offer cash purses as large as those the thoroughbred racing industry, though a few of the biggest show jumping, cutting and reining competitions may offer purse money into the low five figures. However, most show horses in the United States, especially those at the amateur levels, rarely win significant cash prizes during their show career. At best, a solid competitor might break even on entry fees and, if they are quite lucky, cover some travel expenses. Most money made from showing horses is indirectly earned by breeding fees paid for top horses, the sale of their offspring, or from the training fees paid to top trainers.

Trophies

Trophies are usually awarded to the first place horse in a class, depending on the size of the show. In a championship event, trophies may be awarded to both the champion and the reserve champion, and at a national or international show, trophies are sometimes given to the top five to ten competitors.

Medals

Medals are given at international events such as the World Equestrian Games and the Olympics. Usually only three medals, Gold, Silver, and Bronze, are awarded to the top three individuals or teams.

Ribbons

Ribbons are often given for the top placings in a class. Often ribbons are given through the top six place entries, although some of the larger shows may award ribbons to the top ten. Ribbon colour varies from country to country.

RINGMASTER (HORSE SHOW)

A horse show ringmaster, sometimes also called a ring steward, is an individual who works in the centre of an arena at a horse show and carries out many duties to assist the judge and other officials. Unlike a *Horse show steward* or the judge, the ringmaster is not a licensed official of the show. At the biggest shows, the ringmaster may be a paid employee of the show, but at smaller shows is apt to be a volunteer.

In a few competitions, usually national championships or other shows of national importance, the ringmaster may be colourfully attired in a manner similar to the ringmastger of a circus or the bugler at a horse race. In such cases, this official wears a top hat (or hunting cap for hunting and jumping classes), white jodhpurs, and scarlet ('pink') guard coat. More commonly, at ordinary horse shows, the ringmaster will simply wear neat clothing and comfortable shoes, similar to the attire of the judge.

Rarer still, is the practice of having the ringmaster summon each class of exhibitors and horses, usually by blowing a trumpet, fox horn, or carriage or coach horn. More commonly, the show announcer simply performs the task, simply calling each class by number and title over the public address system.

The duties and responsibilities of a ringmaster of a horse show varies by discipline and geographical region. These can include:

- summoning the class;
- keeping the show running smoothly and listening to the judge. The ringmaster does not help to judge the class in any way;
- policing the ring by being alert to safety issues and watching the horses, riders or drivers;
- passing communications from the judge to the announcer to call for specific gaits in a class, for the line up, etc.;
- transmitting the judges' cards to the scorers or the announcer; acting as a scribe (trail or reining usually);
- restraining an unruly horse (they should be physically able horsemen), helping a rider or driver that is in trouble, etc.;

- serving as a timer when a shoe has been thrown during a class and a specified time is allowed to find and have the farrier replace the shoe;
- working with ring crew for each class set up;
- pinning ribbons or distributing ribbons to winners;
- supporting the steward(s) in identifying questionable equipment and attire.

In Tennessee, the ringmaster has a legal duty under cruelty to animals statutes to disqualify and report to authorities certain animal abuses.

Some notable individuals who have served long careers as ringmasters in the United States include Dutch White, Honey Craven, Vincent Wholey, and Paul Copanas.

CHAPTER 16

Horse Artillery

Horse artillery was a type of light, fast-moving and fast-firing artillery which provided highly mobile fire support to European and American armies (especially to cavalry units) from the 17th to the early 20th century. A precursor of modern self-propelled artillery, it consisted of light cannons or howitzers attached to light but sturdy two-wheeled carriages called caissons or limbers, with the individual crewmen riding either the horses or the caissons into battle. This was in contrast to field artillery where the pieces were heavier and the crew marched on foot.

Once in position, horse artillery crews were trained to quickly dismount, deploy or 'unlimber' their guns, then rapidly fire grapeshot, shells or round shot at the enemy. They could then just as rapidly 'limber-up' (reattach the guns to the caissons), remount, and be ready to move to a new position, similar to the shoot-and-scoot tactics of their modern counterparts.

Horse artillery was highly versatile and often supported friendly cavalry units by disrupting enemy infantry formations such as infantry squares with rapid concentrated fire. This would leave the enemy infantry vulnerable to cavalry charges. Their mobility also enabled them to outmaneuver enemy foot artillery units, and to act as a rearguard (in concert with friendly cavalry) to cover the retreat of slower units. A full battery could have a combined front of riders over 50 men strong. If the horse artillery was mistaken for cavalry, the enemy might receive an unpleasant surprise when the towed batteries wheeled around, unlimbered, loaded, sighted and opened fire in less than a minute.

History

Essentially a hybrid of cavalry and artillery, irregular horse artillery units were first used in the 17th century during the Thirty Years' War by Lennart Torstenson. Torstenson was the artillery expert of Gustavus

Adolphus, and used them to provide cavalry with the fire support it needed to deal with massed infantry formations without sacrificing their speed and mobility. Gustavus Adolphus had previously tried intermixing infantry units with cavalry, and this was somewhat successful since the cavalry at that time did not charge the enemy at full gallop.

Others tried to combine firepower with mobility by using novel cavalry tactics such as the caracole, but these slowed the cavalry down and proved largely ineffective. The best solutions involved creating hybrid units of mounted infantry, most notably dragoons. Although they proved highly useful and versatile troops, whether they fired mounted or dismounted, they still had to slow down or stop at least temporarily, and thereby losing their main advantages as cavalry.

In the early 18th century the Russian army began equipping cavalry formations with small units of light horse artillery equipped with 2-pound cannons, and portable 3-pound mortars which were transported on horseback (the weights refer to the size of the projectiles, not the artillery pieces.) Though not decisive by themselves, these units inflicted losses on Prussian troops and influenced Frederick the Great to form the first regular horse artillery unit in 1759.

18th Century Modernization

Frederick understood that the greatest threat to massed infantry was concentrated artillery fire. He realized that even small and relatively light guns could severely disrupt or destroy infantry units if they could be brought in close enough and fire often enough. But since even light foot artillery travelled at the speed of a marching soldier, the solution was to make every artilleryman a part-time horseman. Through relentless drill and discipline Frederick emphasized mobility and speed in all phases of their operations. The unit consisted of a battery of six 6-pound cannons with 48 men, including 3 officers. The battery was wiped out and reformed twice in that same year at the Battle of Kunersdorf and the Battle of Maxen. Despite the setbacks, the new arm had proved so successful that it was quickly reorganized and by the start of the French Revolutionary Wars in 1792 consisted of three companies of 605 men and batteries consisting of eight 6-pound guns and one 7-pound mortar each.

French artillery, engineer and general had served with the military mission to Prussia as well as fought against Frederick in the Seven Years' War. After that war he made numerous technical improvements to French cannons which made them lighter, faster and much easier to aim. These improvements proved a great advantage to horse artillery as well. Later, the British army officer invented a deadly new type of ammunition that was put to effective use by horse artillery units.

The popularity of the new type of unit caught on quickly with other armies. Austria organized a limited amount of 'cavalry artillery' in 1778 where most of the gun crew rode specially designed, padded gun carriages called *Wursts* ('sausages'), rather than on separate horses, into battle. Hanover formed its first cavalry batteries in 1786 and the Hanoverian general Victor von Trew performed several trials in 1791 which proved the great speed and efficiency by which an all-mounted crew could operate. At this time the Danish army had also formed mounted artillery units and by 1792 Sweden had formed its first regular riding batteries, followed by Great Britain in 1793, Russia in 1794 and Portugal in 1796.

19th Century Zenith

During the Napoleonic Wars, horse artillery would be used extensively and effectively in every major battle and campaign. The largest and probably most efficient horse artillery of any nation was that of the French revolutionary army which was first formed in 1792. The French units were especially well-trained and disciplined since the newly-formed arm had proved very popular and could draw on a considerable number of recruits. By 1795 it had grown to eight regiments of six six-gun batteries each, making it the largest horse artillery force ever assembled.

Horse artillery units generally used lighter pieces, pulled by six horses. 9-pounders were pulled by eight horses, and heavier artillery pieces needed a team of twelve. With the individual riding horses required for officers, surgeons and other support staff, as well as those pulling the artillery guns and supply wagons, an artillery battery of six guns could require 160 to 200 horses. Horse artillery usually came under the command of cavalry divisions, but in some battles, such as Waterloo, horse artillery was used as a rapid response force, repulsing attacks and assisting the infantry. Agility was important; the ideal artillery horse was around 15-16 hands high (150-160 cm, 60 to 64 inches), strongly built, but able to move quickly.

In the Mexican-American War, the U.S. Army horse artillery, or 'flying artillery' played a decisive role in several key battles. In the American Civil War, various elements of the horse artillery of the Army of the Potomac were at times grouped together in the U.S. Horse Artillery Brigade.

Modern Decline

As technology advanced and the firepower of infantry and foot artillery increased, the role of cavalry, and thus the horse artillery, began to decline. It continued to be used and improved into the early 20th century, seeing action during and in between both world wars. In the First World War Russia, like some other countries, equipped the artillery batteries of its cavalry divisions with the same field gun used by other units. France and the United Kingdom, however, used specialist horse guns.

Subsequently, the cavalry and horse artillery units rearmed with tanks and self-propelled artillery. As with the cavalry, though, certain artillery units, for instance the Royal Horse Artillery, retain their old designations. Among the last genuine regular horse artillery units were the Wendes Ridande Artilleri of the Swedish Army, which was finally disbanded in 1927. A form of riding artillery using heavy machine guns called tachankas were used by the Polish and Russian in I World War, the Russian Civil War and the German invasion of Poland. The German army used similar units for anti-aircraft defense throughout II World War. In the United Kingdom, the King's Troop, Royal Horse Artillery retains six traditional teams of six horses each and 13-pounder guns for ceremonial duties to this day.

CHAPTER 17

Horses in Warfare

The first use of horses in warfare occurred over 5000 years ago. The earliest evidence of horses ridden in warfare dates from Eurasia between 4000 and 3000 BC. A Sumerian illustration of warfare from 2500 BC depicts some type of equine pulling wagons. By 1600 BC, improved harness and chariot designs made chariot warfare common throughout the Ancient Near East, and the earliest written training manual for war horses was a guide for training chariot horses written about 1350 BC. As formal cavalry tactics replaced the chariot, so did new training methods, and by 360 BC, the Greek cavalry officer Xenophon had written an extensive treatise on horsemanship. The effectiveness of horses in battle was also revolutionized by improvements in technology, including the invention of the saddle, the stirrup, and later, the horse collar.

Many different types and sizes of horse were used in war, depending on the form of warfare. The type used varied with whether the horse was being ridden or driven, and whether they were being used for reconnaissance, cavalry charges, raiding, communication, or supply. Throughout history, mules and donkeys as well as horses played a crucial role in providing support to armies in the field.

Horses were well suited to the warfare tactics of the nomadic cultures from the steppes of Central Asia. Several East Asian cultures made extensive use of cavalry and chariots. Muslim warriors relied upon light cavalry in their campaigns throughout North Africa, Asia, and Europe beginning in the 7th and 8th centuries AD. Europeans used several types of war horses in the Middle Ages, and the best-known heavy cavalry warrior of the period was the armoured knight. With the decline of the knight and rise of gunpowder in warfare, light cavalry again rose to prominence, used in both European warfare and in the conquest of the Americas. Battle cavalry developed to take on a multitude of roles in the late 18th century and early 19th century and was often crucial for victory in the Napoleonic wars. In the Americas, the use of horses and development of mounted warfare tactics were learned by several tribes of indigenous people and in turn, highly mobile horse regiments were critical in the American Civil War.

Horse cavalry began to be phased out after World War I in favour of tank warfare, though a few horse cavalry units were still used into II World War, especially as scouts. By the end of World War II, horses were seldom seen in battle, but were still used extensively for the transport of troops and supplies. Today, formal battle ready horse cavalry units have almost disappeared, although horses are still seen in use by organised armed fighters in Third World countries. Many nations still maintain small units of mounted riders for patrol and reconnaissance, and military horse units are also used for ceremonial and educational purposes. Horses are also used for historical reenactment of battles, law enforcement, and in equestrian competitions derived from the riding and training skills once used by the military.

Types of Horse used in Warfare

A fundamental principle of equine conformation is 'form to function'. Therefore, the type of horse used for various forms of warfare depended on the work performed, the weight a horse needed to carry or pull, and distance travelled. Weight affects speed and endurance, creating a trade-off: armour added protection, but added weight reduces maximum speed. Therefore, various cultures had different military needs. In some situations, one primary type of horse was favoured over all others. In other places, multiple types were needed; warriors would travel to battle riding a lighter horse of greater speed and endurance, and then switch to a heavier horse, with greater weight-carrying capacity, when wearing heavy armour in actual combat.

The average horse can carry up to approximately 30 per cent of its body weight. While all horses can pull more than they can carry, the weight horses can pull varies widely, depending on the build of the horse, the type of vehicle, road conditions, and other factors. Horses harnessed to a wheeled vehicle on a paved road can pull as much as eight times their weight, but far less if pulling wheelless loads over unpaved terrain. Thus, horses that were driven varied in size and had to make a trade-off between speed and weight, just as did riding animals. Light horses could pull a small war chariot at speed. Heavy supply wagons, artillery, and support vehicles were pulled by heavier horses or a larger number of horses. The method by which a horse was hitched to a vehicle also mattered: horses could pull greater weight with a horse collar than they could with a breast collar, and even less with an ox yoke.

Light-weight

Light, oriental horses such as the ancestors of the modern Arabian, Barb, and Akhal-Teke were used for warfare that required speed, endurance and agility. Such horses ranged from about 12 hands to just under 15 hands

[48 to 60 inches (1.2 to 1.5 m)], weighing approximately 800 to 1000 pounds (360 to 450 kg). To move quickly, riders had to use lightweight tack and carry relatively light weapons such as bows, light spears, javelins, or, later, rifles. This was the original horse used for early chariot warfare, raiding, and light cavalry.

Relatively light horses were used by many cultures, including the Ancient Egyptians, the Mongols, the Arabs, and the Native Americans. Throughout the Ancient Near East, small, light animals were used to pull chariots designed to carry no more than two passengers, a driver and a warrior. In the European Middle Ages, a light weight war horse became known as the rouncey.

Medium-weight

Medium-weight horses developed as early as the Iron Age with the needs of various civilisations to pull heavier loads, such as chariots capable of holding more than two people, and, as light cavalry evolved into heavy cavalry, to carry heavily-armoured riders. The Scythians were among the earliest cultures to produce taller, heavier horses. Larger horses were also needed to pull supply wagons and, later on, artillery pieces. In Europe, horses were also used to a limited extent to manoeuvre cannon on the battlefield as part of dedicated horse artillery units. Medium-weight horses had the greatest range in size, from about 14.2 hands but stocky, to as much as 16 hands (58 to 64 inches (1.5 to 1.6 m)), weighing approximately 1,000 to 1,200 pounds (450 to 540 kg). They generally were quite agile in combat, though they did not have the raw speed or endurance of a lighter horse. By the Middle Ages, larger horses in this class were sometimes called destriers. They may have resembled modern Baroque or heavy warmblood breeds. Later, horses similar to the modern warmblood often carried European cavalry.

Heavy-weight

Large, heavy horses, weighing from 1500 to 2000 pounds (680 to 910 kg), the ancestors of today's draught horses, were used, particularly in Europe, from the Middle Ages onward. They pulled heavy loads, having the power to pull weapons or supply wagons and disposition to remain calm under fire. Some historians believe they may have carried the heaviest-armoured knights of the European Late Middle Ages though others dispute this claim, indicating that the destrier, or knight's battle horse, was a medium-weight animal. It is also disputed whether the destrier class included draught animals or not. Breeds at the smaller end of the heavyweight category may have included the ancestors of the Percheron, agile for their size and physically able to manoeuvre in battle.

Other Equids

Horses were not the only equids used to support human warfare. Donkeys have been used as pack animals from antiquity to the present. Mules were also commonly used, especially as pack animals and to pull wagons, but also occasionally for riding. Because mules are often both calmer and hardier than horses, they were particularly useful for strenuous support tasks, such as hauling supplies over difficult terrain. However, under gunfire, they were less cooperative than horses, so were not used to haul artillery on battlefields. The size of a mule and work to which it was put depended largely on the breeding of the mare that produced the mule. Mules could be lightweight, medium weight, or even, when produced from draught horse mares, of moderate heavy weight.

Training and Deployment

The oldest known manual on training horses for chariot warfare was written c. 1350 BC by the Hittite horsemaster, Kikkuli. An ancient manual on the subject of training riding horses, particularly for the Ancient Greek cavalry is *Hippike* (*On Horsemanship*) written about 360 BC by the Greek cavalry officer Xenophon. One of the earliest texts from Asia was that of Kautilya, written about 323 BC.

Whether horses were trained to pull chariots, to be ridden as light or heavy cavalry, or to carry the armoured knight, much training was required to overcome the horse's natural instinct to flee from noise, the smell of blood, and the confusion of combat. They also learned to accept any sudden or unusual movements of humans while using a weapon or avoiding one. Horses used in close combat may have been taught, or at least permitted, to kick, strike, and even bite, thus becoming weapons themselves for the warriors they carried.

In most cultures, a war horse used as a riding animal was trained to be controlled with limited use of reins, responding primarily to the rider's legs and weight. The horse became accustomed to any necessary tack and protective armour placed upon it, and learned to balance under a rider who would also be laden with weapons and armour. Developing the balance and agility of the horse was crucial. The origins of the discipline of dressage came from the need to train horses to be both obedient and manoeuvrable. The *Haute ecole* or 'High School' movements of classical dressage taught today at the Spanish Riding School have their roots in manoeuvres designed for the battlefield. However, the *airs above the ground* were unlikely to have been used in actual combat, as most would have exposed the unprotected underbelly of the horse to the weapons of foot soldiers.

Horses used for chariot warfare were not only trained for combat conditions, but because many chariots were pulled by a team of two to four horses, they also had to learn to work together with other animals in close quarters under chaotic conditions.

Technological Innovations

Horses were probably ridden in prehistory before they were driven. However, evidence is scant, mostly simple images of human figures on horse-like animals drawn on rock or clay. The earliest tools used to control horses were bridles of various sorts, which were invented nearly as soon as the horse was domesticated. Evidence of bit wear appears on the teeth of horses excavated at the archaeology sites of the Botai culture in northern Kazakhstan, dated 3500-3000 BC.

Harness and Vehicles

The invention of the wheel was a major technological innovation that gave rise to chariot warfare. At first, equines, both horses and onagers, were hitched to wheeled carts by means of a yoke around their necks in a manner similar to that of oxen. However, such a design is incompatible with equine anatomy, limiting both the strength and mobility of the animal. By the time of the Hyksos invasions of Egypt, c. 1600 BC, horses were pulling chariots with an improved harness design that made use of a breastcollar and breeching, which allowed a horse to move faster and pull more weight.

Even after the chariot had become obsolete as a tool of war, there still was a need for technological innovations in pulling technologies; horses were needed to pull heavy loads of supplies and weapons. The invention of the horse collar in China during the 5th century AD (Southern and Northern Dynasties) allowed horses to pull greater weight than they could when hitched to a vehicle with the ox yokes or breast collars used in earlier times. The horse collar arrived in Europe during the 9th century, and became widespread by the 12th century.

Riding Equipment

Two major innovations that revolutionised the effectiveness of mounted warriors in battle were the saddle and the stirrup. Riders quickly learned to pad their horse's backs to protect themselves from the horse's spine and withers, and fought on horseback for centuries with little more than a blanket or pad on the horse's back and a rudimentary bridle. To help distribute the rider's weight and protect the horse's back, some cultures created stuffed padding that resembles the panels of today's English saddle. Both the Scythians and Assyrians used pads with added felt attached with a surcingle or girth around the horse's barrel for increased security and comfort. Xenophon mentioned the use of a padded cloth on cavalry mounts as early as the 4th century BC.

The saddle with a solid framework, or 'tree', provided a bearing surface to protect the horse from the weight of the rider, but was not widespread until the 2nd century AD. However, it made a critical difference, as horses could carry more weight when distributed across a solid saddle tree. A solid tree, the predecessor of today's Western saddle, also allowed a more built-up seat to give the rider greater security in the saddle. The Romans are credited with the invention of the solid-treed saddle.

An invention that made cavalry particularly effective was the stirrup. A toe loop that held the big toe was used in India possibly as early as 500 BC, and later a single stirrup was used as a mounting aid. The first set of paired stirrups appeared in China about AD 322 during the Jin Dynasty. Following the invention of paired stirrups, which allowed a rider greater leverage with weapons, as well as both increased stability and mobility while mounted, nomadic groups such as the Mongols adopted this technology and developed a decisive military advantage. By the 7th century, due primarily to invaders from Central Asia, stirrup technology spread from Asia to Europe. The Avar invaders are viewed as primarily responsible for spreading the use of the stirrup into central Europe. However, while stirrups were known in Europe in the 8th century, pictorial and literary references to their use date only from the 9th century. Widespread use in Northern Europe, including England, is credited to the Vikings, who spread the stirrup in the 9th and 10th centuries to those areas.

Tactics

The first archaeological evidence of horses used in warfare dates from between 4000 and 3000 BC in the steppes of Eurasia, in what today is Ukraine, Hungary, and Romania. Not long after domestication of the horse, people in these locations began to live together in large fortified towns for protection from the threat of horseback-riding raiders, who could attack and escape faster than people of more sedentary cultures could follow. The use of horses in organised warfare was also documented early in recorded history. One of the first depictions of equids is the 'war panel' of the Standard of Ur, in Sumer, dated c. 2500 BC, showing horses (or possibly onagers or mules) pulling a four-wheeled wagon.

Chariot Warfare

Among the earliest evidence of chariot use are the burials of horse and chariot remains by the Andronovo (Sintashta-Petrovka) culture in modern Russia and Kazakhstan, dated to approximately 2000 BC. The oldest documentary evidence of what was probably chariot warfare in the Ancient Near East is the Old Hittite Anitta text, of the 18th century BC, which mentioned 40 teams of horses at the siege of Salatiwara. The Hittites became well known throughout the ancient world for their prowess with the chariot. Widespread use of the chariot in warfare across most of Eurasia coincides approximately with the development of the composite bow, known from c. 1600 BC. Further improvements in wheels and axles, as well as innovations in weaponry, soon resulted in chariots being driven in battle by Bronze Age societies from China to Egypt.

The Hyksos invaders brought the chariot to Ancient Egypt in the 16th century BC and the Egyptians adopted its use from that time forward. The oldest preserved text related to the handling of war horses in the ancient world is the Hittite manual of Kikkuli, which dates to about 1350 BC, and describes the conditioning of chariot horses.

Chariots existed in the Minoan civilization, as they were inventoried on storage lists from Knossos in Crete, dating to around 1450 BC. Chariots were also used in China as far back as the Shang Dynasty (c. 1600-1050 BC), where they appear in burials. The high point of chariot use in China was in the Spring and Autumn Period (770-476 BC), although they continued in use up until the 2nd century BC.

Descriptions of the tactical role of chariots in Ancient Greece and Rome are rare. The Iliad, possibly referring to Mycenaen practices used c. 1250 BC, describes the use of chariots for transporting warriors to and from battle, rather than for actual fighting. Later, Julius Caesar, invading Britain in 55 and 54 BC, noted British charioteers throwing javelins, then leaving their chariots to fight on foot.

Cavalry

Some of the earliest examples of horses being ridden in warfare were horse-mounted archers or spear-throwers, dating to the reigns of the Assyrian rulers Ashurnasirpal II and Shalmaneser III. However, these riders sat far back on their horses, a precarious position for moving quickly, and the horses were held by a handler on the ground, keeping the archer free to use the bow. Thus, these archers were more a type of mounted infantry than true cavalry. The Assyrians developed cavalry in response to invasions by nomadic people from the north, such as the Cimmerians, who entered Asia Minor in the 8th century BC and took over parts of Urartu during the reign of Sargon II, approximately 721 BC. Mounted warriors such as the Scythians also had an influence on the region in the 7th century BC. By the reign of Ashurbanipal in 669 BC, the Assyrians had learned to sit forward on their horses in the classic riding position still seen today and could be said to be true light cavalry. The ancient Greeks used both light horse scouts and heavy cavalry, although not extensively, possibly due to the cost of keeping horses.

Heavy cavalry was believed to have been developed by the Ancient Persians, although others argue for the Sarmatians. By the time of Darius (558-486 BC), Persian military tactics required horses and riders that were completely armoured, and selectively bred a heavier, more muscled horse to carry the additional weight. The cataphract was a type of heavily armored cavalry with distinct tactics, armour, and weaponry used from the time of the Persians up until the Middle Ages.

In Ancient Greece, Phillip of Macedon is credited with developing tactics allowing massed cavalry charges. The most famous Greek heavy cavalry units were the companion cavalry of Alexander the Great. The Chinese of the 4th century BC during the Warring States Period (403-221 BC) began to use cavalry against rival states. To fight nomadic raiders from the north and west, the Chinese of the Han Dynasty (202 BC-220 AD) developed effective mounted units. Cavalry was not used extensively by the Romans during the Roman Republic period, but by the time of the Roman Empire, they made use of heavy cavalry. However, the backbone of the Roman army was the infantry.

Horse Artillery

Once gunpowder was invented, another major use of horses was as draught animals for heavy artillery, or cannons. In addition to field artillery, where horse-drawn guns were attended by gunners on foot, many armies had artillery batteries where each gunner was provided with a mount. Horse artillery units generally used lighter pieces, pulled by six horses. '9-pounders' were pulled by eight horses, and heavier artillery pieces needed a team of twelve. Congreve rockets, a type of rocket artillery, required about 25 horses. With the individual riding horses required for officers, surgeons and other support staff, as well as those pulling the artillery guns and supply wagons, an artillery battery of six guns could require 160 to 200 horses. Horse artillery usually came under the command of cavalry divisions, but in some battles, such as Waterloo, the horse artillery were used as a rapid response force, repulsing attacks and assisting the infantry. Agility was important; the ideal artillery horse was 15 to 16 hands high, strongly built, but able to move quickly.

Asia

India

The literature of ancient India describes numerous horse nomads. Some of the earliest references to the use of horses in South Asian warfare are Puranic texts, which refer to an invasion of India by the joint cavalry forces of the Sakas, Kambojas, Yavanas, Pahlavas, and Paradas, called the 'five hordes' (*pañca.ganah*) or 'Ksatriya' hordes (*Kshatriya ganah*). About 1600 BC, they captured the throne of Ayodhya by dethroning the Vedic king, Bahu. Later texts, such as the *Mahabharata*, c. 950 BC, appear to recognise efforts taken to breed war horses and develop trained mounted warriors, stating that the horses of the Sindhu and Kamboja regions were of the finest quality, and the Kambojas, Gandharas, and Yavanas were expert in fighting from horses.

In technological innovation, the early toe loop stirrup is credited to the cultures of India, and may have been in use as early as 500 BC. Not long after, the cultures of Mesopotamia and Ancient Greece clashed with those of central Asia and India. Herodotus (484-425 BC) wrote that Gandarian mercenaries of the Achaemenid Empire were recruited into the army of emperor Xerxes I of Persia (486-465 BC), which he led against the Greeks. A century later, the 'Men of the Mountain Land', from north of Kabul River, served in the army of Darius III of Persia when he fought against Alexander the Great at Arbela in 331 BC. In battle against Alexander at Massaga in 326 BC, the Assakenoi forces included 20,000 cavalry. The Mudra-Rakshasa recounted how cavalry of the Shakas, Yavanas, Kambojas, Kiratas, Parasikas, and Bahlikas helped Chandragupta Maurya (c. 320-298 BC) defeat the ruler of Magadha and take the throne, thus laying the foundations of Mauryan Dynasty in Northern India.

Mughal cavalry used gunpowder weapons, but were slow to replace the traditional composite bow. Under the impact of European military successes in India, some Indian rulers adopted the European system of massed cavalry charges, although others did not. By the 18th century, Indian armies continued to field cavalry, but mainly of the heavy variety.

East Asia

The Chinese used chariots for horse-based warfare until light cavalry forces became common during the Warring States era (402-221 BC). A major proponent of the change to riding horses from chariots was Wu Ling, c. 320 BC. However, conservative forces in China often opposed change, and cavalry never became as dominant as in Europe. Cavalry in China also did not benefit from the additional cachet attached to being the military branch dominated by the nobility.

The Japanese samurai fought as cavalry for many centuries. They were particularly skilled in the art of using archery from horseback. The archery skills of mounted samurai were developed by training such as Yabusame, which originated in AD 530 and reached its peak under Minamoto Yoritomo (AD 1147-1199) in the Kamakura Period. They switched from an emphasis on mounted bowmen to mounted spearmen during the Sengoku period (AD 1467-1615).

Middle East

During the period when various Islamic empires controlled much of the Middle East as well as parts of West Africa and the Iberian peninsula, Muslim armies consisted mostly of cavalry, made up of fighters from various local groups, mercenaries and Turkoman tribesmen. The latter were considered particularly skilled as both lancers and mounted archers. In the 9th century the use of Mamluks, slaves raised to be soldiers for various Muslim rulers, became increasingly common. Mobile tactics, advanced breeding of horses, and detailed training manuals made Mamluk cavalry a highly efficient fighting force. The use of armies consisting mostly of cavalry continued among the Turkish people who founded the Ottoman Empire. Their need for large mounted forces lead to an establishment of the sipahi, cavalry soldiers who were granted lands in exchange for providing military service in times of war.

Mounted Muslim warriors conquered North Africa and the Iberian Peninsula during the 7th and 8th centuries AD following the Hegira, or Hijra, of Muhammad in AD 622. By AD 630, their influence expanded across the Middle East and into western North Africa. By AD 711, the light cavalry of Muslim warriors had reached Spain, and controlled most of the Iberian peninsula by 720. Their mounts were of various oriental types, including the North African Barb. A few Arabian horses may have come with the Ummayads who settled in the Guadalquivir valley. Another strain of horse that came with Islamic invaders was the Turkoman horse. Muslim invaders travelled north from nowadays Spain into France, where they were defeated by the Frankish ruler Charles Martel at the Battle of Tours in AD 732.

Europe the Middle Ages

During the European Middle Ages, there were three primary types of war horses: The destrier, the courser, and the rouncey, which differed in size and usage. A generic word used to describe medieval war horses was *charger,* which appears interchangeable with the other terms. The medieval war horse was of moderate size, rarely exceeding 15.2 hands [62 inches (1.6 m)]. Heavy horses were logistically difficult to maintain and less adaptable to varied terrains. The destrier of the early Middle Ages was moderately larger than the courser or rouncey, in part to accommodate heavier armoured knights. However, destriers were not as large as draught horses, averaging between 14.2 hands and 15 hands [58 to 60 inches (1.5 to 1.5 m)]. On the European continent, the need to carry more armour against mounted enemies such as the Lombards and Frisians led to the Franks developing heavier, bigger horses. As the amount of armour and equipment increased in the later Middle Ages, the height of the horses increased; some late medieval horse skeletons were of horses over 15 hands.

Stallions were often used as destriers due to their natural aggression. However, the use of mares by European warriors cannot be discounted from literary references, and mares, who were quieter and less likely to call out and betray their position to the enemy, were the preferred war horse of the Moors, Muslims who invaded various parts of Southern Europe from 700 AD through the 15th century.

Uses

The heavy cavalry charge, while it could be effective, was not a common occurrence. Battles were rarely fought on land suitable for heavy cavalry. While mounted riders remained effective for initial attacks, by the end of the 14th century, it was common for knights to dismount to fight, while their horses were sent to the rear, kept ready for pursuit. Pitched battles were avoided if possible, with most offensive warfare in the early Middle Ages taking the form of sieges, and in the later Middle Ages as swift mounted raids called *chevauchées,* with lightly armed warriors on swift horses.

The war horse was also seen in hastiludes—martial war games such as the joust, which began in the 11th century both as sport and to provide training for battle. Specialised destriers were bred for the purpose, although the expense of keeping, training, and outfitting them kept the majority of the population from owning one. While some historians suggest that the tournament had become a theatrical event by the 15th and 16th centuries, others argue that jousting continued to help cavalry train for battle until the Thirty Years' War.

Transition

The decline of the armoured knight was probably linked to changing structures of armies and various economic factors, and not obsolescence due to new technologies. However, some historians attribute the demise of the knight to the invention of gunpowder, or to the English longbow. Some link the decline to both technologies. Others argue these technologies actually contributed to the development of knights: Plate armour was first developed to resist early medieval crossbow bolts, and the full harness worn by the early 15th century developed to resist longbow arrows. From the 14th century on, most plate was made from hardened steel, which resisted early musket ammunition. In addition, stronger designs did not make plate heavier; a full harness of musket-proof plate from the 17th century weighed 70 pounds (32 kg), significantly less than 16th century tournament armour.

The move to predominately infantry-based battles from 1300–1550 was linked to both improved infantry tactics and changes in weaponry. By the 16th century, the concept of a combined-arms professional army had spread throughout Europe. Professional armies emphasized training, and were paid via contracts, a change from the ransom and pillaging which reimbursed knights in the past. When coupled with the rising costs involved in outfitting and maintaining armour and horses, the traditional knightly classes began to abandon their profession. Light horses, or *prickers*, were still used for scouting and reconnaissance; they also provided a defensive screen for marching armies. Large teams of draught horses or oxen pulled the heavy early cannon. Other horses pulled wagons and carried supplies for the armies.

Early Modern Period

During the early modern period the shift continued from heavy cavalry and the armoured knight to unarmoured light cavalry, including Hussars and Chasseurs à cheval. Light cavalry facilitated better communication, using fast, agile horses to move quickly across battlefields. The ratio of footmen to horsemen also increased over the period as infantry weapons improved and footmen became more mobile and versatile, particularly once the musket bayonet replaced the more cumbersome pike. During the Elizabethan era, mounted units included cuirassiers, heavily armoured and equipped with lances; light cavalry, who wore mail and bore light lances and pistols; and 'petronels', who carried an early carbine. As heavy cavalry use declined, armour was increasingly abandoned, and dragoons, whose horses were rarely used in combat, became more common: mounted infantry provided reconnaissance, escort and security. However, many generals still used the heavy mounted charge, from the late 17th century and early 18th century, where sword-wielding wedge-formation shock troops penetrated enemy lines, to the early 19th century, where armoured heavy cuirassiers were employed.

Light cavalry continued to play a major role, particularly after the Seven Years War when Hussars started to play a larger part in battles. Though some leaders preferred tall horses for their mounted troops, this was as much for prestige as for increased shock ability, and many troops used more typical horses, averaging 15 hands. Cavalry tactics altered, with fewer mounted charges, more reliance on drilled manoeuvres at the trot, and use of firearms once within range. Ever-more elaborate movements, such as wheeling and caracole, were developed to facilitate the use of firearms from horseback. These tactics were not greatly successful in battle, since pikemen protected by musketeers could deny cavalry room to manoeuvre. However, the advanced equestrianism required survives into the modern world as dressage. While restricted, cavalry was not rendered obsolete. As infantry formations developed in tactics and skills, artillery became essential to break formations; in turn, cavalry was required to both combat enemy artillery, which was susceptible to cavalry while deploying, and to charge enemy infantry formations broken by artillery fire. Thus, successful warfare depended in a balance of the three arms: cavalry, artillery and infantry.

As regimental structures developed, many units selected horses of uniform type. Some, such as the Royal Scots Greys even specified colour. Trumpeters often rode distinctive horses, so they stood out. Regional armies developed type preferences, such as British hunters, German Hanoverians, and steppe ponies of the Cossacks, but once in the field, the lack of supplies typical of wartime meant that horses of all types were used. Since horses were such a vital component of most armies in early modern Europe, many instituted state stud farms to breed horses for the military. However, in wartime, supply rarely matched the demand, resulting in some cavalry troops fighting on foot.

19th Century

In the 19th century, distinctions between heavy and light cavalry became less significant; by the end of the Peninsular War, heavy cavalry were performing the scouting and outpost duties previously undertaken by light cavalry, and by the end of the 19th century the roles had effectively merged. Most armies at the time preferred cavalry horses to stand 15.2 hands [62 inches (160 cm)] and weigh 990 to 1,100 pounds (450 to 500 kg), although cuirassiers frequently had heavier horses. Lighter horses were used for scouting and raiding. Cavalry horses were generally obtained at 5 years of age, and were in service from 10 or 12 years, barring loss. However, losses of 30-40 per cent were common during a campaign, due to conditions of the march as well as enemy action. Mares and geldings were preferred over less-easily managed stallions.

During the French Revolutionary Wars and the Napoleonic Wars, the cavalry's main offensive role were as shock troops. In defence, cavalry were used to attack and harass the enemy's infantry flanks as they advanced.

Cavalry were frequently used prior to an infantry assault, to force an infantry line to break and reform into formations vulnerable to infantry or artillery. Frequently, infantry followed behind in order to secure any ground won. Conversely, cavalry also broke up enemy lines following successful infantry action.

Mounted charges were carefully managed. A charge's maximum speed was 20 km/h; moving faster resulted in a break in formation and fatigued horses. Charges occurred across clear rising ground, and were effective against infantry both on the march and when deployed in a line or column. A foot battalion formed in line was vulnerable to cavalry, and could be broken or destroyed by a well-formed charge. Traditional cavalry functions altered by the end of the 19th century. Many cavalry units transferred in title and role to "mounted rifles": troops trained to fight on foot, but retaining mounts for rapid deployment, as well as for patrols, scouting, communications, and defensive screening. These troops differed from mounted infantry, who used horses for transport but did not perform the old cavalry roles of reconnaissance and support.

Sub-Saharan Africa

Horses were used for warfare in the central Sudan since the 9th century, where they were considered 'the most precious commodity following the slave'. The first conclusive evidence of horses playing a major role in the warfare of West Africa dates to the 11th century when the region was controlled by the Almoravids, a Muslim Berber dynasty. During the 13th and 14th centuries, cavalry became an important factor in the area. This coincided with the introduction of larger breeds of horse and the widespread adoption of saddles and stirrups. Increased mobility played a part in the formation of new power centres, such as the Oyo Empire in what today is Nigeria. The authority of many African Islamic states such as the Bornu Empire also rested in large part on their ability to subject neighboring peoples with cavalry. Despite harsh climate conditions, endemic diseases such as trypanosomiasis the African horse sickness and unsuitable terrain that limited the effectiveness of horses in many parts of Africa, horses were continuously imported and were, in some areas, a vital instrument of war. The introduction of horses also intensified existing conflicts, such as those between the Herero and Nama people in Namibia during the 19th century.

The African slave trade was closely tied to the imports of war horses, and as the prevalence of slaving decreased, fewer horses were needed for raiding. This significantly decreased the amount of mounted warfare seen in West Africa. By the time of the Scramble for Africa and the introduction of modern firearms in the 1880s, the use of horses in African warfare had lost most of its effectiveness. Nonetheless, in South Africa during the Second Boer War (1899-1902), cavalry and other mounted troops were the major combat force for the British, since the horse-mounted Boers moved too quickly for infantry to engage. The Boers presented a mobile and innovative approach to warfare, drawing on strategies that had first appeared in the American Civil War. The terrain was not well-suited to the British horses, resulting in the loss of over 300,000 animals. As the campaign wore on, losses were replaced by more durable African Basuto ponies, and Waler horses from Australia.

The Americas

The horse had been extinct in the Western Hemisphere for approximately 10,000 years prior to the arrival of Spanish Conquistadors in the early 16th century. Consequently, the Indigenous peoples of the Americas had no warfare technologies that could overcome the considerable advantage provided by European horses and gunpowder weapons. In particular this resulted in the conquest of the Aztec and Inca empires. The speed and increased impact of cavalry contributed to a number of early victories by European fighters in open terrain, though their success was limited in more mountainous regions. The Incas' well-maintained roads in the Andes enabled quick mounted raids, such as those undertaken by the Spanish while resisting the siege of Cuzco in 1536-7.

Indigenous populations of South America soon learned to use horses. In Chile, the Mapuche began using cavalry in the Arauco War in 1586. They drove the Spanish out of Araucanía at the beginning of the 17th century. Later, the Mapuche conducted mounted raids known as Malónes, first on Spanish, then on Chilean and Argentine settlements until well into the 19th century. In North America, Native Americans also quickly learned to use horses. In particular, the people of the Great Plains, such as the Comanche and the Cheyenne, became renowned horseback fighters. By the 19th century, they presented a formidable force against the United States Army.

During the American Revolutionary War (1775-1783), the Continental Army made relatively little use of cavalry, primarily relying on infantry and a few dragoon regiments. The United States Congress eventually authorized federal horse regiments in 1855. The newly-formed American cavalry adopted tactics based on experiences fighting over vast distances during the Mexican War (1846-1848) and against indigenous peoples on the western frontier, abandoning some European traditions.

During the American Civil War (1861-1865), cavalry held the most important and respected role it would ever hold in the American military. Field artillery in the American Civil War was also highly mobile. Both horses and mules pulled the guns, though only horses were used on the battlefield. At the beginning of the war, most of the experienced cavalry officers were from the South and thus joined the Confederacy, leading to the Confederate Army's initial battlefield superiority. The tide turned at the 1863 Battle of Brandy Station, part of the Gettysburg campaign, where the Union cavalry, in the largest cavalry battle ever fought on the North American continent, ended the dominance of the South. By 1865, Union cavalry were decisive in achieving victory. So important were horses to individual soldiers that the surrender terms at Appomattox allowed every Confederate cavalryman to take his horse home with him.

20th Century

Although cavalry was used extensively throughout the world during the 19th century, horses became less important to warfare after the beginning of the 20th century. Light cavalry was still seen on the battlefield at the beginning of the 20th century, but formal mounted cavalry began to be phased out for combat during and immediately after World War I, although units that included horses still had military uses well into World War II.

First World War saw great changes in the use of cavalry. The mode of warfare changed, and the use of trench warfare, barbed wire and machine guns rendered traditional cavalry almost obsolete. Tanks, introduced in 1917, began to take over the role of shock combat.

Early in the War, cavalry skirmishes were common, and horse-mounted troops widely used for reconnaissance. On the Western Front cavalry were an effective flanking force during the 'Race to the Sea' in 1914, but were less useful once trench warfare was established. There a few examples of successful shock combat, and cavalry divisions also provided important mobile fire power. Cavalry played a greater role on the Eastern Front, where trench warfare was less common. On the Eastern Front, and also against the Ottomans, the 'cavalry was literally indispensable'. British Empire cavalry proved adaptable, since they were trained to fight both on foot and while mounted, while other European cavalry relied primarily on shock action.

On both fronts, the horse was also used as a pack animal. Because railway lines could not withstand artillery bombardments, horses carried ammunition and supplies between the railheads and the rear trenches, though the horses generally were not used in the actual trench zone. This role of horses was critical, and thus horse fodder was the single largest commodity shipped to the front by some countries. Following the war, many cavalry regiments were converted to mechanised, armoured divisions, with light tanks developed to perform many of the cavalry's original roles.

World War II

Several nations used horse units during World War II. The Polish army used cavalry to defend against the armies of Nazi Germany during the 1939 invasion. Both the Germans and the Soviet Union maintained cavalry units throughout the war, particularly on the Eastern Front. The British Army used horses early in the war, and the final British cavalry charge was on March 21, 1942, when the Burma Frontier Force encountered Japanese infantry in central Burma. The only American cavalry unit during World War II was the 26th Cavalry. They challenged the Japanese invaders of Luzon, holding off armoured and infantry regiments during the invasion of the Philippines, repelled a unit of tanks in Binalonan, and successfully held ground for the Allied armies' retreat to Bataan.

Throughout the war, horses and mules were an essential form of transport, especially in by the British in the rough terrain of Italy and the Middle East. The United States Army utilised a few cavalry and supply units during the war, but there were concerns that the Americans did not use horses often enough. In the campaigns in North Africa, generals such as researcher lamented their lack, saying, 'had we possessed an American cavalry division with pack artillery in Tunisia and in Sicily, not a German would have escaped".

The German and the Soviet armies used horses until the end of the war for transportation of troops and supplies. The German Army, strapped for motorised transport because its factories were needed to produce tanks and aircraft, used around 2.75 million horses—more than it had used in World War I. One German infantry division in Normandy in 1944 had 5,000 horses. The Soviets used 3.5 million horses.

Recognition

While many statues and memorials have been erected to human heroes of war, often shown with horses, a few have also been created specifically to honor horses or animals in general. One example is the Horse Memorial in Port Elizabeth in the Eastern Cape province of South Africa. Both horses and mules are honored in the Animals in War Memorial in London's Hyde Park.

Horses have also at times received medals for extraordinary deeds. After the Charge of the Light Brigade during the Crimean War, a surviving horse named Drummer Boy, ridden by an officer of the 8th Hussars, was given an unofficial campaign medal by his rider that was identical to those awarded to British troops who served in the Crimea, engraved with the horse's name and an inscription of his service. A more formal award was the PDSA Dickin Medal, an animals' equivalent of the Victoria Cross, awarded by the People's Dispensary for Sick Animals charity in the United Kingdom to three horses that served in World War II.

Modern Uses

Today, many of the historical military uses of the horse have evolved into peacetime applications, including exhibitions, historical reenactments, work of peace officers, and competitive events. Formal combat units of mounted cavalry are mostly a thing of the past, with horseback units within the modern military used for reconnaissance, ceremonial, or crowd control purposes. With the rise of mechanised technology, horses in formal national militias were displaced by tanks and armored fighting vehicles, sometimes still referred to as 'cavalry'.

Active Military

Organised armed fighters on horseback are occasionally seen. The best-known current examples are the Janjaweed, militia groups seen in the Darfur region of Sudan, who became notorious for their attacks upon unarmed civilian populations in the Darfur conflict. Many nations still maintain small numbers of mounted military units for certain types of patrol and reconnaissance duties in extremely rugged terrain, including the current conflict in Afghanistan. The only remaining operationally-ready, fully horse-mounted regular regiment in the world is the Indian Army's 61st Cavalry.

Law Enforcement and Public Safety

Mounted police have been used since the 18th century, and still are used worldwide to control traffic and crowds, patrol public parks, keep order in processionals and during ceremonies and perform general street patrol duties. Today, many cities still have mounted police units. In rural areas, horses are used by law enforcement for mounted patrols over rugged terrain, crowd control at religious shrines, and border patrol.

In rural areas, law enforcement that operates outside of incorporated cities may also have mounted units. These include specially deputised, paid or volunteer mounted search and rescue units sent into roadless areas on horseback to locate missing people. Law enforcement in protected areas may use horses in places where mechanised transport is difficult or prohibited. Horses can be an essential part of an overall team effort as they can move faster on the ground than a human on foot, can transport heavy equipment, and provide a more rested rescue worker when a subject is found.

Educational and Ceremonial Uses

Many countries throughout the world maintain traditionally-trained and historically uniformed cavalry units for ceremonial, exhibition, or educational purposes. One example is the Horse Cavalry Detachment of the U.S. Army's 1st Cavalry Division. This unit of active duty soldiers approximates the weapons, tools, equipment and techniques used by the United States Cavalry in the 1880s. It is seen at change of command ceremonies and other public appearances. A similar detachment is the Governor General's Horse Guards, Canada's Household Cavalry regiment, the last remaining mounted cavalry unit in the Canadian Forces. Nepal's King's Household Cavalry is a ceremonial unit with over 100 horses and is the remainder of the Nepalese cavalry that existed since the 19th century. An important ceremonial use is in military funerals, which often have a caparisoned horse as part of the procession, 'to symbolize that the warrior will never ride again'.

Horses are also used in many historical reenactments. Reenactors try to recreate the conditions of the battle or tournament with equipment that is as authentic as possible.

Equestrian Sport

Modern-day Olympic equestrian events are rooted in cavalry skills and classical horsemanship. The first equestrian events at the Olympics were introduced in 1912, and through 1948, competition was restricted to active-duty officers on military horses. Only after 1952, as mechanisation of warfare reduced the number of military riders, were civilian riders allowed to compete. Dressage traces its origins to Xenophon and his works on cavalry training methods, developing further during the Renaissance in response to a need for different tactics in battles where firearms were used. The three-phase competition known as Eventing developed out of cavalry officers' needs for versatile, well-schooled horses. Though show jumping developed largely from fox hunting, the cavalry considered jumping to be good training for their horses, and leaders in the development of modern riding techniques over fences, such as Federico Caprilli, came from military ranks. Beyond the Olympic disciplines are other events with military roots. Competitions with weapons, such as mounted shooting and tent pegging, test the combat skills of mounted riders.

CHAPTER 18

Mounted Archery and Cavalry

Mounted Archery

A horse archer, horsed archer, or mounted archer is a cavalryman armed with a bow, able to shoot while riding from horseback. Archery has occasionally been used from the backs of other riding animals. Mounted archery was a defining characteristic of Steppe warfare throughout Central Asia, and throughout the prairies of America after the adoption of the horse, used by peoples including the Scythians, Sarmatians, Parthians, Sassanids, Huns, Byzantines, Bulgars, Cumans, Kipchaks, Magyars, Japanese, Mongols, Turks, Russians, Rajputs, Comanches, and others. It was also adopted by other peoples and armies, notably Chinese and Romans who both suffered serious conflict with peoples practising horse archery. It developed separately among the peoples of the South American pampas and the North American prairies; the Comanches were especially skilled. Horse archery was also particularly honoured in the samurai tradition of Japan, where mounted archery is called Yabusame. In some places, such as in Germany, Scandinavia and Portugal, the crossbow was favoured over composite bow. Horse archery was never widely used south of the Sahara in Africa, where the ecosystem was less suitable for domestic horses. This was presumably due to factors such as the tsetse fly and lack of suitable fodder. Though some African kingdoms south of the Sahara used horses, they were less useful and had a high mortality rate in these regions.

Basic Features

The natives of large grassland areas developed mounted archery for hunting, and for war. The buffalo hunts of the North American prairies may have been the most spectacular and best-recorded examples of bowhunting by mounted archers. Since using a bow requires the rider to let go of the reins with both hands, horse archers need superb equestrian skills if they are to shoot on the move. It is thought that the Ancient Greeks invented the mythical Centaurs as the perfect union of an archer and a fast moving horseman.

Horse archers may be either light, such as Scythian, Hun, Parthian, Cuman or Pecheneg horsemen; or heavy, such as Byzantine kavallarioi, Russian druzhina and Japanese samurai. Some nations, like Medieval Mongols and Hungarians, fielded both light and heavy cavalry. In some armies, such as Parthians, Teutonic Order and Palmyrans, the mounted part of the army consisted of both super-heavy (cataphracts, knights) and ultra-light cavalry.

In battle, light horse archers were typically skirmishers; lightly armed missile troops capable of moving swiftly to avoid close combat or to deliver a rapid blow to the flanks or rear of the foe. In the tactic of the Parthian shot the rider would retreat from the enemy while turning his upper body and shooting backwards. Due to the superior speed of mounted archers, troops under attack from horse archers were unable to respond to the threat if they did not have ranged weapons of their own. Constant harassment would result in casualties, morale drop and disruption of the formation. Any attempts to charge the archers would also slow the entire army down.

An example comes from an attack on Comanche horse archers by Texas Rangers who were saved by their muzzle-loading firearms and by a convenient terrain feature. Captain John Bird rode up the Little River with fifty Rangers. They met some twenty Comanches hunting buffalo, and attacked them. The Comanches fled, easily keeping clear of the Rangers, for several miles across the open prairie before Bird noticed that he was now chasing some two hundred Indians. He immediately retreated, only to discover his classic error in fighting mounted archers. The Comanches pursued in turn, screaming and loosing what seemed like clouds of arrows. Bird's command happened across a ravine where they could shoot from cover. They fired carefully to keep the Indians at long range, always making sure they kept a few of their rifles loaded in case of an assault. The horse archers did not charge, but kept the Rangers under siege until seven of them, including Captain Bird, were dead or dying. The Rangers retreated to the east and claimed victory. Comanches set out on large-scale raids, destroying and torturing over a wide area.

Heavy horse archers, such as Byzantine kavallarioi, Turkish timariots or Japanese samurai, instead fought as disciplined units. Instead of harassment, they shot at volleys, with intention of weakening the enemy before charging him. The heavy horse archers intended to contact the enemy in melee. In addition to bows, they often also carried close combat weapons, such as lances or spears.

Early horse archery, depicted on the Assyrian carvings, involved two riders, one controlling both horses while the second shot.

One of the few commanders who won his first battle against horse archers was Alexander the Great. He defeated Scythians in 329 BCE at the Battle of Jaxartes (the Syr Darya river). Even so, the Jaxartes marked the north-easternmost border of Alexander's realm in Asia, and he never ventured beyond into the heartlands of the horse nomads. Other commanders of heavy troops with few or no archers of their own had often disastrous experiences, including Crassus at the Battle of Carrhae. The medieval Battle of Liegnitz is a classic example of horse archers contributing to the defeat of armoured troops, via demoralization and continued harassment. The Mongol armies used similar tactics to create the enormous Mongol Empires from China to Eastern Europe.

Skirmishing requires vast areas of free space to run, manoeuvre and flee, and if the terrain is close, light horse archers can be charged and defeated easily. Light horse archers are also very vulnerable to foot archers and crossbowmen, who can easily outshoot them by shooting on volleys.

The heavy horse archers first appeared in the Assyrian army in the 7th century BC after abandoning the chariot warfare and formed a link between light skirmishing cavalrymen and heavy cataphract cavalry. The heavy horse archers usually had mail or lamellar armour and helmets, and sometimes even their horses were armoured. Heavy horse archers, instead of skirmishing and hit-and-run tactics, formed in disciplined formations and units, sometimes intermixed with lancers as in Byzantine and Turkish armies, and shot as volleys instead of shooting as individuals. The usual tactic was to first shoot five or six volleys at the enemy to weaken him and to disorganise them, and then charge. Heavy horse archers often carried spears or lances for close combat, or formed mixed units with lancers.

Heavy horse archers could usually outshoot their light counterparts, and wearing armour, could stand their shooting. The Russian druzhina cavalry developed as a countermeasure for the Tatar light troops. Likewise, the Turkish timariots and qapikulu were often as heavily armoured as Western knights, and could stand the Hungarian, Albanian and Mongol horse archers.

An army could also consist of both heavy and light horse archers, such as the Mongol armies.

The German and Scandinavian Medieval armies made extensive use of mounted crossbowmen. They would act not only as scouts and skirmishers, but also protecting the flanks of the knights and infantry, and chasing away the enemy light cavalry. When the battle was fully engaged, they would charge at the enemy flank, shoot a single devastating volley at point-blank range and then attack the enemy with swords, without reloading. The invention of ratchet cranequin allowed the mounted crossbowmen to use heavy crossbows on horseback.

Decline of Mounted Archery

Mounted archery was usually ineffective against massed foot archery. The foot archers or crossbowmen could outshoot the horse archers with sheer fire volume by shooting on volleys, and a horseman and a horse provide a larger target than a man alone. The Crusaders countered the Turkoman horse archery with their crossbowmen, and Genoese crossbowmen were favoured mercenaries in both Mamluk and Mongol armies. Likewise the Chinese armies consisted of massed crossbowmen to counter the nomad armies. A nomad army that wanted to engage in an archery exchange with foot archers would itself normally dismount. The typical Mongol archer shot from a sitting position when dismounted.

Horse archers were eventually rendered obsolete by the development of modern firearms. In the 16th and subsequent centuries, various cavalry forces armed with firearms gradually started appearing. Because the conventional arquebus and musket were too awkward for a cavalryman to use, lighter weapons such as the carbine had to be developed, that could be effectively used from horseback, much in the same manner as the composite recurve bow presumably developed from earlier bows. The 16th century Dragoons and Carabiniers were heavier cavalry equipped with firearms. Pistols coexisted with the composite bow, often used by the same rider, well into the 17th c. in Eastern European cavalry, including Muscovites, Kalmycks, Turks and Cossacks.

Mounted archery remained an effective tactical system in open country until the introduction of repeating firearms. The Comanches of North America found their bows more effective than muzzleloading guns. 'After... about 1800, most Comanches began to discard muskets and pistols and to rely on their older weapons'.

Technology

The weapon of choice for horse archers was most commonly a composite recurve bow, because it was compact enough to shoot conveniently from a horse while retaining sufficient range and penetrating power. North Americans used short wooden bows often backed with sinew, but never developed the full three-layer composite bow.

Modern Revival of Mounted Archery

Mounted archery and associated skills were revived in Mongolia after independence in 1921 and are displayed at festivals, in particular the Naadam. Horseback archery has also been revived by Kassai Lajos and other modern Hungarians. European horseback archery as a growing sport and equestrian skill is principally based on the Kassai, or "Hungarian" system. There are several competitions and meetings around the world in any given year – mostly in Hungary, Germany and other Central European countries, but also in Canada (Mt Currie, BC), the United States (notably Fort Dodge in Iowa) and also in South Korea. Amongst participants of this growing sport there is a dream of one day finding acceptance as a Olympic equestrian event.

The Korean and the Hungarian styles of competition are the two most widely practiced forms.

It is also interesting to note that while the Mongolian horse archers were probably the most feared and successful of all horse archers, the sport is very limited in Mongolia itself today and at most Naadam festivals the archery and horse-riding competitions are conducted independently; the horses are raced with one another, and the archery is traditionally practiced from a standing position rather than mounted. In the past five years a desire to revive the tradition seems to have been addressed with the foundation of the Mongolian Horseback Archery Association whose members have competed in South Korea and Europe.

Kassai School of Horseback Archery

A horseback archery competition course, as defined by Kassai, is ninetynine metres long. There is one target with a rotating face on the course at its centre point – its diametre is ninety centimetres. An electronic timing system gives the archer a maximum of 20 seconds to cover the course; to encourage speed as well as accuracy, the number of seconds less than 20 is added to the score reached on the targets. Any traditional bow or a modern fibreglass replica can be used, and with the exception of the nocking point, use of any other devices is strictly forbidden.

Originally the Scythians, Mongols and some of the Turkish archers, all used variants of a thumb ring and they released arrows from 'inside' the bow. (e.g. for a right-handed archer holding the bow in their left hand, the arrow sits across the left hand's thumb and on the right side of the bow). Kassai however uses the later, Western method of shooting 'around the bow' and a three-fingered release (for a right-handed archer, the arrow rests over the back of the left hand holding the bow, and is released round the left side of the bow).

The bows are generally fairly light (from about 30-40 lbs) and Kassai uses carbon arrows rather than the more traditional wooden shafts. The 'release' has been significantly modified from a traditional Western release and involves a rather emphatic extension of the release hand (the right hand in the case of a right-handed archer) after releasing the arrow. This helps balance on horseback by allowing a slower adjustment to the transfer of momentum as the arrow leaves the bow.

For fast shooting, Kassai has developed a technique of holding up to a dozen arrows in the bow-hand from which the archer can reload quickly. Kassai's research has shown that the process of pulling arrows from a back quiver or saddle quiver is too cumbersome and slow - it is not known how the Mongols or their predecessors managed the task as no records remain. Kassai places great emphasis on this technique and can shoot up to 12 arrows in 17.80 seconds, while mounted.

Kassai places great emphasis on horsemanship. The aspiring horseback archer must practice first 'bare-back' (without any saddle) to promote good balance. Once past a certain level the archer may graduate to use a specially modified Eastern Saddle. Previously it was thought that the optimum time to release the arrow was rising in the stirrups at the height of the horse's rise in the canter, but as is regularly demonstrated the archer can shoot without stirrups (although generally the top of the rise, when all four horse's hooves are out of contact with the ground, is still the best point for release.)

Traditional Korean School of Horseback Archery

Korea has a fine tradition of horseback archery. In 2007 the Korean government passed a law to preserve and encourage development of traditional Korean martial arts - including Horseback Archery.

In Korean archery competitions there are 5 disciplines that are competed separately. The major difference in Korean archery is that all arrows must be stowed somewhere on the archer or horse - unlike Hungarian style where the archer can take the arrows from the bow hand. Traditionally this is a quiver on the right thigh, but it may also be through a belt, a sash, a saddle quiver or even held in a boot or arm quiver.

The first competition is a single shot to the side. The track is 90 metres long (as in the Hungarian method) but carries only one target set back around 5-10m from the track. This has a unique facia - consisting of 5 square concentric rings which increase in point score from the outer to inner, with the inner (often decorated with a 'Tiger' face) being worth the maximum 5 points. Each archer has two passes to complete, each run has to be completed within 16 seconds (or penalty points are incurred).

The next competition is very similar but is known as the 'double shot' which features one target in the first 30m, slightly angled forwards, and a second target in the last 30m, slightly angled backwards.

The final competition for the static targets is the 'serial shot' which consists of 5 targets evenly spaced along a 110m track - approximately one target every 20 metres or so. In all 3 static target competitions additional bonus points are awarded for style and form.

Another major difference in Korean archery style is the 'Mogu' or moving target competition. This consists of one rider towing a large cotton-and-bamboo ball behind their horse while another archer attempts to shoot the ball (with special turnip-headed arrows which have been dipped in ink). The archer attempts to hit the ball as many times as possible. A second 'Mo Gu' event consists of a team of two trying to hit the target towed by a third rider. Points are awarded for how many arrows strike the ball (verified by the ink stains on the Mogu).

Traditional Japanese Horseback Archery

The history of Japanese horseback archery dates back to the 4th century. It became popular in Japan, attracting crowds; because of its solemn and sacred nature the Emperor found this inappropriate and banned public displays in 698. Horseback archery was a widely-used combat technique from the Heian Period to the Sengoku Period. Nasu no Yoichi, a samurai of the Kamakura Period is the most famous horseback archer in Japan. Three kinds of Japanese horseback archery (Kasagake, Yabusame, and Inuoumono) were defined.

When the arquebus was introduced to Japan in the 16th century, archery became outdated. To maintain traditional Japanese horseback archery, Tokugawa Yoshimune, the eighth Tokugawa shogun, ordered the Ogasawara clan to found a school. Current Japanese horseback archery succeeds to the technique reformed by the Ogasawara clan.

Traditionally, women were barred from performing in yabusame, but in 1963 female archers participated in a yabusame demonstration for the first time.

CAVALRY

Cavalry (from French *cavalerie,* cf. *cheval* 'horse') were soldiers or warriors who fought mounted on horseback. Cavalry were historically the third oldest (after infantry and chariotry) and the most mobile of the combat arms. A soldier in the cavalry is known by a number of designations such as cavalryman or trooper.

The designation of cavalry was not usually given to any military force that used other animals, such as camels or mules. Infantry who moved on horseback, but dismounted to fight on foot, were known in the 17th and early 18th centuries as dragoons, a class of mounted infantry which later evolved into cavalry proper while retaining their historic title.

From earliest times cavalry had the advantage of improved mobility, making it an "instrument which multiplied the fighting value of even the smallest forces, allowing them to outflank and avoid, to surprise and overpower, to retreat and escape according to the requirements of the moment".

A man fighting from horseback also had the advantages of greater height, speed, and inertial mass over an opponent on foot. Another element of horse mounted warfare is the psychological impact a mounted soldier can inflict on an opponent.

The mobility and shock value of the cavalry was greatly appreciated and exploited in armed forces in the Ancient and Middle Ages; some forces were mostly cavalry, particularly in nomadic societies of Asia, notably the Mongol armies. In Europe cavalry became increasingly armoured (heavy), and eventually became known for the mounted knights. During the 17th century cavalry in Europe lost most of its armor, ineffective against the muskets and cannon which were coming into use, and by the mid-19th century armor had mainly fallen into disuse, with some regiments retained a small thickened cuirass that offered some protection against shot.

In the period between the World Wars many cavalry units were converted into motorised infantry and mechanised infantry units, or reformed as tank troops. However some cavalry still served during the Second World War, notably in the Red Army and the Italian Royal Army. Most cavalry units that are horse-mounted in modern armies serve in purely ceremonial roles, or as mounted infantry in difficult terrain such as mountains or heavily forested areas.

Role of Cavalry

In many modern armies, the term *cavalry* is still often used to refer to units that are a combat arm of the armed forces which in the past filled the traditional horse-borne land combat light cavalry roles. These include scouting, skirmishing with enemy reconnaissance elements to deny them knowledge of own disposition of troops, forward security, offensive reconnaissance by combat, defensive screening of friendly forces during retrograde movement, retreat, restoration of command and control, deception, battle handover and passage of lines, relief in place, linkup, breakout operations, and raiding. The shock role, traditionally filled by heavy cavalry, is generally filled by units with the 'armored' designation.

Origins

Before the Iron Age, the role of cavalry on the battlefield was largely performed by light chariots. The chariot originated with the Sintashta-Petrovka culture in Central Asia and spread by nomadic or semi-nomadic Indo-Iranians. The chariot was quickly adopted by settled peoples both as a military technology and an object of ceremonial status, especially by the Pharaohs of the New Kingdom of Egypt as well as Assyrian and Babylonian royalty.

The power of mobility given by mounted units was recognized early on, but was offset by the difficulty of raising large forces and by the inability of horses (then mostly small) to carry heavy armor. Cavalry techniques were an innovation of equestrian nomads of the Central Asian and Iranian steppe and pastoralist tribes such as the Persian Parthians and Sarmatians.

Fighting from the back of a horse was much more difficult than mere riding. The cavalry acted in pairs; the reins of the mounted archer were controlled by his neighbour's hand. Even at this early time, cavalry used swords, shields, and bows. The sculpture implies two types of cavalry, but this might be a simplification by the artist. Later images of Assyrian cavalry show saddle cloths as primitive saddles, allowing each archer to control his own horse.

As early as 490 BC a breed of large horses was bred in the Nisaean plain in Media to carry men with increasing amounts of armour. But large horses were still very exceptional at this time. Excepting a few ineffective trials of scythed chariots, the use of chariots in battle was obsolete in civilized nations by the time of the Persian defeat at the hands of Alexander the Great, but chariots remained in use for ceremonial purposes such as carrying the victorious general in a Roman triumph, or for racing. The southern Britons met Julius Caesar with chariots in 55 and 54 BC, but by the time of the Roman conquest of Britain a century later chariots were obsolete even in Britannia.

Ancient Greek

Cavalry played a relatively minor role in ancient Greek city-states, with conflicts decided by massed armored infantry. However, Thebes produced Pelopidas, her first great cavalry commander, whose tactics and skills were absorbed by Phillip II of Macedon when Phillip was a guest-hostage in Thebes. Thessaly was widely known for producing competent cavalrymen, and later experiences in wars both with and against the Persians taught the Greeks the value of cavalry in skirmishing and pursuit. The Athenian author and soldier Xenophon in particular advocated the creation of a small but well-trained cavalry force; to that end, he wrote several manuals on horsemanship and cavalry operations.

The Macedonian kingdom in the north, on the other hand, developed a strong cavalry force that culminated in the *hetairoi* (Companion cavalry) of Philip II and Alexander the Great. In addition to these heavy cavalry, the Macedonian combined arms army also employed lighter horsemen called prodromoi for scouting and screening, as well as the Macedonian pike phalanx and various kinds of light infantry. There were also the *Ippiko* (or 'Horserider'), Greek 'heavy' cavalry, armed with kontos (or cavalry lance), and sword. They wore leather armour or mail and hat. They were medium cavalry, rather than heavy cavalry. They were good scouts, skirmishers, and chasers.

Roman Republic and Early Empire

The cavalry in the early Roman Republic remained the preserve of the wealthy landed class known as the *equites*—men who could afford the expense of maintaining a horse in addition to arms and armor heavier than those of the common legions. As the class grew to be more of a social elite instead of a functional property-based military grouping, the Romans began to employ Italian socii for filling the ranks of their cavalry. At about the same time the Romans began to recruit foreign auxiliary cavalry from among Gauls, Iberians, and Numidians, the last being highly valued as mounted skirmishers and scouts. Julius Caesar himself was known for his admiration of his escort of Germanic mixed cavalry, giving rise to the *Cohortae Equitates*. Early emperors maintained an ala of Batavian cavalry as their bodyguards until the unit was dismissed by Galba after the Batavian Rebellion.

For the most part, Roman cavalry during the Republic functioned as an adjunct to the legionary infantry and formed only one-fifth of the showing force. This does not mean that its utility could be underestimated, though, as its strategic role in scouting, skirmishing, and outpost duties was crucial to the Romans' capability to conduct operations over long distances in hostile or unfamiliar territory. In some occasions it also proved its ability to strike a decisive tactical blow against a weakened or unprepared enemy, such as the final charge at the Battle of Aquilonia.

After defeats such as the Battle of Carrhae, the Romans learned the importance of large cavalry formations from the Parthians. They would begin to substantially increase both the numbers and the training standards of the cavalry in their employ, just as nearly a thousand years earlier the first Iranians to reach the Iranian Plateau forced the Assyrians to a similar reform. Nonetheless, they would continue to rely mainly on their heavy infantry supported by auxiliary cavalry.

Late Roman Empire and the Migration Empire

In the army of the late Roman Empire, cavalry played an increasingly important role. The Spatha, the classical sword throughout most of the 1st millennium was adopted as the standard model for the Empire's cavalry forces.

The most widespread employment of heavy cavalry at this time was found in the forces of the Parthians and their Iranian Sassanid successors. Both, but especially the latter, were famed for the cataphract (fully armored cavalry armed with lances) even though the majority of their forces consisted of lighter horse archers. The West first encountered this eastern heavy cavalry during the Hellenistic period with further intensive contacts during the eight centuries of the Roman–Persian wars. At first the Parthians' mobility greatly confounded the Romans, whose armoured close-order infantry proved unable to match the speed of the Parthians. However, later the Romans would successfully adapt such heavy armor and cavalry tactics by creating their own units of cataphracts and *clibanarii.*

The decline of the Roman infrastructure made it more difficult to field large infantry forces, and during the 4th and 5th centuries cavalry began to take a more dominant role on the European battlefield, also in part made possible by the appearance of new, larger breeds of horses. The replacement of the Roman saddle by variants on the Scythian model, with pommel and cantle, was also a significant factor as was the adoption of stirrups and the concomitant increase in stability of the rider's seat. Armored Cataphracts began to be deployed in eastern Europe and the near East, following the precedents established by Persian forces, as the main striking force of the armies in contrast to the earlier roles of cavalry as scouts, raiders, and outflankers.

The late Roman cavalry tradition and the mounted nobility of the Germanic invaders both contributed to the development of mediaeval knightly cavalry.

Arabs

Early organised Arab cavalry under the Rashidun caliphate was a light cavalry armed with lance and sword; its main role was to attack the enemy flanks and rear. Armor was relatively light. The Muslims' light cavalry during the later years of Islamic conquest of Levant became the most powerful section of army. The best use of this lightly armed fast moving cavalry was revealed at the Battle of Yarmouk (AD 636) in which Khalid ibn Walid, knowing the importance and ability of his cavalry, used them to turn the tables at every critical instance of the battle with their ability to engage and disengage and turn back and attack again from the flank or rear. A strong cavalry regiment was formed by Khalid ibn Walid which included the veterans of the campaign of Iraq and Syria. Early Muslim historians have given it the name *Mutaharrik tulai'a*, or the Mobile guard. This was used as an advance guard and a strong striking force to route the opposing armies with its greater mobility that give it an upper hand when maneuvering against any Byzantine army. With this mobile striking force, the conquest of Syria was made easy.

The Battle of Talas in 751 CE was a conflict between the Arab Abbasid Caliphate and the Chinese Tang Dynasty over the control of Central Asia. Chinese infantry were routed by Arab cavalry near the bank of the River Talas.

Later Mamluks were trained as cavalry soldiers. Mamluks were to follow the dictates of al-furusiyya, a code of conduct that included values like courage and generosity but also doctrine of cavalry tactics, horsemanship, archery and treatment of wounds.

Asia

Central Asia

Xiongnu or Hun, Tujue, Avars, Kipchaks, Mongols, Cossacks and the various Turkic peoples are also examples of the horse-mounted peoples that managed to gain substantial successes in military conflicts with settled agrarian and urban societies, due to their strategic and tactical mobility. As European states began to assume the character of bureaucratic nation-states supporting professional standing armies, recruitment of these mounted warriors was undertaken in order to fill the strategic roles of scouts and raiders. The best known instance of the continued employment of mounted tribal auxiliaries were the Cossack cavalry regiments of Tsarist Russia. In eastern Europe, Russia, and out onto the steppes, cavalry remained important much longer and dominated the scene of warfare until the early 17th century and even beyond, as the strategic mobility of cavalry was crucial for the semi-nomadic pastoralist lives that many steppe cultures led.

Tibetans also had a tradition of cavalry warfare, in several military engagements early on with the Chinese Tang Dynasty (AD 618-907), including Emperor Taizong's campaign against Tufan in 638.

East Asia

Further east, the military history of China, specifically northern China, held a long tradition of intense military exchange between Han Chinese infantry forces of the settled dynastic empires and the mounted nomads or "barbarians" of the north. The naval history of China was centreed more to the south, where mountains, rivers, and large lakes necessitated the employment of a large and well-kept navy.

In 307 BC, King Wuling of Zhao, the ancient Chinese ruler of the former State of Jin territory, ordered his military commanders and troops to adopt the trousers of the nomads as well as practice the nomads' form of mounted archery to hone their new cavalry skills. Soon afterwards the cavalry tactics employed by the State of Zhao forced their enemies in the other Warring States to adopt the same techniques in order to mount any effective attack against their swift movements on the battlefield.

The adoption of massed cavalry in China also broke the tradition of the chariot-riding Chinese aristocracy in battle, which had been in use since the ancient Shang Dynasty (c. 1600 BC-1050 BC). By this time large Chinese infantry-based armies of 100,000 to 200,000 troops were now buttressed with several hundred thousand mounted cavalry in support or as an effective striking force. The handheld pistol-and-trigger crossbow was invented in China in the 4th century BC; it was written by the Song Dynasty scholars Zeng Gongliang, Ding Du, and Yang Weide in their book *Wujing Zongyao* (1044 AD) that massed missile fire by crossbowmen was the most effective defense against enemy cavalry charges.

On many occasions the Chinese studied nomadic cavalry tactics and applied the lessons in creating their own potent cavalry forces, while in others they simply recruited the tribal horsemen wholesale into their armies; and in yet other cases nomadic empires proved eager to enlist Chinese infantry and engineering, as in the case of the Mongol Empire and its sinicized part, the Yuan Dynasty (1279-1368). The Chinese recognized early on during the Han Dynasty (202 BC-AD 220) that they were at a disadvantage in lacking the number of horses the northern nomadic peoples mustered in their armies. Emperor Wu of Han (r. 141 BC-87 BC) went to war with the Dayuan for this reason, since the Dayuan were hording a massive amount of tall, strong, Central Asian bred horses in the Hellenized–Greek region of Fergana (established slightly earlier by Alexander the Great). Although experiencing some defeats early on in the campaign, Emperor Wu's war from 104 BC to 102 BC succeeded in gathering the prized tribute of horses from Fergana.

Cavalry tactics in China were enhanced by the invention of the saddle-attached stirrup by at least the 4th century, as the oldest reliable depiction of a rider with paired stirrups was found in a Jin Dynasty tomb of the year AD 322. The Chinese invention of the horse collar by the 5th century was also a great improvement from the breast harness, allowing the horse to haul greater weight without heavy burden on its skeletal structure.

The horse warfare of Korea was first started during the ancient Korean kingdom Gojoseon. Since at least the 3rd century BC, there was influence of northern nomadic peoples and Yemaek peoples on Korean Warfare. By roughly the 1st century BC, the ancient kingdom of Buyeo also had mounted warriors. The cavalry of Goguryeo, one of the Three Kingdoms of Korea, were called *Gaemamusa*. King Gwanggaeto the Great often led expeditions into the Baekje, Gaya confederacy, Buyeo, Later Yan and against Japanese invaders with his cavalry.

In the 12th century, Jurchen tribes began to violate the Goryeo-Jurchen borders, and eventually invaded Goryeo Korea. After experiencing the invasion by the Jurchen, Korean general Yun Gwan realized that Goryeo lacked efficient cavalry units. He reorganized the Goryeo military into a professional army that would contain decent and well-trained cavalry units. In 1107, the Jurchen were ultimately defeated, and surrendered to Yun Gwan. To mark the victory, General Yun built nine fortresses to the northeast of the Goryeo-Jurchen borders.

South Asia

In the Indian subcontinent, cavalry played a major role from the Gupta Dynasty (320-600) period onwards. India has also the oldest evidence for the introduction of toe-stirrups.

Indian literature contains numerous references to the cavalry forces of the Central Asian horse nomads like the Sakas, Kambojas, Yavanas, Pahlavas and Paradas. Numerous Puranic texts refer to a conflict in ancient India (16th c. BC) in which the cavalry forces of five nations, called five hordes (*pañcaganan*) or Ksatriya hordes (*Ksatriya ganah*), attacked and captured the throne of Ayudhya by dethroning its VedicKing Bahu.

The *Mahabharata, Ramayana,* numerous *Puranas* and some foreign sources numerously attest that Kamboja cavalry was frequently requisitioned in ancient wars. Historians writes:

> "Both the Puranas and the epics agree that the horses of the Sindhu and Kamboja regions were of the finest breed, and that the services of the Kambojas as cavalry troopers were requisitioned in ancient wars".
>
> "Most famous horses are said to come either from Sindhu or Kamboja; of the latter (i.e the Kamboja), the Indian epic *Mahabharata* speaks among the finest horsemen".

Mahabharata (950 c BC) speaks of the esteemed cavalry of the Kambojas, Sakas, Yavanas and Tusharas, all of whom had participated in the Kurukshetra war under the supreme command of Kamboja ruler Sudakshin Kamboj. Mahabharata and Vishnudharmotari Purana especially styles the Kambojas, Yavansa, Gandharas etc. as 'Ashva.yuddha.kushalah' (expert cavalrymen). In the *Mahabharata* war, the Kamboja cavalry along with that of the Sakas, Yavanas is reported to have been enlisted by the Kuru king Duryodhana of Hastinapura.

Herodotus (484 c BC-425 c BC) attests that the Gandarian mercenaries (i.e. *Gandharans/Kambojans* of Gandari Strapy of Achaemenids) from the 20th strapy of the Achaemenids were recruited in the army of emperor Xerxes I (486-465 BC), which he led against the Hellas. Similarly, the *men of the Mountain Land* from north of Kabol-River equivalent to medieval Kohistan (Pakistan), figure in the army of Darius III against Alexander at Arbela with a cavalry and fifteen elephants. This obviously refers to Kamboja cavalry south of Hindukush.

The Kambojas were famous for their horses, as well as cavalry-men (*asva-yuddha-Kushalah*). On account of their supreme position in horse (*ashva*) culture, they were also popularly known as Ashvakas, i.e. the 'horsemen' and their land was known as 'Home of Horses'. They are the Assakenoi and Aspasioi of the Classical writings, and the *Ashvakayanas* and *Ashvayanas* in Panini's *Ashtadhyayi*. The Assakenoi had faced Alexander with 30,000 infantry, 20,000 cavalry and 30 war elephants. Scholars have identified the Assakenoi and Aspasioi clans of Kunar and Swat valleys as a section of the Kambojas. These hardy tribes had offered stubborn resistance to Alexander (326 c BC) during latter's campaign of the Kabul, Kunar and Swat valleys and had even extracted the praise of the Alexander's historians. These highlanders, designated as *"parvatiya Ayudhajivinah"* in Panini's *Astadhyayi*, were rebellious, fiercely independent and freedom-loving cavalrymen who never easily yielded to any overlord.

The Sanskrit drama *Mudra-rakashas* by Visakha Dutta and the Jaina work *Parisishtaparvan* refer to Chandragupta's (320 C BC-298 c BC) alliance with Himalayan king *Parvataka*. The Himalayan alliance gave Chandragupta a formidable composite army made up of the cavalry forces of the Shakas, Yavanas, Kambojas, Kiratas, Parasikas and Bahlikas as attested by Mudra-*Rakashas* (*Mudra-Rakshasa* 2). These hordes had helped Chandragupta Maurya defeat the ruler of Magadha and placed Vhandragupta on the throne, thus laying the foundations of Mauryan Dynasty in Northern India.

The cavalry of Hunas and the Kambojas is also attested in the *Raghu Vamsa* epic poem of Sanskrit poet Kalidasa. Raghu of Kalidasa is believed to be Chandragupta II (*Vikaramaditya*) (AD 375-413/15), of the well-known Gupta Dynasty.

As late as mediaeval era, the Kamboja cavalry had also formed part of the Gurjara-Pratihara armed forces in 8th/10th centuries AD. They had come to Bengal with the Pratiharas when the latter conquered part of the province.

Ancient Kambojas were constituted into military *Sanghas* and *Srenis* (Corporations) to manage their political and military affairs, as *Arthashastra* of Kautiliya as well as the *Mahabharata* amply attest for us. They are attested to be living as *Ayuddha-jivi* or *Shastr-opajivis* (Nation-in-arms), which also means that the Kamboja cavalry offered its military services to other nations as well. There are numerous references to Kambojas having been requisitioned as cavalry troopers in ancient wars by outside nations.

European Middle Ages

Although Roman cavalry had no stirrups, their horned saddle allowed the combination of a firm seat with substantial flexibility. But the introduction of the wraparound saddle during the Middle Ages provided greater efficiency in mounted shock combat and the important invention of the stirrup enabled a broader array of attacks to be delivered from the back of a horse. As a greater weight of man and armor could be supported in the saddle, the probability of being dismounted in combat was significantly reduced.

In particular, a charge with the lance couched under the armpit would no longer turn into pole vaulting; this eventually led to an enormous increase in the impact of the charge. Last but not least, the introduction of spurs allowed better control of the mount during the 'knightly charge' in full gallop. In western Europe there emerged what is considered the 'ultimate' heavy cavalry, the knight. The knights and other similarly equipped mounted men-at-arms charged in close formation, exchanging flexibility for a massive, irresistible first charge.

The mounted men-at-arms quickly became an important force in Western European tactics. Medieval military doctrine employed them as part of a combined-arms force along with various kinds of foot troops; however medieval chroniclers tended to pay undue attention to the knights at the expense of the rank and file, which led early students of military history to suppose that this heavy cavalry was the only force that mattered on medieval European battlefields, which was not the case.

Massed English longbowmen triumphed over French cavalry at Crécy, Poitiers and Agincourt, while at Gisors (1188), Bannockburn (1314), and Laupen (1339), foot-soldiers proved their invulnerability to cavalry charges as long as they held their formation. Once the Swiss developed their pike squares for offensive as well as defensive use, infantry started to become the principal arm. This aggressive new doctrine gave the Swiss victory over a range of adversaries, and their enemies found that the only reliable way to defeat them was by the use of an even more comprehensive combined arms doctrine, as evidenced in the Battle of Marignano. The introduction of missile weapons that required less skill than the longbow, such as the crossbow and hand cannon, also helped remove the focus somewhat from cavalry elites to masses of cheap infantry equipped with easy-to-learn weapons. These missile weapons were very successfully used in the Hussite Wars, in combination with Wagenburg tactics.

This gradual rise in the dominance of infantry led to the adoption of dismounted tactics. From the earliest times knights and mounted men-at-arms had frequently dismounted to handle enemies they could not overcome on horseback, such as in the Battle of the Dyle (891) and the Battle of Bremule (1119), but after 1350s this trend became more marked with the dismounted men-at-arms fighting as super-heavy infantry with two-handed swords and poleaxes. In any case, warfare in the Middle Ages tended to be dominated by raids and sieges rather than pitched battles, and mounted men-at-arms rarely had any choice other than dismounting when faced with the prospect of assaulting a fortified position.

Renaissance Europe

Ironically, the rise of infantry in the early 16th century coincided with the 'golden age' of heavy cavalry; a French or Spanish army at the beginning of the century could have up to half its numbers made up of various kinds of light and heavy cavalry, whereas in earlier medieval and later 17th century armies the proportion of cavalry was seldom more than a quarter.

Knighthood largely lost its military functions and became more closely tied to social and economic prestige in an increasingly capitalistic Western society. With the rise of drilled and trained infantry, the mounted men-at-arms, now sometimes called *gendarmes* and often part of the standing army themselves, adopted the same role as in the Hellenistic age, that of delivering a decisive blow once the battle was already engaged, either by charging the enemy in the flank or attacking their commander-in-chief. From the 1550s onwards, the use of gunpowder weapons solidified infantry's dominance of the battlefield and began to allow true mass armies to develop. This is closely related to the increase in the size of armies throughout the early modern period; heavily armored cavalrymen were expensive to raise and maintain and it took years to replace a skilled horseman or a trained horse, while arquebusiers and later musketeers could be trained and kept in the field at much lower cost, and were much easier to replace.

The Spanish tercio and later formations relegated cavalry to a supporting role. The pistol was specifically developed to try and bring cavalry back into the conflict, together with manoeuvres such as the caracole. The caracole was not particularly successful, however, and the charge (whether with sword, pistol, or lance) remained as the primary mode of employment for many types of European cavalry, although by this time it was delivered in much deeper formations and with greater discipline than before. The demi-lancers and the heavily armored sword-and-pistol reiters were among the types of cavalry whose heyday was in the 16th and 17th centuries, as for the Polish winged hussars, a heavy cavalry force that achieved great success against Swedes, Russians, and Turks.

18th Century Europe and Napoleonic Wars

Cavalry retained an important role in this age of regularization and standardization across European armies. First and foremost they remained the primary choice for confronting enemy cavalry. Attacking an unbroken infantry force head-on usually resulted in failure, but extended linear infantry formations were vulnerable to flank or rear attacks. Cavalry was important at Blenheim (1704), Rossbach (1757), Eylau and Friedland (1807), remaining significant throughout the Napoleonic Wars.

Massed infantry was deadly to cavalry, but offered an excellent target for artillery. Once the bombardment had disordered the infantry formation, cavalry were able to rout and pursue the scattered foot soldiers. It was not until individual firearms gained accuracy and improved rates of fire that cavalry was diminished in this role as well. Even then light cavalry remained an indispensable tool for scouting, screening the army's movements, and harassing the enemy's supply lines until military aircraft supplanted them in this role in the early stages of World War I.

The greatest cavalry charge of modern history was at the 1807 battle of Eylau, when the entire 11,000-strong French cavalry reserve, led by Maréchal Murat, launched a huge charge on and through the Russian infantry lines. The French horsemen also proved that cavalry could be a decisive element during the Peninsular War in Spain.

19th Century

By the 19th century, European cavalry fell into four main categories:

- Cuirassiers, heavy cavalry.
- Dragoons, originally mounted infantry but later regarded as medium cavalry.
- Hussars, light cavalry.
- Lancers or Uhlans, light cavalry armed with lances.

There were cavalry variations for individual nations as well: France had the *chasseurs à cheval*; Germany had the *Jäger zu Pferd*; Bavaria had the *Chevaulegers*; and Russia had Cossacks. Britain's only cuirassiers were the Household Cavalry, but Dragoon Guards regiments were classed as heavy cavalry. In the United States Army the cavalry were almost always dragoons. The Imperial Japanese Army had its cavalry uniformed as hussars, but they fought as dragoons.

In the early American Civil War the regular United States Army mounted rifle, dragoon, and two existing cavalry regiments were reorganized and renamed cavalry regiments, of which there were six. Over a hundred other federal and state cavalry regiments were organized, but the infantry played a much larger role in many battles due to its larger numbers, lower cost per rifle fielded, and much easier recruitment. However, cavalry saw a role as part of screening forces and in foraging and scouting. The later phases of the war saw the Federal army developing a truly effective cavalry force fighting as scouts, raiders, and, with repeating rifles, as mounted infantry.

Post-civil War, as the volunteer armies disbanded, the regular army cavalry regiments increased in number from six to ten, among them the U.S. 7th Cavalry Regiment of Little Bighorn fame, and the African-American U.S. 9th Cavalry Regiment and U.S. 10th Cavalry Regiment. These units, along with others (both cavalry and infantry), collectively became known as the Buffalo Soldiers. These regiments, which rarely took the field as complete organisations, served throughout the Indian Wars through the close of the frontier in the 1890s.

19th Century Imperial Expansion

Cavalry found new success in Imperial operations (irregular warfare), where modern weapons were lacking and the slow moving infantry-artillery train or fixed fortifications were often ineffective against native insurgents (unless the natives offered a fight on an equal footing, as at Tel-el-Kebir, Omdurman, etc.). Cavalry 'flying columns' proved effective, or at least cost-effective, in many campaigns—although an astute native commander (like Samori in western Africa, Shamil in the Caucasus, or any of the better Boer commanders) could turn the tables and use the greater mobility of their cavalry to offset their relative lack of firepower compared to European forces.

The British Indian Army maintained about forty regiments of cavalry, officered by British and manned by Indian sowars (cavalrymen). The legendary exploits of this branch lives on in literature and early films. Among the more famous regiments in the lineages of modern Indian and Pakistani Armies are:

- The charge of the 21st Lancers at Omdurman.
- Governor General's Bodyguard (now President's Bodyguard).
- Skinner's Horse [now India's 1st Horse (Skinner's Horse)].
- Gardner's Lancers [now India's 2nd Lancers (Gardner's Horse)].
- Hodson's Horse [now India's rd Horse (Hodson's)] of the Bengal Lancers fame.
- 6th Bengal Cavalry (later amalgamated with 7th Hariana Lancers to form 18th King Edward's Own Cavalry) now 18th Cavalry of the Indian Army.
- Probyn's Horse (now Pakistani).
- Royal Deccan Horse (now India's The Deccan Horse).
- Poona Horse (now India's The Poona Horse).
- Scinde Horse (now India's The Scinde Horse).
- Queen's Own Guides Cavalry (now partitioned between Pakistan and India).

Several of these formations are still active, though they now are armoured formations, for example Guides Cavalry in Pakistan.

The French Army maintained substantial cavalry forces in Algeria and Morocco from 1830 until the Second World War. Much of the Mediterranean coastal terrain was suitable for mounted action and there was a long established culture of horsemanship amongst the Arab and Berber inhabitants. The French forces included Spahis, Chasseurs d' Afrique, Foreign Legion cavalry and mounted Goumiers.

First World War/Pre-war Development

At the beginning of the 20th century all armies still maintained substantial cavalry forces, although there was contention over whether their role should revert to that of mounted infantry (the historic dragoon function). Following the experience of the South African War of 1899-1902 (where mounted Boer citizen commandos fighting on foot from cover proved superior to regular cavalry) the British Army withdrew lances for all but ceremonial purposes and placed a new emphasis on training for dismounted action.

In 1908 however the six British lancer regiments in existence resumed use of this impressive but obsolete weapon for active service. In 1882 the Imperial Russian Army converted all its line hussar and lancer regiments to dragoons, with an emphasis on mounted infantry training. In 1910 these regiments reverted to their historic roles, designations and uniforms.

Cavalry during Opening Stages

In August 1914 all combatant armies still retained substantial numbers of cavalry and the mobile nature of the opening battles on both Eastern and Western Fronts provided a number of instances of traditional cavalry actions, though on a smaller and more scattered scale than those of previous wars. The Imperial German Cavalry, while as colourful and traditional as any in peacetime appearance, had adopted a practice of falling back on infantry support when any substantial opposition was encountered. These cautious tactics aroused derision amongst their more conservative French and Russian opponents but proved appropriate to the new nature of warfare. Once the front lines stabilised, a combination of barbed wire, machine guns and rapid fire rifles proved deadly to horse mounted troops.

Cavalry in Europe 1915-18

For the remainder of the War on the Western Front cavalry had virtually no role to play. The British and French armies dismounted many of their cavalry regiments and used them in infantry and other roles: the Life Guards for example spent the last months of the War as a machine gun corps; and the Australian Light Horse served as light infantry during the Gallipoli campaign. In September 1914 cavalry comprised 9.28 per cent of the total manpower of the British Expeditionary Force in France - by July 1918 this proportion had fallen to 1.65 per cent. The German Army dismounted nearly all their cavalry in the West.

Some cavalry were retained as mounted troops behind the lines in anticipation of a penetration of the opposing trenches that it seemed would never come. Tanks, introduced on the Western Front in September 1916, had the capacity to achieve such breakthroughs but did not have the reliable range to exploit them. Since mounted troops were too vulnerable and slow moving to act in effective support of the new weapon, history recorded no significant role for cavalry in mechanized warfare, and post war planning in the allied nations replaced horse cavalry with mechanized cavalry.

In the wider spaces of the Eastern Front a more fluid form of warfare continued and there was still a use for mounted troops. Some wide-ranging actions were fought, again mostly in the early months of the war. However, even here the value of cavalry was over-rated and the maintenance of large mounted formations at the front by the Russian Army put a major strain on the railway system, to little strategic advantage.

Post World War I

Combination of military conservatism in almost all armies and post-war financial constraints prevented the lessons of 1914-18 being acted on immediately. There was a general reduction in the number of cavalry regiments in the British, French, Italian and other Western armies but it was still argued with conviction (for example in the 1922 edition of the *Encyclopædia Britannica*) that mounted troops had a major role to play in future warfare. The 1920s saw an interim period during which cavalry remained as a proud and conspicuous element of all major armies, though much less so than prior to 1914.

Cavalry was extensively used in the Russian Civil War and the Soviet-Polish War. The last major cavalry battle was the Battle of Komarów in 1920, between Poland and the Russian Bolsheviks. Colonial warfare in Morocco, Syria, the Middle East and the North West Frontier of India provided some opportunities for mounted action against enemies lacking advanced weaponry.

The post-war German Army (Reichsheer) was permitted a large proportion of cavalry (18 regiments or 16.4 per cent of total manpower) under the conditions of the Treaty of Versailles. The U.S. Cavalry abandoned its sabres in 1934 and commenced the conversion of its horsed regiments to mechanized cavalry, starting with the First Regiment of Cavalry in January 1933.

In the British Army, all cavalry regiments were mechanised between 1929 and 1941, redefining their role from horse to armoured vehicles to form the Royal Armoured Corps together with the Royal Tank Regiment.

The thirty-nine regiments of the Indian Army were reduced to twenty-one as the result of a series of amalgamations immediately following I World War. The new establishment remained unchanged until 1936 when three regiments were redesignated as permanent training units, each with six, still mounted, regiments linked to them. In 1938 the process of mechanism began with the conversion of a full cavalry brigade (two Indian regiments and one British) to armoured car and tank units. By the end of 1940 all of the Indian cavalry had been mechanised, receiving light tanks, armoured cars or 15cwt trucks.

The last horsed regiment of the Indian Army (other than the Viceregal Bodyguard and some Indian States Forces regiments) was the 19th King George's Own Lancers which had its last mounted parade at Rawalpindi on 28 October 1939. This unit still exists (though in the Pakistan Army) with an armour TOE.

During the 1930s the French Army experimented with integrating mounted and mechanised cavalry units into larger formations. Dragoon regiments were converted to motorised infantry (trucks and motor cycles), and cuirassiers to armoured units; while light cavalry (Chasseurs a' Cheval, Hussars and Spahis) remained as mounted sabre squadrons. The theory was that mixed forces comprising these diverse units could utilise the strengths of each according to circumstances. In practice mounted troops proved unable to keep up with fast moving mechanised units over any distance.

World War II Cavalry

While most armies still maintained cavalry units at the outbreak of World War II in 1939, significant mounted action was largely restricted to the Polish, Balkan and Soviet campaigns.

Polish

A popular myth is that Polish cavalry armed with lances charged German tanks during the September 1939 campaign. This arose from misreporting of a single clash on 1 September near Krojanty, when two squadrons of the Polish 18th Lancers armed with sabres scattered German infantry before being caught in the open by German armoured cars.

Two examples illustrate how the myth developed. First, because motorised vehicles were in short supply, the Poles used horses to pull anti-tank weapons into position. Second, there were a few incidents when Polish cavalry was trapped by German tanks, and attempted to fight free. However, this did not mean that the Polish army chose to attack tanks with horse cavalry. Later, on the Eastern Front, the Red Army did deploy cavalry units effectively against the Germans.

A more correct term should be 'mounted infantry' instead of 'cavalry', as horses were primarily used as a means of transportation, for which they were very suitable in view of the very poor road conditions in pre-war Poland. Another myth describes Polish cavalry as being armed with both sabres and lances; lances were used for peacetime ceremonial purposes only and the primary weapon of the Polish cavalryman in 1939 was a rifle. Individual equipment did include a sabre, probably because of well-established tradition, but in the case of a melee combat this secondary weapon would probably be more effective than a rifle and bayonet. Moreover, the Polish cavalry brigade order of battle of 1939 included, apart from the mounted soldiers themselves, light and heavy machine guns (wheeled), Anti-tank rifle, model 35, anti-aircraft weapon, artillery like Bofors 37 mm anti tank gun or light and scout tanks, etc. The last, in Europe, cavalry vs. cavalry mutual charge took place in Poland during the battle of Krasnobrod when the Polish and German cavalry units charged each other.

Greek

The Italian invasion of Greece in October 1940 saw mounted cavalry used effectively by the Greek defenders along the mountainous frontier with Albania. Three Greek cavalry regiments (two mounted and one partially mechanised) played an important role in the Italian defeat in this difficult terrain.

Soviet

By the final stages of the war only the Soviet Union was still fielding mounted units in substantial numbers, some in combined mechanized and horse units. The advantage of this approach was that in exploitation mounted infantry could keep pace with advancing tanks.

Other factors favouring the retention of mounted forces included the high quality of Russian Cossacks and other horse cavalry; and the relative lack of roads suitable for wheeled vehicles in many parts of the Eastern Front. Another consideration was that the logistic capacity required to support very large motorised forces exceeded that necessary for mounted troops.

Other Axis

Romanian, Hungarian and Italian cavalry had been dispersed or disbanded following the retreat of the Axis forces from Russia. Germany still maintained some mounted (mixed with bicycles) SS and Cossack units until the last days of the War.

U.S.

The U.S. Army's last horse cavalry actions were fought during II World War:

(a) by the 26th Cavalry Regiment (PS) in II World War - a small mounted regiment of Philippine Scouts which fought the Japanese during the retreat down the Bataan peninsula, until it was effectively destroyed by January 1942; and

(b) on captured German horses by the mounted reconnaissance section of the U.S. 10th Mountain Division in a spearhead pursuit of the German Army across the Po Valley in Italy in April 1945. The last horsed U.S. Cavalry (the Second Cavalry Division) were dismounted in March 1944.

British Empire

All British Army cavalry regiments had been mechanised since 1 March 1942 when the Queen's Own Yorkshire Dragoons (Yeomanry) was converted to a motorised role, following mounted service against the Vichy French in Syria the previous year. The final cavalry charge by British Empire forces occurred on 21 March 1942 when a 60 strong patrol of the Burma Frontier Force encountered Japanese infantry near Toungoo airfield in central Burma. The Sikh sowars of the Frontier Force cavalry, led by Captain Arthur Sandeman, charged in the old style with sabres and most were killed.

Post World War II to Present Day

The Soviet Army retained horse cavalry divisions until 1955, and even at the dissolution of the Soviet Union in 1991, there was an independent horse mounted cavalry squadron in Kyrgyzstan.

Several armored units of the modern United States Army retain the designation of 'Armoured cavalry'. The United States also had 'air cavalry' units equipped with helicopters, though that designation has fallen out of use, with the term Air Assault coined for that mission and modern 'cavalry' being retained for ground-based mobility.

While most modern 'cavalry' units have some historic connection with formerly mounted troops this is not always the case. The modern Irish Defence Force (IDF) includes a 'Cavalry Corps' equipped with Panhard armoured cars and Scorpion tracked combat reconnaissance vehicles. The Irish Defense Force has never included horse cavalry since its establishment in 1922 (other than a small mounted escort drawn from the Artillery Corps when required for ceremonial occasions). However, the mystique of the cavalry is such that the name has been introduced for what was always a mechanised force.

Some engagements in late 20th and early 21st century guerrilla wars involved mounted troops, particularly against partisan or guerrilla fighters in areas with poor transport infrastructure. Such units were not used as cavalry but rather as mounted infantry. Examples occurred in Afghanistan, Portuguese Africa and Rhodesia. The French Army used existing mounted squadrons of Spahis to a limited extent for patrol work during the Algerian War (1954-62) and the Swiss Army maintained a mounted dragoon regiment for combat purposes until 1973.

There were reports of Chinese mounted troops in action during frontier clashes with Vietnam in the mid/late 1970s. The Portuguese Army used horse mounted cavalry with some success in the wars of independence in Angola and Mozambique in the 1960s and 1970s. During the 1964-79 Rhodesian Bush War the Rhodesian Army created an elite mounted infantry unit called Grey's Scouts to fight unconventional actions against the rebel forces of Robert Mugabe and Joshua Nkomo. The horse mounted infantry of the Scouts were very effective and feared by their opponents in the rebel African forces. In the 1978 to present Afghan Civil War there have been several instances of horse mounted combat.

South and Central American armies maintained mounted cavalry longer than those of Europe, Asia or North America. The Mexican Army included a number of horse mounted cavalry regiments as late as the mid 1990s and the Chilean Army had five such regiments in 1983 as mounted mountain troops.

A number of armored regiments in the British Army retain the historic designations of Hussars, Dragoons, Dragoon Guards or Lancers. Only the Household Cavalry squadrons maintained for ceremonial duties in London are mounted.

Cavalry or mounted gendarmerie units continue to be maintained for purely or primarily ceremonial purposes by the United States, British, French, Italian, Danish, Swedish, Dutch, Chilean, Portuguese, Moroccan, Nigerian, Venezuelan, Brazilian, Peruvian, Paraguayan, Polish, Argentine, Senegalese, Jordanian, Pakistani, Indian, Spanish and Bulgarian armed forces. The Army of the Russian Federation has recently reintroduced a ceremonial mounted squadron wearing historic uniforms.

In the United States, the Horse Cavalry Detachment of the U.S. Army's 1st Cavalry Division is made up of active duty soldiers, still functions as an active unit, trained to approximate the weapons, tools, equipment and techniques used by the United States Cavalry in the 1880s. In addition, the Parsons' Mounted Cavalry is a Reserve Officer Training Corps unit which forms part of the Corps of Cadets at Texas A&M University.

The French Army still has regiments with the historic designations of Cuirassiers, Hussars, Chasseurs, Dragoons and Spahis. Only the cavalry of the Republican Guard and a ceremonial fanfare (trumpeters) for the cavalry/ armoured branch as a whole are now mounted.

In the Canadian Army, a number of regular and reserve units have cavalry roots, including The Royal Canadian Hussars (Montreal), the Governor General's Horse Guards, Lord Strathcona's Horse, the Royal Canadian Dragoons, and the South Alberta Light Horse. Of these, only the Lord Strathcona's Horse and the Governor General's Horse Guards maintain an official ceremonial horse-mounted cavalry troop or squadron.

Both the Australian and New Zealand armies follow the British practice of maintaining traditional titles (Light Horse or Mounted Rifles) for modern mechanised units. However, neither country retains a horse-mounted unit.

Today, the Indian Army's 61st Cavalry is reported to be the largest remaining non-ceremonial horse-mounted cavalry in the world. It was raised in 1951 from the amalgamated state cavalry squadrons of Gwailior, Jodhpur, and Mysore. The 61st Cavalry and the President's Body Guard parade in full dress uniform in New Delhi each year in what is probably the largest assembly of traditional cavalry still to be seen in the world. Both the Indian and the Pakistani armies maintain armoured regiments with the titles of Lancers or Horse, dating back to the 19th century.

As of 2007 the Chinese People's Liberation Army employs two battalions of horse cavalry in Xinjing Military District for border patrol work (see China-Defense.com website). In the wake of the 2008 Sichuan earthquake, there have been calls to rebuild the army horse inventory for disaster relief in difficult terrain.

Light and Armoured Cavalry

Historically, cavalry was divided into light and armoured cavalry and Horse archers. The differences were their role in combat, the size of the mount, and how much armor was worn by the mount and rider.

Early light cavalry (like the auxiliaries of the Roman army) were typically used to scout and skirmish, to cut down retreating infantry, and for defeating enemy missile troops. Armoured cavalry such as the Byzantine Cataphract were used as shock troops—they would charge the main body of the enemy and, in many cases, their actions decided the outcome of the battle, hence the later term 'battle cavalry'.

During the Gunpowder Age, armored cavalry become obsolescent. However, many units retained cuirasses and helmets for their protective value against sword and bayonet strikes and the morale boost these provide to the wearers. By this time the main difference between light and battle cavalry was their training; the former was regarded as a tool for harassment and reconnaissance, while the latter was considered best for close-order charges.

Since the development of armored warfare the distinction between light and heavy armor has persisted basically along the same lines. Armored cars and light tanks have adopted the reconnaissance role while medium and heavy tanks are regarded as the decisive shock troops.

Social Status

From the beginning of civilization to the 20th century, ownership of heavy cavalry horses has been a mark of wealth amongst settled peoples. A cavalry horse involves considerable expense in breeding, training, feeding, and equipment, and has very little productive use except as a mode of transport.

For this reason, and because of their often decisive military role, the cavalry has typically been associated with high social status. This was most clearly seen in the feudal system, where a lord was expected to enter combat armored and on horseback and bring with him an entourage of peasants on foot. If landlords and peasants came into conflict, the peasants would be ill-equipped to defeat armored knights.

In later national armies, service as an officer in the cavalry was generally a badge of high social status. For instance prior to 1914 most officers of British cavalry regiments came from a socially privileged background and the considerable expenses associated with their role generally required private means, even after it became possible for officers of the line infantry regiments to live on their pay.

Options open to poorer cavalry officers in the various European armies included service with less fashionable (though often highly professional) frontier or colonial units. These included the British Indian cavalry, the Russian Cossacks or the French Chasseurs d' Afrique.

During the 19th and early 20th centuries most monarchies maintained a mounted cavalry element in their royal or imperial guards. These ranged from small units providing ceremonial escorts and palace guards through to large formations intended for active service. The mounted escort of the Spanish Royal Household provided an example of the former and the twelve cavalry regiments of the Prussian Imperial Guard an example of the latter. In either case the officers of such units were likely to be drawn from the aristocracies of their respective societies.

CHAPTER 19

Pony

A pony is a small horse (*Equus ferus caballus*). Depending on context, a pony may be a horse that is under an approximate or exact height at the withers, or a small horse with a specific conformation and temperament. There are many different breeds. Compared to other horses, ponies often exhibit thicker manes, tails and overall coat, as well as proportionally shorter legs, wider barrels, heavier bone, thicker necks, and shorter heads with broader foreheads. The word 'pony' derives from the old French *poulenet*, meaning foal, a young, immature horse, but this is not the modern meaning; unlike a horse foal, a pony remains small when fully grown. However, on occasion, people who are unfamiliar with horses may confuse an adult pony with a foal.

The ancestors of most modern ponies developed small stature due to living on the margins of livable horse habitat. These smaller animals were domesticated and bred for various purposes all over the Northern hemisphere. Ponies were historically used for driving and freight transport, as children's mounts, for recreational riding, and later as competitors and performers in their own right. During the Industrial Revolution, particularly in Great Britain, a significant number were used as pit ponies, hauling loads of coal in the mines.

Ponies are generally considered intelligent and friendly, though sometimes they also are described as stubborn or cunning. Properly trained ponies are appropriate mounts for children who are learning to ride. Larger ponies can be ridden by adults, as ponies are usually strong for their size. In modern use, many organisations define a pony as a mature horse that measures less than 14.2 hands (58 inches, 147 cm) at the withers, but there are a number of exceptions. Different organisations that use a strict measurement model vary from 14 hands (56 inches, 142 cm) to nearly 14.3 hands (59 inches, 150 cm). Many breeds classify an animal as either horse or pony based on pedigree and phenotype, no matter its height. Some full-sized horses may be called "ponies" for various reasons of tradition or as a term of endearment.

For many forms of competition, the official definition of a pony is a horse that measures less than 14.2 hands (58 inches, 147 cm) at the withers. Horses are 14.2 or taller. The International Federation for Equestrian Sports defines the official cutoff point at 148 centimetres (58.27 in) (just over 14.2 h) without shoes and 149 centimetres (58.66 in) (just over 14.2-1/2 h) with shoes, though allows a margin for competition measurement of up to 150 centimetres (59.1 in) (14.3 h) without shoes, or 151 centimetres (59.45 in) (just under 14.3-1/2 h) with shoes. However, the term 'pony' can be used in general (or affectionately) for any small horse, regardless of its actual size or breed. Furthermore, some horse breeds may have individuals who mature under that height but are still called 'horses' and are allowed to compete as horses. In Australia horses that measure from 14 hands to 15 hands are known as a 'galloway', and ponies in Australia measure under 14 hands.

People who are unfamiliar with horses may confuse an adult pony with a young, immature horse. While foals that will grow up to be horse-sized may be no taller than some ponies in their first months of life, their body proportions are very different. A pony can be ridden and put to work, while a foal is too young to be ridden or used as a working animal. Foals, whether they grow up to be horse or pony-sized, can be distinguished from adult horses by their extremely long legs and slim bodies. Their heads and eyes also exhibit juvenile characteristics. Furthermore, in most cases, nursing foals will be in very close proximity to a mare who is the mother (dam) of the foal. While ponies exhibit some neoteny with the wide foreheads and small size, their body proportions are similar to that of an adult horse.

History

Ponies originally developed as a landrace adapted to a harsh natural environment, and were considered part of the 'draft' subtype typical of Northern Europe. At one time, it was hypothesized that they may have descended from a wild 'draft' subspecies of *Equus ferus*. Studies of mitochondrial DNA (which is passed on though the female line) indicate that a large number of wild mares have contributed to modern domestic breeds; in contrast, studies of y-DNA (passed down the male line) suggest that there was possibly just one single male ancestor of all domesticated breeds. Domestication of the horse probably first occurred in the Eurasian steppes with horses of between 13 hands (52 inches, 132 cm) to over 14 hands (56 inches, 142 cm), and as horse domestication spread, the male descendents of the original stallion went on to be bred with local wild mares.

Domesticated ponies of all breeds originally developed mainly from the need for a working animal that could fulfill specific local draft and transportation needs while surviving in harsh environments. The usefulness of the pony was noted by farmers who observed that a pony could outperform a draft horse on small farms.

By the 20th century, many pony breeds had Arabian and other blood added to make a more refined pony suitable for riding.

Use of Ponies

Ponies are seen in many different equestrian pursuits. Some breeds, such as the Hackney pony, are primarily used for driving, while other breeds, such as the Connemara pony and Australian Pony, are used primarily for riding. Others, such as the Welsh pony, are used for both riding and driving.

There is no direct correlation between a horse's size and its inherent athletic ability. Ponies compete at events that include show hunter, English riding on the flat, driving, and western riding classes at horse shows, as well as other competitive events such as gymkhana and combined driving. They are seen in casual pursuits such as trail riding. but a few ponies have performed in international-level competition. Though many exhibitors confine themselves to classes just for ponies, some top ponies are competitive against full-sized horses. For example, a 14.1 hand pony named Stroller was a member of the British Equestrian show jumping team, and won the silver medal at the 1968 Summer Olympics. More recently, the 14.1-3/4 hand pony Theodore O'Connor won the gold medal in eventing at the 2007 Pan American Games.

Pony Clubs, open to young people who own either horses or ponies, are formed worldwide to educate young people about horses, promote responsible horse ownership, and also sponsor competitive events for young people and smaller horses.

In many parts of the world ponies are also still used as working animals, as pack animals and for pulling various horse-drawn vehicles. They are used for children's pony rides at traveling carnivals and at children's private parties where small children can take short rides on ponies that are saddled and then either led individually or hitched to a 'pony wheel' (a non-motorized device akin to a hot walker) that leads six to eight ponies at a time. Ponies are sometimes seen at summer camps for children, and are widely used for pony trekking and other forms of Equitourism riding holidays, often carrying adults as well as children.

Characteristics

Ponies are often distinguished by their phenotype, a stocky body, dense bone, round shape and well-sprung ribs. They have a short head, large eyes and small ears. In addition to being smaller than a horse, their legs are proportionately shorter. They have strong hooves and grow a heavier hair coat, seen in a thicker mane and tail as well as a particularly heavy winter coat.

Pony breeds have developed all over the world, particularly in cold and harsh climates where hardy, sturdy working animals were needed. They are remarkably strong for their size. Breeds such as the Connemara pony, are recognized for their ability to carry a full-sized adult rider. Pound for pound ponies can pull and carry more weight than a horse. Draft-type ponies are able to pull loads significantly greater than their own weight, with larger ponies capable of pulling loads comparable to those pulled by full-sized draft horses, and even very small ponies able to pull as much as 450 per cent of their own weight.

Nearly all pony breeds are very hardy, easy keepers that share the ability to thrive on a more limited diet than that of a regular-sized horse, requiring half the hay for their weight as a horse, and often not needing grain at all. However, for the same reason, they are also more vulnerable to laminitis and Cushing's syndrome. They may also have problems with hyperlipemia.

Ponies are generally considered intelligent and friendly, though sometimes they also are described as stubborn or cunning. The differences of opinion often result from an individual pony's degree of proper training. Ponies trained by inexperienced individuals, or only ridden by beginners, can turn out to be spoiled because their riders typically lack the experience base to correct bad habits. Properly trained ponies are appropriate mounts for children who are learning to ride. Larger ponies can be ridden by adults, as ponies are usually strong for their size.

For showing purposes, ponies are often grouped into small, medium, and large sizes. Small ponies are 12.2 hands (50 inches (130 cm)) and under, medium ponies are over 12.2 but no taller than 13.2 hands [54 inches (140 cm)] and large ponies are over 13.2 hands but no taller than 14.2 hands.

The smallest equines are called miniature horses by many of their breeders and breed organisations, rather than ponies, even though stand smaller than small ponies, usually no taller than 38 inches (97 cm) at the withers. However, there are also miniature pony breeds.

Types and Breeds that are not Ponies

Some horse breeds are not defined as ponies, even when they have some animals that measure under 14.2 hands. This is usually due to body build, traditional uses and overall physiology. Breeds that are considered horses regardless of height include the Arabian horse, American Quarter Horse and the Morgan horse, all of which have individual members both over and under 14.2 hands.

Other horse breeds, such as Icelandic Horse and Fjord Horse, may sometimes be pony-sized or have some pony characteristics, such as a heavy coat, thick mane, and heavy bone, but are generally classified as 'horses' by their respective registries. In cases such as these, there can be considerable debate over whether to call certain breeds 'horses' or 'ponies'. However, individual breed registries usually are the arbiters of such debates, weighing the relative horse and pony characteristics of a breed. In some breeds, such as the Welsh pony, the horse-versus-pony controversy is resolved by creating separate divisions for consistently horse-sized animals.

Some horses may be pony height due to environment more than genetics. For example, the Chincoteague pony, a feral horse that lives on Assateague Island off the coast of Virginia, often matures to the height of an average small horse when raised from a foal under domesticated conditions.

Conversely, the term 'pony' is occasionally used to describe horses of normal height. Horses used for polo are often called 'polo ponies' regardless of height, even though they are often of Thoroughbred breeding and often well over 14.2 hands. American Indian tribes also have the tradition of referring to their horses as 'ponies', when speaking in English, even though many of the Mustang horses they used in the 19th century were close to or over 14.2 hh, and most horses owned and bred by Native peoples today are of full horse height. The term 'pony' is also sometimes used to describe a full-sized horse in a humorous or affectionate sense.

The United States Pony Club defines 'pony' to be any mount that is ridden by a member regardless of its breed or size. Persons up to 25 years old are eligible for membership, and some of the members' 'ponies' actually are full-size horses.

CHAPTER 20

Longeing

Longeing (USA) or lungeing (UK English, informal USA) is a technique for training horses, where a horse is asked to work at the end of a long line and respond to commands from a handler on the ground who holds the line. It is also a critical component of the sport of equestrian vaulting. Longeing is performed on a large circle with the horse traveling around the outside edge of a real or imaginary ring with the trainer in the middle.

The classic spelling of the word in English is 'longeing', pronounced, 'lunjing'. However, because of the pronunciation it is common throughout the English-speaking world for the term to be spelled 'lungeing', even in a significant number of books and magazine articles on the subject. Though inaccurate as a term of art, the more phonetic spelling dates to the 1800s, and particularly since the late 20th century, has been used to such an extent that it is now often considered correct, even in some (though not all) dictionaries. The majority of dressage masters of the 20th century and earlier used the spelling "longeing". In modern times, books aimed at the mass market are published with either spelling, but organisations in the United States that are devoted to traditional horsemanship, including the United States Pony Clubs continues to utilize the spelling 'longeing', as do most practitioners of equestrian vaulting and classical dressage. In the United Kingdom, usage is split to a greater extent, even among major organisations, with the British Horse Society using the spelling 'lungeing' in its materials, while the Association of British Riding Schools (ABRS) uses 'longeing'. In New Zealand and Australia, 'lungeing' is the common spelling used in both nations.

Historically, the word is believed to be derived from either the French word *allonge,* meaning 'to lengthen', or the Latin *longa* ('long'). In both cases, the root word featured spelling with an 'o' and emphasize lengthening and extension.

Reasons for Longeing

Longeing has many benefits for both horses and riders.

For a young or green (inexperienced) horse, longeing is used to teach a horse to respond to voice commands and the trainer's body language, to accustom them to the feel of a saddle and bridle, and to begin their introduction to the feel of reins and bit pressure. In many training stables, a horse is first introduced on the longe to nearly everything it is going to be asked to do under saddle, including movement at all gaits, response to hand and voice commands (called riding aids), and remaining calm in unusual or stressful situations.

On horses of any age or level of experience, longeing is used to exercise a horse when it cannot be ridden, or when additional work is needed to develop balance, rhythm, and to improve the horse's gaits. It is also useful to help settle a horse before riding, especially a high-strung horse, a young horse, or a horse that has been confined more than usual. However, longeing should not be used to tire a horse out, as long sessions can cause joint strain. It can be used to 'blow off steam' or 'get the bucks out' before a rider gets on, though proper turnout or liberty work is a better alternative, because the horse should think of a longeing session as training time, not play time.

Longeing a rider is very valuable for teaching, as the rider may develop their seat and position without having to worry about controlling the horse. Classical schools of riding and training, such as the Spanish Riding School, require new riders to work extensively on the longe before they are allowed reins or stirrups, and riders are required to periodically return to longe work to refine their seat and balance.

Equipment for Longeing

Longe Line

The longe line (or longe) should be about 30 feet (10 m) long, so the longeing circle can have a diametre of 60 feet (20 m). It is usually a flat woven webbing made of nylon, cotton, or Dacron. In the natural horsemanship tradition, the longe line is usually made of round cotton rope, and often much shorter, as short as 15 or 20 feet. In general, cotton longe lines are less likely to burn the trainer's hands than nylon, but nylon is more durable and less likely to break.

It may have a snap, buckle, or chain on one end to attach to a longeing cavesson or bridle. A chain, although sometimes used with difficult horses, has no subtly of contact and is quite severe. In most cases, it is best to use a snap-end longe line. Many longe lines have a loop handle at the other end, but this should not be used, as a person's hand can be trapped in the handle and be injured should the horse bolt.

The longe line takes the place of the rein aids while longeing. It can be held in a rein hold (coming out the bottom of the hand) or a driving hold (coming out the top of the hand), and the extra line should always be folded back and forth rather than coiled, as coiled line can tighten and trap the trainer's hand or fingers should the horse take off.

Longe Whip

The whip usually has a stock of 6 feet (1.8 m), with a lash of 5-6 feet (1.5-1.8 m) (although some are longer). The whip should be light, easy to handle, and well balanced. It is not safe to use a riding or driving whip for longeing because they are too short to reach the horse without bringing the handler close enough to the horse's hindquarters to risk being kicked by the horse.

Longeing Cavesson

A longeing cavesson or caveson is the most commonly used piece of equipment. It is a type of headstall with three rings on the noseband to which the longe line is attached. The most common point of attachment is the centre ring at the top of the cavesson, which allows the horse to go both directions without having to stop and change the adjustment of the line. The two side rings are occasionally used for attachment of the longe line, but more often are used for attachment of side reins or long lines.

The classic design is made of leather, and noseband is usually metal on top with padding beneath, providing good control of the horse, but no risk of injury to the head. Unlike a bridle, there is no chance of damaging the horse's mouth. Newer designs are made of nylon web, similar to some types of halter, with three rings and fleece padding underneath the noseband, often without the metal component. This style is less bulky, less expensive, and available in a very wide range of sizes, but offers less precise control.

A longeing cavesson may be used with or without a bridle. When used with a bridle containing a snaffle bit, the noseband of the bridle is removed, and the bridle goes over the longeing cavesson, to prevent pinching. The bridle cheekpieces sometimes need to be lengthened so that the bit still rests correctly in the mouth.

When fitting a longe cavesson, the noseband must be on the nasal bone of the horse's nose, not on the cartilage. Nosebands that are too low are very uncomfortable for the horse and, in extreme cases, can cause damage to the cartilage if misused. The throatlatch of the cavesson must be snug enough to keep it from slipping over the horse's eye, or from falling off altogether, but not so tight as to restrict the windpipe if the horse flexes its neck properly in response to pressure from the bit and side reins.

Use of a Bridle Alone

On a fully trained horse, a bridle may be used in lieu of a cavesson. However, it is possible to injure a horse's mouth if the line is incorrectly attached or misused. Some sensitive horses may react badly to the attachment of the line to the bit, and some classical dressage masters considered this method to be crude.

The bit used is a snaffle bit. Bit shanks of any kind are dangerous; the line can tangle in them, causing injury to the horse's mouth. The reins should be kept out of the way, either by removing them, or by twisting them once or twice over the neck and then running the throatlatch of the bridle under the reins before buckling it.

The correct method is to run the longe line through the inside bit ring, over the poll, and attach it to the outside bit ring. This method of attaching the line requires it to be changed each time the horse changes direction. This method has a slight gag effect, raising the bit up and applying pressure on the corners of the mouth and placing pressure on the poll, but puts less lateral pressure on the bit. It is best for horses that pull, or when the trainer is longeing a rider, to ensure maximum control of the horse.

If the longe line is attached just to the inside bit ring, the outside ring can slide through the mouth when the line is pulled and damage the horse's mouth.

If the line is run through the inside bit ring, under the chin, and attached to the outside bit ring, the bit can pinch the horse's jaw, and it alters the action of the bit to put pressure on the roof of the horse's mouth. When a method of attachment causes more pain than control, the horse often resists the pressure and will not perform properly.

Halter

A halter should only be used for basic exercise when a longeing cavesson or a bridle is not available. It offers very little control, less finesse, and does not give signals as clearly. If a halter is used, it should fit snugly.

When used with a bridle, the halter is placed on over the bridle. This is generally not advisable, but sometimes is done when warming up a horse just prior to competition.

Always attach the longe line to the inside side ring of the halter noseband on a flat web halter, not the ring under the jaw. If it is attached under the jaw, not only is the halter apt to twist and slip out of place, possibly rubbing the horse in the eye and risking injury, but if the horse is disobedient, the handler has virtually no lateral leverage or control. Some rope halters have knots placed on the noseband and crownpiece that may apply some additional pressure if a longe line is placed under the jaw, which is the only place possible on a rope halter. However, it is still difficult to stop a horse that bolts.

Protective Boots or Bandages

Horse's legs are often protected while longeing, as they are more likely to interfere when on a circle. Both Bell boots and 'brushing' or 'splint' boots are often put on the front legs. Brushing boots are sometimes on the hind legs as well. Polo wraps are sometimes used instead of brushing boots.

Saddles and Surcingles

A saddle is often worn when a horse is longeing. If a horse is longed with a saddle, it is important to make sure the stirrups do not bang against the horse's side. On an English saddle, the stirrups are 'run up'. To do this, run up the stirrups as they are kept when the saddle is off the horse, then bring the loop of stirrup leather around the stirrup iron before bringing it under the back branch and attaching looping the end of the leather (with the holes in it) through the stirrup leather keeper. Stirrups on a western saddle cannot be run up, so they are usually tied together under the belly of the horse with a piece of twine or rope, though for a very skittish young horse they also can be thrown up over the top of the saddle and tied down in that fashion.

A surcingle or roller is a padded band that straps around the horse's girth area, and has rings around on its side for side reins, or long reins or other training equipment, such as an overcheck. It may also be used on a young horse to get it used to girth pressure. It may be used with or without an English saddle underneath. When used without a saddle, it is best to use a pad underneath, and to fit it as you would a saddle. When used with a saddle, the stirrups should be removed.

Side Reins

Side reins are usually used for more advanced horses. They give the horse something to take contact with, encourage balance and correct head carriage, help a horse develop self-carriage, and keep the horse from putting its head too low. Side reins may be attached from the bit to the surcingle rings, or from the bit to the billets of the girth.

Side reins are adjusted longer for less-experienced horses, and gradually shortened, and raised higher (from point of shoulder up to the point of hip) as a horse becomes better trained. In any case, the horse should never have its head pulled behind the vertical. For green horses, the side reins should be adjusted so that the horse can take contact with the bit, but does not have to flex beyond its abilities. A good starting point is to adjust the reins so the green horse carries its head approximately 4 inches in front of the vertical.

Side reins are adjusted so they are the same length on either side, or slightly shorter on the inside. Side reins adjusted too tightly can cause a horse to go behind the bit, deaden the mouth and in extreme cases cause the horse to feel trapped, leading to rearing and the possibility that the horse will flip over.

A horse is warmed up and cooled down without the side reins, allowing the neck to stretch down and the back muscles to relax. Side reins are most useful for work in the trot and canter, where the neck, back and hindquarter muscles are engaged. Working a horse in side reins at the walk actually discourages a relaxed, forward-moving gait. Side reins are not used for jumping, as they restrict the use of the neck too much, and may even cause the horse to fall.

Equipment for the Trainer

The trainer should wear gloves when longeing, to help prevent rope burns if the horse pulls the line hard. Proper boots are also necessary, and at a minimum, shoes with an enclosed toe are a must. A helmet is also sometimes worn, especially if the horse tends to kick at the trainer. It is wise not to wear spurs, which can get caught on the line and cause the trainer to trip.

Use of the Aids

Longe Line

The longe line takes the place of the rider's rein aids. It may be held like a riding rein, with the line running to the horse held between the fourth and fifth finger, or held like a driving rein, with it running between the thumb and pointer finger. The elbow should be softly bent, and the arm at an approximately 90-degree angle. The horse and handler should not pull, jerk, or "hang" on the line. Like rein aids while riding, signals should be given smoothly and as softly as possible to get the desired response, with aids given by squeezing or turning the hand.

The longe line traveling from the horse to the hand is held in the hand in which direction the horse is moving (so if the horse is working clockwise to the right, the right hand is the leading hand). The extra longe line should be folded, never coiled, in the other hand. If the horse were to take off, a coiled line could tighten around the trainer's hand, dragging the trainer and possibly leading to life-threatening injuries. The loops should not be too large, as they could be stepped on or caught on something.

- *Opening rein:* where the lead hand moves to the side and out, away from the trainer's body. It helps to lead the horse forward.
- *Direct rein:* a squeeze and release on the line backwards helps to keep the horse from moving out on the circle, causes the horse to bend inward, or asks the horse to make the circle smaller.
- *Indirect rein:* where the longe hand moves back and sideways towards the other hip. It asks the horse to slow or halt.
- *Giving the longe:* briefly releasing the line towards the horse's head, before re-establishing contact. Acts as a reward, asks the horse to lower its head, or asks the horse to move out onto a larger circle. The line should not drag or become very loose when this is performed.
- *Vibrating:* several short, brief squeezes of the longe line. Used to halt or slow the horse down without pulling.
- *Half-halting:* as in riding, it is used for re-balancing the horse, calling his attention to the trainer, and prepares him for a command. Must be used in conjunction with the whip and voice.

Whip

The longe whip takes the place of the rider's legs, asking the horse to move forward or out. It should be held with the tip low, pointing towards the horse's hocks, with the lash dragging on the ground. The whip is held in the hand that the horse is not going (so if the horse were going to the right, the whip would be held in the lunger's left hand). The horse should accept the whip as an aid, but should not be fearful. When the lunger goes toward the horse to adjust equipment, the lash should be caught up and the whip turned backward, under the lunger's arm, so that it does not interfere with the horse.

- Pointing the whip at the shoulder is used to make the horse move out or stops him from moving inward on the circle.
- Pointing the whip, and making a forward rotating movement, at the hocks asks the horse to increase speed or impulsion.
- Pointing the whip in front of the head, going under the longe line, can be used to ask a horse to slow or halt.
- Cracking the whip should be reserved for extreme cases, such as a horse that refuses to move forward. It should not be overused, or the horse may begin to ignore it. Cracking upsets some horses. If a crack is needed, it should be done behind the hindquarters.
- Touching the horse with the lash is used to make the horse move strongly forward. The lash is usually applied where the rider's leg would be, in the girth area. It may also be used on the hindquarters, although this causes some horses to kick, or on the shoulder, to prevent the horse from running inward. It is usually used only lightly, in an upward motion. Stinging snaps should be reserved for emergencies.

Voice

The voice is used in the same manner as when riding. It is used mainly for transitions, praise, or to express displeasure. Although the voice is not commonly used for riding, it is very important in longeing and should be used frequently. Voice commands used in longeing should be identical to any voice commands used when leading or riding the horse, but the most voice commands are used when longeing than at other times. All words used in transitions for longeing should be spoken slowly, clearly and each command should be phonetically distinct from and others. For upward transitions the voice should raise to a higher pitch, downward transitions should lower the pitch.

- A word, such as the name of the horse, or simply a word like 'and...' should be used as a 'half-halt', essentially to warn the horse that a command is coming. For example, to ask for walk to trot transition, one would say 'and trot'. A word other than whoa should be reserved to calm a horse (such as 'easy' or 'steady'), This word should be spoken in a low tone and calm manner. A word for praise (such as 'good boy') should be used frequently whenever the horse responds correctly to a command. A word such as 'out' should be used to ask the horse to increase the circle size or to help stop the horse from cutting in. It must be used firmly.

- A trainer may cluck or make another type of chirping or kissing sound to increase speed or impulsion. It is best to cluck when the inside hind leg begins to move forward. Overuse of voice to encourage impulsion will cause a horse to ignore the trainer.

Longe Area

It is best to longe in an enclosed area. If the horse escapes, it will be easier to catch, and an enclosed area will make him easier to control on the longe. Ideally, a 60 to 70-foot (20-25 m) round pen is used. However, the corner of any enclosed arena or small field may also be used. For safety, it is best if there is no one riding in the longeing area.

The footing should not be slippery or deep, to help prevent slipping and injuries. The ground should be relatively flat (don't longe on a hill), for the horse's balance.

The circle should be large (approx. 20 metres), as smaller circles tend to increase strain on the horse's joints and ligaments.

Free Longeing

In the field of natural horsemanship, it is a common practice to work a horse loose in a round pen 40 to 70 feet in diametre. (50 to 60 feet is considered standard). This is sometimes called *free longeing* or work *at liberty,* because the horse is asked to travel in a circle and obey human commands, only without a longe line attached. The handler uses voice, body language and a lariat or a longe whip to give commands to the horse, eventually teaching it to speed up, slow down, stop and change direction on command.

A variation of these techniques are also used by circus trainers to train horses and other animals, such as elephants to work in a ring for exhibition purposes. Both single animals and groups of animals can be trained to perform at liberty.

These types of liberty work are considered schooling disciplines and to simply turn a horse loose in a small pen and make it run around to get exercise is not free longeing.

Time Limits

Work in small circles is stressful on a horse's legs, so it is best to limit a longeing session to about 20 minutes. Gaits should be changed frequently, and the horse should be worked for equal time in both directions so that both sides of the horse are worked evenly and to keep the work interesting for the horse.

CHAPTER 21

Horse Tack

Tack is a term used to describe any of the various equipment and accessories worn by horses in the course of their use as domesticated animals. Saddles, stirrups, bridles, halters, reins, bits, harnesses, martingales, and breastplates are all forms of horse tack. Equipping a horse is often referred to as tacking up.

Saddles

Saddles are seats for the rider, fastened to the horse's back by means of a *girth* (English-style riding), known as a *cinch* in the Western US, a wide strap that goes around the horse at a point about four inches behind the forelegs. Some western saddles will also have a second strap known as a *flank* or *back cinch* that fastens at the rear of the saddle and goes around the widest part of the horse's belly.

It is important that the saddle be comfortable for both the rider and the horse as an improperly fitting saddle may create pressure points on the horse's back muscle (*Latissimus dorsi*) and cause the horse pain and can lead to the horse, rider, or both getting injured.

There are many types of saddle, each specially designed for its given task. Saddles are usually divided into two major categories: 'English saddles' and 'Western saddles' according to the riding discipline they are used in. Other types of saddles, such as racing saddles, Australian saddles, sidesaddles and endurance saddles do not necessarily fit neatly in either category.

Saddle Accessories

- Breastplate or breastcollar: Prevents saddles of all styles from sliding sideways or backward on a horse's back.
- Surcingle
- Pack saddle
- Crupper
- Breeching, also called 'Britching'

Stirrups

Stirrups are supports for the rider's feet that hang down on either side of the saddle. They provide greater stability for the rider but can have safety concerns due to the potential for a rider's feet to get stuck in them. If a rider is thrown from a horse but has a foot caught in the stirrup, they could be dragged if the horse runs away. To minimize this risk, a number of safety precautions are taken. First, most riders wear riding boots with a heel and a smooth sole. Next, some saddles, particularly English saddles, have safety bars that allow a stirrup leather to fall off the saddle if pulled backwards by a falling rider. Other precautions are done with stirrup design itself. Western saddles have wide stirrup treads that make it more difficult for the foot to become trapped. A number of saddle styles incorporate a tapedero, which is covering over the front of the stirrup that keeps the foot from sliding all the way through the stirrup. The English stirrup (or 'iron') has several design variations which are either shaped to allow the rider's foot to slip out easily or are closed with a very heavy rubber band. The invention of stirrups was of great historic significance in mounted combat, giving the rider secure foot support while on horseback.

Headgear

Bridles, hackamores, *halters* or *headcollars,* and similar equipment consist of various arrangements of straps around the horse's head, and are used for control and communication with the animal.

Halters

A *halter* (US) or *headcollar* (BI) (occasionally *headstall*) consists of a noseband and headstall that buckles around the horse's head and allows the horse to be led or tied. The lead rope is separate, and it may be short (from six to ten feet, two to three metres) for everyday leading and tying, or much longer (up to 25 feet (7.6 m), eight metres) for tasks such as for leading packhorses or for picketing a horse out to graze.

Some horses, particularly stallions, may have a chain attached to the lead rope and placed over the nose or under the jaw to increase the control provided by a halter while being led. Most of the time, horses are not ridden with a halter, as it offers insufficient precision and control. Halters have no bit.

In Australian and British English, a *halter* is a rope with a spliced running loop around the nose and another over the poll, used mainly for unbroken horses or for cattle. The lead rope cannot be removed from the halter. A show halter is made from rolled leather and the lead attaches to form the chinpiece of the noseband. These halters are not suitable for paddock usage or in loose stalls. An *underhalter* is a lightweight halter or headcollar which is made with only one small buckle, and can be worn under a bridle for tethering a horse without untacking.

Bridles

Bridles usually have a *bit* attached to *reins* and are used for riding and driving horses.

- *English Bridles* have a *cavesson* style noseband and are seen in English riding. Their reins are buckled to one another, and they have little adornment or flashy hardware.
- *Western Bridles* used in Western riding usually have no noseband, are made of thin bridle leather. They may have long, separated 'Split' reins or shorter closed reins, which sometimes include an attached *Romal*. Western bridles are often adorned with silver or other decorative features.
- *Double bridles* are a type of English bridle that use two bits in the mouth at once, a snaffle and a curb. The two bits allow the rider to have very precise control of the horse. As a rule, only very advanced horses and riders use double bridles. Double bridles are usually seen in the top levels of dressage, but also are seen in certain types of show hack and Saddle seat competition.

Hackamores and Other Bitless Designs

A *hackamore* is a headgear that utilizes a heavy noseband of some sort, rather than a bit, most often used to train young horses or to go easy on an older horse's mouth. Hackamores are more often seen in western riding. Some related styles of headgear that control a horse with a noseband rather than a bit are known as bitless bridles.

The word 'hackamore' is derived from the Spanish word *jaquima*. Hackamores are seen in western riding disciplines, as well as in endurance riding and English riding disciplines such as show jumping and the stadium phase of eventing. While the classic bosal-style hackamore is usually used to start young horses, other designs, such as various bitless bridles and the mechanical hackamore are often seen on mature horses with dental issues that make bit use painful, horses with certain training problems, and on horses with mouth or tongue injuries. Some riders also like to use them in the winter to avoid putting a frozen metal bit into a horse's mouth.

Like bitted bridles, noseband-based designs can be gentle or harsh, depending on the hands of the rider. It is a myth that a bit is cruel and a hackamore is gentler. The horse's face is very soft and sensitive with many nerve endings. Misuse of a hackamore can cause swelling on the nose, scraping on the nose and jawbone, and extreme misuse may cause damage to the bones and cartilage of the horse's head.

Other Headgear

A *longeing cavesson* (UK: *lungeing*) is a special type of halter or noseband used for longeing a horse. Longeing is the activity of having a horse walk, trot and/or canter in a large circle around the handler at the end of a rope that is 25 to 30 feet (9.1 m) long. It is used for training and exercise.

Reins

Reins consist of leather straps or rope attached to the outer ends of a *bit* and extend to the rider's or driver's hands. Reins are the means by which a horse rider or driver communicates directional commands to the horse's head. Pulling on the reins can be used to steer or stop the horse. The sides of a horse's mouth are sensitive, so pulling on the reins pulls the bit, which then pulls the horse's head from side to side, which is how the horse is controlled.

On some types of harnesses there might be supporting rings to carry the reins over the horse's back. When pairs of horses are used in drawing a wagon or coach it is usual for the outer side of each pair to be connected to reins and the inside of the bits connected by a short bridging strap or rope. The driver carries 'four-in-hand' or 'six-in-hand' being the number of reins connecting to the pairs of horses.

A rein may be attached to a halter to lead or guide the horse in a circle for training purposes or to lead a packhorse, but a simple lead rope is more often used for these purposes. A longe line is sometimes called a 'longe rein', but it is actually a flat line about 30 feet (9.1 m) long, usually made of nylon or cotton web, about one inch wide, thus longer and wider than even a driving rein.

Horses should never be tied by the reins. Not only do they break easily, but, being attached to a bit in the horse's sensitive mouth, a great deal of pain can be inflicted if a bridled horse sets back against being tied.

Harness

A horse harness is a set of devices and straps that attaches a horse to a cart, carriage, sledge or any other load. There are two main styles of harnesses - breaststrap and collar and hames style. These differ in how the weight of the load is attached.

A breaststrap harness has a wide leather strap going horizontally across the horses' breast, attached to the traces and then to the load. This is used only for lighter loads.

A collar and hames harness has a collar around the horses' neck with wood or metal hames in the collar. The traces attach from the hames to the load. This type of harness is needed for heavy draft work.

A hybrid type, known as a 'brollar', increases the bearing area of the breastcollar around the shoulder of the horse, but does not have rigid hames.

Both types will also have a bridle & reins. A harness that is used to support shafts, such as on a cart pulled by a single horse, will also have a *saddle* attached to the harness to help the horse support the shafts and *breeching* to brake the forward motion of the vehicle, especially when stopping or moving downhill. Horses guiding vehicles by means of a pole, such as two-horse teams pulling a wagon, a hay-mower, or a dray, will have *pole-straps* attached to the lower part of the horse collar.

Breastplates and Martingales

Breastplates, breastcollars or breastgirths attach to the front of the saddle, cross the horse's chest, and usually have a strap that runs between the horse's front legs and attaches to the girth. They keep the saddle from sliding back or sideways. They are usually seen in demanding, fast-paced sports. They are crucial pieces of safety equipment for English riding activities requiring jumping, such as eventing, show jumping, polo, and fox hunting. They are also seen in Western riding events, particularly in rodeo, reining and cutting, where it is particularly important to prevent a saddle from shifting. They may also be worn in other horse show classes for decorative purposes.

A martingale is a piece of equipment that keeps a horse from raising its head too high. Various styles can be used as a control measure, to prevent the horse from avoiding rider commands by raising its head out of position; or as a safety measure to keep the horse from tossing its head high or hard enough to smack its rider in the face.

They are allowed in many types of competition, especially those where speed or jumping may be required, but are not allowed in most 'flat' classes at horse shows, though an exception is made in a few classes limited exclusively to young or 'green' horses who may not yet be fully trained.

Martingales are usually attached to the horse one of two ways. They are either attached to the centre chest ring of a breastplate or, if no breastplate is worn, they are attached by two straps, one that goes around the horse's neck, and the other that attaches to the girth, with the martingale itself beginning at the point in the centre of the chest where the neck and girth straps intersect.

Martingale types include:

- *Running martingale:* This design adds leverage to a bit and features a split *fork* beginning at the chest with a ring on each side of the *fork* through which the reins pass, enabling the rider to more easily keep the horse under control, but also allowing the horse freedom of movement when needed. Fitted correctly, the running martingale only controls how high the horse carries its head when the rider tightens the reins. The standard adjustment of a running martingale is to set the rings at a height where they do not engage and add leverage to the reins when the horse carries its head at the proper height. Sometimes a running martingale may be adjusted at a greater or lesser length depending on the needs of the horse and rider.
- *Standing martingale:* A design with one strap that runs from the girth or the chest and attaches to the noseband of the bridle. The standing martingale acts on the horse's nose and creates an absolute limit to how high a horse can raise its head. The term used in western riding for this piece of equipment is the *tie down*. Standard adjustment of a standing

martingale allows enough slack to bring the strap to the horse's throatlatch when the animal has its head in a relaxed, natural position. However, it is sometimes adjusted shorter. Unlike the running martingale, it limits the freedom of the horse's head, no matter how long or short the reins may be. While standing martingales are common in show hunter and equitation classes, the limits placed on the horse's movement are dangerous for cross-country riding or show jumping. Therefore, in these disciplines, a running martingale is necessary for safety reasons, if a martingale is used at all.

- *German martingale* or *Market Harborough:* This design consists of a split fork that comes up from the chest, runs through the rings of the bit and attaches to the reins of the bridle between the bit and the rider's hand. It acts in a manner similar to a running martingale, but with greater leverage. It is not usually considered show legal and is used primarily as a training aid.
- *Irish martingale:* Unlike the previous designs, this very simple 'martingale' does not control the height of the horse's head, but merely keeps the reins from going over the horse's head in the result of a fall. It consists of a piece of leather with a ring on each end through which each rein runs.

There are other training devices that fall loosely in the martingale category, in that they use straps attached to the reins or bit which limit the movement of the horse's head or add leverage to the rider's hands in order to control the horse's head. Common devices of this nature include the overcheck, the chambon, de Gogue, grazing reins, draw reins and the 'bitting harness' or 'bitting rig'. However, most of this equipment is used for training purposes and is not legal in any competition. In some disciplines, use of leverage devices, even in training, is controversial.

Bit (Horse)

A bit is a device placed in a horse's mouth, kept on a horse's head by means of a headstall. There are many types, each useful for specific types of riding and training.

The mouthpiece of the bit does not rest on the teeth of the horse, but rather rests on the gums or 'bars' of the horse's mouth in an interdental space behind the front incisors and in front of the back molars. It is important that the style of bit is appropriate to the horse's needs and is fitted properly for it to function properly and be as comfortable as possible for the horse.

The basic 'classic' styles of bits are:

- Curb bit
- Snaffle bit
- Pelham bit
- Weymouth or double bridle

While there are literally hundreds of types of bit mouthpieces, bit rings and bit shanks, essentially there are really only two broad categories: direct pressure bits, broadly termed snaffle bits; and leverage bits, usually termed curbs.

Bits that act with direct pressure on the tongue and lips of the bit are in the general category of *snaffle* bits. Snaffle bits commonly have a single jointed mouthpiece and act with a nutcracker effect on the bars, tongue and occasionally roof of the mouth. However, regardless of mouthpiece, any bit that operates only on direct pressure is a 'snaffle' bit.

Leverage bits have shanks coming off the mouthpiece to create leverage that applies pressure to the poll, chin groove and mouth of the horse are in the category of *curb* bits. Any bit with shanks that works off of leverage is a 'curb' bit, regardless of whether the mouthpiece is solid or jointed.

Some combination or hybrid bits combine direct pressure and leverage, such as the Kimblewick or Kimberwicke, which adds slight leverage to a two-rein design that resembles a snaffle; and the four rein designs such as the single mouthpiece Pelham bit and the double bridle, which places a curb and a snaffle bit simultaneously in the horse's mouth.

In the wrong hands even the mildest bit can hurt the horse. Conversely, a very severe bit, in the right hands, can transmit subtle commands that cause no pain to the horse. Bit commands should be given with only the quietest movements of the hands, and much steering and stopping should be done with the legs and seat.

Basic Tyes

Although there are hundreds of design variations, the basic families of bits are defined by the way in which they use or do not use leverage. They include:

- Direct pressure bits without leverage.
  - *Snaffle bit:* Uses a bit ring at the mouthpiece to apply direct pressure on the bars, tongue and corner of the mouth.
- Leverage bits:
  - *Curb bit:* A bit that uses a type of lever called a shank that puts pressure not only on the mouth, but also on the poll and chin groove.
  - *Pelham bit:* A single curb bit with two sets of reins attached to rings at the mouthpiece and end of the shank. Partly combines snaffle and curb pressure.
- *Kimblewick or Kimberwicke:* A hybrid design that uses a slight amount of mild curb leverage on a bit ring by use of set rein placement on the ring.
- Bit combinations

- A type of bridle that carries two bits, a bradoon and a curb, and is ridden with two sets of reins is called a Weymouth or double bridle, after the customary use of the Weymouth-style curb bit in a double bridle.

- Non-curb leverage designs:
  - *Gag bit:* A bit that, depending on design, may outwardly resemble a snaffle or a curb, but with added slots or rings that provide leverage by sliding the bit up in the horse's mouth, a very severe design.
- In-hand bits are designed for leading horses only, and include the:
  - *Chifney Anti-Rearing Bit:* This is a semi-circular-shaped bit with three rings and a port or straight mouth piece used when leading horses. The port or straight piece goes inside the mouth, and the circular part lies under the jaw. The bit is attached to separate head piece or the head collar and the lead is clipped onto the bit and headcollar to limit the severity.
  - Tattersall ring bit.
  - Horse-shoe stallion bit.

Bits are further described by the style of mouthpiece that goes inside the horse's mouth as well as by the type of bit ring or bit shank that is outside the mouth, to which the reins are attached.

Types of headgear for horses that exert control with a noseband rather than a bit are usually called hackamores, though the term 'bitless bridle' has become a popular colloquialism in recent years.

History

It is likely that the first domesticated horses were ridden with some type of bitless headgear made of sinew, leather, or rope. Components of the earliest headgear may be difficult to determine, as the materials would not have held up over time. For this reason, no one can say with certainty which came first, the bitted or the bitless bridle. There is evidence of the use of bits, located in two sites of the Botai, dated about 3500-3000 BC. Nose rings were used on the equids portrayed on the Standard of Ur, circa 2600 BCE - 2400 BCE. To date, the earliest artistic evidence of use of some form of bitless bridle was found in illustrations of Synian horseman, dated approximately 1400 BC.

The first bits were made of rope, bone, horn, or hard wood. Metal bits came into use between 1300 and 1200 BC, originally made of bronze. In modern times, nickel was a favoured material until about 1940, when it was largely replaced by stainless steel. Copper, aurigan and sweet iron (cold rolled steel) are incorporated into some bits to encourage salivation in the mouth of the horse, which encourages a softer mouth and more relaxed jaw. Bits also can be made of other materials such as rubber or plastic, sometimes in combination with metals.

Throughout history, the need for control of horses in warfare drove extensive innovation in bit design, producing a variety of prototypes and styles over the centuries, from Ancient Greece into modern day use.

A bit consists of two basic components, the bit mouthpiece that goes inside the horse's mouth, and the *bit rings* of a snaffle bit or *shanks* of a curb bit, to which the bridle and reins attach.

Design

All bits act with some combination of pressure and leverage, often in conjunction with pressure applied by other parts of the bridle such as the curb chain on the chin, noseband on the jaw and face, or pressure on the poll from the headstall. Particular mouthpieces do not define the type of bit. It is the sidepieces and the leverage these rings or shanks use to act on a horse's mouth that determines if a bit is in the curb or snaffle family, and has a great impact on the severity of the mouthpiece.

The *mouthpiece* of a horse's bit is the first factor most people think of when assessing the severity and action of the bit. Therefore, it is carefully considered when choosing a bit for a horse. Many mouthpieces are not allowed in certain competitions. Bit mouthpieces may be single jointed, double-jointed, "mullen" (a straight bar), or have an arched port in the centre of varying height, with or without joints. Some have rollers, rings or small "keys" that the horse can move with its tongue. Mouthpieces may be smooth, wire-wrapped or otherwise roughened, or of twisted wire or metal.

Often, bits with shanks and single- or double-jointed mouthpieces are incorrectly referred to as snaffles. However, because of the presence of a shank, they are actually in the curb bit family.

Effects

The mouthpiece of the bit does not rest on the teeth of the horse, but rather rests on the gums or 'bars' of the horse's mouth in an interdental space behind the front incisors and in front of the back molars.

When a horse is said to 'grab the bit in its teeth' they actually mean that the horse tenses its lips and mouth against the bit to ignore the rider's commands (although some horses may actually learn to get the bit between their molars).

Bits are designed to work by pressure, not pain. Depending on the style of bit, pressure can be brought to bear on the bars, tongue, and roof of the mouth, as well as the lips, chin groove and poll. Bits offer varying degrees of control and communication between rider and horse depending upon their design and on the skill of the rider. It is important that the style of bit is appropriate to the horse's needs and is fitted properly for it to function properly and be as comfortable as possible for the horse.

In the wrong hands even the mildest bit can hurt the horse. Conversely, a very severe bit, in the right hands, can transmit extremely subtle, nuanced signals that cause no pain to the horse. Commands should be given with only the quietest movements of the hands, and most steering is done with the legs and seat.

Thus, instead of pulling or jerking the horse's head to change direction by force, a skilled rider indicates the desired direction by tightening and loosening the grip on the reins. The calf of the leg is used to push the body of the horse in a certain direction while the other one is used as a pivot and to provide the correct amount of impulsion required to keep the horse moving. Likewise, when slowing or stopping, a rider sits deeper in the saddle and closes their hands on the reins, avoiding jerking on the horse or hauling back on the reins in a "heavy-handed" fashion. Change of position of the seat and the pressure of the rider's seat bones are also extremely useful for turning, speeding up and slowing down.

There are many factors in the bitting equation which must be considered to get a true estimate of the action and severity of a bit. Although some mouthpieces are marketed as 'correction' (a euphemism for 'severe') bits or 'training' (implying a mild bit), the terms are relative.

The bit always rests on the sensitive bars of a horse's mouth. A hard-handed rider can make even the mildest bit painful, and a skilled, light-handed rider can ride in a much harsher mouthpiece without damaging the mouth or causing any distress in the horse. Additionally, the shank or ring has a great impact on the action of the mouthpiece. Snaffles are generally considered the mildest, curbs and gags the harshest. It is difficult, therefore, to compare a harsher-type bit with a mild mouthpiece (such as a pelham with a rubber mullen mouth), and a milder-type bit with a harsher mouthpiece (like a thin snaffle with a slow twist).

In general, however, the mouthpiece can have a marked difference on the severity. Snaffles with twisted wires are never considered mild, whereas a pelham with a low port could.

Snaffle or Direct Pressure Bits

All bits work with either direct pressure or leverage. Bits that act with direct pressure on the tongue and lips are in the general category of *snaffle* bits. Snaffle bits most commonly have a single jointed mouthpiece and act with a nutcracker effect on the bars, tongue and occasionally roof of the mouth. However, any bit that operates only on direct pressure is a 'snaffle' bit, regardless of mouthpiece.

Curb or Leverage Bits

Bits that have shanks coming off the bit mouthpiece to create leverage that applies pressure to the poll, chin groove and mouth of the horse are in the category of curb bits. Most curb bit mouthpieces are solid without joints, ranging from a straight bar with a slight arch, called a 'mullen' mouthpiece, through a 'ported' bit that is slightly arched in the middle to provide tongue relief, to the full spade bit of the Vaquero style of western riding which combines both a straight bar and a very high 'spoon' or 'spade' extension that contacts the roof of the mouth.

The length of the shank determines the degree of leverage put on the horse's head and mouth. Again, a bit with shanks and leverage is always a 'curb' type bit, even when it has a jointed mouthpiece more commonly seen on a snaffle (such bits are sometimes—incorrectly—called 'cowboy snaffles'). All shanked bits require the use of a curb chain or curb strap for proper action and safe use.

Combination Designs

Some bits combine both direct pressure and leverage, the most common examples being the Pelham bit, which has shanks and rings allowing both direct and leverage pressure on a single bit and is ridden with four reins; the Kimblewick or Kimberwicke, a hybrid bit that uses minimal leverage on a modified snaffle-type ring combined with a mouthpiece that is usually seen more often on curb bits, ridden with two reins; and the double bridle, which places a curb and a snaffle bit simultaneously in the horse's mouth so that each may act independently of the other, ridden with four reins.

Another bit that combines direct pressure and leverage in a unique manner is the Gag bit, a bit derived from the snaffle that, instead of having a rein attached to the mouthpiece, runs the rein through a set of rings that attach directly to the headstall, creating extra pressure on the lips and poll when applied. Usually used for correction of specific problems, the gag bit is generally illegal in the show ring and racecourse.

Idiomatic Usage

Bits and the behaviour of horses while wearing bits have made their way into popular culture outside of the horse world.

- *Took the bit in his teeth*, a phrase that describes a horse that sets its jaw against the bit and cannot be controlled (rarely does the horse actually grab the bit with its molars), is used today to refer to a person who cannot be controlled or who is charging ahead without consideration of the consequences.
- *Champing at the bit* (or mistakenly as *chomping at the bit*) refers to a tendency of some horses, when impatient or nervous, and especially if being held back by their riders, to chew on the bit, often salivating excessively. This behaviour is sometimes accompanied by head-tossing or pawing at the ground. Because this behaviour was most often seen by the general public in horses who were anxious to begin a horse race in the days before the invention of the starting gate, the term has become popular in everyday speech to refer to a person who is anxious to get started or to do something. Because some impatient horses, when held back, would also occasionally rear, a related phrase, 'raring to go', is also derived from observations of equine behaviour.

CHAPTER 22

Horses in the Middle Ages

Horses in the Middle Ages differed in size, build and breed from the modern horse, and were, on average, smaller. They were also more central to society than their modern counterparts, being essential for war, agriculture, and transport.

Consequently, specific types of horse developed, many of which have no modern equivalent. While an understanding of modern horse breeds and equestrianism is vital for any analysis of the medieval horse, researchers also need to consider documentary (both written and pictorial) and archeological evidence.

Horses in the Middle Ages were rarely differentiated by breed, but rather by use. This led them to be described, for example, as 'chargers' (war horses), 'palfreys' (riding horses), cart horses or packhorses. Reference is also given to their place of origin, such as 'Spanish horses', but whether this referred to one breed or several is unknown. Another difficulty arising during any study of medieval documents or literature is the flexibility of the medieval languages, where several words can be used for one thing (or, conversely, several objects are described by one word). Words such as 'courser' and 'charger' are used interchangeably (even within one document), and where one epic may speak disparagingly of a rouncey, another praises its skill and swiftness.

Significant technological advances in equestrian equipment, often introduced from other cultures, allowed for significant changes in both warfare and agriculture. In particular, improved designs for the solid-treed saddle as well as the arrival of the stirrup, horseshoe and horse collar were significant advances in medieval society.

Consequently, the assumptions and theories developed by historians are not definitive, and debate still rages on many issues, such as the breeding or size of the horse, and a number of sources must be consulted in order to understand the breadth of the subject.

Breeding

During the decline of the Roman Empire and the Early Middle Ages, much of the quality breeding stock developed during the classical period was lost due to uncontrolled breeding and had to be built up again over the following centuries. In the west, this may have been due in part to the reliance of the British and Scandinavians on infantry-based warfare, where horses were only used for riding and pursuit.

However, there were exceptions; in the 7th century a Merovingian kingdom still retained at least one active Roman horse breeding centre. The Spanish also retained many quality horses, in part due to the historic reputation of the region as a horse-breeding land, and partially due to the cultural influences related to the Islamic conquest of the Iberian peninsula between the 8th and 15th centuries.

The origins of the medieval war horse are obscure, although it is believed they had some Barb and Arabian blood, through the Spanish Jennet, a forerunner to the modern Friesian and Andalusian horse. It is also possible that other sources of oriental bloodstock came from what was called the *Nisaean breed* (possibly akin to the Turkoman horse) from Iran and Anatolia, another type of oriental horse brought back from the Crusades. 'Spanish' horses, whatever their breeding, were the most expensive. In fact, in Germany the word *spanjol* became the term used to describe quality war horses. However, German literary sources also refer to fine horses from Scandinavia. France also produced good war horses. Some scholars attribute this to the strong Feudal society there, but an equally probable explanation is the historic influence of the Roman horse breeding traditions preserved by the Merovingians, combined with the addition of valuable Spanish and oriental bloodstock captured in the wake of the victory of Charles Martel over the Islamic Umayyad invaders at the Battle of Tours in 732. Following this battle, the Carolingians began to increase their heavy cavalry, which resulted in the seizure of land (for fodder production), and a change in tribute payment from cattle to horses.

As the importance of horse breeding to successful warfare was realized, planned breeding programmes increased. Many changes were due to the influence of Islamic culture through both the Crusades and the Moorish invasions of Spain; the Arabs kept extensive pedigrees of their Barb and Arabian horses via an oral tradition. Some of the earliest written pedigrees in recorded European history were kept by Carthusian monks, who were among those who bred the Spanish Jennet. Because they could read and write, thus kept careful records, monastics were given the responsibility for horse breeding by certain members of the nobility, particularly in Spain. In England, a common source of warhorses were the wild moorland ponies, which were rounded up annually by horse-breeders, including the Cistercians, for use as campaign riding horses, or light cavalry; one such breed was the Fell pony, which had similar ancestry to the Friesian horse.

It is also hard to trace what happened to the bloodlines of destriers when this type seems to disappear from record during the seventeenth century. Many modern draft breeds claim some link to the medieval "great horse," with some historians considering breeds such as the Percheron, Belgian and Suffolk Punch likely descendants of the destrier. However, other historians discount this theory, since the historical record suggests the medieval warhorse was quite a different 'type' to the modern draught horse Such a theory would suggest the war horses were crossed once again with 'cold blooded' work horses, since war horses, and the destrier in particular, were renowned for their hot-blooded nature.

Types of Horse

Throughout the period, horses were rarely described by breed, but rather by *type*: by describing their purpose, or their physical attributes. Many of the definitions were not precise, or were interchangeable. Prior to approximately the 13th century, few pedigrees were written down. Thus, many terms for horses in the Middle Ages did not describe breeds as we know them today, but rather described appearance or purpose.

One of the best-known of the medieval horses was the destrier, renowned and admired for its capabilities in war. It was well trained, and was required to be strong, fast and agile. A fourteenth century writer described them as 'tall and majestic and with great strength'. In contemporary sources, the destrier was frequently referred to as the 'great horse' because of its size and reputation. Being a subjective term, it gives no firm information about its actual height or weight, but since the average horse of the time was 12 to 14 hands [48 to 56 inches (120 to 140 cm)], thus a 'great horse' by medieval standards might appear small to our modern eyes. The destrier was highly prized by knights and men-at-arms, but was actually not very common, and appears to have been most suited to the joust.

Coursers were generally preferred for hard battle as they were light, fast and strong. They were valuable, but not as costly as the destrier. They were also used frequently for hunting.

A more general-purpose horse was the rouncey (also *rounsey*), which could be kept as a riding horse or trained for war. It was commonly used by squires, men-at-arms or poorer knights. A wealthy knight would keep rounceys for his retinue. Sometimes the expected nature of warfare dictated the choice of horse; when a summons to war was sent out in England, in 1327, it expressly requested rounceys, for swift pursuit, rather than destriers. Rounceys were sometimes used as pack horses (but never as cart horses).

The well-bred palfrey, which could equal a destrier in price, was popular with nobles and highly-ranked knights for riding, hunting and ceremonial use. Ambling was a desirable trait in a palfrey, as the smooth gait allowed the rider to cover long distances quickly in relative comfort. Other horse types included the jennet, a small horse first bred in Spain from Barb and

Arabian bloodstock. Their quiet and dependable nature, as well as size, made them popular as riding horses for ladies; however, they were also used as cavalry horses by the Spanish.

Horses in Warfare

The hobby was a lightweight horse, about 13 to 14 hands [52 to 56 inches (130 to 140 cm)], developed in Ireland from Spanish or Libyan (Barb) bloodstock. This type of quick and agile horse was popular for skirmishing, and was often ridden by light cavalry known as *Hobelars*. Hobbies were used successfully by both sides during the Wars of Scottish Independence, with Edward I of England trying to gain advantage by preventing Irish exports of the horses to Scotland. Robert Bruce employed the hobby for his guerilla warfare and mounted raids, covering 60 to 70 miles (97 to 110 km) a day.

While light cavalry had been used in warfare for many centuries, the medieval era saw the rise of heavy cavalry, particularly the European knight. Historians are uncertain when the use of heavy cavalry in the form of mounted shock troops first occurred, but the technique had become widespread by the mid 12th Century. The heavy cavalry charge itself was not a common occurrence in warfare. Pitched battles were avoided, if at all possible, with most offensive warfare in the early Middle Ages taking the form of sieges, or swift mounted raids called *chevauchées*, with the warriors lightly armed on swift horses and their heavy war horses safely in the stable. Pitched battles were sometimes unavoidable, but were rarely fought on land suitable for heavy cavalry. While mounted riders remained effective for initial attacks, by the fourteenth century, it was common for knights to dismount to fight. Horses were sent to the rear, and kept ready for pursuit. By the Late Middle Ages (approx 1300-1550), large battles became more common, probably because of the success of infantry tactics and changes in weaponry. However, because such tactics left the knight unmounted, the role of the war horse also changed. By the 17th century, the medieval charger had become a thing of the past, replaced by lighter, unarmoured horses. Throughout the period, light horse, or *prickers*, were used for scouting and reconnaissance; they also provided a defensive screen for marching armies. Large teams of draught horses, or oxen, were used for pulling the heavy early cannon. Other horses pulled wagons and carried supplies for the armies.

Tournaments

Tournaments and hastiludes began in the eleventh century as both a sport and to provide training for battle. Usually taking the form of a melee, the participants used the horses, armour and weapons of war. The sport of jousting grew out of the tournament and, by the fifteenth century, the art of tilting became quite sophisticated. In the process, the pageantry and specialization became less war-like, perhaps because of the knight's changing role in war.

Horses were specially bred for the joust, and heavier armour developed. However, this did not necessarily lead to significantly larger horses. Interpreters at the Royal Armouries, Leeds, have re-created the joust, using specially bred horses and replica armour. Their horses are 15-16 hands high (60 to 64 inches (150 to 160 cm)), and approximately 1,100 pounds (500 kg), and perform well in the joust.

Types of War Horses

This 13th century manuscript shows an approximate height of the medieval horse at the time, note the knights' legs extending well below the horses' barrels.

The most well known horse of the medieval era of Europe is the destrier, known for carrying knights into war. However, most knights and mounted men-at-arms rode smaller horses known as coursers and rounceys. (A generic name often used to describe medieval war horses is *charger,* which appears interchangeable with the other terms). In Spain, the jennet was used as a light cavalry horse.

Stallions were often used as war horses in Europe due to their natural aggression and hot-blooded tendencies. A thirteenth century work describes destriers 'biting and kicking' on the battlefield, and, in the heat of battle, war horses were often seen fighting each other. However, the use of mares by European warriors cannot be discounted from literary references. Mares were the preferred war horse of the Moors, the Islamic invaders who attacked various European nations from A.D. 700 through the 15th Century.

War horses were more expensive than normal riding horses, and destriers the most prized, but figures vary greatly from source to source. Destriers are given a values ranging from seven times the price of an ordinary horse to 700 times. The Bohemian king Wenzel II rode a horse 'valued at one thousand marks' in 1298. At the other extreme, a 1265 French ordinance ruled that a squire could not spend more than twenty marks on a rouncey. Knights were expected to have at least one war horse (as well as riding horses and packhorses), with some records from the later Middle Ages showing knights bringing twenty-four horses on campaign. Five horses was perhaps the standard.

Size of War Horses

There is dispute in medievalist circles over the size of the war horse, with some notable historians claiming a size of 17 to 18 hands [68 to 72 inches (170 to 180 cm)], as large as a modern Shire horse. However, there are practical reasons for dispute over size. Analysis of existing horse armour located in the Royal Armouries indicates the equipment was originally worn by horses of 15 to 16 hands [60 to 64 inches (150 to 160 cm)], or about the size and build of a modern field hunter or ordinary riding horse. Research undertaken at the Museum of London, using literary, pictorial and archeological sources, supports military horses of 14-15 hands [56 to 60 inches

(140 to 150 cm)], distinguished from a riding horse by its strength and skill, rather than its size. This average does not seem to vary greatly across the medieval period. Horses appear to have been selectively bred for increased size from the ninth and tenth centuries, and by the eleventh century the average warhorse was probably 14.2 to 15 hh [58 to 60 inches (150 to 150 cm)], a size verified by studies of Norman horseshoes as well as the depictions of horses on the Bayeux Tapestry. Analysis of horse transports suggests thirteenth century destriers were a stocky build, and no more than 15-15.2 hands [60 to 62 inches (150 to 160 cm)]. Three centuries later, warhorses were not significantly bigger; the Royal Armouries used a 15.2 hand [62 inches (160 cm)] Lithuanian Heavy Draught mare as a model for the statues displaying various fifteenth-sixteenth century horse armours, as her body shape was an excellent fit.

Perhaps one reason for the pervasive belief that the medieval war horse had to be of draught horse type is the assumption, still held by many, that medieval armour was heavy. In fact, even the heaviest tournament armour (for knights) weighed little more than 90 pounds (41 kg), and field (war) armour 40 to 70 pounds (18 to 32 kg); barding, or horse armour, more common in tournaments than war, rarely weighed more than 70 pounds (32 kg). For horses, *Cuir bouilli* (a type of hardened leather), and padded caparisons would have been more common, and probably as effective. Allowing for the weight of the rider and other equipment, horses can carry approximately 30 per cent of their weight; thus such loads could certainly be carried by a heavy riding horse in the 1,200 to 1,300 pounds (540 to 590 kg) range, and a draught horse was not needed.

Although a large horse is not required to carry an armoured knight, it is held by some historians that a large horse was desirable to increase the power of a lance strike. However, practical experiments by re-enactors have suggested that the rider's weight and strength is of more relevance than the size of the mount, and that little of the horse's weight is translated to the lance.

Further evidence for a 14-16 hand (56 to 64 inches (140 to 160 cm)) war horse is that it was a matter of pride to a knight to be able to vault onto his horse in full armour, without touching the stirrup. This arose not from vanity, but necessity: if unhorsed during battle, a knight would remain vulnerable if unable to mount by himself. In reality, of course, a wounded or weary knight might find it difficult, and rely on a vigilant squire to assist him. Incidentally, a knight's armour served in his favour in any fall. With his long hair twisted on his head to form a springy padding under his padded-linen hood, and his helm placed on top, he had head protection not dissimilar to a modern bicycle or equestrian helmet.

Transportation

Throughout the Middle Ages it was customary for people of all classes and background to travel, often widely. The households of the upper classes and royal courts moved between manors and estates; the demands of diplomacy, war and crusades took men to distant countries; priests travelled between churches, monasteries and formed emissaries to Rome; people of all classes went on pilgrimage, or travelled to find work; others travelled as a pastime. Most people undertook small journeys on foot and hired horses for longer journeys. For the upper classes, travel was accompanied by a great deal of pomp and display, with fine horses, large retinues and magnificent cavalcades in order to display their wealth as well as to ensure personal comfort. For example, in 1445, the English royal household contained 60 horses in the king's stable and 186 kept for 'chariots' (carriages) and carts.

During much of the Middle Ages, there was no system of interconnected roads and bridges. Though parts of Europe still had remnants of Roman roads built before the collapse of the Roman Empire, most had long fallen into disrepair. Because of the necessity to ride long distances over uncertain roads, smooth-gaited horses were preferred, and most ordinary riding horses were of greater value if they could do one of the smooth but ground-covering four-beat gaits collectively known as an *amble* rather than the more jarring trot.

Mule trains, for land travel, and barges, for river and canal travel, were the most common form of long-distance haulage, although wheeled horse-drawn vehicles were used for shorter journeys. In areas with good roads, regular carrier services were established between major towns. However, because medieval roads were generally so poor, carriages for human passengers were rare. When roads permitted, early carriages were developed from freight wagons. Carriage travel was made more comfortable in the late fourteenth century with the introduction of the *chariot branlant,* which had strap suspension.

The speed of travel varied greatly. Large retinues could be slowed by the presence of slow-paced carts and litters, or by servants and attendants on foot, and could rarely cover more than fifteen to twenty miles a day. Small mounted companies might travel 30 miles a day. However, there were exceptions: stopping only for a change of horses midway, Richard II of England once managed the 70 miles between Daventry and Westminster in a night.

For breeding, war and travel purposes, it was also necessary to be able to transport horses themselves. For this purpose, boats were adapted and built to be used as horse transports. William of Normandy's 1066 invasion of England required the transfer of over 2000 horses from Normandy. Similarly, when travelling to France in 1285-6, Edward I of England ferried over 1000 horses across the English Channel to provide the royal party with transport.

Riding Horses

Riding horses were used by a variety of people during the Middle Ages, and so varied greatly in quality, size and breeding. Knights and nobles kept riding horses in their war-trains, saving their warhorses for the battle. The names of horses referred to a *type* of horse, rather than a breed. Many horses were described by the region where they or their immediate ancestors were foaled. For example, in Germany, Hungarian horses were commonly used for riding. Individual horses were often described by their gait ('trotters' or 'amblers'), by their colouring, or by the name of their breeder.

The best riding horses were known as palfreys; other riding horses were often called *hackneys*, from which the modern term "hack" is derived. Women sometimes rode palfreys or small quiet horses known as jennets.

Harness and Pack Horses

A variety of work horses were used throughout the Middle Ages. The pack horse (or 'sumpter horse') carried equipment and belongings. Common riding horses, often called "hackneys", could be used as pack horses. Cart horses pulled wagons for trading and freight haulage, on farms, or as part of a military campaign. These draught horses were smaller than their modern counterparts; pictorial and archeological evidence suggests that they were stout but short, approximately 13-14 hands (52 to 56 inches (130 to 140 cm)), and capable of drawing a load of 500 to 600 pounds (230 to 270 kg) per horse. Four-wheeled wagons and two-wheeled carts were more common in towns, such as London and, depending on type of vehicle and weight of the load, were usually pulled by teams of two, three, or four horses harnessed in tandem. Starting in the 12th century, in England the use of oxen to pull carts was gradually superseded by the use of horses, a process that extended through the 13th century. This change came because horse-drawn transport moved goods quicker and over greater distances than ox-drawn methods of transport.

Agriculture

The Romans had used a two-field crop rotation agricultural system, but from the 8th century on, a three-field system became more common. One field would be sown with a winter crop, the second with a spring crop, and the third left fallow. This allowed a greater amount of spring crop of oats to be grown, which provided fodder for horses. Another advance during the Middle Ages was the development of the heavy mouldboard plough, which allowed dense and heavy soils to be tilled easily; this technology required the use of larger teams of draught animals including oxen and horses, as well as the adoption of larger fields. Particularly after the 12th Century, the increased use of both the horse collar and use of iron horse shoes allowed horsepower to be directed more efficiently. Horse teams usually were four horses, or perhaps six, as compared to eight oxen, and the lesser numbers compensated for the fact that the horses needed to be fed grain on top of pasture, unlike oxen. The increased speed of horses also allowed more land to be ploughed in a day, with a eight ox plough team averaging a half an acre a day, but a horse team averaged an acre a day.

For farm work, such as ploughing and harrowing, the draught horse used was called an *affrus* (or *stott*), which was usually smaller and cheaper than the cart horse. While oxen were traditionally used as work animals on farms, horses began to be used in greater numbers after the development of the horse collar. Oxen and horses were sometimes harnessed together. The transition from oxen to horses for farm work was documented in pictorial sources (for example, the 11th century Bayeux tapestry depicts working horses), and also clear from the change from the Roman two-field crop-rotation system to a new three-field system, which increased the cultivation of fodder crops (predominantly oats, barley and beans). Horses were also used to process crops; they were used to turn the wheels in mills (such as corn mills), and transport crops to market. The change to horse-drawn teams also meant a change in ploughs, as horses were more suited to a wheeled plough, unlike oxen.

Equestrian Technology

The development of equestrian technology proceeded at a similar pace as the development of horse breeding and utilisation. The changes in warfare during the Early Middle Ages to heavy cavalry both precipitated and relied on the arrival of the stirrup, solid-treed saddle, and horseshoe from other cultures.

The development of the nailed horseshoe enabled longer, faster journeys on horseback, particularly in the wetter lands in northern Europe, and were useful for campaigns on varied terrains. By providing protection and support, nailed horse shoes also improved the efficiency of draught horse teams. Though the Romans had developed an iron 'hipposandal' that resembled a hoof boot, there is much debate over the actual origins of the nailed horseshoe, though it does appear to be of European origin. There is little evidence of nailed-on shoes prior to AD 500 or 600, though there is speculation that the Celtic Gauls were the first to nail on metal horseshoes. The earliest clear written record of iron horseshoes is a reference to 'crescent figured irons and their nails' in a list of cavalry equipment from AD 910. Additional archaeological evidence suggests they were used in Siberia during the 9th and 10th centuries, and had spread to Byzantium soon afterward; by the 11th century, horseshoes were commonly used in Europe. By the time the Crusades began in 1096, horseshoes were widespread and frequently mentioned in various written sources.

Riding Technology

The saddle with a solid tree provided a bearing surface to protect the horse from the weight of the rider. The Romans are credited with the invention of the solid-treed saddle, possibly as early as the first century BC, and it was widespread by the 2nd century A.D. Early medieval saddles resembled the Roman "four-horn" saddle, and were used without stirrups. The development of the solid saddle tree was significant; it raised the rider above the horse's back, and distributed the rider's weight, reducing the pounds per square inch carried on any one part of the horse's back, thus greatly increasing the comfort of the horse and prolonging its useful life. Horses could carry more weight when distributed across a solid saddle tree. It also allowed a more built up seat to give the rider greater security in the saddle. From the twelfth century, on the high war-saddle became more common, providing protection as well as added security. The built up cantle of a solid-treed saddle enabled horsemen to use lance more effectively.

Beneath the saddle, caparisons or saddle cloths were sometimes worn; these could be decorated or embroidered with heraldic colours and arms. War horses could be equipped with additional covers, blankets and armour collectively referred to as barding; this could be for decorative or protective purposes. Early forms of horse armour, usually restricted to tournaments, comprised padded leather pieces, covered by a trapper (a decorated cloth), which was not particularly heavy. Mail and plate armour was also occasionally used; there are literary references to horse armour (an 'iron blanket') starting in the late twelfth century.

The solid tree allowed for effective use of the stirrup The stirrup was developed in China and in widespread use there by AD 477. By the 7th century, primarily due to invaders from Central Asia, such as the Avars, stirrups arrived in Europe, and European riders had adopted them by the 8th century. Among other advantages, stirrups provided greater balance and support to the rider, which allowed the knight to use a sword more efficiently without falling, especially against infantry.

The increased use of the stirrup from the eighth century on aided the warrior's stability and security in the saddle when fighting. This may have led to greater use of shock tactics, although a couched lance could be used effectively without stirrups. In particular, Charles Martel recognized the military potential of the stirrup, and distributed seized lands to his retainers on condition that they serve him by fighting in the new manner.

A theory known as The Great Stirrup Controversy argues that the advantages in warfare that stemmed from use of the stirrup led to the birth of feudalism itself. Other scholars, however, dispute this assertion, suggesting that stirrups provided little advantage in shock warfare, being useful primarily for allowing a rider to lean farther to the left and right on the saddle while fighting, and simply reduce the risk of falling off. Therefore, it is argued, they are not the reason for the switch from infantry to cavalry in Medieval militaries, nor the reason for the emergence of Feudalism.

There was a variety of headgear used to control horses, predominantly bridles with assorted designs of bits. Many of the bits used during the Middle Ages resemble the bradoon, snaffle bit and curb bit that are still in common use today. However, they often were decorated to a greater degree: the bit rings or shanks were frequently covered with large, ornamental 'bosses'. Some designs were also more extreme and severe than those used today.The curb bit was known during the classical period, but was not generally used during the Middle Ages until the mid-14th century. Some styles of snaffle bit used during the Middle Ages had the lower cheek extended, in the manner of the modern half-cheek or full cheek snaffle. Until the late 13th century, bridles generally had a single pair of reins; after this period it became more common for knights to use two sets of reins, similar to that of the modern double bridle, and often at least one set was decorated.

Spurs were commonly used throughout the period, especially by knights, with whom they were regularly associated. A young man was said to have 'won his spurs' when he achieved knighthood. Wealthy knights and riders frequently wore decorated and filigreed spurs. Attached to the rider's heel by straps, spurs could be used both to encourage horses to quickly move forward or to direct lateral movement. Early spurs had a short shanks or 'neck', placing the rowel relatively close to the rider's heel; further developments in the spur shape lengthened the neck, making it easier to touch the horse with less leg movement on the part of the rider.

Harness Technology

A significant development which increased the importance and use of horses in harness, particularly for ploughing and other farm work, was the horse collar. The horse collar was invented in China during the 5th century, arrived in Europe during the 9th century, and became widespread throughout Europe by the 12th century. It allowed horses to pull greater weight than they could when hitched to a vehicle by means of yokes or breastcollars used in earlier times. The yoke was designed for oxen and not suited to the anatomy of horses, it required horses to pull with their shoulders rather than using the power of their hindquarters. Harnessed in such a manner, horse teams could pull no more than 500 kg. The breastplate-style harness that had flat straps across the neck and chest of the animal, while useful for pulling light vehicles, was of little use for heavy work. These straps pressed against the horse's sterno-cephalicus muscle and trachea, which restricted breathing and reduced the pulling power of the horse. Two horses harnessed with a breastcollar harness were limited to pulling a combined total of about 1,100 pounds (500 kg). In contrast, the horse collar rested on horses' shoulders and did not impede breathing. It allowed a horse to use its full strength, by pushing forward with its hindquarters into the collar rather than to pull with its shoulders. With the horse collar, a horse could provide a work effort of 50 per cent more foot-pounds per second than an ox, because it could move at a greater speed, as well as having generally greater endurance and the ability to work more hours in a day. A single horse with a more efficient collar harness could draw a weight of about 1,500 pounds (680 kg).

A further improvement was managed by altering the arrangement of the teams; by hitching horses one behind the other, rather than side by side, weight could be distributed more evenly, and pulling power increased. This increase in horse power is demonstrated in the building accounts of Troyes, which show carters hauling stone from quarries 50 miles (80 km) distant; the carts weighed, on average, 5,500 pounds (2,500 kg), on which 5,500 pounds (2,500 kg) of stone was regularly loaded, sometimes increasing to 8,600 pounds (3,900 kg) – a significant increase from Roman-era loads.

Horse Trades and Professions

The elite horseman of the Middle Ages was the knight. Generally raised from the middle and upper classes, the knight was trained from childhood in the arts of war and management of the horse. In most languages, the term for knight reflects his status as a horseman: the French *chevalier*, Spanish *caballero* and German *Ritter*. The French word for horse-mastery – *chevalerie* – gave its name to the highest concept of knighthood: chivalry.

A large number of trades and positions arose to ensure the appropriate management and care of horses. In great households, the marshal was responsible for all aspects relating to horses: the care and management of all horses from the chargers to the pack horses, as well as all travel logistics. The position of marshal (literally 'horse servant') was a high one in court circles and the king's marshal (such as the Earl Marshal in England) was also responsible for managing many military matters. Also present within the great households was the constable (or 'count of the stable'), who was responsible for protection and the maintenance of order within the household and commanding the military component and, with marshals, might organise hastiludes and other chivalrous events. Within lower social groupings, the 'marshal' acted as a farrier. The highly-skilled marshal made and fitted horseshoes, cared for the hoof, and provided general veterinary care for horses; throughout the Middle Ages, a distinction was drawn between the marshal and the blacksmith, whose work was more limited.

A number of tradesmen dealt with the provision of horses. Horse dealers (frequently called "horse coursers" in England) bought and sold horses, and frequently had the reputation as dishonest figures, responsible for the brisk trade in stolen horses. Others, such as the 'hackneymen' offered horses for hire, and many formed large establishments on busy roads, often branding their horses to deter theft.

Women and Horses

It was not uncommon for a girl to learn her father's trade, and for a woman to share her husband's trade; many guilds also accepted the membership of widows, so they might continue their husband's business. Under this system, some women trained in horse-related trades, and there are records of women working as farriers and saddle-makers. On farms, where every hand was needed, excessive emphasis on division of labour was impracticable, and women often worked alongside men (on their own farms or as hired help), leading the farmhorses and oxen, and managing their care.

Despite the difficulties of travel, it was customary for many people, including women, to travel long distances. Upper-class wives frequently accompanied their husbands on crusade or to tournaments, and many women travelled for social or family engagements; both nuns and laywomen would perform pilgrimages. When not on foot, women would usually travel on horseback or, if weakened or infirm, be carried in a wagon or a litter. If roads permitted, women sometimes rode in early carriages developed from freight wagons, pulled by three or four horses. After the invention of better suspension systems, travel in carriages became more comfortable. Women of the nobility also rode horses for sport, accompanying men in activities that included hunting and hawking.

Most medieval women rode astride. While an early chair-like sidesaddle with handles and a footrest was available by the 13th century and allowed women of the nobility to ride while wearing elaborate gowns, they were not universally adopted during the Middle Ages. This was largely due to the insecure seat they offered, which necessitated a smooth-gaited horse being led by another handler. The sidesaddle did not become practical for everyday riding until the 16th century development of the pommel horn that allowed a woman to hook her leg around the saddle and hence use the reins to control her own horse. Even then, sidesaddle riding remained a precarious activity until the invention of the second, 'leaping horn' in the 19th century.

It was not unknown for women to ride war horses, and take their part in warfare. Joan of Arc is probably the most famous female warrior of the medieval period, but there were many others, including the Empress Matilda who, armoured and mounted, led an army against her cousin Stephen of Blois, and Stephen's wife Matilda of Boulogne in the 12th Century. The fifteenth-century writer Christine de Pizan advised aristocratic ladies that they must 'know the laws of arms and all things pertaining to warfare, ever prepared to command her men if there is need of it'.

CHAPTER 23

Popular Breeds of Horses Around the World

Horses are described in numerous ways; breeds, types, 'bloods' and purposes. When looking at shows or sales descriptions its very easy to be confused by the different descriptions used. We have complied a short list of some of the more popular horse breeds with a picture, so that you can more easily identify the breed types we are referencing.

Popular Breeds of Horses

- • *American Paint Horse:* American Paint Horse has an easy going temperament & used for cattle work.
- *American Quarter Horse:* American quarter horse Versatile, popular equine breed that's great for new riders.
- *American Saddlebred Horse:* American saddlebred horse result of selective breeding of four breeds of horses.
- *American Standardbred Horse:* Most of this breed complete a mile race in 3 minutes.
- *Appaloosa Horse:* This horse's spotted coat and fur is its most recognize characteristic.
- *Arabian Horse:* Arabians are know for being affectionate and a dished head profile.
- *Clydesdale Horses:* Known for their large frames and study working abilities.
- *Ponies:* Distinctive pony breed (breeding two ponies) & is less than 14.2 hand high.
- *Hanoverian Horse:* This breed of horse excels in jumping, dressage, and eventing.
- *Missouri Fox Trotter:* Breed named after its unusual gait and smooth movement.
- *Morgan Horse:* Historically the official horse breed of the United States.

- *Palomino Horse:* Breed admired for their beauty, versatility, & endurance.
- *Peruvian Paso/Paso Fino:* Breed known for an easy ride on rocky terrain.
- *Tennessee Walking Horse:* Distinct breed with no trot - only a 'running walk'.
- *Thoroughbred Horse:* Horse of choice for racing and speed related equestrian sports.
- *Miniature Horses:* Miniature Horse Breed Makes a Great Household Pet.
- *Pinto Horses:* Their colouring provided a degree of natural camouflage.
- *Mustang Horses:* Mustangs can range in size of between 13 and 16 hands.

Types of Equine Breeds

- Coldbloods - Larger, gentle horses for working or hauling.
- Hotbloods - Swift, fast horses used for racing and speed.
- Warmbloods - Great breed for equestrian sports and competitions.

From cave paintings it is believed that the equid from which modern horses are derived resemble the modern Przewalski Horse. The large strong heads and erect manes depicted in these paintings bear a striking resemblance to this modern breed.

The first domestication of the horses was probably in the steppes of central Asia between 3000 and 4000 B.C. These first animals were kept for meat and milk. As early man became more mobile undoubtedly horses began to be used as pack animals.

Oxen were being used in the Middle East at approximately 4000 B.C. for plowing. Progressively they were used on sleds, which were eventually mounted on rollers, with the final evolution of wheels. Early in the 3rd millennium B.C. there is archeological evidence that vehicles drawn by equid, generally onagers or ass hybrids, were being used in warfare. As horses from the north became more numerous the carts moved to the familiar two-wheeled chariot with spoked wheels. Due to his greater speed the horse rapidly replaced other equid as harness animals.

What is a Breed?

The classic definition of a 'breed' is usually stated as a variation of this statement.

Animals that, through selection and breeding, have come to resemble one another and pass those traits uniformly to their offspring.

Unfortunately this definition leaves some unanswered questions. For example, when is a crossbred animal considered a composite breed and when do we stop thinking about them as composites? Perhaps this definition from *The Genetics of Populations* by researcher helps explain why a good definition of 'breed' is elusive.

A breed is a group of domestic animals, termed such by common consent of the breeders, . . . a term which arose among breeders of livestock, created one might say, for their own use, and no one is warranted in assigning to this word a scientific definition and in calling the breeders wrong when they deviate from the formulated definition. It is their word and the breeders common usage is what we must accept as the correct definition.

Researcher defined that it is at least in part the perception of the breeders and the livestock industry which decides when a group of individuals constitutes a 'breed'.

The development of the breeds takes different routes also. In some breeds you can see the amount of change that can occur as the result of selection for a small number of traits. As an example, Holstein cattle have been selected primarily for milk production and are the highest milk producing cattle in the world. Other breeds have traits that result from natural selection pressure based upon the environment in which they were developed. An example of this might be the N'dama cattle from west Africa. These animals have, through the centuries, developed a resistance to trypanosomiasis or sleeping sickness spread by the tse-tse fly, which is fatal to most other breeds of cattle.

American Paint Horse

The American Paint descended from horses introduced by the Spanish conquistadors. Paints became part of the herds of wild horses that roamed the Western plains. Native Americans widely used the Paint, and some even believed this horse to possess magical powers.

The Paint was cherished by cowboys for cattle work because they were nimble and worked hard. American Paint Horses are easy-going, friendly and intelligent.

The Paint has distinctive colouring. Their coat markings fall into two classes- *tobiano* (white with dark markings) or *overo* (dark with light markings).

The overo (pronounced: oh vair' oh) pattern may also be either predominantly dark or white. But typically, the white on an overo will not cross the back of the horse between its withers and its tail.

Not all coat patterns fit neatly into the tobiano or overo categories. For this reason, a number of years ago the classifications have been expanded to include 'tovero' (pronounced: tow vair' oh) to describe horses that have characteristics of both the tobiano and overo patterns.

The American Paint Horse is an excellent horse for ranch work, rodeo, trail riding, showing, or simply as a friendly mount for the kids.

Pintos Mean 'Paint' Too

The Pinto is the Spanish word for 'paint'. Most Paints are also Pintos, but not all Pintos are Paints, since the Pinto Horse Association of America allows different breeding restrictions than the American Paint Horse Association.

American Quarter Horse

The adaptability of the quarter horse breed has allowed it to be used in other occupations such as trail riding and for use by many urban mounted police units. Their even temperament makes them a great animal for new riders learning about horses and their breeding ability has made several stud farm owners both famous and wealthy. It is by far the most popular breed and currently boasts a population of about 3.2 million.

The quarter horse breeds usually shown in competition are larger, more muscular horses with wide jowls. Those for reining and cutting are smaller with more powerful hindquarters very agile and quick on their feet. The show type resembles the running quarter horse though some may be taller and slimmer. All quarter horses however have speed, power and are more than willing to please their owners.

Their popularity also has them working in rodeo and on ranches and as show horses in show and pleasure events.

Their colouring varies from bay, black and brown and includes chestnut, palomino, buckskin and grey. The quarter horse breed is known for its small, short and refined head and straight profile as well as its broad chest and powerful hindquarters. Standing between 14 and 16 hands, about five-feet-tall at the withers, they are bred with two main body types. The stock type, which is more compact and muscular yet extremely agile, and the racing type that may be slightly taller with smoother muscles typically trained for running quarter mile sprints.

Back in the late 1700s the colonists came across a horse breed that combined the English horses with the Chickasaw breed, which was a descendent of the Arabia and Barb, brought into the southeast United States by the Spanish Conquistadors. What they had was a small, sturdy horse that was quick and nimble and showed signs of superior intelligence and a willingness to work. As flat land horse racing became popular, this fast animal, achieving speeds of up to 55 miles per hour over short distances soon dominated the quarter mile track and was aptly named the quarter miler, or quarter horse. As the quarter horse breed continued to gain popularity, its gentle nature led it to be used as a riding horse and due to its strength was soon performing other work on many of the early farms. The breed seemed to have a natural instinct for working around cattle as well. When the settlers began surging west in the 1800s, the quarter horse breed was the horse of choice of the early cowboys, being used for cattle round-up due to their speed and agile maneuverability and quickly became the horses that cowboys counted on for their daily duties on cattle ranches. As with most activities undertaken by the early cowboys, the duties performed by them and their horses, quickly turned into competition, setting the stage for rodeo riding, and the quarter horse breed excelled at calf roping, team roping and barrel racing. Today, these horses are still in demand for these events.

American Saddlebred Horse

- The American Saddlebred evolved during the 1800's in the Southern States, primarily in Kentucky.
- Originally known as the Kentucky Saddler, it was the result of selective breeding of the Canadian and Narragansett Pacers, the Morgan Horse, and the Thouroughbred. It was an elegant horse, and looked wonderful pulling a carraige to church on Sundays.
- Although fine as a harness horse, the modern Saddlebred is the premiere showring horse, exhibited under saddle. As a five-gaited horse, it is shown with a full mane and tail. In addition to the usual walk, trot, and cantor, the Saddlebred performs the slow gait, a prancing four-beat motion with a deliberate pause before each foot-fall, and the 'rack', a full-speed flashy four-beat gait.
- The American Saddlebred stands at 16 hands, and in addition to the show ring, can cut cattle, jump well, and is a pleasure to trail ride. It is an excellent competitor in dressage.
- This is an intelligent horse with a good dispostion, has good stamina, well balanced, with good jumping ability - a real pleasureable horse to own.

American Standardbred Horse

- The American Standardbred was based on an English Thoroughbred by the name of Messenger. Messenger was brought to America in 1788, and was bred with all sorts of mares including many Morgans.
- Never actually racing, Messenger died at the age of 28 in 1808, and was buried on Long Island. His grandson Hambletorian, sired 1,355 offspring. Hambletorian also never raced, but his son Dexter trotted the mile in a record 2 minutes 17 seconds.
- Early Standardbreds, to be included in the registry, had to complete a mile in less than 3 minutes, but today many are able to go this distance in less that 1 minute and 55 seconds.
- The Standardbred has a lateral pacing gait, where both legs on one side move forward or back at the same time, that is ideal for harness racing. Although they are extremely fast trotters and virtually all European trotters have the Standardbred bloodline, pacers now outnumber the trotters about 4 to 1.
- American Standardbreds stand at about 15.2 to 15.9 hands in height, and are found in all shades of bay, brown, and blcak. Most of the finest are raised in Kentucky.

Appaloosa Horse

- The wonderful Appaloosa horse was the result of selective breeding by the Nez Perce Indians of Idaho, Northeast Oregon, and Southeast Washington. They based the breed on Spanish stock. The word

'Appaloosa' came from the Palouse River, which runs through the area. These spotted horses were mentioned in Lewis and Clark's journal from their 1806 expedition.

- The breed almost died out after the U.S. calvary slaughtered the Indian's horses after chasing the tribe into the Bear Paw mountains of Montana. In 1938, a group of concerned horse people in Moscow, Idaho began a registry, the Appaloosa Horse Club, to save the breed. It now has the third largest registry in the world.
- Probably the Appaloosa's most distinguishing feature is its spotted coat, which can be found in various patterns. The more common patterns are a dark body colour with light spots (snowflake), and a white body with dark spots (leopard). There are also a frost coat with white specks, marble which is molted all over, and a blanket, which is all white (usually with dark spots) over the hips. Their hooves generally have black or white stripes.
- There are a number of types today, as there has been some cross-breeding with the Quarter Horse. Many Appaloosas have thin manes and tails, and some believe that their eyes have an almost human look to them. The height range is from 14.3 to 15.4 hands.
- Appaloosas are known for their quiet temperment. They are versatile, able jumpers, and do well in Western events and three day eventing. They make good trail and long distance riders.

Arabian Horse

- There are several characteristics that set the Arabian horse apart from other breeds, the most noticeable being their face. "The Arabian's head has a characteristic dished profile with a prominent eye, large nostrils and small teacup muzzle".
- Arabian horses are well known for being affectionate and bonding well with humans. Arabians have also become the breed of choice in the endurance world because of their stamina and agility. Due to their friendly nature and willingness to work, Arabians are a popular choice for instructional programmes and therapeutic riding.
- It is unknown whether the Arabian was first needed for work or riding, but by 1500 B.C. the people of the Middle East had domesticated the Arabian horse.
- In 1725, Nathan Harrison of Virginia imported the first Arabian stallion into the American colonies. In 1873, General Ulysses S. Grant was given two purebred Arabian stallions, Leopard and Lindentree, on a trip to the Middle East by Sulton, Abdul Hamid II of Turkey. Leopard was then passed to Randolph Huntington, who then imported two more stallions and two mares in 1888 from England. This became the first purebred Arabian breeding programme in the United States.

- On September 2, 1908, the Arabian Horse Club of America, Inc. (now called the Arabian Horse Registry of America), was founded in New York State. It is now located in Colorado.
- Arabian horses come in many colours, grey, chestnut, bay, roan, brown, and occasionally black. Most Arabians stand between 14.1 and 15.2 hands and weigh between 800 and 1,000 pounds as adults.

Clydesdale Working Horse

- The Clydesdale horse breed is best known for its size, over 18 hands, about six-feet and the feather above the hooves. This long hair covering their ankles makes this breed easily recognizable and it is thought the feather was developed during the first breedings with the Fleming and English Breeds. This feather, a thick mane and heavy coat helped the breed survive in the Scottish climate. Intelligent eyes peer from the Clydesdale horse breed's large head with small ears a deep chest and heavy bone structure in the shoulders. Growing to over 2,000 pounds and having a high wither; this large beast is also known for its grace. With a seemingly eager gait, this horse always presents a positive attitude as it raises it feet cleanly from the ground before continuing with a long stride.
- Colouring of the Clydesdale horse breed varies from different shades of bay, brown, chestnut and black, predominantly with one solid colour, often with a white underbelly as well as a white feather.
- Although horses with black legs may sometimes also offer a black feather. Originally developed for protection against harsh weather, the feather is manly for show.
- Horses with a white muzzle typically have black spots around the chin and lips and a white mask usually covers the face. White feet may extend up to merge with the white underbelly, they can also end at the top of the feather. Another characteristic of the Clydesdale horse breed are black and white striped hooves.
- Queen Elizabeth II saw a colourful Clydesdale pulling a milk cart and was so impressed with the animal she pressed it into royal service as a drum carrier to haul a 90-pound silver kettle used by the Household Cavalry band. Similarly, colourful horses today are referred to as drum horses or gypsy horses and are bred for their colour, long mane and tail.

Breed History

From their use as warhorses in the 17th century to their work in advertising today, the Clydesdale horse breed has undergone powerful changes. In Clydesdale, Scotland, now known as Lanarkshire, the animal was named for the town where it was used as a draft horse on area farms. Believed to have a history of over 300 years, the strong yet amiable animal was used in farming as well as pulling heavy loads in rural settings, as well as is urban and industrial areas.

As recently as the 1960's they could been seen pulling carts of milk and vegetable and are perhaps better known as the advertising celebrity for Anheuser-Busch Brewing Company. Right after then-president August A. Busch II admonished his son for buying a new Lincoln Town Car during the depression, he found outside the brewery in St. Louis, Missouri a Studebaker beer wagon with an eight-horse hitch of Clydesdales. The horses remain today as the company's mascot.

The Clydesdale population dipped to a low of about 80 animals and in 1975 was on the vulnerable list for survival. With the Clydesdale horse breed's growing popularity, their population is estimated at over 5,000 and growing with an estimated 600 foals each year.

Traditionally used for heavy labour, the Clydesdale horse breed has been mostly replaced by tractors and other machinery except by farmers who reject the industrial way of life and on eco-friendly farms, as well as in some remaining logging operations.

Ponies

A pony is a small type of horse that stands less than 14.2 hands high. This doesn't mean that a midget horse is automatically a pony. Ponies are members of distinctive breeds, and you get a pony by breeding two ponies.

There are numerous breeds from all around the world. In the show ring, ponies are divided into three height classes: up to 12.2 hands high, up to 13.2 hands high, and up to 14.2 hands.

The Shetland Pony

This is the one that most people seem to think of when they here the word pony. These are really short ponies, usually about 11 hands tall - great for small children. They come in many colours.

Welsh Pony

There are actually 4 kinds of welsh ponies, the Welsh Mountain Pony, the Welsh Pony, the Welsh Pony of Cob Type, and the Welsh Cob. These are listed from the shortest to the tallest.

Pony of the Americas

These originated by crossing the Appaloosa and the Shetland pony, and usually have Appaloosa markings. These are good ponies for kids. They are commonly referred to as a POA.

Connemara Pony

This is a refined looking-pony, one of the taller ones and so is suitable for many adults. The Connemara makes an excellent jumping pony.

Chincoteague Pony

The Chincoteague is a feral pony living on two islands off the Virginia coast. First discovered there in the late 1700's, the herds are managed by the Chincoteague fire department, who rounds them up the ones on Assateague Island on the fourth of July, and swims them across the little stretch of ocean to Chincoteague Island for auction.

This is a rather stubborn pony, but they are broken for riding. They come in all colours, with pinto being the most common.

Other Ponies

- American Walking Pony
- Australian Pony
- Dales Pony
- Dartmoor Pony
- Dulmen
- Exmoor Pony
- Falabella
- Fell Pony
- Gotland
- Highland
- Icelandic Horse
- Merens
- New Forest Pony
- Norwegian Fjord
- Prezlwalski's Horse
- Rocky Mountain Pony
- Tarpan

Hanoverian Horse

The Hanoverian is the best known of the European Warmbloods, and has become very popular in the United States.

The Hanoverian horse excels in the equestrian disciplines of jumping, dressage, and eventing.

The success of Hanoverian horses in competition proves the soundness of the breed - 13 medals in the 1992 Olympics and four consecutive World Breeding Championships as well as five gold, one silver and two bronze medals in dressage and show jumping at the 1996 Olympics.

The American Hanoverian Society was established in 1978.

History of the Breed

The breed originated in northern Germany in the state of Lower Saxony, the former kingdom of Hannover. A flourishing horse-breeding industry has existed here for almost 300 years at Celle. Although the Hanoverian Studbook was officially begun in 1888, detailed pedigrees have been kept since the late 1700's.

Orinially, Thoroughbreds were crossed with Holsteiner mares to improve the quality of horses for cavalry and farming. In the past 70 years, the Hanoverian breeding programme has adapted to the need for a more athletic riding horse, introducing other breeds as appropriate. The result is the modern Hanoverian horse.

Breed Characteristics

The Hanoverian has elastic gaits characterized by an elastic ground-covering walk, a floating trot, and a round, rhythmic canter.

The Hanoverian stands at 15.3 to 16.2 hands. They are strong and athletic, and are quite even-tempered.

Missouri Fox Trotter

- This wonderful breed was developed by early American settlers, originally mixing Morgans and Thoroughbreds beginning in the 1820's. Later, they introduced the Saddlebred and Tennessee Walking Horse blood.
- This breed gets its name from its unusual gait where it walks quickly with its forelegs and trots with its hind legs. It can sustain this smooth movement for a long period of time.
- Usually ridden in Western saddle, it is a sure-footed trail horse over rough ground, and a common show horse. At show no artificial appliances such as false tails are allowed, and no weighting of the hooves.
- You would think with the unusal gait that the rider might be uncomfortable. But just the opposit is true, the rider does not feel the effects of the movement.
- Other gaits of the Fox Trotter include the cantor, and the 'four-time walk', performed with the hind feet overriding the front track.

The Missouri Fox Trotter comes in all colours, but mainly chestnet, and stands at 14-16 hands in height.

Morgan Horse

- The Morgan Horse is the first documented American breed, and began with a stallion by the name of Justin Morgan. Foaled at Randolph, Vermont in 1789, he was originally name Figure, but was given his owner's name (a teacher and music composer named Justin Morgan) after his owner passed away.
- His new owner, Robert Evans, discovered that this little horse at only 14 hands could out-run and out-haul all challengers.
- Because of this ability, Justin Morgan was used for hauling freight and plowing, clearing logs, and all kinds of draft work.
- Justin Morgan competed throughout his life in every kind of racing and hauling contest. He was never beaten.
- This wonderful horse died in 1821 when he ws 32 years old, from an untreated kick received from another horse.
- All modern day Morgan's are traced to Justin Morgan's most famous three sons, Sherman, Woodbury,and Bullrush. Justin Morgan himself, was probably a combination of a Welsh Cob, and possibly a thoroughbred.

- The American Saddlebred and Standardbred, and the Tennessee Walking Horse, all have some Morgan blood in their lines.
- The Morgan is used in both ridden and harness classes, and pleasure riding too. At one time, the Morgan was the official horse of the United States Army.

Palomino

- The place of origin of the Palomino probably never will be conclusively determined. Myths and legends of various countries shroud the beginnings of the golden horse. The golden horse with ivory-coloured mane and tail appears in ancient tapestries and paintings of Europe and Asia, Asia.
- The Palomino has come down through the pages of history. During the days of the Crusades, the Emir Saladin presented Richard-Coeur-de-Lion with two splendid war horses, one was a gray and the other a Golden Palomino.
- These splendid golden horses were favoured by her Majesty Isabella de-Bourbon, that beloved queen who pawned her jewels so that the expenses of the expedition which discovered the New World might be paid. Queen Isabella kept a full hundred of these animals and as the chosen favourites. A commoner was not allowed to even own
- It is recorded that Queen Isabella sent a Palomino stallion and five mares to her Viceroy in New Spain (now Mexico). From there, the blood spread into Texas, and from Texas it came to California.
- The word 'Palomino' is a Spanish surname. Many feel that Palomino is only a colour and not a breed, which is true that the colour of Palomino comes in all breeds, but the Palomino of Spanish times, the Golden Dorado, was as close to being a breed as any strain of horse. The Dorado was of Arabic-Moorish-Spanish blood and breeding, closely akin to the Arabian and the Moorish Barb. This point has been noted in an old book and printed in Barcelona in 1774.
- The Palomino is a multi-purpose horse. They are admired not only for their beauty but for their versatility, maneuverability, and endurance. They are to be found in ranching, racing, rodeos, pleasure riding, parades, shows, fiestas, jumping, trail rides, and all other equine activities.
- We even have a few movie stars including, Mr. Ed and Trigger, who were registered with The Palomino Horse Association.

Peruvian Paso

- The Peruvian Paso was bred from Spanish stock brought to South America by the conquistadors in the 1500's. The people of this area need a horse that would be easy to ride for long distances over high mountain terrain.
- During the Middle ages, the Barbs and Palfreys bred in Spain were considered the finest and most beautiful in the world. They were called

Spanish Jennets and when Spanish nobelmen first settled in South America and the Caribbean Islands, they took many of these prized horses with them. Today, the descendents of those early Spanish Jennets are known as Paso Finos and Peruvian Pasos.

- The Peruvain Paso, one of the world's last remaining naturally gaited breeds, is becoming very popular among American horse enthusiasts for several good reasons.
- This horse provides riding comfort, strength and stamina for the avid trail rider and has a calm disposition. Its flashy presence and gait have a natural tendancy to set the exhibitor and parader apart from others. No special training is necessary to enable the Peruvian Paso to perform its specialty - a natural four-beat footfall that provides a ride of incomparable smoothness.
- Peruvian Paso horses come in all basic, solid colours as well as greys and roans. The breed, because of its direct link to the Barb horse, has some striking colour tones and shades.
- The average height of the Peruvian Paso is between 14 and 15 hands and the weight is commonly between 900 and 1,100 pounds, about the same as Morgans and Arabians.

Paso Fino

- The Paso Fino is the American-bred equivalent of the Peruvian Paso, with all the same fine qualities
- Although some outside blood was occasionally added to gain size, usually Arabian, Morgan or American Saddlebred, the modern Paso Fino is a close representation of the old Spanish Jennet and still can be thought of as one of the world's most coveted palfreys.
- There is probably no smoother horse to be ridden than a Peruvian Paso or Paso Fino.

Tennessee Walking Horse

- The Tennessee Walking Horse is a distinct breed that does not trot, but has a gait called a 'running walk'. This gait provides the rider with a smooth comfortable ride, no bounce for the rider. To ride a Tennessee Walking Horse, the rider just has to sit quiet in the saddle. No posting is necessary.
- Besides their smooth gaits, the Tennessee Walking Horse is known world wide for their great dispositions, gentle manners, and good looks.
- The Tennessee Walking Horse was developed in Tennessee in the late 1800's, by farmers who wanted to develop a breed of horse that could work in the fields during the day, and give the owner a comfortable saddle gait. They crossed their Thoroughbreds, Saddlebreds, Morgans, Standardbreds, and Narranganett Pacers.
- The Tennessee Walking Horse Breeders & Exhibitors Association was formed in 1935, and currently have more than 20,000 members.

- Most Tennessee Walking Horses are born with he ability to do other gaits in addition to the running walk, such as the rack, pace, and foxtrot. The Tennessee Walking Horse is also famous for their 'rocking chair' canter.
- Tennessee Walking Horse comes in all sizes and colours. Besides being great performance horses in the show ring, they are currently being shown.in barrels, poles, jumping, dressage, driving and trail classes. They are also being used on ranches as working horses.

Thoroughbred Horse

The Thoroughbred was originally bred in England due to the Englishmen's emerging passion for fast race-horses.

Three that founded the Thoroughbred bloodline were Byerley Turk, Darley Arabian, and Godolphin Arabian, all imported to England between 1670 and 1710. About 90 per cent of modern Thoroughbreds have descended from Eclipse (his grandsire was Darley Arabian), who was never beaten in 18 races.

Another descendant of Darley Arabian was Diomed, who won the first running of the Derby, held in 1780. At 21 years old, he was sent to the United States, where he founded the male line through his son, Sir Archie.

Thoroughbreds are the horse of choice for track racing, the best known race being the Kentucky Derby.

The Thoroughbred has also had influence on other breeds such as the American Standardbred, the popular choice for harness racing. In fact, many of the world's horse breeds have benefited at some time from the addition of Thoroughbred blood.

Thoroughbreds in America are born in the spring, but regardless of the actual date, January 1st is their official birthday.

Having spent its first year developing size and power, the young Thoroughbred begins training as a yearling. The animal learns to accept a saddle and bridle, a rider on its back and ultimately to break from a starting gate and run around a track.

Kentucky has more Thoroughbred horse farms than anywhere else in the world. Most of the racetrack champions come from Kentucky.

Miniature Horse

Originally bred as pets for the children of royalty in the 1600's, the miniature horse breed also spent time working in the mines and now mainly appear in their own shows. They are considered gentle animals that are affectionate and genuinely eager to please still making them perfect pets. In addition to their role as pets, they were also kept as curiosities and appeared in circuses where their reputation as performers grew. It was not until the late 18th century that they because used as pit ponies, working the mines in Wales and in Great Britain.

In the 1800's, because of their size, they were imported to the United States to work in the coal mines of Appalachia. American breeders took an interest in the miniature horse breed and began selective breeding practices to breed a miniature with perfect proportions to the larger animals. The American Miniature Horse Association, founded in 1978, lists two classes of miniatures, class A being 34 inches tall or less, and class B ranging from 34 to 38 inches tall. In order to appear in horse shows as a miniature, the animal can be no taller than 34 inches, which is eight and half hands. Today, the AMHA registers about 140,000 animals around the world. Their breeding goal is to develop the smallest possible horse that maintains the correct conformity and the smallest of the breed is considered more desirable.

They are found in a variety of colours including bay, black, buckskin, chestnut, grey, palomino, pinto and white. They should have a head in proportion to the body and neck with a broad forehead and eyes widely spaced. Medium sized ears should be pointed with a long, flexible neck. Hooves should be rounded with legs straight and parallel to each other and the animal's croup should be the same height as the withers.

Many times the miniature horse breed is confused with dwarf horses and although dwarfs may be cute, they are not considered as miniatures due to irregularities in conformity. Their strength is also in proportion to their build and are capable of pulling loads that are also in proportion and as such are still used as circus attractions, often dressed in colourful costumes and pulling miniature carts.

Because of their gentle nature, many still own miniature horses as pets as they thrive on attention with a great display of curiosity and intelligence. While many people have always wanted to own a horse, but had reservations of owning, handling and caring for an animal that could weight over 1,000 pounds, are finding the miniature horse breed ideal. About an acre of land is usually sufficient roaming territory for exercise and outdoor feeding and caring for a miniature is the same as for any other horse breeds, only on a much smaller scale.

They are also used in therapeutic value is also growing for use with disabled children and adults and they are used for people of all walks of life in stressful jobs or situations. The lifespan of a miniature horse is about 30 years, although on miniature in North Carolina's protective area attained the age of 50.

Mustang Horse

Mustangs have no specific conformation and can range in size of between 13 and 16 hands, but on average stand about 14 hands. While their colourings of appaloosa, palomino, buckskin and black seem to have been bred from the breed over the years, it is still possible to see these colours. Shapes and the horse's physical build will vary as they have mostly been bred in the wild. During the early colonial days and going through the westward expansion, horses that escaped from their owners or were purposely set free became part of the mustang reproductive family. Some ranchers also would allow their horses to roam free during the winter to basically fend for themselves, food wise, and then recapture them in the spring. Other ranchers attempted to improve the breeding of local mustang herds by killing off the dominant male in the herd and replacing him with males with a pedigree. In many parts of the country the wild mustangs are kept in preserves as part of the 1971 federal protection law, but they can be found in the southwest roaming free on open plains. The term wild may not be completely accurate, however as all horses in North America are descended from animals which were originally domesticated and trained by humans. The correct term for this type animal would be feral as they are wild with domesticated ancestors.

Until the early 16th century horses were extinct in North America, brought to this country by the Spanish Conquistadors in the early 1500's. When the Pueblo Indians learned to tame and ride horses, they passed this lesson to other Indians and when they revolted against Spanish rule in 1680, the Spanish left thousands of horses behind as they fled.

While the Indians could have rounded up the wild horses and trained them, they found it easier to raid the Spanish fort and steal their horses. To combat this, Spain shipped thousands of the animals to North America, flooding the country with new rides in hopes the Indians would then go after the wild ones and leave their horses alone.

Wild Spanish horses were herded to the Rio Grande area and turned loose over 200 years so that by 1900, there was an estimated two million roaming free throughout the plains. Cattle farmers began to kill them off as a threat to their grazing land until only about 17,000 remained as recently as 1970. The Wild Free-Roaming Horse and Burro Act, passed in 1971 gave the Mustangs, which means free roaming or ownerless in Spanish, freedom to roam as they please. It is estimated that 41,000 mustangs are alive today, although it is doubtful many remain with their original Spanish blood.

In 1977, a Mustang called Tang was born and raised in Texas has become a national celebrity representing the Mustang Horse in the Big D Charity Horse Show in Texas and in 1992 was featured in Car and Driver Magazine when they compared the Mustang Horse with Mustang Car. In 1997 Tang was featured on its own trading card.

Coldblood Horses

Large horses with a gentle disposition and a placid interactive style are usually referred to as cold bloods. Cold blooded horses are descendants of the ancient European breeds used for farming, hauling and other types of heavy work. Early cold blooded horses were also used for war: Medieval knights needed heavy, strong mounts that could be armored and carry a heavily armored man. Charging with a lance also required a horse with weight, and the heavy cold blooded horses proved equal to the task.

Draft horses are considered coldbloods; they tend to be larger than warm and hot blooded horses by a couple of hands and may weight two hundred pounds or more than warm blooded horses. Examples of cold blooded horses include the Clydesdale, the Shire and the Belgian.

Cold blooded horses, because of their stolid demeanor and great weight are not suitable for sports other than hauling or pulling competitions at farm shows.

Some people love the look of draft horses, who have thicker coats and manes to enable them to endure rough weather more readily than sleeker horses. Their heads and eyes are large, their legs and shoulders massive, for pulling wagons filled with hay or dung or for being in harness. The horses that once drew wagons of kegged beer or produce through the streets of the major cities of the western world were draft horses. Today, you're most likely to encounter them at working historic farms, in the Amish towns of the Midwest, or at country farm shows.

If you want a horse to work plowing or hauling on your farm or for occasional riding, a cold-blooded horse is a fine choice. Their easy manner makes them gentle with children, and it takes a lot to spook them. Some people mistake their easy going temperament for thick-headedness, but in fact draft horses are very intelligent. Built for endurance, these horses tend to have stronger limbs, often with long, thick hair around their lower legs and hooves for added warmth. These most ancient breeds were used in Europe for all kinds of work and are still bred and worked by enthusiasts.

Here breed considered cold bloods:

- American cream draft
- Belgian heavy draft
- Black forest chestnut
- Clydesdale
- Friesian
- Haflinger
- Noriker
- Percheron
- Poitevin
- Shire
- Suffolk punch
- Swedish Ardennes

Hot-blooded Horses

Hot blooded horses are used for racing in the West, but the tribes who still roam the reaches of outer Mongolia breed and ride these horses as a way of life. Arabians have a long history of domestication. In the Middle Ages, Arabs were breeding their horses according to what is now long-established practice: for speed, strength, conformation and temperament.

Several hundred years later, Arabians are the most prized and costly horse breed. 'Hot blooded' refers to their temperament, which has been described as difficult by some and passionate by others.

There are only two recognized hot-blood breeds; the Arabian and the Thoroughbred. Arabians didn't reach the European continent until the 16th or 17th Centuries, but once they did, they revolutionized horse breeding.

Breeding the Arabians with English horses created the Thoroughbred, which is used for racing and other sporting events. Hot blooded horses are known for their speed: with lighter bodies and a passion that outstrips other breeds, their quickness makes them ideal race horses. But the same fire that makes them fast makes them high strung or fiery tempered. Hotbloods, often likened to passionate human artists by those who understand their temperaments, can injure themselves in training or racing when their need for speed outpaces their bodies' capacity for endurance. Because they are high strung, hot blooded horses may also be injured when trying to escape from something frightening, when upset at being transported or when faced with a new situation.

Race horses demand a lot from their owners and handlers. For the specialist with the money for training, stabling and racing, hot blooded horses can be an exciting life. But these horses have to be handled by people who know what they're doing; experts with plenty of experience. Because of their sensitivity, hot blooded horses can be too easily harmed by ineffective or inexpert handling. Their legs are delicate and must be protected by careful handling and the right kind of support. They are the most expensive horses, being costly to breed and buy, which makes them the playthings of the very wealthy and the backbone of the extremely lucrative worldwide racing industry.

Here are some horse breeds considered hot bloods:

- Akhi-Teke
- Anglo-Arabian
- Arabian
- Moroccan Barb
- Pintabian
- Shagya Arabian
- Spanish Barb
- Thoroughbred

Warmblooded Horses

The warm blooded breeds were created when warriors returned to Europe from the Middle East and Africa with hot blooded Arabian horses captured in battle. Breeding the large, heavy war horses of northern Europe with the lighter, faster and fiery tempered hot bloods from the Mongolian steppes created horse breeds that combine the quickness and agility of race horses with the larger build and milder temperament of cold bloods. Over time, the draft horses of Europe were increasingly bred with hot blooded imports, creating the forerunners of dozens of breeds in existence today. Warmbloods have smaller heads and bodies than draft horses and tend to be less excitable than hot blooded horses, making them good all-round horses for riding and light work.

Warm blooded horses are popular in Olympic sporting events such as dressage, and many European breeders are breeding warmbloods for competition. The Hanoverian is one currently breed popular for eventing. Warm-blooded horses are also considered perfect for riding, and in America, the West was won on the backs of warmblood breeds. Considered perfect for roping, cutting and herding, the fortunes of cattle owners increased by the warm bloods and the cowboys who rode them, pushing thousands of head of cattle to the rapidly populating and hungry Western city centres. Most popular American breeds—the Quarter horse, the Tennessee Walking horse and the Palomino—are all examples of excellent horses derived from the original breeding of draft horses and Arabians.

If you plan to ride as a sport but aren't looking for a heavy work horse, you will probably buy a warmblood breed.

They aren't quick-tempered as hot bloods, but they have a different life's purpose from cold bloods. Excellent for riding, dressage and other events, warm bloods are also the breeds for people who want their children to experience the joys of horseback riding.

CHAPTER 24

Horses in India

According to the National Commission on Agriculture (1976), horses in India can be placed broadly in two classes viz. the slow moving pack ponies and the fast running saddle horses used for riding or for drawing carriages. The indigenous breeds of horses/ponies include Marwari, Kathiawari, Manipuri, Spiti, Bhutia and Zanskari. Among these, Marwari and Kathiawari are considered as two distinct breeds or types although they have several characteristics in common. Kathiawar (Gujarat) and Rajasthan are the homes of Kathiawari and Marwari breeds, respectively. These breeds have been selected both for utility and beauty. Bhutia, Spiti and Zanskari ponies, mainly found in the hilly areas of Himalayan ranges are slow moving horses. The Manipuri horses having qualities of both hill and plain breeds of horses have been bred over centuries in the Manipur area of the northeast. Manipuri horses reputed for their intelligence are used for polo and racing. Three other breeds of India namely Deccani, Chummarti and Sikang are considered to be on the verge of extinction.

The exotic breeds of horses introduced in India include English thoroughbred, Water, Arab, Polish, Connemera and Halflinger. The Arab, the first to be introduced,is believed to have contributed substantially for the evolution of Kathiawari, Marwari, Sindhi, Malani and Manipuri horses. It is believed that all the indigenous breeds of the horses are rapidly deteriorating in quality as a result of lack of organized systematic breeding and availability of good specimen animals. Unless huge financial commitment is made, there is a possibility of the breeds losing their identity even in their home tract.

Kathiawari Horses

The superintendent of Gaekwar Contingent in 1880 suggested that the Kathiawari breed may have sprung from the wild horses of Kathiawar. The breeding tract of the breed is Saurashtra province of Gujarat which comprises of Rajkot, Bhavnagar, Surendranagar Junagarh and Amreli districts of Gujarat.

The most prominent body colour in Kathiawari horses is chestnut followed by bay (body chestnut, Foreleg up to knee and fetlock are black, Keshwali black, Hairs of tail and neck are black), grey (complete white colour) and dun (light chestnut). The physical characteristics of Kathiawari horses are concave profile, long neck, short leg and squared quarters. Face is dry and short, triangular from pale to forehead and small muzzle, big nostrils, edge of nostril is thin; small, fine and curved upright ears on 90° axis that can rotate at 180°, broad forehead and large expressive sensitive eyes. Tail is long, not bushy, curved well and touching to the ground, foot round and broad. Kathiawari horses have on an average 119 cm long body, 147 cm height and 160 cm heart girth. The average ear length is 15 cm. The average face length and width are 53 and 21 cm, respectively. The tail length without switch is 42 cm.

Marwari Horse

The Marwari or Malani is a rare breed of horse from the Marwar (or Jodhpur) region of India. Known for its inward-turning ear tips, it comes in all equine colours, although pinto patterns tend to be the most popular with buyers and breeders. It is known for its hardiness, and is quite similar to the Kathiawari, another Indian breed from the Kathiawar region southwest of Marwar. Many breed members exhibit a natural ambling gait. The Marwari are descended from native Indian ponies crossed with Arabian horses, possibly with some Mongolian influence.

The Rathores, traditional rulers of the Marwar region of western India, were the first to breed the Marwari. Beginning in the 12th century, they espoused strict breeding that promoted purity and hardiness. Used throughout history as a cavalry horse by the people of the Marwar region, the Marwari was noted for its loyalty and bravery in battle. The breed deteriorated in the 1930s, when poor management practices resulted in a reduction of the breeding stock, but today has regained some of its popularity. The Marwari is used for light draught and agricultural work, as well as riding and packing. In 1995, a breed society was formed for the Marwari in India, and in the 2000s horses have begun to be exported to the United States and Europe.

The Marwari averages between 15 and 16 hands (60 and 64 inches, 152 and 163 cm) high. Horses originating in different parts of India tend to be of different heights, with the breed having an outside range of 14 to 17 hands (56 to 68 inches, 142 to 173 cm) high. They can be bay, grey, chestnut, palomino, piebald, or skewbald. Although white horses are bred specifically for religious use in India, they are generally not accepted into Marwari stud books. Gray horses are considered auspicious, and tend to be the most valuable, with piebald and skewbald horses the second-most favoured. Black horses are considered unlucky, as the colour is a symbol of death and darkness. Horses that have the white markings of a blaze and four white socks are considered lucky.

The facial profile is straight, and the ears are pointed with inward turning tips. The neck is slender, running into pronounced withers, a deep chest, and fairly straight shoulders. Marwaris generally have a long back and sloping croup. The legs tend to be slender and the hooves small but well-formed. Members of the breed are hardy and easy keepers, but they can also be of tenacious and unpredictable temperaments. They are quite similar to the Kathiawari horse, another breed from India, having much of the same history and physical features. The main difference between the Marwari and the Kathiawari is their original geographic origin – Marwaris are mainly from the Marwar region while Kathiawaris are from the Kathiawar peninsula. Kathiawaris tend to have slight facial differences from the Marwari, and are slightly taller in general.

The Marwari often exhibits a natural ambling gait, close to a pace, called the *revaal*, *aphcal*, or *rehwal*. Hair whorls and their placement are important to breeders of Marwaris. Horses with long whorls down the neck are called *devman* and considered lucky, while horses with whorls below their eyes are called *anusudhal* and are unpopular with buyers. Whorls on the fetlocks are thought to bring victory. There are correct proportions that horses are expected to have, based on the width of a finger, said to be the equal of five grains of barley. For example, the length of the face should be between 28 and 40 fingers, and the length from the poll to the dock should be four times the length of the face.

The Marwari is descended from native Indian ponies crossed with Arabian horses. The ponies were small and hardy, but with poor conformation; the influence of the Arabian blood improved the appearance without compromising the hardiness. The Arabians possibly came ashore from a cargo ship wrecked off India's west coast. Legend in India states that the Arabian ship, containing seven Arabian horses of good breeding, was shipwrecked off the shore of the Kutch District. These horses were then taken to the Marwar district and used as foundation bloodstock for the Marwari. There is also the possibility of some Mongolian influence from the north. The breed probably originated in northwest India on the Afghanistan border, as well as in Uzbekistan, Kazakhstan, and Turkmenistan, and takes its name from the Marwar region (also called the Jodhpur region) of India.

The Rathores, rulers of Marwar and successful Rajput cavalry, were the traditional breeders of the Marwari. The Rathores were forced from their Kingdom of Kanauj in 1193, and withdrew into the Great Indian and Thar Deserts. The Marwari was vital to their survival, and during the 12th century they followed strict selective breeding processes, keeping the finest stallions for the use of their subjects. During this time, the horses were considered divine beings, and at times they were only allowed to be ridden by members of the Rajput families and the Kshatriyas warrior caste. When the Moguls captured northern India in the early 16th century they brought Turkoman horses that were probably used to supplement the breeding of the Marwari. Marwaris were renowned during this period for their bravery and courage in battle, as well as their loyalty to their riders. During the late 16th century, the Rajputs of Marwar, under the leadership of Moghul emperor Akbar, formed a cavalry force over 50,000 strong. The Rathores believed that the Marwari horse could only leave a battlefield under one of three conditions – victory, death, or carrying a wounded master to safety. The horses were trained to be extremely responsive in battlefield conditions, and were practised in complex riding maneuvers. Over 300 years later, during the First World War.

1900s to Today

The period of the British Raj hastened the Marwari's downfall, as did the eventual independence of India. The British occupiers preferred other breeds, and tried to eliminate the Marwari, along with the Kathiawari. The British instead preferred Thoroughbreds and polo ponies, and reduced the reputation of the Marwari to the point where even the inward-turning ears of the breed were mocked as the 'mark of a native horse'. During the 1930s the Marwari deteriorated, with breeding stock diminishing and becoming of poorer quality due to poor breeding practices. Indian independence, along with the obsolescence of warriors on horseback, led to a decreased need for the Marwari and many animals were subsequently killed. In the 1950s many Indian noblemen lost their land and hence much of their ability to take care of animals, resulting in many Marwari horses being sold as pack horses, castrated, or killed. The breed was on the verge of extinction until the intervention of Maharaja Umaid Singhji in the first half of the 20th century saved the Marwari, work that was carried on by his grandson, Maharaja Gaj Singh II. As a direct result of indiscriminate breeding practices, as of 2001 only a few thousand purebred Marwaris existed.

A British horsewoman named Francesca Kelly founded a group called Marwari Bloodlines in 1995, with the goal of promoting and preserving the Marwari horse around the world. In 1999, Kelly and Raghuvendra Singh Dundlod, a descendant of Indian nobility, led a group that founded the Indigenous Horse Society of India (of which the Marwari Horse Society is part), a group that works with the government, breeders, and the public to promote and conserve the breed. Kelly and Dunlod also entered and won endurance races at the Indian national equestrian games, convincing the Equestrian Federation of India to sanction a national show for indigenous horses – the first in the country. The pair worked with other experts from the Indigenous Horse Society to develop the first breed standards. Kelly imported the first Marwari horse into the United States in 2000; the first Marwari was exported to Europe in 2006, when a stallion was given to the French Living Museum of the Horse.

In late 2007 plans were announced to create a stud book for the breed, a collaborative venture between the Marwari Horse Society of India and the

Indian government. A registration process was initiated in 2009, when it was announced that the Marwari Horse Society had become a government body, the only government-authorized registration society for Marwari horses. The registration process includes an evaluation of the horse against the breed standards, during which unique identification marks and physical dimensions are recorded. After the evaluation, the horse is cold branded with its registration number and photographed. In late 2009 the Indian government announced that the Marwari horse, along with other Indian horse breeds, would be commemorated on a set of stamps issued by that country. In early 2010, the UK-based Friends of Marwari/Kathiawari Horse asked for donations of used bits. These would be given to owners of horses, including Marwaris, in India in place of home-made bits that often have sharp edges that can injure the horse.

Research studies have been conducted to examine the genetics of the Marwari and its relationship to other Indian and non-Indian horse breeds. Six different breeds have been identified in India: the Marwari, Kathiawari, Spiti pony, Bhutia pony, Manipuri Pony, and Zanskari. These six are distinct from each other in terms of unique performance traits and different agroclimactic conditions in the various areas of India where they originated. A 2005 study was conducted to identify past genetic bottlenecks in the Marwari. The study found that, in the DNA of the horses tested, there was no evidence of a genetic bottleneck in the breed's history. However, since the population has decreased rapidly in past decades, bottlenecks may have occurred that were not identified in the study. In 2007, a study was conducted to assess genetic variation among all Indian horse breeds except the Kathiawari. Based on analysis of microsatellite DNA, the Marwari was found to be the most genetically distinct breed of the five studied, and was most distant from the Manipuri; none of the breeds were found to have close genetic ties to the Thoroughbred. The Marwari was distinguishable from the other breeds in terms of both physical characteristics (mainly height) and environmental adaptability. The physical differences were attributed to differing ancestries: the Marwari are closely associated with the Arabian horse, while the four other breeds are supposedly descended from the Tibetan pony.

Uses

The Marwari is used for riding, packing and light draught, and agricultural work. Marwaris are often crossed with Thoroughbreds to produce a larger horse with more versatility. Despite the fact that the breed is indigenous to the country, cavalry units of the Indian military make little use of the horses, although they are popular in the Jodhpur and Jaipur areas of Rajasthan, India. They are particularly suited to dressage, in part due to a natural tendency to perform. Marwaris are also used to play polo, sometimes playing against Thoroughbreds. Within the Marwari breed was a strain known as the Natchni, believed by local people to be 'born to dance'.

Decorated in silver, jewels, and bells, these horses were trained to perform complex prancing and leaping movements at many ceremonies, including weddings. Although the Natchni strain is extinct today, horses trained in those skills are still in demand in rural India.

Spiti Horses

The Spiti horses are distributed in Spiti valley and adjoining areas of Kullu and Kinnaur divisions of Himachal Pradesh. These horses are smaller in height.

The Spiti ponies have two strains, Spiti pure and Konimare. The Konimare ponies are comparatively taller. They are capable of thriving in cold regions under adverse conditions of scarcity of food, low temperature and long journeys at high altitude. The Spiti horses are used for riding and as pack animals. The predominant body colour is grey (complete white) followed by black, black flay bone (white body with black patches), brown and bay. The Spiti horses are hardy and surefooted. Body is well developed with fairly strong bones. The legs are thick and covered with long coarse hairs. The mane is longer having 20 to 30 cm long hairs. Solid and compact body, convex face, erect ears, black eyes, straight back, long and straight tail, alert looking and short height are some of the important breed characteristics. The horses are nervous in temperament. The Spiti horses have on average 97 cm body length, 127 cm height, 150 cm paunch girth, 15 cm long ear, 49 cm face length and 20 cm face width. It has been observed that females have shorter body, height, heart girth and paunch girth.

Zanskari Horses

Zanskari horses are available in Leh and Laddakh area of Jammu and Kashmir. The predominant body colour is grey followed by black and copper. The horses are known for their ability to work, run adequately and carry loads at high altitude. Horses are medium in size, well built and 120 to 140 cm high. The Zanskari horses have predominant eyes, heavy and long tail and uniform gait. The body hairs are fine, long and glossy. Only a few hundred horses at present exist in the Zanskar and other valleys of Laddakh. Large scale breeding with non descript ponies has endangered this breed. The Animal Husbandry Department, Jammu and Kashmir has recently established a Zanskari horse Breeding farm at Padum Zanskar in Kargil district of Ladakh for breed improvement and conservation through selective breeding.

Manipuri Horses

Manipuri breed of ponies is one of the purest and prestigious breed of equines of India. It is a strong and hardy breed and has very good adaptability to extreme geo-climatic conditions. It is one of the well-known breeds of India and has been claimed as the oldest polo pony. They are found in Manipur and Assâm, and are similar to the south-east Asian type pony.Generally the Manipuri ponies are of 11-13 hands high at wither with a good shoulder, short back, well developed quarters and strong limbs. Mane is generally coarse and upright. It has small pointed prsicked ears, eyes are alert and slightly slant .The area between the nostrils is flat not crispy. Withers are not prominent. Face is concave and tail is well set and commensurate with height. Manipuri ponies are intelligent and extremely tough, and have tremendous endurance. Perhaps all these good qualities made it suitable for polo game for which it is globally famous. The breed is available in 14 different colours viz Bay, Black, Gray, Mora white, Leiphon white, Sinai White, Stocking, liver chestnut, Roan, light gray, Reddish brown and dark bay. The pony undoubtly played significant role in the field of war and play.

It has close association with the socioeconomic life of the people of hilly region through travel, transport and hunting. It is a matter of concern that the number of Manipuri has decreased drastically. As per latest data the population of Manipuri pony is 2327 only. Thus, immediate attention and efforts are required to conserve this precious breed of ponies in India.ng.

Bhutia Horses

Bhutia horses are distributed in Sikkim and Darjeeling. They are usually grey or bay coloured and similar to the Tibetan pony.

Bibliography

Anthony, David W. (1996). "Bridling Horse Power: The Domestication of the Horse". *Horses Through Time* (First ed.). Boulder, CO: Roberts Rinehart Publishers. ISBN 1570980608.

Apperson, George Latimer and Martin Manser (2006). *Dictionary of Proverbs.* Wordsworth Editions. ISBN 1840223111.

Belknap, Maria (2004). *Horsewords: The Equine Dictionary* (Second ed.). North Pomfret, VT: Trafalgar Square Publishing. ISBN 1-57076-274-0.

Bennett, Deb (1998). *Conquerors: The Roots of New World Horsemanship* (First ed.). Solvang, CA: Amigo Publications, Inc.. ISBN 0-9658533-0-6.

Bongianni, Maurizio (1987). *Simon & Schuster's Guide to Horses and Ponies.* New York: Fireside. ISBN 0-671-66068-3.

British Horse Society (1966). *The Manual of Horsemanship of the British Horse Society and the Pony Club* (6th Edition, reprinted 1970 ed.). Kenilworth, UK: British Horse Society. ISBN 0954886313.

Bryant, Jennifer Olson and George Williams (2006). *The USDF Guide to Dressage.* Storey Publishing. ISBN 1580175295.

Budiansky, Stephen (1997). *The Nature of Horses.* New York: NY Free Press. ISBN 0-684-82768-9.

Bush, Karen and Julian Marczak (2005). *The Principles of Teaching Riding: The Official Manual of the Association of British Riding Schools.* David & Charles. ISBN 0715319027.

Campbell, B.N. (2001). *National Gambling Impact Study Commission Final Report (1999).* Darby, PA: DIANE Publishing. ISBN 0756707013.

Chamberlin, J. Edward (2006). *Horse: How the Horse Has Shaped Civilizations.* New York, NY: Bluebridge. ISBN 0-9742405-9-1.

Collins, Tony, John Martin, Wray Vamplew (2005). *Encyclopedia of Traditional British Rural Sports.* London, UK: Routledge. ISBN 041535224X.

Evans, J. *et al.* (1990). *The Horse* (Second ed.). New York, NY: Freeman. ISBN 0-7167-1811-1.

Evans, James Warren (1992). *Horse Breeding and Management*. Amsterdam: Elsevier Health Sciences. ISBN 0444882820.

Fear, Sally (2006). *New Forest Drift: A Photographic Portrait of Life in the National Park*. Perspective Photo Press. ISBN 0-9553253-0-7.

Fort, Matthew (2005). *Eating Up Italy: Voyages on a Vespa*. London, UK: Centro Books. ISBN 0-00-721481-2.

Fox-Davies, Arthur Charles (2007). *A Complete Guide to Heraldry*. Skyhorse Publishing Inc. ISBN 1602390010.

Giffin, M.D., James M. and Tom Gore, D.V.M. (1998). *Horse Owner's Veterinary Handbook* (Second ed.). New York: Howell Book House. ISBN 0-87605-606-0.

Gifford, Angela (1998, reprinted 2000). 'Working Draught Horses As Singles and Pairs'. *The Working Horse Manual*. Tonbridge, UK: Farming Press. ISBN 0852364016.

Gifford, Angela (1998, reprinted 2000). 'Working Horses in Forestry'. *The Working Horse Manual*. Tonbridge, UK: Farming Press. ISBN 0852364016.

Hairston, Rachel and Madelyn Larsen (2004). *The Essentials of Horsekeeping*. New York, NY: Sterling Publishing Company, Inc.. ISBN 0806988177.

Hammond, Gerald (2000). *The Language of Horse Racing*. London: Taylor & Francis. ISBN 1579582761.

Harris, Susan E. (1993). *Horse Gaits, Balance and Movement*. New York: Howell Book House. ISBN 0-87605-955-8.

Harris, Susan E. (1994). *The United States Pony Club Manual of Horsemanship: Basics for Beginners - D Level*. Howell Book House. ISBN 0876059523.

Kreling, Kai (2005). "The Horse's Teeth". *Horses' Teeth and Their Problems: Prevention, Recognition, and Treatment*. Guilford, CT: Globe Pequot. ISBN 1592286968.

MacGregor, Arthur (1985). *Bone, Antler, Ivory and Horn: Technology of Skeletal Materials Since the Roman Period*. Totowa, NJ: Barnes & Noble. ISBN 0389205311.

Matossian, Mary Kilbourne (1997). *Shaping World History: Breakthroughs in Ecology, Technology, Science, and Politics*. Armonk, NY: M.E. Sharpe. ISBN 0585023972.

McBane, Susan (1992). *A Natural Approach to Horse Management*. London: Methuen. ISBN 0-413-62370-X.

McBane, Susan (1997). *The Illustrated Encyclopedia of Horse Breeds*. Edison, NJ: Wellfleet Press. ISBN 0-7858-0604-0.

Mettler, John J. Jr. (1989). *Horse Sense: A Complete Guide to Horse Selection and Care*. Pownal, VT: Storey Communications, Inc. ISBN 0882665499.

Miller, Lynn R. (1981, reprinted 2000). *Work Horse Handbook* (First Edition, Fifteenth Impression ed.). Sisters, or: *Small Farmer's Journal* Inc. ISBN 0960726802.

Miller, Robert M. (1999). *Understanding the Ancient Secrets of the Horse's Mind.* Neenah, WI: Russell Meerdink Company Ltd. ISBN 0929346653.

Miller, Robert M. and Rick Lamb (2005). *Revolution in Horsemanship and What it Means to Mankind.* Guilford, Connecticut: Lyons Press. ISBN 159228387x.

Mills, Bruce and Barbara Carne (1988). *A Basic Guide to Horse Care and Management.* New York, NY: Howell Book House. ISBN 0876058713.

Myers, Jane (2005). *Horse Safe: A Complete Guide to Equine Safety.* Collingwood, UK: CSIRO Publishing. ISBN 0643092455.

Ockerman, Herbert W.; Hansen, Conly L. (2000). *Animal By-product Processing & Utilization.* Lancaster, PA: CRC Press. ISBN 1566767776.

Olsen, Sandra L. (1996). "Horse Hunters of the Ice Age". *Horses Through Time* (First ed.). Boulder, CO: Roberts Rinehart Publishers. ISBN 1570980608.

Olsen, Sandra L. (1996). 'In the Winner's Circle: The History of Equestrian Sports'. *Horses Through Time* (First ed.). Boulder, CO: Roberts Rinehart Publishers. ISBN 1570980608.

Thorson, Juli S. (2006). 'Rugged Lark'. In Martindale, Cathy and Kathy Swan (editors). *Legends 7: Outstanding Quarter Horse Stallions and Mares.* Colorado Springs, CO: Western Horseman. ISBN 0-911647-79-1.

Vogel, Colin B.V.M (1995). *The Complete Horse Care Manual.* New York, NY: Dorling Kindersley Publishing, Inc.. ISBN 0789401703.

Wheeler, Eileen (2006). "Fence Planning". *Horse Stable And Riding Arena Design.* Armes, IA: Blackwell Publishing. ISBN 0813828597.

Whitaker, Julie; Whitelaw, Ian (2007). *The Horse: A Miscellany of Equine Knowledge.* New York: St. Martin's Press. ISBN 0-312-37108-X.

Index

I

J

K